The Aztecs

The Peoples of America

This series is about the native peoples and civilizations of the Americas, from their origins in ancient times to the present day. Drawing on archaeological, historical, and anthropological evidence, each volume presents a fresh and absorbing account of a group's culture, society, and history.

Accessible and scholarly, and well illustrated with maps and photographs, the volumes of *The Peoples of America* will together provide a comprehensive and vivid picture of the character and variety of the societies of the American past.

Published

The Tiwanaku: A Portrait of an Andean Civilization
Alan Kolata

The Timucua
Jerald T. Milanich

The Cheyenne
John Moore

The Iroquois
Dean Snow

The Moche
Garth Bawden

The Incas
Terence N. D'Altroy

The Nasca
Helaine Silverman and Donald A. Proulx

The Aztecs, Second Edition
Michael E. Smith

The Aztecs

Second Edition

Michael E. Smith

BLACKWELL PUBLISHING
350 Main Street, Malden, MA 02148-5020, USA
9600 Garsington Road, Oxford OX4 2DQ, UK
550 Swanston Street, Carlton, Victoria 3053, Australia

First edition published 1996
Second edition published 2003 by Blackwell Publishing Ltd

9   2010

Library of Congress Cataloging-in-Publication Data

   Smith, Michael Ernest, 1953–.
      The Aztecs / Michael E. Smith. — 2nd ed.
         p.   cm. — (The peoples of America)
      Includes bibliographical references and index.
      ISBN: 978-0-631-23015-1 (alk. paper) — ISBN: 978-0-631-23016-8 (alk. paper)
         1. Aztecs—History.   2. Aztecs—Antiquities.   3. Aztecs—Social life
      and customs.   4. Mexico—Antiquities.   I. Title.   II. Series.
      F1219.73.S58   2002
      972'.018—dc21

                                                              2001006950

A catalogue record for this title is available from the British Library.

Set in 10 on 12 pt Sabon
by Ace Filmsetting Ltd, Frome, Somerset
Printed and bound in Singapore
by Fabulous Printers Pte Ltd

The publisher's policy is to use permanent paper from mills that operate a sustainable
forestry policy, and which has been manufactured from pulp processed using
acid-free and elementary chlorine-free practices. Furthermore, the publisher ensures
that the text paper and cover board used have met acceptable environmental
accreditation standards.

For further information on
Blackwell Publishing, visit our website:
www.blackwellpublishing.com

*To the memory of my mother, Esther O. Smith,
and my stepmother, Carolyn S. Smith.*

Contents

Figures

Tables

Preface

Is there perchance any truth to our words here?
All seems so like a dream, only do we rise from sleep, only on earth
do our words remain.

Cantares Mexicanos

Words were important to the Aztecs, and we are fortunate today that many of their own words were preserved after the Spanish Conquest. Also preserved were examples of the Aztecs' picture-writing as well as descriptions by Spanish conquerors and observers. These written sources have been available for four centuries, and many works on the Aztecs make use of them. But they are not the only window into the Aztec past; words are not all that remain on earth.

Paradoxically, the oldest information on the Aztecs is also the most recent to be discovered. I refer to the ruins of houses, temples, and towns that make up the archaeological record of Aztec civilization. Aztec archaeology is a relatively new field of study. Many exciting new discoveries over the past two decades have revolutionized our understanding of Aztec civilization, but until now most of this information has appeared only in technical reports and professional journals. A major goal of this book is to make these discoveries known to a wider audience. As a participant in this work, I try to communicate something of the excitement and significance of our research. In preparing the second edition, I have updated the text and notes in all chapters and reorganized and expanded my discussion of religion. But the biggest change is an increased attention to specific Aztec archaeological sites. This edition describes many more sites than the first edition, with accompanying photographs and maps.

In the pages that follow I draw heavily upon the results of fieldwork that I have directed at Aztec sites in the Mexican state of Morelos. I would like to acknowledge the following institutions and agencies for providing funding for that fieldwork: the National Science Foundation, the National Endowment for the Humanities, the Wenner-Gren Foundation for Anthropological Research, the National Geographic Society, the Heinz

Charitable Trust, Loyola University of Chicago, the University at Albany (State University of New York), and the Institute for Mesoamerican Studies. My research in Mexico has been greatly facilitated by Mexican colleagues and officials, particularly Joaquim García-Cook, Lorena Mirambell, Mari Carmen Serra Puche, Norberto González C., and Hortensia de Vega Nova. I thank the following students who participatd in the fieldwork for their contributions to its overall success: Patricia Aguirre, Martín Antonio, Robert Austin, Courtney Brown, Elizabeth DiPippo, Ruth Fauman-Fichman, Timothy Hare, Kathleen Haynie, Kathryn Hirst, Kori Kaufman, Ronald Kohler, Annette McLeod, Samantha Miller, Lisa Montiel, Susan Norris, Joan Odess, Jan Marie Olson, Scott O'Mack, Jennifer Pinson, T. Jeffrey Price, Colleen Rhodes, David Shafer, Margaret Shiels, Jerrell Sorensen, Sharon Spanogle, Osvaldo Sterpone, Timothy Sullivan, Cheryl Sutherland, Deborah Szymborski, and Brian Tomaslewski. I also must thank my excellent field crews from the Morelos towns of Tetlama and Yautepec. My later father, Dudley B. Smith, deserves acknowledgment for providing pickup trucks for our fieldwork.

My understanding of Aztec civilization has benefited greatly from interaction with my colleagues. Although these are too numerous to list, I do want to acknowledge an intellectual debt to the following scholars: Jorge Angulo, Carlos Barreto M., Juan José Batalla Rosado, Francis F. Berdan, Richard E. Blanton, Elizabeth H. Boone, Elizabeth M. Brumfiel, Louise M. Burkhart, Robert M. Carmack, Thomas H. Charlton, George L. Cowgill, Ann Cyphers, Hortensia de Vega Nova, Susan T. Evans, Silvia Garza de González, Susan D. Gillespie, Norberto González C., Gary H. Gossen, Michel Graulich, David C. Grove, Rafael Gutierrez, Cynthia Health-Smith, Frederic Hicks, Kenneth G. Hirth, Mary G. Hodge, Dorothy Hosler, John S. Justeson, Susan Kepecs, Leonardo López Luján, Druzo Maldonado J., Marilyn A. Masson, Deborah L. Nichols, Cynthia Otis Charlton, Jeffrey R. Parsons, Ana Maria Pelz, John Pohl, Helen Pollard, José Luis de Rojas, William T. Sanders, Juan Antonio Siller, Wanda Tommasi de Magrelli, Emily Umberger, and James Wessman.

I want to thank the following colleagues for providing comments on specific chapters: Louise Burkhart (chapters 8, 9, 10, 11), Thomas H. Charlton (chapters 3–5), William E. Doolittle (chapter 3), Susan T. Evans (chapter 6), Mary G. Hodge (chapter 7), Dorothy Hosler (chapter 4), and Cynthia Otis Charlton (chapters 3–5). I am particularly grateful to the following readers who provided comments on many or all of the chapters of the first or second editions: Elizabeth DiPippo, Elizabeth Graham, Cynthia Heath-Smith, Alan Kolata, Maxine S. Heath, Carolyn Smith and Megan Snedden. The editing of Cynthia Heath-Smith has improved my prose greatly. I thank these colleagues for responding to my requests for help with illustrations: Frances F. Berdan, Elizabeth H. Boone, Louise

Burkhart, Davíd Carrasco, Thomas H. Charlton, Phil Crossley, William E. Doolittle, Susan T. Evans, Judith Friedlander, Janine Gasco, Salvador Guilliem Arroyo, Mary G. Hodge, Dean Lambert, Eduardo Matos Moctezuma, Cynthia Otis Charlton, Richard Perry, Christopher Pool, Timothy J. Smith, and Emily Umberger. I also wish to acknowledge the help of Dorothy Christiansen of the Special Collections Department, University Library, and Mark Schmidt of the University Graphics Office, University at Albany. I thank Marnie DiStefano, April N. Smith, and Heather C. Smith for their help with the preparation of the manuscript, and Ellen Cesarski, Kori Kaufman, and Pam Headrick for help with drafting. I also thank my copy editor Eldo Barkhuizen for his fine work and attention to detail.

Last but not least, I owe the greatest debt to my wife, Cynthia Heath-Smith, and our daughters April Nicole and Heather Colleen. Cindy is a superb archaeologist who has contributed greatly to our fieldwork, and is the best editor I know. She has also helped create a happy and stable home during our many moves between the US and Mexico. April and Heather have assisted during some of the fieldwork described here, but more than that they help make the life of an archaeologist worthwhile and fulfilling.

Guide to Pronunciation and Spelling

In Nahuatl, the language of the Aztecs, most consonants are pronounced as in English, and vowels are pronounced as in Spanish. The major exceptions are:

h	pronounced 'hw' (Huitzilopochtli; macehualli)
qua, quo	pronounced 'kw' (quachtli)
que, qui	pronounced 'k' (Quetzalcoatl; pulque)
tl	pronounced like the English 'atlas' (Tlaloc), even at the end of a word, where it is unvoiced (Nahuatl; coatl)
x	pronounced 'sh' (Xipe Totec; Mexica)

chapter one
The Aztecs of Mesoamerica

*Next morning, we came to a broad causeway and continued our
march towards Iztapalapa. And when we saw all those cities and
villages built in the water, and other great towns on dry land, and
that straight and level causeway leading to Mexico, we were astounded. These great towns and cues [temple-pyramids] and buildings rising from the water, all made of stone, seemed like an
enchanted vision from the tale of Amadis. Indeed, some of our
soldiers asked whether it was not all a dream. It is not surprising
therefore that I should write in this vein. It was all so wonderful
that I do not know how to describe this first glimpse of things
never heard of, seen or dreamed of before.*
Bernal Díaz del Castillo, The Conquest of New Spain

With these words Bernal Díaz del Castillo, a soldier in Hernando Cortés's
conquering army, expressed his amazement at the Aztec capital city. When
the Spaniards approached Tenochtitlan in 1519, it was one of the most popu-
lous cities in the world, the largest ever to flourish in the pre-Hispanic New
World, and far richer and more grandiose than any community the Spanish
soldiers had ever beheld in their home country (figure 1.1). Expecting to find
a simple, backward people, the conquerors were awed by the civilized nature
of Aztec society. The kings and royal courts, the huge bustling marketplaces
with their orderly layouts, the wealth of the nobility, the detailed scientific
and technical knowledge of the priests and artisans, these and many other
features of Aztec civilization filled the conquerors with awe.

Much about the Aztecs continues to amaze us today. When workmen in
Mexico City accidentally uncovered a huge Aztec sculpture in 1978, the
Mexican government quickly mounted one of the largest excavations in the
country's history. What emerged from these diggings was the so-called

Figure 1.1   Artist's reconstruction of the Templo Mayor and the sacred precinct in the heart of Tenochtitlan (After Marquina 1951: lámina 55)

"Templo Mayor," a huge temple-pyramid that had served as the sacred center of the Aztec empire. The sculpture was an offering buried in front of the pyramid. This pyramid (figure 1.1) and the thousands of rich and exotic offerings uncovered in and around it are now open to the public, and millions of visitors express their interest and appreciation every year.

Human sacrifice was a central ritual at the Templo Mayor, as it was at most Aztec temple-pyramids. Each year hundreds or perhaps thousands of victims had their chests cut open, and their still-beating hearts ripped out by knife-wielding priests, as throngs of spectators looked on. Today we find these bloody rituals horrifying but morbidly fascinating. Yet the same people who produced this sacrificial blood and gore wrote some of the most beautiful and poignant lyric poetry ever recorded. Here is a poem attributed to the philosopher-king Nezahualcoyotl of Texcoco:

> Is it true that on earth one lives?
> Not forever on earth, only a little while.
> Though jade it may be, it breaks;
> though gold it may be, it is crushed;
> though it be quetzal plumes, it shall not last.
> Not forever on earth, only a little while.
> *Cantares Mexicanos*[1]

Today we find this contrast intriguing – blood and sacrifice versus beauty and sensitivity.

As an archaeologist, I used to feel a different sort of fascination toward the Aztecs: why was there so little fieldwork at Aztec sites? Spectacular discoveries had been made for over a century at Maya sites in southern Mexico, Guatemala, and Belize, but little effort was directed at the remains of the Aztecs. Nearly all of our information about the Aztecs came from ethnohistoric documents, but these left gaping holes in our reconstructions of Aztec society. Ironically, many of these gaps in the written record were topics for which the methods of modern archaeology were uniquely suited to study. If archaeologists could now provide detailed information on the agricultural systems, craft production, cities, houses, and rituals of other ancient civilizations, why were these methods not being applied toward understanding the Aztecs? This question had two answers: first, most scholars assumed that nearly all Aztec sites had been destroyed, either by the Spanish conquerors or by modern urban expansion; and second, those sites known to have survived were small and unassuming, unlike the large and impressive jungle cities of the Maya.

Two breakthroughs – the excavations of the Templo Mayor starting in 1978 and the work of a group of Mexican and American archaeologists at smaller sites – showed that it was still possible to map and excavate Aztec sites, and the results of recent work have revolutionized our understanding of Aztec civilization. The Templo Mayor excavations are now complete, and a number of books and articles describe this work for specialists and non-specialists alike. Fieldwork in Tenochtitlan and at smaller Aztec sites continues unabated, but so far most of this research has been described only in technical reports and articles. Although archaeological fieldwork outside of Tenochtitlan has yet to turn up any finds as spectacular as the Templo Mayor, recent discoveries have led to exciting new views of Aztec social, economic, and religious life. My goal in writing this book is to draw upon both the ongoing archaeological study of Aztec sites and the continuing tradition of ethnohistoric scholarship in order to arrive at a more complete and comprehensive picture of Aztec society as it existed on the eve of Spanish conquest. As a participant in Aztec archaeology, I hope to communicate something of the excitement and significance of our work and its contribution to a new understanding of Aztec life before 1519.

Who Were the Aztecs?

I take a wider and more inclusive view of the Aztecs, both geographically and socially, than most authors. For many, the term "Aztec" refers strictly to the inhabitants of Tenochtitlan (the Mexica people) or perhaps the inhabitants of the Valley of Mexico, the highland basin where the Mexica and certain other Aztec groups lived. I believe it makes more sense to expand the definition of "Aztec" to include the peoples of nearby highland valleys in addition to the inhabitants of the Valley of Mexico. In the final few centuries before the arrival of the Spaniards in 1519, the peoples of this wider area all spoke the Nahuatl language (the language of the Aztecs), and they all traced their origins to a mythical place in the north called Aztlan (Aztlan is the origin of the term "Aztec," a modern label that was not used by the people themselves).[2]

The several million Aztecs were divided into 20 or so ethnic groups (such as the Mexica, Tepanecs, or Tlahuica). Although people identified themselves by their ethnic group and by the city-state in which they resided, they were tied together by a common language, origin myths, and cultural patterns. Ethnohistorian James Lockhart has found many cultural similarities among these peoples at the time of the Spanish conquest, and he uses the term "Nahuas" to describe the central Mexican Nahuatl-speaking peoples. My use of the term "Aztecs" parallels Lockhart's term for the period before 1519; after that I switch to "Nahuas" to describe these peoples following the Spanish conquest.[3]

This book also takes a more inclusive social perspective than most other works on the Aztecs. Much of the available written documentation of Aztec society is flawed by two biases. First, the lives and conditions of nobles are heavily emphasized, whereas the situation of commoners is given short shrift. Second, life in Tenochtitlan is described in detail, whereas rural life is almost ignored. These biases ensure that any account of Aztec society based entirely on historical records will be incomplete. At this point, however, archaeology comes to the rescue. Recent methodological and conceptual changes in the discipline now permit archaeologists to recover rather detailed information on the lives of commoners and social conditions outside of Tenochtitlan.

The archaeological study of the everyday lives of peasants and other commoners is a relatively new development in the history of the discipline. It is understandable that early archaeologists with an interest in the high civilizations – ancient Egypt, Sumeria, the Inca, Maya, and others – chose to devote their energy to the grand monuments of these cultures. For two centuries, archaeologists excavated pyramids, palaces, tombs, and temples, the highly visible remains of ancient power. They searched for artistic masterpieces to bring back to European or American museums. This style of fieldwork, which I call "monumental archaeology," still goes on today, but it has been supplemented by a newer approach, "social archaeology."

Social archaeology develops its mission from a close interaction between archaeology and anthropology and draws its methods from the physical and biological sciences. This approach views archaeology as a social science whose goal is to reconstruct and explain the workings of past cultures. Pyramids and palaces were certainly important parts of ancient cultures, but so were peasant houses, foods and crops, merchants and markets, and other aspects of everyday life that the monumental archaeology approach omits. The social archaeology approach depends upon the principle that the everyday actions of ordinary people are important parts of any culture.[4] These things can be reconstructed for the Aztecs or any ancient civilization if the appropriate methods and theories are used to guide archaeological fieldwork and analysis. One of the main tasks of this book is to bring the Aztec people – commoners as well as lords – into the light of modern knowledge, and archaeology is the primary means for accomplishing this.

Mesoamerican Context

The Aztecs were a Mesoamerican civilization. Mesoamerica is the term for a distinctive cultural area that extends from north-central Mexico to Pacific Costa Rica (figure 1.2). Mesoamerica first took form with the initial spread of farming villages soon after 2000 BC. By the year AD 1519, the area was composed of a large variety of peoples whose cultures resembled one another far more than they resembled other New World cultures. Even in the face of Spanish conquest and colonization, the native Mesoamerican peoples managed to maintain fundamental beliefs and practices. In Mesoamerica today many distinct native languages are still spoken; the most common are Nahuatl, Yucatec Maya (there are many Maya languages), Zapotec, Mixtec, and Otomi. Nevertheless, the different Mesoamerican cultures share many characteristics, and key traits can be traced to their origin several thousand years ago.[5]

Early definitions of Mesoamerica focused on the identification of cultural traits unique to the area, which included economic features such as periodic markets, obsidian tools, plaster floors, and digging sticks, and religious traits such as human sacrifice, use of 13 as a sacred number, and a 260-day ritual calendar. Today, scholars are less interested in the compilation of lists of Mesoamerican traits and more concerned with the processes and mechanisms by which the diverse Mesoamerican cultures interacted with one another to maintain their cultural similarities and differences.[6]

Mesoamerican environments

The hallmark of Mesoamerica as a setting for cultural development is its diversity. The area includes many different environmental zones, from steamy lowland jungles to cold, windy highland plains. This

Figure 1.2   Map of Mesoamerica showing the location of central Mexico, the Aztec heartland (Drawing by Ellen Cesarski and Kori Kaufman)

environmental diversity was matched by linguistic and cultural variation. Mesoamerican environments, which set the scene for the expansion of the Aztec empire, are best discussed in terms of elevation above sea level.[7]

The tropical lowlands. Mesoamerica lies entirely within the tropical latitudes, and areas of low elevation tend to be hot and humid. Lands under 1,000 m in elevation are referred to by Mexican geographers as *tierra caliente* or the hot country. Rainfall is heavy in most lowland areas, producing either tropical forest vegetation (figure 1.3) or else savanna grasslands. Two Mesoamerican civilizations that evolved in tropical lowland environments were the Formative-period Olmec and the Classic-period Maya. The Aztecs were a highland civilization, yet they were dependent upon the tropical lowlands for a number of critical goods, including colorful feathers from parrots and quetzal birds (important in ritual and art), jaguar skins, cacao, tobacco, and jade.

Highland Mesoamerica. Areas lying between 1,000 and 2,000 m above sea level are called the *tierra templada* or temperate country. Many Mesoamerican civilizations, including the Mixtecs, Zapotecs, Tarascans, and highland Maya, flourished in this zone. Temperatures are more moderate than in the lowlands, with many areas averaging in the 70s (Fahren-

Figure 1.3   A Mesoamerican tropical forest at the Maya ruins of Tikal in Guatemala (Photograph by Michael E. Smith)

heit) year round. Most places have enough rain to grow crops successfully. Rainfall is highly seasonal, with a wet season from June to October and a dry season from January to May. Much of the Mesoamerican highlands consist of steep mountains; human settlement was concentrated in river valleys with expanses of flat terrain. The southern portion of the Aztec heartland in central Mexico falls into this highland temperate zone.

The Central Mexican Plateau. Lands above 2,000 m in elevation are called the *tierra fria*, or cold lands. This zone includes the central Valley of Mexico and adjacent valleys to the north, east, and west. Rainfall varies from levels adequate for farming to levels that will not support maize agriculture. Average temperatures are much cooler than the other zones, and frost is a problem for farmers between October and March. The shorter growing season makes agriculture more risky than at lower elevations and limits the number and variety of crops that can be grown.

The Aztec Environment

Central Mexico, the home of the Aztecs, is a mountainous area, with much of the land surface taken up by steep wooded slopes. The highest mountain in Mexico, Pico de Orizaba (5,700 m elevation), sits at the eastern edge of the region. Human settlement in central Mexico has always been concentrated in the large highland valleys, whose fertile soils and abundant resources made them home to a series of complex ancient cultures beginning before 1000 BC and leading up to Aztec civilization.

The Valley of Mexico

The Valley of Mexico was the heartland of Aztec civilization, and in 1519 it was home to approximately one million Aztecs. It is a large internally drained basin ringed by volcanic mountains that reach over 3,000 m in elevation. Millennia of soil erosion from the mountainsides have produced deep, rich soils in the Valley and a system of shallow, swampy, saline lakes in its center (figure 1.4). These salty lakes furnished various types of food to the Aztecs, including fish, turtles, insect larvae, blue-green algae, and salt. The outcast Mexica peoples chose an island in the central lake (Lake Texcoco) to found their town Tenochtitlan, which later grew into the huge imperial capital. The southern arm of the lake system, Lakes Chalco and Xochimilco, was higher in elevation than Lake Texcoco and consequently less saline. The freshwater swamps of this arm proved to be ideal for the construction of *chinampas* or raised fields, a highly productive form of agriculture used to feed the large Aztec population (see chapter 3).[8]

Surrounding the lakes is a band of alluvial plains with deep, rich soils. Where springs or rivers could be tapped for canal irrigation, the flat alluvium became a highly productive zone. Most of the Aztec cities in the Valley (except for Tenochtitlan) were located in this environmental zone. Beyond the flat alluvium are piedmont foothills that lead up to the volcanic mountains ringing the Valley of Mexico. The soils on these gentle slopes are rich and easy to work using hand tools, but they are shallow and prone to erosion. The Aztecs made use of stone terrace walls to check erosion and create fields in this area. Few large settlements were located in the foothills, but this zone was crowded with dispersed rural houses of peasant farmers. A major outcrop of obsidian, the volcanic glass that was important to Aztec technology, is located in the foothills of Otumba in the Teotihuacan subvalley (see chapter 4).

The steep mountain slopes above the piedmont were not farmed and had little settlement. These areas were covered with a pine and oak forest exploited for wood for lumber, firewood, and charcoal production. Deer and various smaller mammals were hunted in these forests, although much of the game had been depleted by hunters of pre-Aztec cultures. A few shrines have been found on mountaintops above the treeline (4,000 m). In

Figure 1.4   Map of Aztec central Mexico (Drawing by Ellen Cesarski)

the southeast corner of the Valley the two towering volcanoes Popocatepetl (5,450 m) and Ixtacihuatl (5,290 m) are covered with snow year round.

Surrounding valleys

The highland valleys and plains that surround the Valley of Mexico were home to the remaining two million Aztecs. The Toluca Valley to the west and the Puebla Valley to the east have environments similar to the Valley of Mexico. The lands north and south are considerably different.

Northern plains. Unlike the eastern, southern, and western borders, the northern edge of the Valley of Mexico does not have a steep mountain range to set it off from adjacent areas. The climate to the north becomes increasingly drier, and the northern border of Mesoamerica is soon reached. The agricultural potential of this area, now part of the Mexican state of Hidalgo, is poor and one of the major crops for the Aztecs of this region was the hardy maguey plant, cultivated for fiber and syrup. The Toltec capital Tula was located in this northern zone, as were several geological sources of obsidian.

East and west valley. The Toluca and Puebla valleys are at a similar elevation and have environments and climates comparable to the Valley of Mexico. Like the central Valley, the foothills were terraced and the alluvial areas irrigated during Aztec times. The Toluca Valley, to the west of the Valley of Mexico, is a large, flat plain in the modern state of Mexico. The headwaters of the Lerma River are in this valley. During the Aztec period, Nahuatl speakers shared the valley with other groups including Otomi and Matlatzinca speakers. The Puebla Valley, east of the Valley of Mexico, is located in the modern states of Tlaxcala and Puebla. Several Aztec city-states in the northern part of this area (including Tlaxcalla and Huexotzinco) successfully resisted attempts by the Triple Alliance (Aztec) empire to conquer them and remained independent until the arrival of the Spaniards.

The southern valleys. South of the Valley of Mexico, elevation drops off more quickly and the valleys of the modern state of Morelos and the southern part of Puebla lie about 1,000 m lower than the other central Mexican valleys. A warmer climate permits cultivation of a number of tropical crops such as cotton and many fruits. Otherwise, this area has similar environmental zones to the rest of central Mexico (figure 1.5). The Aztecs built terraces on hillsides and irrigation canals in the valleys, making Morelos one of the most fertile areas of central Mexico. Beyond the agricultural productivity of Morelos is its archaeological richness; Aztec sites are abundant and well preserved here.

The social landscape

The natural environment of central Mexico is unique within Mesoamerica, and its qualities go a long way toward explaining why the area was a center for advanced civilizations for over two thousand years. The close juxtaposition of many diverse environmental zones encouraged communication and exchange among groups and enabled settlements to

Figure 1.5   Typical central Mexican countryside (in southern Puebla). The field in the foreground is planted in maize (Photograph by Michael E. Smith)

obtain readily a wide variety of goods. Unlike most highland areas in Mesoamerica, central Mexico has numerous flat valleys and plains. Rainfall is adequate for maize agriculture, though not abundant. This environment easily supported small agricultural populations for many centuries, but larger numbers of people, with more complex institutions such as cities and states, required higher levels of food production. Fortunately, many central Mexican regions could be made more productive with only modest investments of labor. Barren hillsides could be transformed into fertile plots by construction of terrace walls; valley plots could be improved with canal irrigation; and swamps could be turned into high-yielding farms by adoption of the ancient Maya technique of raised field agriculture (*chinampas*).[9]

The Aztecs did in fact adopt all of these innovations in farming. They were carried out in response to two dramatic developments during the final centuries before Spanish conquest: an explosion of population and an expansion of city-states and empires across the region. One result of these changes in agriculture, demography, and politics was the spread of Aztec peoples across the face of the land. By the time the Spaniards arrived in 1519, central Mexico had been transformed into a social landscape filled with villages, towns, and cities set within a greatly modified agricultural countryside. Although I do not wish to invoke any sense of environmental determinism, it is clear that the unique characteristics of the central Mexican environment were crucial in order for this social and ecological transformation to occur.

Sources of Information

The Aztecs are long gone, yet we know quite a bit about them today. Our knowledge comes from two sources: ethnohistory, the study of written documents, and archaeology, the study of material objects or artifacts. At first glance, the use of this information seems straightforward. What could be clearer than a firsthand Spanish description of an Aztec town or ritual, or an archaeological interpretation of an Aztec temple or cookpot? Yet as we look closer at the evidence, the picture begins to blur.

The conqueror Hernando Cortés sought to glorify his accomplishments by inflating the sizes of the towns he conquered, and he justified his destruction of Aztec culture by exaggerating its more savage elements. Similarly, a 500-year old pot does not have a label telling us whether it was used to store grain, to serve wine, or to cook human flesh. The archaeologist must infer its use and significance from fragmentary evidence.

In other words, scholars cannot simply leap from primary evidence – written or material – to believable interpretations of Aztec culture. We must consider the origin and nature of the evidence, we must apply rigorous methods to its study, and we must report the evidence and our methods objectively so that others may judge our interpretations on their merit.[10] Let us now take a look at the sources and methods used by ethnohistorians and archaeologists to create our understanding of Aztec civilization.

Ethnohistory

The use of documents and other written materials to study the anthropology of past cultures is known as ethnohistory. Ethnohistorians typically use the writings of explorers, soldiers, missionaries, diplomats, and others to reconstruct cultures at the time of contact with the west. Unlike many of the cultures studied by ethnohistorians, those of Mesoamerica were literate. For the Aztecs and other Mesoamerican peoples, the scope of ethnohistory is therefore broadened to include all written texts by and about these cultures. Ethnohistoric documents on the Aztecs can be divided into four types: native pictorial documents, reports of the Spanish conquerors, compilations of early colonial chroniclers, and Colonial-period administrative documents.

Pictorial codices

The Aztecs used one of the five known writing systems of ancient Mesoamerica; the others are Maya, Zapotec, Mixtec, and Epi-Olmec.

Unlike Mayan writing, which could record anything that could be spoken, Aztec writing could only depict a limited repertoire of names and concepts. Most Aztec texts comprised pictorial images of persons, places, and things augmented with limited glyphic elements. Texts served as mnemonic devices – the readers (typically nobles, priests, and scribes) used the images as clues or keys and filled out the interpretation with their own personal knowledge. Manuscripts or codices (singular, codex) were written on bark paper or animal skins (see chapter 11). Only a few pre-Colonial examples have survived, but scribes continued to paint manuscripts in the Aztec style for several generations after the Spanish conquest, and several types of these still exist.

Pictorial histories depicted significant events in the history of a dynasty or city state. In the most common form, a continuous series of year-glyphs was painted across the page, and depictions of events were drawn next to the year in which they occurred or were connected to the year by a line. Aztec history was related in oral form, with the historian using these manuscripts as a framework. The *Anales de Cuauhtitlan*, an early colonial, Nahuatl-language narrative that describes the events illustrated in a now-lost pictorial history, gives an idea of the content of these histories:

> **2 House [1481]** was when the ruler Axayacatl died. Then Tizoc was inaugurated as ruler of Tenochtitlan. Also, there was an eclipse of the sun.
> **3 Rabbit [1482].** At this time the Colhuacan ruler called Tlatolcaltzin died. Then his son, called Tezozomoctli, was inaugurated as ruler of Colhuacan.
> **4 Reed [1483].** At this time, in Tenochtitlan, the foundation was laid for the house of the devil Huitzilopochtli [i.e., the Templo Mayor], started by the ruler Tizoc.[11]

An example of a pictorial history codex is provided in chapter 2 (figure 2.11 and box, p. 53 below).

Ritual almanacs helped priests to manage the ritual calendar, a sacred 260-day cycle (figure 1.6; see box; see also figures 11.1, 11.5). These depictions of gods and rituals were used for divination and to keep records of ceremonies and cycles of time. *Tribute records* were lists of payments due by individuals to their lords and by city-states to the Aztec empire (figure 7.4), and maps were records of land held by individual families.

For sheer quantity of information, the Codex Mendoza is perhaps the most important Aztec pictorial document. This three-part manuscript was commissioned in the 1540s by the Spanish viceroy (Antonio de Mendoza) to show the king of Spain something of Aztec culture. The manuscript was painted in Aztec style, and then a scribe wrote short descriptions (in Spanish) of each element. The first part of the Codex Mendoza is a pictorial history showing the conquests of the Mexica emperors. The second part is a record of the tribute paid by each province of the Aztec empire

Figure 1.6   Page from an Aztec ritual almanac (Codex Borgia 1976:f.62). This shows a 13-day period known as a *trecena*; the 13 day names are arranged across the bottom and right, starting with the day 1 jaguar in the lower right. This *trecena* is ruled by the god Quetzalcoatl, who is seated on a throne. A supplicant and a variety of cult items and offerings are shown in front of the deity (After Seler 1963)

(figure 7.4). These two sections are based on pre-Hispanic manuscript formats and are similar to other pictorial histories and tribute records. The third part of the Codex Mendoza is an innovation without any known pre-Hispanic antecedents – an account of the Aztec life cycle from birth to death (figures 4.4, 4.9, 6.1, 6.2, 11.6).

The Codex Mendoza has had a colorful history. It contains a note from the scribe stating that he did not have sufficient time to complete the job to his satisfaction because the royal galleon was about to sail for Spain. French pirates hijacked the ship, and the Codex ended up in the possession of an aide to the French king. After a number of transfers, it came to rest at Oxford University, where it remains today.[12]

Reports of the conquerors

Hernando Cortés and several of his soldiers recorded accounts of the conquest of the Aztecs. Bernal Díaz del Castillo, whose description of the approach to Tenochtitlan opens this chapter, wrote a particularly vivid account of his experiences. Cortés's lengthy reports to the king of Spain, Charles V, were filled with information on the Aztecs.

As helpful as these documents are to modern scholars, they are biased

Reading a Ritual Codex

Priests used ritual codices for divination and to keep track of lucky and unlucky days in a type of astrology. The most common theme in these codices is the *tonalpohualli*, the 260-day ritual calendar. The operation of this calendar is explained in chapter 11; here we only need to know that the calendar was divided into 20 groups of 13 days called by the Spanish term *trecenas*, and that the days of a *trecena* shared a patron god and various symbolic associations. The *trecena* in figure 1.6 is called 1 jaguar, after the first day name in the sequence of 13 days (lower right). The 13 days of this *trecena* are listed across the bottom and up the left side.

On the right of the main panel the god Quetzalcoatl sits on a throne; he is the patron of the *trecena* 1 jaguar. A supplicant offers weapons and a bowl of precious objects (such as feathers) to the god. A sun disk half obscured by the starry night sky suggests dusk or nightfall. In the center is a temple with a ball of rubber before it. The identification of these elements and their meanings are not certain; no Aztec priest ever revealed his or her secrets to a Spanish or native chronicler. The meanings of these items have been reconstructed by scholars using myths and other pictorial and written accounts. According to Eduard Seler (1963), the foremost interpreter of the Codex Borgia, these elements all relate to myths about Quetzalcoatl, who ruled over the 13 days of the *trecena* 1 jaguar.

in several ways and must be treated with caution. The Spaniards, Cortés in particular, were trying to justify and glorify their actions, and they slanted their accounts accordingly. Cortés gained greater glory by inflating the size of the armies he defeated, or the size of the cities he converted. Furthermore, Cortés and his army were criticized by priests and others for their wanton destruction of the Aztec people and their property, and he tried to justify his actions by portraying the Aztecs as terrible savages in great need of civilizing and conversion by the Spaniards. So long as these biases are taken into consideration, however, the lengthy reports of Cortés, Díaz del Castillo, and others are essential sources of information on the Aztecs.[13]

Accounts of the chroniclers

The term "chronicler" refers to anyone who wrote a description of Aztec culture in the decades immediately following the Spanish conquest. This is a broad category that includes many authors and diverse types of written accounts. A brief look at four of the more important chroniclers – Durán, Sahagún, Alva Ixtlilxochitl, and Chimalpahin – gives an idea of the nature of these sources. The chroniclers provide some of the richest and most detailed accounts of Aztec culture.

Friar Diego Durán. The Dominican friar Diego Durán was born in Spain around 1537. He was brought to New Spain (central Mexico) as a young boy and spent his youth in Texcoco and Mexico City before entering the priesthood in 1556. Durán traveled extensively throughout central Mexico, where he developed a curiosity about ancient Aztec culture. As research for his three books on the Aztecs, Durán read the earlier accounts of the conquerors, traveled widely to interview natives and Spaniards, and consulted Aztec pictorial manuscripts.

Durán was quite energetic in seeking out knowledge on Aztec culture, and his respect for and objectivity towards Aztec customs and beliefs was unusual among his contemporaries. For example, he describes the practice of human sacrifice almost dispassionately and then goes on to discuss the famous racks of human skulls that were set up outside of temples:

> From pole to pole, through the holes, stretched thin rods strung with numerous human heads pierced through the temple. Each rod held twenty heads. These horizontal rows of skulls rose to the height of the poles of the palisade and filled it from end to end. One of the conquerors assured me that they were so numerous that they were impossible to count, so close together that they caused fright and wonder. These skulls were all that remained of those who had been sacrificed . . . I asked whether they were set up flesh and all, and everyone said no; after the flesh had been eaten, only the skull was brought to the temple. Some were left with their hair on, and they remained until the hair fell off.[14]

Friar Durán interviewed Mexica nobles and commoners and consulted pictorial histories to write the most complete historical account of the Mexica people.

Friar Bernardino de Sahagún. Sahagún was born in Spain in 1499 and traveled to New Spain as a Franciscan monk in 1529. He helped found the College of Santa Cruz in Tlatelolco, where he instructed young Mexica nobles in Spanish and Latin and in turn learned Nahuatl from them. Like

Durán, Sahagún was keenly interested in the precontact culture and strived to learn as much as he could about Aztec history, customs, and especially religion. He began to collect systematic information on these topics, employing a team of Indian assistants and artists. They interviewed surviving Mexica nobles, asking the same questions of a series of different informants. Answers were cross-checked, and informants were reinterviewed to settle conflicting accounts and to amplify previous replies. All the interviews were conducted in Nahuatl, which helped to ensure that Sahagún's account preserved much of the Aztec point of view.

Friar Sahagún produced several distinct, yet overlapping, written accounts of Aztec culture. The most informative, today called the *Florentine Codex: General History of the Things of New Spain*, is a lengthy chronicle written in Nahuatl. Although Sahagún made a hasty Spanish translation of the manuscript, the original Nahuatl version is more complete. It was written in 12 books, some of the titles of which are as follows: The Gods, The Ceremonies, Rhetoric and Moral Philosophy, Kings and Lords, The People, and Earthly Things. Each book was accompanied by numerous drawings illustrating major points. The *Florentine Codex* has been translated into English and published in a bilingual (Nahuatl and English) edition. The work of Bernardino de Sahagún stands as the most detailed and systematic first-hand account of Aztec culture. I make numerous references to Sahagún's writings in the pages that follow, and many of his illustrations are reproduced in this book.[15]

Alva Ixtlilxochitl and Chimalpahin. These two chroniclers, descendants of Aztec nobles and kings, recorded historical accounts of their native towns.[16] Fernando de Alva Ixtlilxochitl (1578–1650) was a mestizo (a person of mixed native and Spanish origins) whose ancestors were kings of Texcoco (his namesake Ixtlilxochitl ruled from 1409 to 1418). He was educated at Sahagún's Colegio de Santa Cruz and wrote his first chronicle, in Spanish, in 1600. His description of the expansion of the Triple Alliance (Aztec) empire provides a non-Mexica point of view of the empire's history to balance the better-known Mexica versions, and gives scholars insight into the nature of Aztec native historical accounts.

Domingo de San Antón Muñón Chimalpahin Quauhtlehuanitzin (1579–1660) was a descendent of a minor branch of the nobility of Amecameca, a city-state in the southeast corner of the Valley of Mexico that was subject to Chalco. He was a caretaker at a Christian church and was in contact with Alva Ixtlilxochitl and other native historians of the early seventeenth century. Chimalpahin wrote several histories of Chalco and Amecameca, in Nahuatl, that cover events from the time of the Toltecs until 1612. These documents are valuable for their historical chronicle of these areas and for their portrayal of the Aztec view of histories and settlements.

Durán, Sahagún, Alva Ixtlilxochitl, and Chimalpahin were only four of the many sixteenth-century chroniclers. Other notable examples are the priests Acosta, Mendieta, Motolinía, Torquemada, and Ruiz de Alarcón; the Aztec noble Alvarado Tezozomoc; and the Spanish administrator Zorita. Taken as a group, the works of the chroniclers are our single most extensive source of information on the Aztecs. Recently, however, ethnohistorians have begun to recognize several serious drawbacks to these accounts. First, the chroniclers describe overwhelmingly the lives and activities of lords and nobles with scant attention to the commoners. Second, most of their descriptions are very generalized and written as if they apply to all parts of the Aztec realm, whereas we now realize that there was considerable variation between regions in customs, beliefs, and social conditions. For example, the chroniclers described Aztec cities as huge, complex urban centers, using the imperial capitals Tenochtitlan and Texcoco as their models. Yet recent research on other Aztec cities shows them to be far smaller and simpler than the imperial capitals. Just how widely can we generalize descriptions of the Mexica of Tenochtitlan to other Aztec peoples and places? Another problem is that the Colonial-period Nahuas sometimes deliberately deceived the Spanish chroniclers to achieve particular objectives, so some of the information in the chronicles is incorrect. There is a growing recognition that the work of the chroniclers is of limited relevance for many Aztec peoples and areas, and this sentiment has led to an increased use of the fourth type of ethnohistoric document.

Colonial-period administrative documents

Once the conquest of the Aztecs was completed in 1521, central Mexico became a province of the Spanish empire called New Spain. The Spaniards ran their empire in a highly bureaucratic fashion, and countless written reports were produced on topics ranging from fruit trees to Aztec land tenure to strategies for converting the natives to Christianity. These documents were stored in archives in Mexico and Spain, where many still remain for scholars to study. Fortunately, a large number of the most informative examples have been transcribed and published, and some have been translated into English.

Documents on the civic administration of New Spain are numerous. Wills, deeds, baptismal and death records all provide information on household and family organization. Many of the most informative records are those written by Nahuas in Nahuatl, using the Spanish alphabet. The Nahuas quickly learned to use the Spanish legal system, and lawsuits with extensive written documentation proliferated. These suits often involved detailed information-gathering actions, and the results are a treasure trove of useful information on local conditions in many areas of central Mexico soon after the Spanish conquest.[17]

The most systematic attempt at gathering information on New Spain and the other Spanish provinces was a questionnaire prepared by the crown in 1577 and sent to all colonial administrators. Fifty questions were included on a variety of topics, from the ancient customs of the area to the natural environment and resources to the Spanish occupants. The often lengthy replies to this questionnaire, called *Relaciones Geográficas*, fill nine books today and furnish detailed pictures of several hundred Aztec towns in the years 1579 to 1581.[18]

Excerpts from the *Relación Geográfica* from Huaxtepec, a town in the modern state of Morelos, give an idea of the information to be found in these documents. The reply was submitted on September 24, 1580, by Juan Gutiérrez de Liébana, mayor of Huaxtepec and other towns.

> **Question 14:** To whom were they subject when they were heathens; what power did their rulers have over them; what did they pay in tribute; what forms of worship, rites, and good or evil customs did they have?
> **Reply:** They say that in this town, although they recognized Montezuma the Elder and his successors as king, they did not pay tribute beyond participation in his campaigns . . . They had another local lord whom they obeyed and recognized as king . . . called Tultecatl tecuhtli. When the king would go out of his house, no one dared look at him except those who accompanied him . . . For affairs of state, they had two officials like judges who ascertained and verified what had to happen when crimes occurred . . . And they say that they had only one idol in the town's public market, called Ichpuchtli Quilaztle . . . to this idol, every 20 days they sacrificed a child, the offspring of slaves they had captured in war.[19]

In addition to the written replies, many of the *Relaciones* are accompanied by maps of the towns and their dependent villages (see chapter 7). Unfortunately, not all Aztec towns are covered by these reports, and some examples that were submitted have since been lost. For towns that do have a surviving report, it is one of the first places ethnohistorians turn for information on local conditions.

Archaeology

The contributions of archaeologists to Aztec studies are quite recent. For decades archaeologists bypassed Aztec sites on their way to the spectacular jungle ruins of Classic Maya civilization. A few surviving Aztec pyramids at sites such as Tenayuca (in Mexico City) and Teopanzolco (in

Cuernavaca, Morelos) were excavated and restored (see chapter 2), but most Aztec sites had little to offer fieldworkers whose focus was on the great monuments of ancient civilizations. In the late 1970s, when the ideas of social archaeology began to bring a more scientific approach to the discipline, archaeologists took another look at the potential of Aztec sites.

Today archaeologists design their fieldwork with clear research problems in mind. Previously, archaeologists would select a site simply because it had large mounds or was conveniently located; they would then excavate it to see what turned up. Sometimes the results were spectacular; sometimes they were meager. Now, we focus on a particular problem and use that to structure the research. We select which sites to study and what methods to use in order to answer specific questions about the past. This change makes fieldwork much more efficient and productive. When this approach is coupled with the latest technical advances in dating methods, fieldwork, and artifact analysis, it allows archaeologists to reconstruct many aspects of Aztec society in great detail. A number of examples of projects that follow the problem-oriented social archaeology approach are discussed in the chapters that follow. Here I review the different fieldwork methods that have contributed to our knowledge of Aztec society.

Regional survey

The goal of regional survey is to locate archaeological sites across the landscape. A team of archaeologists walks over the entire surface of an area, using maps and aerial photographs to plot the locations of sites and features. This method is particularly useful in arid and semiarid environments, such as most of central Mexico, where the surface of the ground can easily be seen. Most of rural central Mexico has been plowed for many years. Although plowing destroys the upper portion of archaeological sites, it also brings buried artifacts to the surface where the survey crew can find them. The team members spread out in a line and walk forward with their "nose to the ground." Sites are identified by either the presence of mounds (usually the ruins of temples or residences) or more commonly by a scatter of potsherds, obsidian tools, and other artifacts (figure 1.7).

Once a site is found, the survey crew measures its size, makes a map, and takes one or more collections of artifacts from the ground surface. Any visible architecture is photographed and/or drawn (figure 1.8). Regional surveys provide information on the number and size of sites in each temporal period and the locations of sites in relation to the natural landscape and to each other. These data are then analyzed to produce population estimates and reconstructions of settlement patterns for each period.

The use of regional survey in highland Mesoamerica was pioneered by

Figure 1.7   A rural Aztec site. The low mound was once an Aztec house or other structure. This site in the Teotihuacan Valley, called TA-27, was discovered in 1957 by a regional survey project directed by William T. Sanders (Evans and Sanders 2000:188).

Figure 1.8   A small temple platform at the site TA-8 in the Teotihuacan Valley. This structure was built of small stones and covered with white lime plaster. It was discovered by a regional survey project directed by William T. Sanders (Evans and Sanders 2000:115).

William T. Sanders in the Teotihuacan subvalley of the Valley of Mexico in the 1960s. As part of this research, Sanders located many Aztec sites, and he used ethnohistoric sources to interpret Aztec settlement patterns. His methods of regional survey were then applied to other parts of the Valley of Mexico by Jeffrey R. Parsons, Richard E. Blanton, and in later fieldwork by Sanders himself. By 1975, several thousand square kilometers had been surveyed, resulting in the identification of nearly four thousand archaeological sites.[20] A major discovery of these projects was a population explosion that took place during the Late Aztec period. The implications of this growth are discussed in chapters 2 and 3.

Intensive site surface studies

At many sites, artifacts are numerous on the surface of the ground, or the foundations of houses and temples may still be visible. Aztec sites are often not deeply buried. In these cases, the mapping of structures and features and the systematic collection of surface artifacts allow archaeologists to reconstruct the ancient activities and lifeways at a site. The surface collections taken during regional survey are usually inadequate for this purpose. Intensive site surface studies typically take hundreds or even thousands of separate artifact collections for thorough coverage of the site (figure 1.9).

Intensive site surface research at Aztec sites was pioneered by Elizabeth M. Brumfiel at the city-state center of Huexotla. Brumfiel took 1,243 artifact collections from the surface of the site and studied changing patterns of resource use, commerce, and craft production between the Early Aztec (AD 1150–1350) and Late Aztec periods (1350–1520). She later applied this method to the sites of Xico and Xaltocan, and I used a similar but less intensive approach at Yautepec (see chapter 8). The most spectacular results from intensive site surface research come from the city-state center of Otumba. Thomas H. Charlton, Deborah L. Nichols, and Cynthia Otis Charlton took 1,150 artifact collections that documented extensive craft production activity, including the manufacture of obsidian tools, pottery figurines and incense burners, textiles, and several types of jewelry. This unexpectedly high degree of craft specialization has changed our views of Aztec urbanism and economics; the Otumba research is discussed in more detail in chapter 4.[21]

Excavation

Beginning with the uncovering of the Templo Mayor in 1978, excavations at Aztec sites have added tremendously to our knowledge of Aztec culture. The Mexican government project at the Templo Mayor, directed

Figure 1.9 Archaeologists collecting surface artifacts from a 2 by 2 m square in a cornfield at the Aztec city of Yautepec (Photograph by Michael E. Smith)

by Eduardo Matos Moctezuma, has produced the most dramatic results. Beyond documenting the history of building and rebuilding of the central temple of Tenochtitlan, these excavations have yielded new information on imperial rituals, tribute from distant lands, and the cosmic symbolism of the Aztec empire (see chapter 10).

Outside of the Templo Mayor project, three types of excavations have been done at Aztec sites: (1) excavations of monumental architecture at major urban centers, (2) large-scale exposure of houses and domestic contexts, and (3) small, problem-oriented test-pit operations. The monumental archaeology approach has been applied to Aztec urban sites since the 1920s, when major excavations were undertaken at Tenayuca in Mexico City and Teopanzolco in Morelos (see chapter 2). Urban architecture has also been studied at Tlatelolco and Santa Cecelia in Mexico and at provincial sites like Malinalco, Calixtlahuaca, Coatetelco, and Yautepec.[22]

House excavations are crucial for the reconstruction of Aztec economic and social patterns (figure 1.10). Except in the largest cities, houses were widely scattered and people simply threw their trash out back. By excavating these trash middens, we can learn of domestic activities and living conditions of individual Aztec households. Susan T. Evans excavated several houses at the rural village of Cihuatecpan in the Teotihuacan Valley,

Figure 1.10   Excavation of an elite residence at the Aztec city of Yautepec. The flat white surfaces are lime plaster floors. This ruin is in a schoolyard today; the modern basketball courts are visible in the background (Photograph by Michael E. Smith)

and I have dug houses at a village (Capilco), a town (Cuexcomate), and a city (Yautepec) in Morelos. Hortensia de Vega Nova and colleagues have excavated part of an Aztec royal palace in Yautepec.[23]

A number of projects have used test excavations to investigate specific issues at Aztec sites. For example, Jeffrey R. Parsons and colleagues tested the *chinampa* agricultural fields in the southern Valley of Mexico to learn how and when these features were constructed. At Otumba, Charlton, Nichols, and Otis Charlton followed up their intensive surface collections at craft workshops with test excavations to better document economic activities at the site. Similarly, Brumfiel used test pits to amplify her intensive surface collections at Xaltocan, and Mary G. Hodge excavated test pits in Chalco to investigate economic and social changes. At Yautepec, I used test excavations to look for buried houses (some were successful, some not), to see whether early Spanish churches were built on top of Aztec temples (they were not), to test (successfully) my earlier reconstruction of the borders of Aztec Yautepec, and to look (unsuccessfully) for evidence of Aztec irrigation canals.[24]

Analysis and interpretation

Artifacts do not speak to us directly. They must be analyzed, and the results must be interpreted. This is the tedious side of archaeology. It is fun and exciting to excavate sites, but then we are faced with the long task of classifying, studying, and describing the artifacts and architecture. The fruits of five months of excavation at Cuexcomate and Capilco (nearly half a million artifacts, mostly potsherds) required my wife and me to spend four years in the laboratory studying artifacts plus several additional years of computer analysis and write-up.

Beyond the basic classification and description of artifacts, new technological analyses have revolutionized the discipline. We routinely use methods such as radiocarbon dating or obsidian hydration dating to determine the ages of artifacts and deposits, and new techniques of chemical analysis permit artifacts to be traced to their often distant points of origin. Some of the advances made possible by these methods are discussed in chapters 4 and 5.

Nearly all of our interpretations of archaeological remains depend upon inductive logic, also called reasoning by analogy. For example, I have interpreted small bowls with tripod supports as tools used in the spinning of cotton thread based on an analogy with modern cotton handspinning techniques. When modern Maya women spin cotton, they use a small bowl to control the twirling spindle. The small Aztec bowls resemble modern spinning bowls, so I argued by analogy that the ancient artifacts functioned in a similar manner. An analogy is a hypothesis, so the next step was to test this interpretation with independent data. Several lines of evidence converge to support this hypothesis: pictorial sources from the Early Colonial period such as the Codex Mendoza show women spinning cotton using a small bowl; the artifacts show traces of abrasion where the spindle has worn away the interior surface of the bowl; and these artifacts are found in domestic contexts where we know from other evidence that spinning took place.[25]

This example shows the importance of modern (and historical) analogues for our interpretation of many aspects of Aztec culture. Thus our knowledge of the Aztecs comes not only from ethnohistory and archaeology but also, indirectly, from Mesoamerican ethnology, the study of modern and historic cultures. Two other branches of modern anthropology – physical anthropology and linguistics – also contribute greatly to Aztec studies. Physical anthropologists study the skeletal remains of the Aztecs in order to determine their sex, age, health and nutrition, and sometimes cause of death. Linguists have expanded greatly our knowledge of Nahuatl and its historical development in Aztec and more recent times. Geographers have also provided new information on the physical environment, farming systems, and settlement patterns.

Art History

After the initial work by the chroniclers in the sixteenth and early seventeenth centuries, scholarly study of the Aztecs started in the eighteenth century with a growing appreciation for Aztec art, particularly stone sculpture and painted codices. An interest in Aztec architecture and archaeological sites did not come until much later. In the nineteenth century, museums in Mexico, the United States, and Europe were busy filling their exhibit halls and back storerooms with Aztec sculpture, ceramic vessels, metal, and other objects. The richest collection was at Mexico's National Museum, where items of Aztec art filled storerooms to their limit (figure 1.11). Today, Aztec art may be found in museums throughout Mexico and in the larger museums in the United States and Europe. The National Museum of Anthropology in Mexico City has an outstanding exhibit of the finest examples of Aztec art, and the Museum of the Templo Mayor has another excellent exhibit. These and other museums also have large collections of objects in storage that are open to researchers.

Ever since the rebirth of interest in Aztec art in the eighteenth century, the rigorous study of Aztec objects by art historians has been one of the major components of Aztec studies. Art historians have made major contributions not only to the historical and aesthetic study of Aztec art, but also to the topics of Aztec religion, writing, cosmology, iconography, astronomy, and social organization.[26]

Aztec Studies Today

If any overarching theme can be identified within the recent boom of research on Aztec civilization, it is an explicit focus on people. Ethnohistorians, archaeologists, and art historians are reconstructing the activities of families, social groups, and villages while they explore the social conditions of the people who lived in all parts of the Aztec world. Whereas many earlier scholars restricted their studies to lords, temples, gods, and cities, the advances of social archaeology and recent trends in ethnohistory and art history now give us access to peasants, workshops, and villages. Themes that were unheard of two decades ago, such as women's roles, farming methods, domestic crafts, and standards of living, are now topics of research.

Figure 1.11   "Mexican antiquities which exist in the National Museum of Mexico, 1857." Lithograph by Casimiro Castro, published in *México y sus alrededores* (Castro 1855–1857)

Modern anthropology, the study of human cultures and their variations over space and time, provides the best framework for our emerging understanding of Aztec civilization, and I use an anthropological approach to structure the narrative that follows. Chapter 2 sets out the historical outline of Aztec culture, from its predecessors through the Spanish conquest. Chapters 3 through 11 discuss specific aspects of Aztec culture, beginning with settlement (chapter 3), followed by economics (chapters 4 and 5), social organization (chapter 6), politics (chapter 7), urbanism (chapter 8), religion (chapters 9 and 10), and intellectual and aesthetic life (chapter 11). Chapter 12 recapitulates the glory of the final century of Aztec civilization, tells the story of the Spanish conquest, and ends with an account of the legacy of the Aztecs today. I begin my account in central Mexico before the Aztecs arrived on the scene.

chapter two
The Rise of Aztec Civilization

So great were the feats and exploits of the Aztecs, so full of adventure, that those who are not acquainted with these exploits and with these people will enjoy hearing of their ancient customs and of their origins and descendants.
Diego Durán, The History of the Indies of New Spain

The evolution of Aztec civilization is partly a rags-to-riches story of the sudden rise of the Nahuatl speakers from obscurity to power and partly a chronicle of continuity in the cultural achievements of central Mexican civilizations. These two themes were important elements in Aztec native historical accounts, and they loomed large in the Aztecs' own sense of identity and heritage. The rags-to-riches theme centers on the Mexica people, following them from their origin as a simple nomadic tribe in the northern desert, their migration to the Valley of Mexico, the founding of Tenochtitlan, and their rise to power as the lords of the Aztec empire. Native historical accounts of this story suggest that the rise of Aztec civilization was due to the genius and accomplishments of the Mexica and their leaders.

In contrast to the rags-to-riches story, the theme of cultural continuity stresses the debt that the Aztecs (Mexica and others) owed to both their Toltec ancestors and the still earlier Teotihuacan culture. The last in a series of advanced urban civilizations, the Aztecs inherited much of their culture from these earlier peoples. Although the progress of the Mexica people may make a more exciting story, most scholars today find the theme of cultural continuity provides a more satisfactory account of cultural evolution in Postclassic central Mexico. The rise of Aztec civilization was due less to the genius and success of one small group (the Mexica) than to the larger social forces that had shaped the rise and fall of central Mexican civilizations over the centuries.

In this chapter I trace the historical course of the Aztec peoples from their predecessors at Classic-period Teotihuacan (AD 150–750) up to their conquest by the Spaniards in 1519. But first I review the archaeological and native historical timetables through which Aztec history is written.

Timetables

The central Mexican archaeological record goes back thousands of years to the small bands of early hunters and gatherers who flourished at the end of the Pleistocene ice age. Maize and other Mesoamerican food crops were first domesticated between 5000 and 7000 BC, but agriculture did not become the main form of subsistence until around 2000 BC. During the next two millennia, a period archaeologists call the Formative or Preclassic, central Mexico was the setting for small villages and towns, a few of which grew into centers of modest-sized chiefdoms. Chalcatzingo in Morelos, for example, became an influential chiefdom during the Middle Formative or Olmec period. Around 100 BC two of these towns – Cuicuilco in the southern Valley of Mexico and Teotihuacan in the northern Valley – became large and powerful enough to be called states. The eruption of the Mount Xitle volcano in the first century AD buried Cuicuilco under a thick mantle of lava, and soon after Teotihuacan grew into the largest urban center in Mesoamerica.[1]

The era of Teotihuacan ascendancy in central Mexico is known as the Classic period (AD 150–750). The burning of Teotihuacan around AD 750 ushered in a time of decentralized city-states called the Epiclassic period (AD 750–950). The final six centuries of pre-Hispanic cultures are known as the Postclassic era (AD 950–1519), which archaeologists divide into Early, Middle, and Late Postclassic periods (figure 2.1).

The Early Postclassic period (AD 950–1150) is sometimes called the Toltec period, since it corresponds to the flourishing of Toltec culture. The story of the Aztecs themselves begins with the arrival of Nahuatl-speaking peoples in central Mexico at the start of the Middle Postclassic period (AD 1150–1350). The "Early Aztec phase" is the term archaeologists use to describe Middle Postclassic sites in the Valley of Mexico, and I use this term for the Middle Postclassic period throughout the Aztec realm. During this crucial epoch most Aztec towns, cities, and dynasties were first established.

The Late Aztec period, part of the wider Mesoamerican Late Postclassic period (AD 1350–1520), includes the growth of Tenochtitlan and the formation and expansion of the Triple Alliance empire. In some regions of

Date AD	Archaeological Period		Event	Year
			Spanish Conquest	1519
1500	Late Aztec B	AZTEC CIVILIZATION		
1400	Late Aztec A		Aztec Empire Established	1428
			Tepanec Empire Established	1370
1300			Tenochtitlan Founded	1325
	Early Aztec		(growth of city-states)	
1200			Arrival of Aztlan Migrants	1200
			Fall of Tula	1175
1100	Early Postclassic		(Toltec civilization)	
1000				
			Start of Toltec Civilization	
900	Epiclassic		Fall of Xochicalco	

Figure 2.1 Archaeological and native historical chronologies for Aztec civilization (Drawing by Michael E. Smith)

central Mexico, archaeologists have subdivided the Late Aztec period into two subperiods (referred to here as "Late Aztec A" and "Late Aztec B") covering the intervals before (1350–1430) and after the formation of the empire (1430–1520). In other regions, including the Valley of Mexico, only a single archaeological phase is in use, which can make fine-grained study of change difficult. Chronological refinement is a topic of research by archaeologists working on the Aztecs.[2]

The native historical timetable for Aztec civilization begins with the Toltecs, but the early part of the historical record is not very reliable. There are fewer native historical sources, and their content is more obviously mythological in character than later documents. For the final century of Aztec civilization, there are numerous independent native historical accounts that can be cross-checked to gauge their accuracy. The expansion of the Aztec empire after 1430 is covered in great detail, and most scholars believe that much of the historical information is correct, if biased. The extent to which the archaeological and native historical records can be compared and correlated is a topic of continuing research, but most authorities agree on the outline of Aztec history presented in figure 2.1.

Pre-Aztec Civilizations

The Aztecs were heirs to a long tradition of central Mexican urban civilizations and owed a great cultural debt to the earlier peoples of Teotihuacan and Tula. The inhabitants of Tula – the Toltecs – figured heavily in Aztec native history, but the more ancient peoples of Teotihuacan were a mystery to the Aztecs. A brief review of these earlier peoples sets the scene for the rise of Aztec civilization.

Teotihuacan

The great Classic-period metropolis of Teotihuacan flourished between AD 150 and 750 in the northeastern Valley of Mexico. At its height between 450 and 650, Teotihuacan's 150,000 inhabitants, spread over 21 sq km, made it one of the largest cities in the world.[3] The city was laid out according to a strict grid pattern, organized around a central north–south avenue called the "Street of the Dead" (figure 2.2). The massive Pyramid of the Sun stood adjacent to the central avenue, with the smaller Pyramid of the Moon at the northern end of the street. Most people lived in large walled apartment compounds, which were tightly packed together, with only narrow alleys and passages between them. The city's rulers and elite class had larger and more elaborate residences along the Street of the Dead.

During the Classic period, Teotihuacan's renown and influence spread over all of Mesoamerica. Within its immediate hinterland in the Valley of Mexico, the city's rulers maintained a tight grip on economic activities and peoples' lives. Outside of the valley, Teotihuacan's armies conquered nearby peoples and forged one of the earliest empires of Mesoamerica. Beyond the reach of its empire, Teotihuacan engaged in trade relationships with many parts of Mesoamerica, and the city was viewed as an important sacred center by peoples as far away as the Maya lowlands in Guatemala.

Figure 2.2   Air photo of the ruins of Classic-period Teotihuacan (Photograph courtesy of Companía Mexicana de Aerofoto)

Teotihuacan's prosperity and success came to an end in the seventh and eighth centuries when the city was burned and largely abandoned for reasons still unknown. A remnant population continued to live on the site of the Classic city throughout the pre-Hispanic era, and there was an Aztec town located at the edge of the old city. But by the time the Aztecs came to power, the city's center had lain in ruins for centuries. To the Aztecs, the city was a mystical and sacred place, the birthplace of the gods, and they named the ruins Teotihuacan, which means "city or place of the gods" in Nahuatl. The modern popular names of the main pyramids (sun and moon) and the "Street of the Dead" are translations of the Aztec terms. We do not know what the city or its buildings were called in the Classic period, nor what languages were spoken there.

A number of Aztec traits can be traced back to Teotihuacan. Among these are a number of religious features, including human sacrifice as a state-sponsored ritual and the worship of a feathered-serpent god (the Aztec god Quetzalcoatl) and a goggle-eyed deity (the Aztec Tlaloc). The Aztecs adapted these older gods to their own purposes. Tlaloc, for example, was a peaceful rain god to the Aztecs, whereas his goggle-eyed predecessor at Teotihuacan was a more militaristic state god. The Aztecs were the only other Mesoamerican culture to build a city as large as Teotihuacan, or to create a zone of economic and political influence as extensive as Teotihuacan's. The Mexica recognized the greatness of the earlier city and used Teotihuacan objects and styles to promote their legitimacy as rulers of an extensive empire. For example, ancient Teotihuacan ceramic vessels were buried in offerings at Tenochtitlan, Mexica sculptors deliberately imitated Teotihuacan styles, and Teotihuacan's planned grid layout was duplicated at Tenochtitlan.[4]

Tula and the Toltecs

The fall of Teotihuacan initiated a period of warfare and disruption throughout central Mexico. A series of large and impressive fortress-cities, protected by walls and ditches, were founded at Xochicalco, Cacaxtla, and Teotenango. Stone carvings and painted murals emphasized military themes and sacrifice. These warring cities flourished between AD 750 and 950 (the Epiclassic period; see figure 2.1), after which time they were largely abandoned.[5] Then in the succeeding Early Postclassic period (AD 950–1150), the city of Tula grew into the first center large and powerful enough to warrant the title of successor to the great Teotihuacan. Modern understanding of Tula's role in Mesoamerican history is made difficult, however, by contradictions between native historical descriptions and the results of archaeological fieldwork. The Aztecs referred to the capital of the Toltecs as Tollan, a term meaning great metropolis.[6] Although scholars have linked the Tollan of the native histories to the ruined city at the site of Tula in the modern state of Hidalgo, other cities were sometimes called by this name as well. To the Aztecs, Tollan was a fantastic city of mythical proportions and qualities, and the Toltecs almost superhuman in their accomplishments. They were said to have invented most of Mesoamerican culture, including all of the arts and crafts, writing, and the calendar. In Aztec eyes, the Toltecs were the wise, healthy, rich and morally superior lords of a far-flung empire ruled by semidivine kings.

Archaeology paints a different picture, however. Mesoamerican crafts, writing, and the calendar originated long before the Toltecs arrived on the scene. Although Tula was the largest city in central Mexico at the time, it was far smaller and more modest than either Teotihuacan or Tenochtitlan. Tula had a population of about 50,000, covering approximately 13 sq km. The central ceremonial core had two large pyramids, two impressive ballcourts, and other civic buildings arranged around a large public plaza (figure 2.3). There is no archaeological evidence for a Toltec empire, and in fact, Toltec artifacts are notable for their absence outside of Tula itself. At Tula, exotic trade goods are rarer than at either Teotihuacan or Tenochtitlan. Although Tula was an important local urban center whose inhabitants traded widely in Mesoamerica, the scale and luxury of the city certainly do not accord with the lavish imaginings of the Aztecs. The end of Toltec civilization came about with the abandonment of Tula in the mid to late twelfth century, although like Teotihuacan, the city continued to have a minor occupation through Aztec times.

The symbolic importance of Tollan and the Toltecs to the Aztecs cannot be overestimated. Aztec rulers traced their genealogy, whether actual or invented, back to the Toltec kings, and this semimythical dynastic origin was a major source of political legitimacy to Mesoamerican kings, both Aztec and non-Aztec, at the time of Spanish conquest. The Aztec emperor Motecuhzoma (sometimes called "Montezuma" in English) sent a party to dig for precious relics at Tula, and Toltec objects were revered as sacred icons by the Aztecs.[7] Although the Aztec kings traced their history to the Toltecs, the Aztec peoples themselves looked to a different source for their origins.

The Aztlan Migrations

According to native historical accounts, the Aztecs migrated into central Mexico from an original home in a place called Aztlan. Some scholars believe that Aztlan was a real place and argue over its exact location (opinions range from just north of the Valley of Mexico to the southwestern

Figure 2.3   Air photo of the ruins of the central ceremonial district of Tula, the Early Postclassic Toltec capital (Photograph courtesy of Companía Mexicana de Aerofoto)

United States). Others argue that Aztlan was a mythical place with no precise location on the map. The term Aztlan, meaning "place of the herons," is the origin of the word "Aztec," a modern label that was not used by the ancient peoples themselves. Whether or not there ever was a place called Aztlan, scholars agree that the Aztec peoples migrated into central Mexico from the north.[8]

Setting out from Aztlan, the migrants visited Chicomoztoc, or "place of seven caves." A number of sources describe seven groups or "tribes" at Chicomoztoc although they disagree over the identity of these groups. When all of the native histories are compared, no fewer than 17 ethnic groups are listed among the original tribes migrating from Aztlan and Chicomoztoc. One version of the seven tribes account is the *Tira de la Peregrinación* (also known as the Codex Boturini), illustrated in figure 2.4. The name glyphs of the groups are translated on the left side. The southward migration of these groups took several generations to complete. The migrants were led by priests, and they stopped periodically to build houses and temples, to gather or cultivate food, and to carry out rituals.

The historical accounts of the Aztlan migrations may vary widely in the

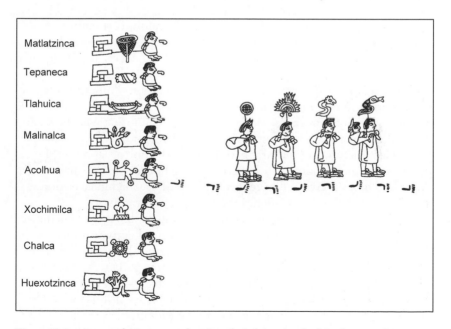

Figure 2.4 Aztec ethnic groups leaving their homeland of Aztlan to migrate south to central Mexico (After the *Tira de la Peregrinación* 1944; drawing by Ellen Cesarski)

content of their lists of the migrating groups and the precise order in which they traveled, but there is consistency in the overall timing of three contingents of migrants. The first groups to arrive in central Mexico settled throughout the Valley of Mexico. The groups that formed part of this initial contingent were the ancestors of the major Nahuatl ethnic groups to be found in the Valley of Mexico in the sixteenth century; they included the Acolhua, Tepaneca, Culhua, Chalca, Xochimilca, and several other groups.

The second contingent of migrants arrived to find the Valley of Mexico settled, so they moved on to occupy the surrounding valleys of central Mexico. These groups included the Tlahuica of Morelos, the Tlaxcalteca and Huexotzinca of Tlaxcala and Puebla, the Matlatzinca of the Toluca Valley and the Malinalca of Malinalco. Historical dates for the arrival of the Aztec migrants fall around AD 1200 for the Valley of Mexico groups and around 1220 for the groups in the surrounding valleys. The last to arrive, around AD 1250, were the Mexica, who found all of the good land occupied and were forced to settle in an undesirable, desolate area of the Valley of Mexico called Chapultepec, "grasshopper hill" or "place of the grasshopper." Far more details are available about the Mexica migration than about the other groups simply because more Mexica-based histories have survived. These sources tell us that the Mexica were guided by their patron god, Huitzilopochtli, whose image was carefully carried from Aztlan to the Valley of Mexico. We know the names of the places where the Mexica stopped on their journey, and some of the events that happened along the way.

Native historical descriptions of the Aztlan migrants contain contradictory information on the cultural sophistication of these peoples. In some accounts they lived in caves, made their living by hunting with bows and arrows, and wore animal skins for clothing. These traits describe peoples known as Chichimecs (barbaric peoples from the north), and the Mexica and other groups claimed to have been Chichimecs before they settled down and became civilized in central Mexico. The Chichimec notion was a major part of the rags-to-riches theme of Aztec origins.

Contrasting with this picture of the migrants as barbaric Chichimecs are descriptions of complex economic and cultural activities such as the planting of maize, the construction of temples, and the use of the ancient Mesoamerican 52-year calendar. Nomadic hunter-gatherers of the north Mexican desert did not have these practices, which suggests that the migrants had experience with Mesoamerican civilization long before they arrived in central Mexico. The presence of these contradictory traits among the Aztlan migrants is part of the dual conception of the cultural origins of the Aztecs, who believed themselves descended from both savage Chichimecs and civilized Toltecs.

The north-to-south movement of the Aztlan groups – described in the native histories – is confirmed by research in historical linguistics. The Nahuatl language, classified in the Nahuan group of the Uto-Aztecan family of languages, is unrelated to most Mesoamerican native languages. Whereas the other major Mesoamerican language families – Mayan, Oto-Mangueyan, and Mixe-Zoquean – had deep roots going back millennia, Nahuatl was a relatively recent intrusion into Mesoamerica.[9] The Uto-Aztecan languages originated in northern Mexico or the southwestern United States, and Nahuatl was brought to central Mexico by peoples moving south. Linguists argue over the exact timing of the arrival of Nahuatl speakers in central Mexico, but most agree that this must have occurred sometime after the collapse of Teotihuacan and before the rise of the Aztecs. Since the descendants of the named Aztlan groups were Nahuatl speakers in 1519, it is reasonable to assume that the Aztlan migrants spoke Nahuatl when they first arrived in central Mexico several centuries earlier. Whether they were the initial speakers of Nahuatl in central Mexico is uncertain, but once the Aztlan migrants arrived, the Nahuatl language spread rapidly through both migration and cultural contact. As the political and economic influence of the Aztec empire expanded, Nahuatl became the language of diplomacy and trade. By the time of the Spanish conquest, Nahuatl had spread far beyond its initial stronghold in the fertile valleys of central Mexico.

The Growth of City-States: The Early Aztec Period

New towns, new dynasties (1150–1350)

The Aztlan migrants arrived in central Mexico during the Early Aztec period (figure 2.1). The countryside was far from empty, and the settlers avoided existing settlements to found their own sites.[10] Most of the indigenous non-Nahuatl-speaking peoples were eventually assimilated into Aztec culture, although some groups, such as the Otomi, managed to retain their separate ethnic identity within Aztec civilization. Many of the new settlements were successful and grew rapidly into towns or cities with regional political and economic significance. Nearly all of the major Aztec cities and towns that existed at the time of Spanish conquest were founded during this time period.

Central Mexico became the arena for a dynamic system of interacting city-states. The rulers of these small polities were petty kings called *tlatoque* (sing. *tlatoani*) who endeavored to establish genealogical links to the Toltec kings through marriage ties with their descendants or through invention. Like systems of city-states in other ancient cultures, the polities of Early

Aztec central Mexico interacted intensively with one another in both friendly and antagonistic fashions. Alliances between dynasties and trade between city-states were accompanied by warfare and aggression.

The native histories are full of accounts of battles among the city-states. During the first century or so after initial settlement, small-scale warfare among the new city-states was frequent, but because of shifting alliances and the small scale of most conflicts, no individual polity succeeded in establishing a tributary empire. Among the more active and influential polities at this time were the cities of Azcapotzalco, Coatlinchan, Culhuacan, Tenayuca, and Xaltocan in the Valley of Mexico, and Cuauhnahuac/Teopanzolco, Calixtlahuaca, Cholula, and Huexotzinco in surrounding areas.[11]

During the Early Aztec period a common Aztec culture emerged among the new settlers of the central Mexican highlands. The use of the Nahuatl language and the acknowledgement of a common Aztlan origin were at the foundation of this widespread culture. The interactions among city-states, particularly through trade and noble marriage alliances, kept far-flung peoples in touch. An important component of this widespread culture was religious ritual. Although individual gods and ceremonies varied slightly from region to region, a common core of ritual and belief united the central Mexican peoples. This religion received concrete material expression in both cult objects – incense burners and figurines – and temple architecture. In contrast to earlier Mesoamerican pyramids with a single temple on top and a single stairway up the side, the pyramids built by the Early Aztec peoples had twin temples and double stairways. Impressive examples of such pyramids have been excavated and restored at the Early Aztec sites of Teopanzolco and Tenayuca.

Figure 2.5   An Early Aztec twin-stair pyramid at Teopanzolco, a site located in the city of Cuernavaca, Morelos (Photograph by Michael E. Smith)

Teopanzolco and Tenayuca: early Aztec cities

Nearly all cities and towns of the Early Aztec period continued to be occupied into Late Aztec times. Unfortunately for archaeologists, Late Aztec urban expansion and renewal obliterated or built over most of the Early Aztec architecture. At Teopanzolco and Tenayuca, however, large Early Aztec twin-stair pyramids survived intact; these were excavated and restored in the early part of the twentieth century.[12] The pyramid at Teopanzolco (figure 2.5) was discovered during the Mexican Revolution (1910–14) when the army of Emiliano Zapata placed canons on top of the mound to shell federalist positions in downtown Cuernavaca. The vibrations from cannon fire shook loose the soil, exposing ancient walls and floors. After the Revolution the pyramid was excavated and restored, along with a series of nearby platforms and buildings. The pyramid had two main stages of construction, and the walls of small temples on top of the earlier (inner) platform have survived. Across the plaza from the pyramid is a row of low platforms that probably served as bases for altars (figure 2.6). The two round altars may have been dedicated to Ehecatl, the wind god (chapters 9 and 10). Inside the southernmost altar archaeologists found a sunken chamber filled with human skulls and offerings of ceramic vessels. The presence of cervical vertebrae with the skulls indicates that these were the victims of decapitation, probably part of a ritual of human sacrifice (chapter 10).

The structures shown in figure 2.6 are the only buildings that survive of Teopanzolco. This ceremonial precinct was almost certainly the center of the city of Cuauhnahuac during the Early Aztec period. Early Aztec ceramics associated with the site have been found in many parts of the modern city of Cuernavaca, suggesting that the city was quite extensive at that time. In Late Aztec times, the civic center of Cuauhnahuac was moved from Teopanzolco to a more defensible location between steep ravines, and this new area was to became the center of the Spanish (and modern) city of Cuernavaca. After the capital was moved, no further construction was carried out at Teopanzolco, although the temples were probably maintained. In the Early Aztec period, Teopanzolco/Cuauhnahuac was the capital of a large and powerful city-state. Its distinctive painted ceramics were widely traded, comprising one of the main imported ceramic types at most Early Aztec sites in Morelos.

The pyramid of Tenayuca (figure 2.7), located in Mexico City, resembles the Teopanzolco pyramid, but is nearly twice as large.[13] Like the Teopanzolco structure it was excavated in the 1920s, but the project was published much more fully. Six construction stages were identified, starting with a small twin-stair pyramid toward the beginning of the Early

Figure 2.6 Map of the central urban district of the Early Aztec city of Teopanzolco (From Smith 2002)

Figure 2.7 A large Early Aztec pyramid at Tenayuca (located within Mexico City), showing one of the two stairways (Photograph by Michael E. Smith)

Aztec period and ending with an impressive, towering structure (figure 2.8). The pyramid is surrounded by a *coatepantli* (serpent wall) made up of nearly 150 carved stone serpents. A number of nearby altars and shrines were also excavated, some with additional serpent sculptures. The pyramid was still standing when the Spaniards arrived, and the conqueror Bernal Díaz del Castillo called Tenayuca "town of the serpents."

Figure 2.8   Construction stages of the Early Aztec pyramid at Tenayuca (After Marquina 1964:169)

According to native historical accounts, Tenayuca was founded as a capital city by the Early Aztec ruler Xolotl, a powerful king who was the ancestor of the Acolhua dynasty. A later king, Quinatzin, moved the capital from Tenayuca to Texcoco. Like Teopanzolco, construction activity at Tenayuca stopped in the Late Aztec period after the capital was moved to another location. Tenayuca maintained its symbolic importance, however. Although the pyramids are almost all that survives of the Early Aztec cities of Teopanzolco (Cuauhnahuac) and Tenayuca, they furnish us with important insights into Aztec civilization at that time. The rulers of these cities were powerful enough to build impressive monumental temples. They forged a new architectural style – the twin-stair pyramid temple – without precedent in earlier cultures. The similarities between Tenayuca and Teopanzolco showed that the various parts of the Aztec realm were in communication with one another and formed a single, extensive culture. The symbolism of the twin-stair pyramid was important enough for the Mexica to copy this style when they started building the Templo Mayor of Tenochtitlan in the Late Aztec period. Their deliberate use of an archaic style may be analogous to the use of Greek and Roman architectural styles in later European cities.

When the Mexica immigrants arrived from Aztlan, Tenayuca was a powerful polity and its pyramid one of the most sacred landmarks in the Valley of Mexico. From this point onward, the story of the Mexica peoples dominates Aztec native history. The Mexica were destined to rule the Aztec empire, and as a result the vast majority of the surviving native histories come from the Mexica tradition. That they held Tenayuca in great esteem is shown on the first page of the Codex Mendoza, where Tenayuca is one of two towns (Culhuacan is the other) shown as the initial conquests in the long process of Tenochtitlan's imperial expansion. We now turn to the Mexica story.

Mexica outcasts (1250–1325)

By the time the Mexica arrived in the Valley of Mexico around 1250, most of the land was already claimed by the city-states of the earlier immigrant groups.[14] The Mexica settled initially in Chapultepec, a hill adjacent to a swamp, because the land was empty and barren. Nearby groups, such as the Tepaneca and Chalca, were wary of the newcomers. The Mexica convinced the reluctant king of Culhuacan to let them settle in an isolated, snake-infested part of his realm called Tizaapan. Culhuacan was an ancient town southeast of Chapultepec that had been settled by both Toltecs and Aztlan migrants, and the Culhua nobles and peoples considered the Mexica newcomers barbaric. The Mexica flourished, supposedly living on a diet of snakes and lizards, prompting the Culhua king to exclaim to his court, "See what rascals they are; have no dealings and do not speak to them."[15] The king's attitude soon changed as the Mexica became good subjects and neighbors of the Culhua. The Culhua king called on the Mexica to come to their aid in a fierce battle with the Xochimilca, and the arrival of Mexica troops turned the tide in favor of the Culhua. This victory was important, for it previewed the later military success of the Mexica as vassals of the Tepanecs.

The Mexica managed to turn the Culhua against them, however. According to the semi-mythical accounts of native history, their god Huitzilopochtli ordered the Mexica to obtain a Culhua princess to be worshiped as a goddess. The Culhua king agreed and sent them his favorite daughter. Some time later, he and the other Culhua lords were invited to witness ceremonies and sacrifices to the new Mexica goddess. On Huitzilopochtli's orders the Mexica had killed and flayed the princess, and a Mexica priest donned her skin to dance in public (a common Aztec ritual practice, see chapter 9). When the Culhua king saw what the Mexica had done, he ordered his nobles and troops to attack, and the Mexica were driven from Tizaapan by force. This was all part of the god Huitzilopochtli's divine plan, however.

The Mexica fled into the wilderness of swamps that ringed the salty lakes of the Valley of Mexico, where they wandered for weeks. Huitzilopochtli appeared in a vision to one of the priests and told the Mexica that they would soon find their promised homeland, in a place where an eagle lived atop a tall nopal cactus. When the Mexica saw the eagle and cactus on a small island in the swamp, they were overjoyed and proceeded to found the site of Tenochtitlan, "place of the cactus fruit," in the year 2 House, AD 1325.[16]

The fourteenth century was a time of rapid and far-reaching transformation among the Aztecs. One of the most striking changes was an unprecedented population explosion. Another dramatic change was the emergence of the first true empire since Teotihuacan. In the native historical record, these changes are best documented for the Mexica and their city, Tenochtitlan. From the beginning, the Mexica saw their history – from migrations to the founding of Tenochtitlan to the expansion of the empire – as ruled by divine destiny.

Tenochtitlan and Empire: The Late Aztec Period

Tenochtitlan's first century (1325–1428)

Tenochtitlan's location on a small island in the middle of a swamp may seem inauspicious, but actually it had numerous advantages for the Mexica.

The salt marshes provided abundant wild plant and animal resources to feed people until agricultural fields could be constructed and become productive. High-yielding *chinampas* or raised fields were built on land reclaimed from the swamp and methods were devised to keep the salty waters of Lake Texcoco apart from the fresh waters of Lakes Chalco and Xochimilco. A system of dikes and canals accomplished this purpose, and gradually the cultivated fields turned the outskirts of Tenochtitlan into a lush green ring around the inner city. Commerce with other towns in the valley was facilitated by the use of canoes and boats; at the same time, the limited access to the city provided protection against military attack.

To build their city, the Mexica obtained construction materials through the market system in exchange for swamp delicacies such as fish, frogs, ducks, and algae. Once the Mexica were able to settle in one place, their numbers began to increase rapidly. Soon the other communities in the Valley of Mexico came to regard the Mexica as equals. During this time, two city-states had begun to expand their reach through conquest: the Tepanecs of Azcapotzalco on the western shore of Lake Texcoco and the Acolhua of Texcoco on the eastern shore. The Mexica, not powerful enough to resist these two incipient empires, allied themselves with the Tepanec ruler Tezozomoc and became tribute-paying subjects. For the most part, their tribute consisted of military service. Tezozomoc was a shrewd leader who put the military abilities of the Mexica to work as part of his imperial plans. From the mid-fourteenth century until the formation of the Aztec empire in 1428, the Mexica fought under the Tepanec banner and helped Tezozomoc forge the first significant empire since Teotihuacan.

The Mexica were becoming an increasingly powerful polity, and in 1372 they sought a legitimate king – a *tlatoani* – of their own to provide leadership and legitimacy. They looked to Culhuacan for help, in spite of their earlier alienation of the Culhua king, because of the prestige of the ancient Toltec dynasty there and the past cooperation between the two peoples. There were four simultaneous royal dynasties at Culhuacan, and one of the Culhua kings gave his daughter in marriage to a high-ranking Mexica. Their son Acamapichtli became the first Mexica *tlatoani*. Acamapichtli led the Mexica for 19 years (1372–91) and then passed the throne to his son Huitzilihuitl, whose mother was also a Culhua princess.

Huitzilihuitl, who ruled from 1391 until 1415 (figure 2.9), presided over one of the most important periods in Mexica history. Under his popular leadership, people from all over the Valley of Mexico came to live in Tenochtitlan, and the city expanded greatly. The Mexica became highly skilled as soldiers and diplomats in their dealings with neighbors. One of Huitzilihuitl's major accomplishments was the establishment of successful marriage alliances with a number of powerful dynasties. Marriage alliances were an important component of diplomacy among Mesoamerican

Figure 2.9   Genealogy of the Mexica kings (Drawing by Ellen Cesarski)

states. Lower ranking kings would endeavor to marry the daughters of more powerful and important kings. A marriage established an alliance between the polities and was a public acknowledgment of the dominant status of the more powerful king. Aztec nobles practiced polygamy, and as time went on, the dynasties of important polities became closely intertwined. Huitzilihuitl planned a strategy to improve his own standing and the political fortunes of the Mexica by marrying princesses from several of the more powerful central Mexican dynasties.

Huitzilihuitl successfully petitioned Tezozomoc himself for the hand of his daughter. She bore a son, Chimalpopoca, who later succeeded Huitzilihuitl as Mexica *tlatoani*. Chimalpopoca's mother died young, and Huitzilihuitl turned to the powerful dynasty of Cuauhnahuac for another wife. The Cuauhnahuac *tlatoani* ruled a large domain from his new palace (recently moved from Teopanzolco). He was said to be a great sorcerer, who used magic to protect his daughter from suitors. He initially refused Huitzilihuitl's petition, asking how his daughter could lead the luxurious life to which she was accustomed in the rustic, swampy town of Tenochtitlan.

According to legend, the Mexica king, following an idea that came to him in a dream, filled a hollow arrow shaft with precious jewels and shot the arrow into the Cuauhnahuac palace where it fell at the feet of the princess. She found the jewels, and soon the couple were wed.[17] This marriage formed the first Mexica royal alliance with a state outside of the Valley of Mexico, and a son of this union, Motecuhzoma Ilhuicamina, would later become one of the great Mexica kings, Motecuhzoma I. In addition to his diplomatic success, Huitzilihuitl also led the Mexica to victory in a number of military campaigns, but the conquered towns became subjects of the Tepanec capital Azcapotzalco, not Tenochtitlan.

Huitzilihuitl died in 1415 and was succeeded by his son Chimalpopoca, who reigned for 11 years. During this time Tenochtitlan continued to grow in size and prosperity. In the northern part of the island, the separate town of Tlatelolco was also growing. Around this time merchants from Tlatelolco began to offer goods such as parrot feathers and jewels for sale in their market. These exotic luxuries signaled a growing economic prosperity and the presence of enough nobles (the consumers of such items) to make the sales worthwhile. The Tlatelolco market later evolved into the largest in the empire (see chapter 5).

At the same time that Chimalpopoca was continuing to help the Tepanecs to expand their domain, the Acolhua of Texcoco were expanding in the eastern Valley to become the only true rivals of the Tepanec empire. When a new Acolhua king, Ixtlilxochitl, challenged Tezozomoc, war broke out between the two states. The Mexica played a major role in the fighting, which resulted in the death of Ixtlilxochitl and victory for the Tepanecs. To reward the Mexica for their services, Tezozomoc granted them the city-state of Texcoco as a tributary subject. For the first time the Mexica had tribute-paying subjects of their own. This was not the only relationship between the Mexica and the Acolhua, however. Ixtlilxochitl had married Chimalpopoca's half-sister, and their son Nezahualcoyotl became the new Acolhua king. These events cemented a special relationship between Texcoco and Tenochtitlan that was to continue until the Spanish conquest.

The death of the Tepanec emperor Tezozomoc in 1426 initiated a series of events that would lead to the formation of the Aztec empire two years later. In the struggle over succession to the Tepanec crown, the Mexica backed Tezozomoc's chosen heir Tayauh. Tayauh's brother Maxtla, a member of an anti-Mexica faction, usurped the throne, however. Soon after, Chimalpopoca was killed under suspicious circumstances, and the Mexica council chose Itzcoatl, brother of Huitzilihuitl (figure 2.9), to be the new *tlatoani*.

Itzcoatl, an experienced soldier and forceful leader, was determined to stand up to Maxtla and the Tepanecs. By now Tenochtitlan was a large and prosperous city, and the Mexica had attained a reputation as the fiercest warriors among the Aztec peoples. The Mexica government was strengthened by Itzcoatl's personality and his use of two able and experienced ministers, Motecuhzoma Ilhuicamina and Tlacaelel. Motecuhzoma, Itzcoatl's nephew, would later succeed Itzcoatl as *tlatoani*. He was an outstanding general, diplomat, and advisor. Itzcoatl created another advisory office, the *cihuacoatl* ("woman serpent"). Tlacaelel, Motecuhzoma's half-brother by still another of Huitzilihuitl's marriage alliances, was its first occupant. This triad of strong leaders – Itzcoatl, Motecuhzoma, and Tlacaelel – were in large part responsible for the creation of the Aztec empire.

The empire of the Triple Alliance, 1428–1519

The establishment of the Triple Alliance empire in 1428 ushered in the final century of Aztec civilization. This period, the Late Aztec B archaeological phase, witnessed the greatest accomplishments of the Aztecs. The story of the foundation of the empire began in 1426 with the escalation of hostilities between the Mexica and the Tepanecs. To counter the growing threat of the Mexica, Maxtla tried to blockade Tenochtitlan, and he demanded increasingly high amounts of tribute from the Mexica. At the same time, Maxtla continued to harass the Acolhua, forcing Nezahualcoyotl to flee his palace in Texcoco. The Acolhua king escaped over the eastern mountains to the Puebla-Tlaxcalla area, where he lobbied the kings of Tlaxcalla and Huexotzinco to come to his aid against the Tepanecs. Meanwhile, Motecuhzoma and Tlacaelel were marshaling support for a Mexica rebellion in the Valley of Mexico; their best aid came from dissident Tepanecs in the town of Tlacopan.

War soon erupted, and in 1428, the combined forces of Tenochtitlan, Texcoco, Tlacopan, and Huexotzinco managed to defeat the Tepanecs of Azcapotzalco. The Huexotzinca returned to their home over the mountains, and the other three polities formed a military-economic alliance. They agreed not to wage war on one another and to cooperate in wars of conquest against other towns. The tribute generated by these conquests was to be divided, with two-fifths to Tenochtitlan, two-fifths to Texcoco, and one-fifth to Tlacopan. This accord, known as the Triple Alliance, would soon rule the largest empire ever forged in ancient Mesoamerica.

The first task of the new alliance was to secure control over the Valley of Mexico. Itzcoatl conquered Coyoacan (an old Tepanec town), and then Xochimilco and Cuitlahuac in the *chinampa* district. The construction of *chinampas* (raised fields) in the freshwater lakes of Chalco and Xochimilco had begun in Early Aztec times and, by 1430, these productive farm plots covered nearly the entire lakebeds (see chapter 3). This district was the breadbasket of the Valley of Mexico, and its conquest gave the allies access to a large supply of tribute in foodstuffs.

Next, Itzcoatl and Nezahualcoyotl initiated expansion of the empire outside of the confines of the Valley of Mexico. Their first targets – Cuauhnahuac and Huaxtepec – offered a number of enticements. These towns were located just over the Ajusco mountain range south of the *chinampa* zone in an area with abundant rainfall and a semi-tropical climate. Like the Valley of Mexico, Morelos was the home of a dense Aztec population organized into city-states and reliant upon intensive agricultural practices. Conquest of this rich area was the logical first step toward forging a tribute empire beyond the Valley of Mexico.

During his reign Itzcoatl began a process of glorifying the Mexica at the expense of earlier Aztec groups, and he burned many historical books written earlier. In the words of Miguel León-Portilla, "With the intention of suppressing the 'lies' of history, Itzcoatl directed himself to the creation of a history which would give an appropriate background to the future glory of the Aztecs [Mexica]." As the Aztec empire expanded during the 91 years between the fall of Azcapotzalco and the arrival of Hernando Cortés, the Mexica increasingly assumed a dominant role, to the point at which some scholars refer to the empire as the "Mexica empire." The formal tribute-sharing arrangement remained in effect to the end, however.[18]

In 1440, soon after the Morelos campaign, Itzcoatl died and Motecuhzoma Ilhuicamina assumed the Mexica throne. Scholars refer to him as Motecuhzoma I to distinguish him from his great-grandson Motecuhzoma Xocoyotzin, ruler of the empire when Cortés arrived in 1519. During his 28 years in office, Motecuhzoma I proved to be one of the two most successful Mexica leaders in furthering the expansion of the empire. A program of political consolidation within the Valley of Mexico occupied the first decade of Motecuhzoma I's rule. The Mexica emperor undertook a series of measures to reduce the threat of rebellion among subject city-states and to ensure the continuity of Mexica rule. Selected kings were replaced by Mexica puppets, new administrative positions were established, and a comprehensive imperial tribute system was initiated. The Mexica installed their own people as tribute collectors, effectively bypassing the existing city-state dynasties. The long-term effect of this strategy of political consolidation was to promote imperial control over the core area and to contribute toward the rising power and influence of the Mexica at the expense of their Acolhua allies.

Motecuhzoma began major construction on the great temple of Tenochtitlan and issued a new legal code that widened the gap between nobles and commoners. Some of its provisions are as follows:

1. The king must never appear in public except when the occasion is extremely important and unavoidable . . .

3. Only the king and the prime minister Tlacaelel may wear sandals within the palace . . .
5. The great lords, who are twelve, may wear special [cotton] mantles of certain make and design, and the minor lords, according to their valor and accomplishments, may wear others . . .
7. The commoners will not be allowed to wear cotton clothing, under pain of death, but can use only garments of maguey fiber . . .
8. Only the great noblemen and valiant warriors are given license to build a house with a second story; for disobeying this law a person receives the death penalty.
9. Only the great lords are to wear labrets [lip plugs], ear plugs, and nose plugs of gold and precious stones . . .
13. All the barrios [*calpolli*] will possess schools or monasteries for young men where they will learn religion and correct comportment.
14. There is to be a rigorous law regarding adulterers. They are to be stoned and thrown into the rivers or to the buzzards.
15. Thieves will be sold for the price of their theft, unless the theft be grave, having been committed many times. Such thieves will be punished by death.[19]

At the same time that he was enlarging the social gulf between nobles and commoners, Motecuhzoma allowed talented commoners to rise to positions of influence by creating a new title, *quauhpilli* (eagle lord). This status, a kind of nobility of achievement, was awarded to the most successful soldiers in the army.

In the years 1450–4 a serious drought hit the Valley of Mexico. For several years running, crops failed and famine was widespread. The royal granaries were opened to feed the public, but the stored food lasted only a few years. By 1454 chaos gripped the Aztecs. Thousands died, and people wandered the countryside looking for any scrap of food to eat. The Totonac peoples of the Gulf Coast were unaffected and took advantage of the famine, bringing grain to the Valley of Mexico in order to purchase slaves. Finally, in 1455, the rains fell again, crops were successful, and the process of rebuilding took place.

Beginning in 1458, Motecuhzoma I and Nezahualcoyotl of Texcoco set out on a series of military campaigns that would expand the empire far beyond the Valley of Mexico. Previously conquered city-states such as Cuauhnahuac (home of Motecuhzoma's mother) were reconquered, and then the Mexica and Acolhua forces subdued the rest of Morelos, the Gulf Coast area, and parts of the modern state of Oaxaca. It is interesting to compare historical accounts of these campaigns. The Mexica histories describe the conquests as carried out largely by Motecuhzoma's forces, with minor help from Nezahualcoyotl, while histories from Texcoco describe the wars as major Acolhua victories, with some help from the Mexica. Taken together, the sources suggest that the Mexica and Acolhua were more-or-less equal partners in the empire at this point. The two kings conquered vast areas of Mesoamerica for the empire. Their victories, together with modest gains made by the next Mexica king, Axayacatl, constituted the first of two great cycles of imperial expansion (figure 2.10).

In 1468 Motecuhzoma I died and was succeeded by Axayacatl. This young prince, whose grandfathers were Motecuhzoma I and Itzcoatl, was selected by a council consisting of the top nobles in Tenochtitlan, Nezahualcoyotl, and the king of Tlacopan. Much of his 13-year reign was occupied with the consolidation of the conquests achieved by his predecessor. Some towns had to be reconquered, and it took time to work out the logistics of a tribute system that covered thousands of square kilometers of the new empire. Three important battles occurred during the reign of Axayacatl: victories over Tlatelolco and Toluca, and defeat at the hands of the Tarascans. A dispute developed between Tenochtitlan and its twin city Tlatelolco, resulting in the conquest of the latter. Axayacatl installed a military governor to rule Tlatelolco in place of the formerly independent *tlatoani*. The Tlatelolco marketplace had developed into the largest in Mesoamerica, and the professional merchants (*pochteca*) who ran the market started working for Axayacatl (see chapter 5).

Figure 2.10   Cycles of expansion of the Triple Alliance empire (Data from Berdan et al. 1996; drawing by Pam Headrick)

Axayacatl's only major addition to the empire was the Toluca Valley, a broad expanse immediately west of the Valley of Mexico. The Toluca Valley was of great strategic importance to the Aztecs since it formed a buffer between the Valley of Mexico and the Tarascan empire of western Mexico. The Tarascans lived in what is now the state of Michoacan, just west of central Mexico. In many ways the Tarascan empire resembled the Aztec empire. Tarascan oral tradition also told of ancestors who were relatively recent immigrants to their home area. They, too, settled in a highland basin with a large lake in the center, the Patzcuaro Basin. There, processes of population growth and cultural evolution led to the development of city-states and then to the expansion of an empire headed by a powerful dynasty.[20]

By the 1470s the Tarascan armies were approaching central Mexico and Axayacatl prepared to do battle from a base in the Toluca Valley. In 1478 or 1479, some 24,000 Aztec soldiers went up against 40,000 Tarascans, resulting in an Aztec loss of 20,000 men either killed or taken prisoner. Axayacatl himself was seriously wounded in the battle. The remaining Aztec forces limped back to Tenochtitlan, and the Aztecs never again dared to engage the Tarascans in a major direct confrontation.

Axayacatl died in 1481 and was replaced by his brother Tizoc. Tizoc proved to be a weak ruler and a poor military leader. He added little new territory to the empire, although this did not prevent him from commissioning a major sculpture, the so-called "Tizoc stone," that depicts him conquering numerous towns.[21] Tizoc died, perhaps assassinated, in 1486 and another brother, Ahuitzotl, was crowned. By this time the title of the Mexica king had changed from simply *tlatoani* to *huehuetlatoani* or "supreme king." The Acolhua *tlatoani* Nezahualpilli, son and successor of the great Nezahualcoyotl, apparently had lost some of his power to the Mexica, although officially the empire was still run by the Triple Alliance.

Ahuitzotl's extravagant coronation was soon followed by another major state celebration upon completion of the Templo Mayor in 1487. One of Ahuitzotl's first tasks was to suppress a rebellion by the Huaxtec peoples of the Gulf Coast. Rebellions were a common occurrence in the Aztec empire because of the indirect nature of imperial rule. Local dynasties were left in place as long as they cooperated with the Triple Alliance and paid their tribute. In many cases, the positions of rulers of provincial city-states were actually strengthened by their participation in the empire since these rulers could call on the empire for aid in the event of local troubles. Periodically, a provincial king would decide that he was strong enough to withhold tribute payments from the empire. This is what the sources refer to as "rebellion." The Triple Alliance would respond by dispatching an army to threaten the errant king and, if necessary, reconquer the city-state. As a result of repeated resistance and rebellion, many towns

Figure 2.11   Page 14 of the *Tira de Tepechpan*, an Aztec historical codex from the city-state of Tepexpan (After Noguez 1978:14)

Reading a Historical Codex

City-state dynasties kept track of their histories on painted historical codices. An Aztec innovation was the adoption of the continuous year-count annal, in which year glyphs extend in a long line and pictures of events were connected to their year of occurrence with lines. This example (figure 2.11) is from the *Tira de Tepechpan* (Noguez 1978), a dynastic record from the Tepexpan city-state which was subject to the kings of Texcoco. In this codex, the line of years runs across the center of the page from left to right; events of the local dynasty are depicted above the line and events from Tenochtitlan and other polities are depicted below the line. The timeline of the codex runs from AD 1298 through 1590; here I show only the interval from 1501 to 1510. I have added the Christian dates next to the Aztec year glyphs (see chapter 11 on the year-count calendar used in this and other codices). This description of people and events is based upon the analysis of ethnohistorian Xavier Noguez (1978:v.1:99–103).

Year		Event
10 rabbit	1502	Death of Ahuitzotl, king of Tenochtitlan. He is shown as a mummy bundle, wrapped in cloth and tied, with no face. The names of individuals are shown above and to the left of their heads.
(same year)		Accession of Motecuhzoma Xocoyotzin. The reed throne and turquoise crown indicate kingship.
2 reed	1507	Celebration of the New Fire ceremony. This is indicated by a knot under the year glyph (the New Fire was known as "the tying of the years").
(same year)		Death of Tencoyotzin, king of Tepexpan.
(same year)		Ometochtzin, widow of Tencoyotzin (and daughter of king Nezahualcoyotl of Texcoco) is pictured at the top. The line of dots shows that she survived her spouse and lived on until 1520.
3 flint-knife	1508	Construction of a temple in Tepexpan.
5 rabbit	1510	Accession of Cuacuahtzin to the throne of Tepexpan. Lines show that he was the son of Tencoyotzin and Ometochtzin.

Readers looking at the *Tira de Tepechpan* could see the outlines of the history of Tepexpan in relation to events elsewhere in central Mexico. Professional historians, however, would use this document as a guide or outline from which they would recount the events depicted in great detail.

reappear in the conquest lists of multiple emperors. For example, Cuauhnahuac, initially conquered by Itzcoatl, had to be reconquered successively by Motecuhzoma I and Axayacatl.[22]

The unstable nature of the Aztec empire should not be taken as an indication that imperial expansion was random or haphazard. The Mexica and Acolhua followed two deliberate strategies in planning and implementing their conquests. The first strategy was economically motivated.

The Aztecs wanted to generate tribute payments and promote trade and marketing throughout the empire. The Mexica rulers sponsored *pochteca* (professional merchants), imposed tribute in nonlocal goods (so that provincial towns had to engage in commerce to obtain their imperial tribute), and protected market towns and trade routes. The second strategy dealt with enemy frontiers. The Aztecs established client states and outposts along imperial borders to help contain their enemies (see chapter 7).

Ahuitzotl began a new cycle of imperial expansion, guided by these two strategies. He brought the Valley of Oaxaca and the Soconusco Coast of southern Mexico (Xoconochco) into the empire for their economic value. Major trade routes ran through the Valley of Oaxaca, and Xoconochco, the most distant province of the empire, was an important source of tropical lowland products such as cacao and feathers. Ahuitzotl pursued the frontier strategy by carrying out conquests and establishing client states along the Tarascan border. He built a fortress at Oztoma, along the southern part of the Tarascan frontier, and sent colonists from the Valley of Mexico to guard it and to settle the immediate area.

Ahuitzotl's reign was a time of unparalleled prosperity and growth in Tenochtitlan, accompanied by major territorial expansion in the empire. Ahuitzotl increasingly took over the duties of running the empire from the other Triple Alliance kings, and by the end of his reign, the Mexica state was clearly dominant over the others in power, prestige, and influence.

Ahuitzotl died in 1502 and was succeeded by his nephew, the son of Axayacatl, Motecuhzoma Xocoyotzin (figure 2.11). Motecuhzoma II was a seasoned general who had participated in many of Ahuitzotl's wars of conquest. His style of rulership was virtually the opposite of Ahuitzotl's. Motecuhzoma II eliminated the status of *quauhpilli* and reserved all important military and government positions for members of the Mexica hereditary nobility. He replaced all of Ahuitzotl's officials and had many of them killed. Instead of ruling through the pride and cooperation of talented officials, Motecuhzoma II controlled his court through terror. Some scholars have seen these actions as steps toward the creation of an absolute monarchy among the Aztecs.[23]

Just as Axayacatl's reign was concerned with the consolidation of his predecessor's conquests, his son Motecuhzoma II's imperial activities centered around the consolidation of Ahuitzotl's conquests. Some of the distant towns had to be reconquered, and Motecuhzoma II continued his predecessors' long-standing war with Tlaxcalla. Like the Tarascan empire, the states of the Tlaxcalla area remained unconquered enemies. The ancestors of the Tlaxcallans had come from Aztlan, but these city-states grew apart culturally from the other Aztec peoples. The Aztec armies were never able to defeat the Tlaxcallans, but the empire did manage to surround the area and reduce its commerce with the outside world. Motecuhzoma II fought a number of battles with the Tlaxcallans in which the Aztecs appeared to have had the upper hand, but victory proved elusive.

According to historical accounts, Motecuhzoma II's reign was plagued by omens of disaster and doom, which appeared to the king, to his priests, and to the public. In 1519 these omens proved all too real in the form of an invading Spanish army under the leadership of Hernando Cortés. The empire was at the height of its glory when it was destroyed by Cortés. Some writers, citing the slowdown of imperial expansion under Motecuhzoma II, have asserted that Aztec culture and the empire had begun a process of decay and decline before 1519, but that was not the case. Motecuhzoma II's relatively modest additions to the empire were simply part of the rhythm of Aztec imperial expansion, in which major conquests by one king were followed by consolidation of control by the next. There were two great cycles of imperial growth (figure 2.10). In the first, Motecuhzoma I added many new areas to the empire and then Axayacatl consolidated these gains. In the second cycle, Ahuitzotl conquered much new territory, which was then organized and secured by Motecuhzoma II. By the year 1519 this was the second-largest empire in the ancient New World (the Inca empire of South America covered more territory), and there were few if any signs of decline or decay.

chapter three
People on the Landscape

In those times these hills and valleys were populated with thousands of souls who lived, following their custom, in many scattered hamlets, a short distance from one another.
Juan de la Cruz y Moya, Historia de la santa y apostólica provincia de Santiago de Predicadores de México en la Nueva España *(author's translation)*

The arrival of the Aztlan migrants and the subsequent development of Aztec civilization transformed the central Mexican countryside from the thinly populated backwater of Toltec times into a densely settled landscape. On the eve of Spanish conquest, the Aztecs had more people, more cities, and larger cities, than any other ancient culture of the New World. This large population was not the result of a gradual build-up over many centuries; rather it expanded in a single dramatic surge between 1200 and 1500. In part, the Aztec population explosion can be attributed to the arrival of the Aztlan migrants at the beginning of this time period, but two other factors were also responsible. First, central Mexico was emerging from five centuries of abnormally dry conditions (AD 600–1100), and rainfall increased significantly.[1] This led to a dramatic improvement in agricultural productivity, and the resulting increased food supply helped set off the population surge. Second, once the Aztec migrants settled in and established their city-states, political and economic conditions encouraged people to have larger families.[2]

The large size of the population influenced many aspects of Aztec society and culture. Although it is no longer fashionable among archaeologists to attribute cultural change and evolution solely to "population pressure," it is difficult to escape the conclusion that the Late Aztec population explosion brought about a series of fundamental changes throughout central Mexican society. The most obvious of these are in the realm of food and agriculture. As their numbers grew, the Aztecs had to adjust their diet by finding new sources of food. They were also forced to increase their farming efforts to produce enough food. This process, known as agricultural intensification, led to a massive modification of the landscape as canals, dams, terraces, and crop beds were constructed all over central Mexico.[3]

The Late Aztec demographic surge also changed the nature of both urban and rural settlement in central Mexico. More cities were founded, and cities grew larger than in earlier times. At the same time, nonurban settlement dispersed across the countryside to the point where people were living almost everywhere (see the quotation at the start of the chapter).

How Many Aztecs?

Just over one million people were living in the Valley of Mexico when Hernando Cortés and his army arrived in 1519, and another two to three million Aztecs dwelt in the surrounding valleys of central Mexico. How have modern scholars arrived at these estimates?

Counting back from colonial census figures

The Aztecs kept several types of census-like written records to keep track of land holdings and tribute obligations (chapter 11), but too few have survived to be of much help in determining the total size of the Aztec population. First-hand accounts by Spanish soldiers and missionaries who saw the Aztecs before they were devastated by smallpox and other diseases are another potential source of information. Unfortunately, these are difficult to use because their descriptions of population sizes vary wildly. For example, Hernando Cortés estimated the size of the Tlaxcaltecan army at 100,000 soldiers, whereas his soldier Bernal Díaz counted the same army at 40,000 soldiers.[4] These men were hardly dispassionate observers since both writers were trying to justify and glorify the Spanish conquest of the Aztecs. Even if such estimates could be trusted, first-hand observations exist for only a few cities and armies, far from complete coverage of the Aztec population.

After the conquest of Mexico in 1521, Spanish administrators began to collect information on their new Nahua subjects. Systematic census-taking began soon after the conquest in some areas, but it was not until 1568 that the entire area of central Mexico was subjected to a comprehensive and standardized census whose findings are known today. In the half century between the Spanish conquest and the 1568 census, however, the Aztec population dropped precipitously owing to the introduction of European diseases (see chapter 12). In 1568 there were 410,000 non-Spanish occupants of the Valley of Mexico and 970,000 in central Mexico as a whole.

Several studies have attacked the problem of measuring the size of the Aztec population in 1519 using these accurate but late Spanish census figures. There are quite a few scattered pieces of information that relate to the sixteenth-century demographic loss, but it is almost impossible to piece these together into a single continuous picture of population loss in any single town or area. All demographic studies of this time period must rely upon a series of assumptions and estimates that are difficult to verify. Table 3.1 lists the most influential estimates of the Aztec population. The size of Native American populations before European conquest and colonization is a contentious issue that has been debated hotly by historians and archaeologists of the 1980s and 1990s. Of the several studies of the historical demography of Early Colonial central Mexico, William T. Sanders uses the most reasonable assumptions and the widest range of information, and Thomas Whitmore employs the most sophisticated methods (computer simulation). For these reasons, most scholars favor their estimates over the very high figures of Woodrow Borah and Sherburne Cook.[5] Although the lower estimates in table 3.1 are the more reasonable ones, these still show a very high Aztec population size and density. These

Table 3.1 Documentary estimates of the Aztec population in 1519

	Borah and Cook	Sanders	Whitmore
Valley of Mexico (area: 7,260 sq km)			
Total population (in millions)	2.96	1.16	1.59
Population density (persons/sq km)	410	160	220
Aztec Central Mexico[a] (area: 20,810 sq km)			
Total population (in millions)	6.40	3.33	(4.56)[b]
Population density (persons/sq km)	310	160	(220)[b]

[a] "Aztec central Mexico" includes most of the Nahuatl-speaking areas of central Mexico except for the Toluca Valley, whose 1568 popuation is not reported in the same format as the other areas.
[b] Whitmore reports figures for the Valley of Mexcio only. I have extended his estimate to the area of central Mexico using his population density figure for the Valley of Mexico.
Sources: Borah and Cook 1963; Sanders 1970; Whitmore 1992

were the highest population levels of any pre-Hispanic time period. Modern population in the Valley of Mexico did not surpass Aztec levels until the mid-twentieth century. The overall population density of 160 persons per square kilometer, which includes uninhabited areas such as the lakes and steep hillsides, is a very high figure for a preindustrial society.

Counting sites

William Sanders' estimate, based on documentary evidence, of one million inhabitants in the Valley of Mexico, is corroborated by results from the Valley of Mexico Archaeological Survey Project. These archaeological population estimates were produced as follows. Based upon the archaeological principle of analogy, the directors of the survey hypothesized that ancient settlements in the Valley of Mexico resembled modern traditional settlements. They carried out studies of the modern traditional settlements and classified them into types such as dispersed village, nucleated village, nucleated town, and hamlet. The settlements composing each type share characteristics such as population density and settlement layout.

Information on the modern settlements was then applied to the ancient sites located in the regional survey. The size of each archaeological site was measured for each of the time periods during which it was occupied. Sites were then assigned to types (again, for each time period) based upon information such as the density of artifacts, the number and arrangements of mounds, and the size of the site. The population of a site in a given time period was estimated by multiplying the population density figure for that type (as determined from the modern settlements) by the total area of the site in that period. The results of this operation for the Early and Late Aztec periods are listed in table 3.2 and are portrayed in the maps of figure 3.1. These findings provided the first indication of the Aztec population explosion mentioned above and are among the most important results yet achieved by archaeologists working in central Mexico.[6]

The high Late Aztec population estimate produced by archaeological survey, 920,000, is consistent with the results of the historical demographic research summarized above. The survey results show that the large Late Aztec population was achieved through a rapid growth during a few centuries rather than a gradual sustained increase over many centuries. The Late Aztec period witnessed a great dispersion of population to all corners of the central Mexican highlands. The large size of the population raises several questions, including: what foods did the Aztecs eat, and how did they grow enough to feed three to four million people in highland central Mexico?

Figure 3.1   Population growth in the Valley of Mexico from the Early Aztec to the Late Aztec period. The dots labeled "small sites" show areas where such sites are numerous; there are far too many small Late Aztec sites to mark each one on a map of this scale (Based upon Sanders et al. 1979: maps 17, 18; drawing by Ellen Cesarski)

The Aztec Diet

Staple foods

Like all Mesoamerican peoples before and since, the Aztecs depended heavily on maize, or corn (*Zea mays*), for their sustenance.[7] Maize is a remarkable plant whose domestication made possible the evolution of Mesoamerican civilizations. Maize exists in many different varieties, adapted to specific local conditions of soil and climate, and can grow nearly everywhere in Mesoamerica except for the cold high mountains. Indeed, the northern boundary of Mesoamerica as a culture area is usually defined as the northern limits of rainfall-based maize cultivation. A highly productive plant, with caloric yields among the highest of any major world food crop, maize is also high in protein. Animal sources of protein

Table 3.2 Aztec archaeological sites and population levels in the Valley of Mexico

Category	Early Aztec	Late Aztec
Type of Site		
Hamlet	258	986
Small village	15	265
Large village	4	89
Regional center	14	41
Supraregional center	0	2
Ceremonial precinct	1	59
Special-use site	1	57
Indeterminate type	105	137
Total sites	398	1,636
Total population	175,000	920,000

Source: Sanders et al. 1979:184–5, 215

were in short supply in ancient Mesoamerica, so maize was an essential component of the diet.

Maize was eaten in a variety of forms. Most common was the *tortilla*, a round, flat, toasted bread that has been a staple of Mesoamerican cuisine from the Classic period through the present. Tortillas were prepared by first soaking the shelled corn in an alkali solution (water with limestone, ashes, or another source of calcium hydroxide); next grinding the wet corn into dough on a *metate* or grinding-stone; then, shaping the tortillas by hand; and finally, cooking them on a clay griddle called a *comalli*. Instruction in tortilla-making was one of the fundamental lessons mothers taught their daughters (figure 3.2). Tortillas could be eaten fresh from the griddle, or they could be stored for later use, including meals eaten away from home by farmers, merchants, soldiers, or other travelers. Also popular were *tamales*, a more ancient, steamed food. Coarse maize dough was shaped into balls, often with some beans, chilis, or sometimes meat in the center, and then wrapped in maize leaves and steamed in a large clay pot. Other forms in which the Aztecs ate maize were *atole*, a thin gruel of fine maize flour in water flavored with chilis or fruits; *pozole*, a soup or stew containing large maize kernels (hominy); and *elote* or corn on the cob.

Maize figured prominently in Aztec religion and thought. A number of deities were devoted specifically to maize and its growth (for example,

Figure 3.2   Mother teaching her 13-year-old daughter to make tortillas (Codex Mendoza 1992:v.4:125; f.60r)

Centeotl, whose name means "corn god," and Chicomecoatl, the goddess "seven serpent"), and many rituals were carried out to propitiate these deities. Farmers requested a successful harvest by addressing the maize seeds formally before planting. Women thanked the maize before preparing it to eat, a practice that survives today in the folk ritual of Mesoamerican peasants. The symbolism of maize permeated Aztec thought, and people were often compared to the maize plant. For example, a person who had achieved honor was said to have "reached the season of the green maize ear."[8]

Beans were second only to maize in the Aztec diet. Like tortillas, they were served at every meal. Tomatoes, avocados, and several varieties of squash were also common, and squash seeds were eaten in several forms. A large variety of chili peppers gave spice and flavor to food. The seeds of the domesticated chia and amaranth plants were ground on a grinding-stone as corn and eaten in several ways. The Aztecs shaped amaranth dough into small figures of the gods and ate them on ritual occasions. Amaranth leaves were also eaten as greens, and chia seeds were pressed to extract the oil.

Nopal, the prickly pear cactus, was cultivated in the Valley of Mexico for its sweet succulent fruit and paddle-shaped leaf, which is a tasty green vegetable once the spines are removed. The *maguey* plant, a member of the *Agave* family, was cultivated for a number of uses. The fresh *maguey* sap was a nutritious beverage and, when allowed to ferment, became *pulque* or *octli*, the only alcoholic drink known to the Axtecs. *Maguey* and *pulque* were sacred to the Aztecs and had their own deities. A number of other products were derived from parts of the maguey plant: rope, textiles, nets, bags, and sandals were made from its coarse fibers, sewing needles from its spines, and medicines from the sap (see chapter 4).

Animal foods

Dogs, turkeys, and the Muscovy duck were the only domesticated animals in ancient Mesoamerica. All were used for food, but they made only a minor contribution to the Aztec diet. This contrasts sharply with the ancient civilizations of the Old World, which exploited a variety of domesticated animals for food, fiber, and work as draft animals. The Aztecs also fished and hunted wild game, but again these sources of food were limited. After more than a millennium of urban civilizations with high populations, central Mexico no longer had significant reserves of game that could be used by the Aztecs. Archaeologists do find the bones of fish, deer, rabbit, iguana, dog, turkey, and other animals in Aztec domestic trash deposits, but rarely in dense concentrations. Meat from large animals was a minor part of the Aztec diet.

Early Spanish observers noted the widespread use of insects among the Aztecs, including ants, grasshoppers, maguey worms, and jumil bugs. Insects are high in protein, tasty, and often could be harvested in large numbers. The Aztecs also gathered great amounts of blue-green spirulina algae (*Spirulina geitlerii*) from the surface of the lakes. This algae, known as *tecuitlatl*, is extremely high in protein, grows rapidly and abundantly, and is easy to gather with fine nets. Bernal Díaz del Castillo said of it, "the fisherwomen and the men . . . sell small cakes made from a sort of weed [algae] which they get out of the great lake, which curdles and forms a kind of bread which tastes rather like cheese."[9] The Spanish soldiers and priests had a low opinion of the palatability of this algae, but it was much prized by the Aztecs. The Aztecs also gathered a wide variety of wild plants for food and medicinal purposes.

Nutritional status

The nutritional status of the Aztecs has been debated for a number of years. Some authors, pointing out the low level of animal protein in the Aztec diet and the large size of the population, argue that the Aztecs (or at least the commoners) must have been severely malnourished. In an extreme version of this argument, the unlikely suggestion has been made that the Aztecs resorted to cannibalism on a large scale to make up protein and calorie deficiencies.[10] The notion that the Aztec diet was poor has been countered by analyses of the composition of Aztec foods, which show that for the most part the diet was nutritionally adequate. Whether or not sufficient *quantities* of food were produced in central Mexico to meet the needs of the burgeoning Aztec population, however, is a more difficult question to answer.

Maize was the key to the nutritional success of the Aztec diet. Most traditional diets around the world depend on low-protein staple grains (such as wheat or rice) to provide the bulk of the calories, but the grain must be supplemented by animal foods that are high in protein. As mentioned above, maize is relatively high in protein for a grain, but by itself is not a complete protein since it does not supply all of the essential amino acids that the human body needs. The ancient Mesoamericans worked out two cultural practices that, when combined, provided them with a complete protein source and greatly reduced their need for meat.

For a food to be a complete protein (i.e., an adequate source of protein for human metabolism), it must supply all 11 of the essential amino acids. Animal flesh is a complete protein, which is why most cultures rely on meat for their protein needs. Maize is high in most of the essential amino acids, but several, including lysine and tryptophan, are chemically bound and not available if the maize is eaten unprocessed. Soaking the shelled kernels in an alkali solution both frees the tryptophan and adds calcium to the mixture.[11] Beans are high in lysine. When beans are eaten together with lime-soaked maize, one has a complete, plant-derived protein source. The Mesoamerican preference for maize and beans at every meal has a solid nutritional basis.

How did these practices originate and become fixed cultural patterns? We can only speculate. Mesoamerican farmers, in the past and today, let the maize dry out and harden in the field before harvesting it in order to store it for the coming year. The hard kernels must be soaked in water to soften them before grinding. Somehow, it was discovered that adding chemical lime to the soaking water, most likely in the form of powdered limestone, improved the maize. I have asked modern Mesoamerican peasant women why they soak the maize before cooking it, and their answer is that the tortillas don't taste right if the maize is not lime soaked. The Aztec ancestors of these women five centuries ago probably would have said the same thing.

Other components of the Aztec diet provided important nutrients as well. For example, chili peppers are high in iron, riboflavin, niacin, and vitamins A and C; chia has high amounts of calcium, phosphorus, and iron; beans are high in niacin; and many of the wild herbs and spices used by the Aztecs are high in calcium and vitamin A. Without the benefit of modern nutritional knowledge, early Mesoamerican peoples managed to work out an adequate diet that suited their environment, and by the time the Aztecs arrived, these patterns were deeply ingrained cultural practices.

The Aztec diet provided adequate amounts of protein and other key nutrients, but were their farmers able to produce enough to feed a population of several million? An important concept here is "carrying capacity," or the total population that a particular environment can support, given the types of crops and farming methods in use. Because the measurement of ancient carrying capacity combines many difficult estimates (e.g., human nutritional requirements, the nature of past environments, ancient crop yields, the technology and organization of labor used in farming and hunting), the whole endeavor is somewhat controversial. Nevertheless, the available evidence suggests that the Aztec population had reached or exceeded the carrying capacity of central Mexico. The Aztecs could easily feed themselves in good years, but when yields were poor, owing to low rainfall, early frosts, or other periodic environmental fluctuations, the Aztec agricultural system did not produce sufficient food to feed adequately the entire population.[12] During the final century of Aztec society, a number of famines and years of poor harvests were reported, and the famine of 1450–4 was disastrous. How did the growing Aztec population attempt to meet its subsistence needs?

Farming Systems

Agricultural intensification

The intensification of agricultural practices was one of the most direct responses to the Late Aztec population explosion. It is also one of the most archaeologically visible responses. Agricultural intensification refers to changes in farming in which additional energy is invested in agriculture in order to secure higher yields from a given unit of land. Nonintensive or extensive agricultural methods, such as slash-and-burn farming or simple rainfall cultivation, are not highly productive in terms of yield per area, but are energy efficient because they do not require large investments of human labor. Extensive agriculture is adaptive where the population density is low and high yields are not necessary to meet subsistence needs. More intensive agricultural methods, such as heavy weeding, fertilization, or irrigation, provide greater amounts of food per area under cultivation, but require that a lot more work be expended in farming.

The intensification of agriculture is a process that goes hand in hand with cultural change. As cultures evolve and their populations grow, they require more food from the land, which forces farmers to intensify their methods. The development of social stratification and the state also stimulates intensive agriculture. Farmers must produce enough to meet the tribute and tax demands of the government and elite class as well as their own subsistence needs. All ancient civilizations relied upon one or more forms of intensive agriculture.[13] In the Aztec case, simple rainfall agriculture was supplemented by terracing, irrigation, raised fields, and houselot garden cultivation. None of these intensive methods was new; they all dated back to earlier Mesoamerican civilizations. What was unique about Aztec agriculture was the *degree* of intensification, which transformed the countryside from its natural condition into a cultivated cultural landscape with little empty or wild land left.

Friar Sahagún described the activities of the Aztec farmer as follows:

> The farmer . . . is bound to the soil; he works – works the soil, stirs the soil anew, prepares the soil; he weeds, breaks up the clods, hoes, levels the soil, makes furrows . . . He sets the boundaries; . . . he works [the soil] during the summer; he takes up the stones; he digs furrows; he makes holes; he plants, hills [up the soil], waters, sprinkles; he broadcasts seed; he sows beans, provides holes for them . . . fills in the holes; he hills [the maize plants], removes the undeveloped maize ears, discards the withered ears . . . gathers the maize, shucks the ears, removes the ears . . .[14]

Rainfall cultivation that involved some fallowing of the land was called *tlacolol*. The basic agricultural tool was a flat, wooden digging stick called a *coa*, which was used to turn over and perforate the soil (figure 3.3). At the start of the Early Aztec period, most farmers practiced extensive rainfall cultivation. As populations grew and city-states expanded their control, more intensive methods were applied. Not every field could be

Figure 3.3   Farmers planting maize with a digging stick (After Sahagún 1950–82:bk.10:fig.70; drawing by Ellen Cesarski)

transformed by intensification, however, and rainfall cultivation continued to be used in many parts of central Mexico.

Farming the hills

Central Mexico is mountainous, but the Aztecs put the gently sloping hillsides to good use. They constructed many miles of stone terrace walls to create level planting surfaces and turned otherwise unusable hillslopes into productive farm fields. Remnants of ancient stone terrace walls are found throughout the Aztec territory, and in some areas, Aztec terraces have been maintained or rebuilt and are still in use today. The Aztecs built three types of terraces, each adapted to different environmental conditions: hillslope contour terraces, semi-terraces, and cross-channel terraces.[15]

The most common type of terrace – *hillslope contour terraces* – had stone walls that ran parallel to the contour of the slope (figure 3.4). The stones were piled up by hand, and the terrace behind the wall was filled in by digging into the hillside or by relying on natural soil erosion from uphill. Today the archaeological remnants of Aztec terrace walls are rough stone alignments rarely having more than a single course or layer of stones.

Figure 3.4   Aztec agricultural terraces at Cerro Texcotzinco in the Valley of Mexico. These terraces, used in the 1400s, were irrigated with water from a spring; the saddle between the hills at top right is an aqueduct that carried the water (Photograph by William E. Doolittle; reproduced with permission)

In comparison with the better-known Inca agricultural terraces of the Andes Mountains, Aztec stone terraces were smaller and built of rougher stones with simpler masonry techniques. Whereas the carefully constructed Inca terraces often extended in parallel rows for hundreds of meters, Aztec terraces typically had an irregular layout, sometimes with a somewhat haphazard look. They do not show the hand of central planning.

On more gentle slopes the Aztecs used low terrace walls made from long lines of maguey plants grown close together. Archaeologists call these *semi-terraces*. The maguey plants held soil erosion in check, creating level planting surfaces on which maize and other crops could be cultivated. The maguey themselves could be exploited for fiber and *pulque*. *Cross-channel terraces* or *check-dams* were built across streambeds in the bottoms of ravines, perpendicular to the stream. As the water flowed over the walls, silt and other sediments carried by the stream were deposited naturally behind the stones to create a level surface. As deposition continued season after season, farmers gradually built the walls higher and the new field surfaces expanded greatly in area. Although check-dams were built in small increments over a period of years, the result could be an impressive stone terrace wall holding back a large level field. I excavated check-dams at the site of Cuexcomate (in Morelos) and found walls over 2 m high. They had been constructed over a long period of time and used for many decades (see discussion below).

Farming the valleys

Irrigation was another method of intensive agriculture used by the Aztecs.[16] In contrast to terracing, which opened up previously unusable land to cultivation, irrigation was applied to already-farmed valley soils to make them more productive. This was done by extending the rainy season (i.e., watering fields before the onset of the summer rains) and by providing additional water to crops during the growing season to supplement the natural rainfall. Although irrigation technology had a long history in central Mexico (it was very important at Teotihuacan), the Aztecs built canal systems that were both larger and more sophisticated than earlier endeavors.

By the time of the Spanish conquest, nearly all available sources of fresh water in central Mexico had been tapped for irrigation. Although archaeological remains of canals and dams are scarce, Spanish administrative documents mention the use of irrigation throughout sixteenth-century central Mexico. In many areas, small-scale irrigation systems were the norm. Dams diverted water from springs or small rivers into simple ditch canals that brought the water to nearby fields. In a variation called flood-

Figure 3.5 Aztec embankment built to contain the new channel of the Cuauhtitlan River in the Valley of Mexico (Photograph by William E. Doolittle; reproduced with permission)

water irrigation, small dams diverted the frequent rainy-season flash floods onto nearby fields.

In some areas the Aztecs built larger and more technologically advanced irrigation systems. For example, a major segment of the Cuauhtitlan River in the northwest Valley of Mexico was diverted and channeled to provide water to a large area of fields. The river channel itself was deepened, widened, and straightened, and the results are impressive even today (figure 3.5) A series of canals were built leading off the river to the fields. In the eastern part of the valley, a complex irrigation network was built in the area of Mount Texcotzinco. Springs were tapped to feed canals, some of which were up to 10 km in length. The longest canals were built of stone and the channels were lined with plaster. Aqueducts carried the canals over ravines and other low points.

Aqueducts were also used to bring water to the city of Tenochtitlan. The swampy island had a limited supply of drinking water, so an aqueduct was built to carry fresh water over the lake from springs at Chapultepec on the mainland. These elaborate hydraulic works were some of the most impressive accomplishments of Aztec technology. This hydrological knowledge was also applied to a third form of intensive agriculture, the *chinampas*.

Farming the swamps

Raised fields, or *chinampas*, were an ancient Mesoamerican technology for turning swamps into highly productive fields.[17] Large straight ditches were dug to drain away excess water. Between the ditches, long narrow artificial islands were built up to form planting surfaces (figure 3.6). Mud and muck from the lake bottom were piled up, along with vegetation and other organic matter, and the fields were held together with wooden stakes driven into the lake bottom. Trees were also planted to help stabilize the fields. The resulting plots were very productive. The muck and organic matter served as fertilizers, and the roots of the maize and other crops drew on abundant ground-water from the naturally high water table. The fields were piled high enough to prevent the roots becoming waterlogged, and fertility was maintained by periodically adding more vegetation and rich muck scraped from the canals. Farmers used canoes to travel on the canals between the fields.

Plants were germinated in seedbeds built on floating reed rafts, and these were pulled by canoe to individual *chinampa* plots for replanting. These floating seedbeds have given rise to the modern term "floating gardens," used mistakenly to refer to the *chinampa* fields themselves. Their high fertility and their location in the frost-free southern Valley of Mexico

Figure 3.6   Modern use of a *chinampa* to cultivate maize (Photograph by Phil Crossley; reproduced with permission)

allowed three or four crops to be grown annually on the *chinampas*. This made them the most intensive and productive of all Mesoamerican agricultural practices.

The Aztecs built *chinampas* throughout Lakes Chalco and Xochimilco, the two lakes that formed the southern arm of the Valley of Mexico lake system. Archaeological surveys that were carried out in this area before the recent urban expansion of Mexico City located many square kilometers of long narrow ridges arranged in an overall grid pattern indicative of Aztec *chinampa* cultivation. According to Early Colonial documents, *chinampas* also were built on the outskirts of Tenochtitlan. The system survives today in a few areas of the southern lakebed, particularly in the modern towns of Xochimilco and Mixquic. The *chinampas* historically have provided vegetables for the Mexico City market, but recent environmental degradation, caused by pollution, urban expansion and a lowered water table, is having a negative affect on their economic viability. The *chinampa* towns have developed into tourist attractions, and for a fee one can travel through the old canals on boats. Although raised field agriculture was practiced throughout Mesoamerica and South America in pre-Hispanic times, the fields were abandoned before or soon after Spanish conquest in all areas except for the southern Valley of Mexico. These modern *chinampas* provide crucial insights on this important and widespread ancient technique of intensive agriculture.

Farming in town

Much of the land devoted to terracing, irrigation, and raised field cultivation was located either away from settlements or adjacent to them. The Aztecs also practiced the intensive cultivation of gardens within their villages, towns, and cities. In most settlements, each family had a substantial garden plot adjacent to the house, which was used to grow some maize, fruits, herbs, medicines, and other useful plants. These houselot gardens, called *calmil*, were intensively cultivated in that they were fertilized with domestic refuse, weeded and carefully tended by family members. Susan T. Evans's archaeological study of the village of Cihuatecpan suggests that much of its surface area was taken up with *calmil* cultivation that used maguey semi-terraces on the gently sloping terrain.[18] This intensive garden cultivation may be one reason for the dispersed nature of most Aztec settlements, from villages to cities.

Household enterprise or state control?

Was the state involved in the management of Aztec intensive agriculture? This is an important question in the study of ancient civilizations, for some scholars have suggested that intensive agricultural methods such as irrigation could only be managed by centralized bureaucratic states, whereas others have argued that independent households could take care of their own intensive agriculture without interference from the state.

Aztec terrace agriculture was similar to terrace systems in many parts of the world today where construction, maintenance, and cultivation is carried out on the household level.[19] The labor of individual families or cooperative groups of a few families was sufficient to build terraces, and most farming was probably done on a small scale by the individual owners of the terraces. The intensive cultivation of terraces and the need for continual maintenance on the walls made it advantageous for farmers to live close to their plots. This contributed to the great dispersion of rural settlement across the landscape during the Late Aztec period. Houselot *calmil* gardens were also organized on a household basis.

Unlike rainfall agriculture or terracing, which are organized on the household level in most societies, irrigation systems normally require cooperative labor for their construction and maintenance and some form of central authority for their management.[20] Irrigation networks must be planned carefully from the start. Considerable labor goes into digging canals and building dams. Canals silt up frequently, and clearing them out is a regular and time-consuming task that goes beyond the abilities of individual households. A common political authority is usually needed to establish water rights and schedules and to settle the numerous disputes that inevitably arise in the operation of any irrigation system. This authority does not have to be the state, however, since in many modern systems the body regulating irrigation is a lower-level local organization.

In Aztec central Mexico, irrigation was most heavily used in the area of the modern state of Morelos. The size and shape of the major Late Aztec states in this area suggest a link between irrigation and state organization.[21] A series of north–south river valleys were extensively irrigated, and the major states, such as Cuauhnahuac, Yautepec, and Huaxtepec, were each confined to individual valleys. Each state could control its own irrigation system without having to rely upon the goodwill of upstream competitors for water. The capital cities of each of these domains were located near the northern or upstream edges of their territory. Irrigation was important to the people of Morelos, and the size and layout of city-states reflected this importance.

The organizational requirements of raised field cultivation were intermediate between those of terracing and irrigation. The initial construction of a system of raised fields required planning and a considerable investment of labor, but once they were built, *chinampas* were easily farmed and maintained by households. Some archaeologists see the hand of the state in the regular gridlike arrangement of *chinampas* in Lakes Chalco and Xochimilco, but documentary sources on the *chinampas* at the edge of Tenochtitlan describe small plots of several fields farmed by individual households who lived among their fields.[22]

In sum, some of the intensive agricultural methods used by the Aztecs required organization and control by a central authority, perhaps local lords or city-state bureaucrats, but other methods were almost certainly organized and operated entirely at the scale of the individual farm household.

Rural Settlement

Settlement patterns

Most of the several million Aztecs in central Mexico were peasants – rural cultivators who farmed land controlled by lords. Rural settlements took a variety of forms, depending upon the local environmental setting, the type of agriculture practiced, and the nature of local social organization. When the Aztlan migrants first arrived in central Mexico, their new settlements were small and scattered widely across the landscape. Only a few large cities – such as Tenayuca (see chapter 2) – existed in the Valley of Mexico during the Early Aztec period. As the population grew, small groups moved into the swampy backwaters of Lakes Chalco and Xochimilco and constructed the earliest *chinampas*. Then, during Late Aztec times, large numbers of people moved onto the lakeshore plain and built irrigation systems, and into the foothills, where they constructed terraces. These farming systems had a major impact on the nature of rural settlement patterns.

Archaeological surveys indicate that much Late Aztec settlement was dispersed. The remains of individual houses and house groups are widely scattered across the landscape, particularly in areas where terrace agriculture was practiced. The Late Aztec settlement of the Buenavista hills, an alluvial fan in western Morelos, is typical. This ancient geological formation of long, gently sloping ridges extends out for several miles from the Ajusco mountain range to the north. Late Aztec house foundations, which are visible on the ground surface, are scattered along the ridge tops. The sloping sides of the ridges are covered with the remnants of stone terrace walls, and check-dams are present in the ravines between the ridges. As one moves along the narrow ridge tops, the density of houses increases periodically, clustering around small groups of mounds, which were probably elite residences and/or small temple-pyramids. Between the mound groups, house density drops off but never to the point where there are large empty areas.[23]

Not all Aztec farmers lived in these dispersed settlements. Nucleated villages and towns were also common, particularly in the *chinampa* zone of the southern Valley of Mexico and in the irrigated valleys of Morelos. In these settlements, houses were packed more closely together, and the communities had clearer boundaries. Towns and some larger villages contained distinctive buildings that had administrative and religious functions. These buildings might include the residence of a village headman or a lord, a temple, or other special structures. Large villages, towns, or areas of dispersed settlement often corresponded to a *calpolli*, a social and territorial unit that helped regulate land tenure and tribute payment (see chapter 6).

Excavations at Cuexcomate and Capilco

Archaeological fieldwork at the rural sites of Cuexcomate and Capilco in western Morelos provides a case study that illustrates some of the topics covered in this chapter. My wife, Cynthia Heath-Smith, and I directed mapping and excavations at these sites in 1985 and 1986 in a project designed to gather information on social and economic conditions among Aztec peasants.[24] Although ethnohistoric sources provide rich data on the lives of Aztec nobles and urban-dwellers (see chapter 6), little was known about the Aztec peasantry. We selected these sites for study because they were not deeply buried, and the foundations of individual houses were visible on the ground surface. Archaeologists have found that the best information on social and economic organization comes from the excavation of houses, and conditions at Cuexcomate and Capilco made them ideal sites. We could begin to excavate houses immediately, without wasting a lot of time and effort looking for buried structures. The sites are located in a rural area today and, at the time of fieldwork, were little disturbed by modern settlement or activities.

Capilco is a small site with 21 house foundations, and Cuexcomate is a larger site with over 150 houses and other structures, including temples, storehouses, and ritual dumps (see figure 3.7). One of our first tasks was to estimate the populations of these sites. Since we were unable to excavate all 164 houses at the two sites, we used the technique of random sampling to select a sample of houses at each site. At Capilco, 8 of the 21 houses (38 percent) were selected in a simple random sample, while at Cuexcomate 21 out of 143 houses (15 percent) were chosen in a stratified

Figure 3.7   Maps of Cuexcomate and Capilco, rural Aztec sites in Morelos. The black squares are houses (Drawing by Michael E. Smith)

random sample.[25]

For each house in the two samples, two test pits were dug: one in the structure to date its construction, and one in a nearby midden (trash deposit) to recover information on domestic artifacts and living conditions. Through a combination of dating methods, we determined in which periods each house was occupied. We used a detailed sequence of temporal phases based upon the types of pottery present. The latter part of the Early Aztec period is represented at these sites in the Temazcalli phase (AD 1200–1350), and the Early Cuauhnahuac (AD 1350–1440) and Late Cuauhnahuac (AD 1440–1550) phases correspond to the Late Aztec A and B periods (figure 2.1).

The use of random sampling to choose the 29 houses to excavate permits us to extrapolate characteristics of the houses in the samples to the total collection of houses at Capilco and Cuexcomate. For example, two of the eight houses (25 percent) tested at Capilco had occupation during the Early Aztec phase. We therefore inferred that 25 percent of the 21 houses at the site, or five houses, were occupied in Early Aztec times. The numbers of houses were then converted into population estimates using average family size figures from Early Colonial census documents from various towns in Morelos.[26]

Patterns of house occupation show a dramatic growth of population

Table 3.3   Population and site areas of Cuexcomate and Capilco

Site	Early Aztec 1150–1350	Late Aztec A 1350–1430	Late Aztec B 1430–1550
Capilco			
Population	28	72	116
Site area (ha)	0.14	0.60	1.15
Cuexcomate			
Population	0	237	803
Site area (ha)	0	9.94	14.58

Source: M. E. Smith 1992a

across the three phases (table 3.3). Although these results pertain only to the two sites, they suggest that the demographic explosion reported for the Valley of Mexico was also taking place in adjacent areas such as western Morelos. When we applied the demographic patterns from Capilco and Cuexcomate to nearby sites in western Morelos, it became obvious that by the Late Aztec B phase, the regional population far exceeded the carrying capacity of rainfall agriculture. This burgeoning population needed intensive agricultural methods to survive, and, in the hilly landscape of western Morelos, terraces and check-dams were the logical choices.

When we mapped these sites, we noticed check-dams at both sites. Although the remains of ancient check-dams and hillside terraces had been reported from various parts of central Mexico, no one had excavated these features to establish their age, construction methods, or use. At Capilco, we excavated two of the seven check-dams, and at Cuexcomate we dug three of the 36 check-dams that crossed a seasonal streambed just southwest of the occupation zone.

We were able to piece together the history of one extensively excavated check-dam at Cuexcomate by using a combination of methods, including stratigraphic analysis, pollen studies, soil chemistry, grain-size analysis, and radiocarbon dating.[27] Its construction was begun sometime in the fifteenth century. A stone wall was built and the upstream side quickly filled up with sediments carried by flash floods. After a period of active use, a flood breached the wall and carried away much of the accumulated deposit. The wall was repaired, and a long period of use followed, during which sediments gradually built up, and the wall was enlarged several times one row of stones at a time. A radiocarbon date of AD 1476 was obtained from a deposit early in this period of gradual expansion. Unfortunately our pollen results were equivocal and do not permit us to state which crops were grown on this or other check-dam fields. The dam was probably abandoned soon after the Spanish conquest, when the occupants of Cuexcomate (those who did not succumb to disease) were forced to move to another community.

Although we had noted the remnants of a few stone terrace walls on hillsides around Cuexcomate and Capilco, they did not seem to cover a large area. The soils are very rocky, and today large and small stones are scattered all over the ground surface, in pastures and plowed fields alike. One of the student excavators first noticed that the sloping flanks of the ridge surrounding the settlement of Cuexcomate had many subtle stone alignments that could only be the bases of ancient terrace walls.[28] The crew had been walking all over these features for months without noticing their existence. We mapped and excavated some of the stone alignments, but soil erosion on the hillsides has been severe since the site was abandoned, and preservation of the terraces is quite poor. The surviving terrace walls consist of rough lines of stones, only a single course high, often resting directly on bedrock.

The Rural Landscape

The peasants who farmed the hills, valleys, swamps, and villages of rural central Mexico were essential participants in the Aztec social order. Their efforts provided food and other products such as cotton to supply the tens of thousands of people who did not farm for a living. The nobility lived off the work of these peasants, as did craft specialists and other inhabitants of cities. Not all Aztec peasants were full-time farmers, however. Women produced textiles for trade and tribute, in addition to their other domestic tasks, and many men took up part-time crafts, producing goods like pottery, stone tools, paper, or rope.

The Aztec countryside did not consist solely of isolated farming families; small home-based cottage industries thrived in many areas, and a large number of lords lived in small towns and country estates. Peasants were well integrated into an extensive system of marketplace trade, and they had access to goods from all over the empire. In short, the Aztec countryside was a thriving and complex social landscape, not a rural backwater of impoverished peasants. The next two chapters describe how agricultural production was complemented by craft industries, and how a dynamic system of markets and merchants served to distribute goods throughout the rural and urban settlements of Aztec central Mexico.

chapter four
Artisans and their Wares

*The last sign, the twentieth, called Xochitl, means Flower . . . and
was a sign which was associated with masters and craftsmen. Thus
it was said that those born under it were to be painters, metalworkers, weavers, sculptors, carvers – that is to say, [workers in]
all the arts that imitate nature.*

**Diego Durán, Book of the Gods and Rites
and the Ancient Calendar**

The producers of goods played an important role in Aztec society. Work
was heavily specialized, and a relatively small group of people was relied
upon to manufacture most of the goods that people used in their homes,
temples, and workplaces. There were two types of craft industries in Aztec central Mexico – utilitarian and luxury – and the nature and organization of work in each of these sectors had very different implications for
the lives of both producers and consumers. Utilitarian goods such as reed
sandals or pottery vessels were produced by part-time artisans, who worked
in their homes and sold their goods in the marketplace. Luxury items such
as gold jewelry or stone sculptures were fashioned in the workshops of
full-time artists who worked directly for elite patrons.[1]

Utilitarian Crafts

Early Spanish observers had little to say about Aztec utilitarian objects
such as kitchen utensils or household tools and even less about how these
items were produced. Archaeologists, on the other hand, can say much
about these objects because the bulk of the artifacts recovered from most

sites are the detritus of mundane, daily activities. Furthermore, the production of utilitarian items often left clear traces in the archaeological record. Increasingly those who study ancient civilizations, including the Aztecs, are turning their attention to issues of utilitarian craft production and specialization.[2]

Obsidian

Obsidian cutting tools are among the finest achievements of Mesoamerican manufacturing technology. Obsidian is a naturally occurring, black volcanic glass which is available in several highland areas of Mesoamerica. Although brittle and easily broken, obsidian can fracture into pieces with extremely sharp edges. In fact, microscopic studies have shown obsidian blades to have the sharpest edges of any known tool, ancient or modern. The edge of a well-made prismatic blade can be sharper than a surgeon's scalpel. No wonder that the earliest Mesoamericans, many millennia before the Aztecs, selected obsidian as the material of choice for the manufacture of stone tools. By Aztec times, the technology of obsidian-working had been perfected, and stoneknappers could produce a wide range of domestic and industrial tools.[3]

Obsidian tools are the second most abundant type of artifact found at Aztec residential sites, surpassed only by ceramic potsherds. Every Aztec household maintained a collection of implements used for a variety of purposes. Prismatic blades – long, thin, parallel-sided flakes with a characteristic prism-shaped cross-section (figure 4.1) – were the most common type. These versatile tools were used chiefly as knives, but hafted onto wooden handles, they also served as sickles and razors. Prismatic blades were often reworked into new tools, including drills, scrapers, and arrow points. Other common obsidian tools were bifacially flaked knives and projectile points, scrapers, and simple unmodified flakes that could be used for a number of cutting jobs.

Implements of obsidian also were used outside of the home. The Spanish conquerors first encountered obsidian in Aztec swords. The *maquahuitl* sword consisted of a stout wooden shaft with opposing rows of prismatic blades (see chapter 7). These swords were sharp enough to decapitate a man. The more mundane industries such as carpentry and woodworking, textile production, basketry, and farming also utilized obsidian tools.

The technology of obsidian tool production began at the mines. The Aztecs were fortunate to have several nearby obsidian sources, both in the Valley of Mexico and in the mountains north of the valley.[4] The Otumba source, located in the Otumba city-state in the Teotihuacan Valley, and the Pachuca source, just north of the Valley of Mexico, were the most

Figure 4.1   Obsidian blade-core and four prismatic blades from Aztec houses at Yautepec (Photograph by Michael E. Smith)

important to the Aztec industry. Because of its chemical composition and crystal structure, Pachuca obsidian was better suited for prismatic blade technology than most other obsidians. The stone was mined from pits and shafts using basalt tools, although in some areas boulders had eroded from the ground and were easily picked up.

Obsidian knapping is a "subtractive" technology in that, during the process of toolmaking, waste flakes are removed or subtracted from a core. Each stage of the process – from quarry to finished tool – produces a distinctive type of waste material, which allows archaeologists to reconstruct the various toolmaking activities that took place at a site. The presence of initial shaping flakes at quarry sites indicates that excess material usually was chipped from the mined chunks at the quarry prior to carrying the obsidian back to the knapper's home or workshop. At the workshops, most nodules were used in one of two basic technologies: biface production or prismatic blade production. A biface tool is flaked on both its upper and lower surfaces. Biface production is an old technology that has been used throughout the world for tens of millennia. Prismatic blade production is far more difficult and has a more limited distribution.

To make prismatic blades, the obsidian first was worked into a rough, cylindrical macrocore, which then was refined into a symmetrical blade-core through careful chipping. The upper, flat surface of the blade-core was ground with a basalt tool to roughen it in preparation for blade making. The actual blades were removed from the core through the application of steady force to a small area on the edge of the core. This step, known as pressure flaking, was the most difficult part of the whole process. The force required is greater than a person's arm-strength, and it must be applied evenly at just the right place on the core. It took archaeologists many years of experimentation to figure out how the Aztecs and other Mesoamerican peoples accomplished the removal of blades.[5] After many blades had been produced from a core, the exhausted core was either discarded or else fashioned into a new tool; figure 4.1 shows one of these exhausted cores.

The high degree of skill required to produce prismatic blades suggests that blade making was done by specialists. Since all households used many blades, which broke easily, the demand for these blades must have been enormous. A skilled blade-maker could produce some 200 blades from a single core in a short period of time, however, so the number of specialists was not necessarily high. It is likely that many obsidian workers, at least in the rural areas, were part-time specialists who used their obsidian work to supplement farming activities. Archaeological excavations confirm that blade production was carried out in only a few places. The city of Otumba, located next to the Otumba obsidian source, had several obsidian blade workshops that supplied the surrounding area (see below). The rural sites Capilco and Cuexcomate (see chapter 3) were not located near an obsidian source, yet their inhabitants had ready access to blades and other tools. More than 12,000 obsidian artifacts were recovered from the excavations at these sites (mostly blade fragments), but there was virtually no evidence for the production of cores or blades. These farmers bought their blades, ready-made, in the marketplace.

Pottery

Aztec kitchens were equipped with a variety of pottery vessels for cooking, preparing, and serving food. Each family probably owned one or two painted water jars; several flat tortilla griddles (*comalli*); cookpots of various shapes and sizes for beans, sauces, and other foods; a pot to soak maize in; a rough-bottom tripod grinding dish for chilis and tomatoes (*molcaxitl*); a salt jar; and various plates, bowls, and cups for meals (figure 4.2). In addition to kitchenware, pottery was used for religious items (figurines and incense burners); tools (spindle whorls and special bowls to support the spindle during the spinning of cotton thread); and a range of small objects, of uncertain uses, such as stamps, disks, bells, balls, tubes, whistles, and miniature cookpots (figure 4.3). With all of these breakable

Figure 4.2   Ceramic vessels from Aztec kitchens (From Smith [n.d.-a])

objects in common use, it is not surprising that broken pieces of pottery, or sherds, are by far the single most abundant type of artifact at Aztec sites.

Aztec pottery was produced by hand. For most objects, the clay was shaped over a mold made of fired clay and then baked in open fires or in kilns. Unfortunately there is little direct archaeological evidence of pottery manufacture among the Aztecs. Unlike subtractive technologies such as obsidian toolmaking, additive technologies like potting leave far less debris for the archaeologist to find. Although molds for figurines, incense burners, and spindle whorls have been recovered from Otumba, Yautepec, and other sites, no Aztec kilns or firing areas have been found, in spite of excavations at a number of sites.

Several lines of indirect evidence provide clues to the techniques of pottery production. For example, sherds from jars sometimes show horizontal join-marks where two halves of a vessel – each formed in a convex mold – were joined together. Small cavities in the body of Aztec orangeware sherds indicate the addition of plant fibers (reeds or grasses) to the clay as temper to improve its workability. A pink tint in many of these sherds, caused by the presence of salt in the moist clay, suggests some potting near the saline lakes. In chapter 5 I discuss chemical analyses of Aztec sherds and the insights they provide into ceramic production.

Ethnohistoric sources contain bits of information on the Aztec pottery industry. In his descriptions of occupations, Sahagún lists two types of potters: a general "clay worker," who made many different types of

Figure 4.3   Small ceramic objects recovered from excavations of houses at
Cuexcomate and Capilco. These are tobacco pipes (upper left), miniature
cookpots (upper right), bells (lower left), and whistles (lower right) (Photograph
by Michael E. Smith)

vessels, and a "griddle-maker," who specialized in tortilla griddles:

> The griddle maker [is] one who moistens clay, kneads it, tempers it with
> [soft pieces of] reed, makes it into a soft paste . . . He makes griddles; he
> beats [the clay], flattens it, polishes it, smoothes it; he applies a slip. He
> places [the unfired pieces] in the oven; he feeds the fire, makes the oven
> smoke, cools the oven.
>   He sells hard-fired [griddles] which ring, [which are] well tempered, [as
> well as those which are] poorly fired, smudged, blackened, discolored, poorly
> made, inferior, sounding as if cracked – cracked in firing.[6]

From this passage, two things may be inferred. One, a griddle-maker was a
specialist who made only one type of vessel, which indicates a division of
labor within the overall pottery industry. Two, some potters sold their own
wares in the market, a common pattern among the artisans described by
Friar Sahagún. Many questions, however, remain unanswered. Did most
towns and villages have some potters, or did a few large production centers
supply all of central Mexico? How large were individual workshops? Were
potters full-time or part-time specialists? Some tentative answers are

suggested below and in chapter 5, but archaeologists continue to search for more evidence concerning the manufacture of Aztec pottery.[7]

Cotton textiles

Cotton cloth had many uses in Aztec Mexico. Much of it was made into clothing for men (loincloths and capes) and women (skirts and *huipils* or pullover shirts). Cloth also was used for bedding, bags, awnings, decorative hangings, battle armor, adornments for statues of the gods, and shrouds for the dead.[8] Cotton textiles served as items of exchange, most commonly in the form of the *quachtli*, a long narrow folded cloth or cape. *Quachtli* served as currency in the markets, were exchanged as gifts among the nobility, and formed the dominant item of tribute payment at all levels. Commoners used them to pay nobles and subordinate city-states to pay the Aztec empire.

Cotton cloth had symbolic importance in addition to its practical uses. Clothing and capes came in both plain and highly decorated styles. Fancy, colorful types were reserved for important nobles or priests, and a special kind of decorated cape was worn exclusively by the Mexica kings. Some sources state that among the Mexica, only nobles were permitted to wear cotton clothing; commoners wore clothing of maguey cloth or animal skins. Thus cotton symbolized the privileges of nobility.

Women made cotton cloth in the home. From ethnohistoric documents, we know that spinning and weaving were viewed as women's work and that all Aztec women, from the lowliest slave to the highest noblewoman, engaged in cloth production. Cloth production was a fundamental part of female gender identity. Newborn girls were presented with miniature spinning and weaving tools to symbolize their later adult activities (see chapter 6). Women worked at these tasks off and on, throughout the day, interspersed with their other domestic activities. Textile production began with the cleaning and combing of the raw cotton. The cleaned cotton was spun by hand into thread, and the thread was twisted into yarn. In the Codex Mendoza an illustration of a women teaching her daughter to spin cotton shows the method and tools that were used (figure 4.4, top). The fibers were drawn out and twisted onto a twirling wooden spindle or distaff. A round ceramic weight, the spindle whorl, gave the spindle momentum and provided a base on which the thread rested. Because cotton fibers are short, the spinner had to use care to control the spindle. A small bowl kept the base of the twirling spindle from sliding out of control.

Two of the spinning tools depicted in figure 4.4 – the spindle whorl and the small bowl – were made of fired clay. These artifacts survive as direct archaeological evidence for Aztec cotton spinning (figure 4.5). Spindle whorls

Mother of the children
shown in this row

One and a half *tortillas*

A 7-year old girl is being
taught how to spin
by her mother

Two *tortillas*

A 14 year-old [girl][2] weaving

Loom for weaving

Figure 4.4   Girls being taught by their mothers to spin and weave cotton. Top: a 7-year-old learns to spin (Codex Mendoza 1992:v.4:123; f.59r); bottom: a 13-year-old learns to weave with a backstrap loom (Codex Mendoza 1992:v.4:125; f.60r)

have been found at almost every excavated Aztec house in central Mexico, which supports the statements in ethnohistoric sources that all women – nobles and commoners, rural and urban – spun thread in their homes.

Once the thread was twisted into yarn, it was dyed if necessary. A variety of plants and insects were crushed and then boiled with water by specialists to extract dyes. The residue was removed in cake form and sold to consumers in the market. Women reconstituted the dyes, soaked the yarn, and then fixed the colors with a mordant. Cloth was woven on a backstrap loom. A woman hooked one end of the loom over a tree branch or pole and attached the other end to a harness that wrapped around her back. She leaned back to weave, using her posture and position to adjust the tension of the loom (figure 4.4, bottom). Unfortunately, the cross-pieces, shuttles, and other parts of the loom were made of wood or bone, and few of these have survived at Aztec archaeological sites.

Cotton is a warm-country crop that does not grow at the chilly, high altitude of the Valley of Mexico. Families in the Aztec heartland obtained

Figure 4.5   Ceramic cotton-spinning tools from the Aztec village of Capilco. Compare these bowls and spindle whorls to those illustrated in the Codex Mendoza (figure 4.4, top) (Photograph by Michael E. Smith)

raw cotton from warmer areas through the market, and cotton was probably somewhat expensive when compared with the fibers of the locally grown maguey plant. Most households in the Valley of Mexico produced more maguey cloth than cotton cloth. In areas of lower elevation, like Morelos, the situation was reversed: cotton was cultivated in great quantities, but the fiber-producing species of maguey did not grow well in the warmer, moister climate. Fortunately for archaeologists, the ceramic spindle whorls used to spin cotton and maguey are easily distinguished by size. At Aztec houses excavated in Morelos, the small, cotton-spinning whorls are ubiquitous, but very few of the large, maguey-spinning whorls are found. In the higher and colder Valleys of Mexico and Toluca, however, maguey whorls are preponderant.

The maguey industries

The maguey plant is a remarkable cultigen whose leaves and sap the Aztecs used for many products (figure 4.6).[9] The sixteenth-century Spanish naturalist Francisco Hernández described its benefits as follows:

Figure 4.6   A maguey plant at the Aztec city of Otumba (Photograph by Michael E. Smith)

> This plant has almost innumerable uses. The plant itself serves as firewood and for fencing fields . . . its leaves serve to cover roofs, as roof tiles, as plates or dishes, to make paper, and to make thread for footwear, cloth, and all kinds of garments . . . They make nails and tacks from the thorns, with which the Indians formerly perforated their ears in order to mortify their flesh when they worshipped demons . . . From the juice that drips out into the plant's central cavity when the interior leaves are cut out with stone knives, they make wine, honey, vinegar, and sugar.[10]

The two major maguey industries were production of fiber and of *pulque* or wine. To make fiber, the long fleshy leaves or *pencas* were cut off the plant and the flesh was loosened by soaking the leaves in a solution or by roasting them in a pit. The fibrous flesh was then scraped from the outer membrane of the leaf with an obsidian scraper and allowed to dry. The dried fibers were spun tightly to make thread or twisted coarsely to make rope or twine. A coarse fiber, with long filaments, maguey thread was spun by hand onto a spindle outfitted with a large, heavy ceramic whorl. Unlike cotton, maguey fiber was drop spun, a method in which the twirling spindle hangs in the air, spinning freely. The thread was woven into clothing and other textiles on a backstrap loom similar to that used for cotton cloth.

Pulque or *octli*, the only alcoholic beverage drunk by the Aztecs, was made from the fermented sap of the maguey plant. When a plant reached maturity, its center was cut out to leave a cavity. The sides of the cavity were then scraped with an obsidian scraper to stimulate the flow of sap into it. The collector extracted the sap by sucking it into a hollow gourd, and then emptied it into a ceramic jar. The sap was brought to the workshop, where it was emptied into large fermentation vats. The plants had to be scraped and emptied two or three times daily for a period of several weeks to six months, and each maguey plant provided two to four liters of sap each day. The sap, called *aguamiel* today, could be drunk both fresh or in its fermented form, *pulque*; it was also used for medicinal purposes.

Although archaeologists have not located *pulque* production workshops at Aztec sites, they have identified the obsidian tools used to scrape the plant for sap extraction. These tools are widely distributed at Aztec sites in the Valley of Mexico, which suggests that *pulque* production was carried out in many local areas. The drink was used in rituals, and the *pulque* cult with numerous deities was a major component of Aztec religion.[11] Drinking to intoxication was restricted by law, but old people were permitted to indulge as a reward for their long lives. *Pulque* is still a popular beverage among central Mexican peasants today; its alcoholic content is similar to that of beer or wine.

Copper and bronze tools

The technology of metallurgy was introduced into Mesoamerica from Andean South America.[12] The ancient ancestors of the Incas had developed sophisticated methods for working gold, silver, and copper, including the ability to produce tools of bronze alloys, several millennia prior to the Spanish conquest. Around AD 700, seaborne traders or artisans introduced the techniques of copper metallurgy from South America to west Mexican cultures. Later, around AD 1200, the methods of bronze working were introduced into west Mexico, again from a South American place of origin. Bronze is an alloy consisting primarily of copper with limited amounts of tin or arsenic that improve its strength and workability. The smelting of bronze is a more complex technology than copper working, requiring greater skills and higher temperatures. This technology flourished in west Mexico, and by the Late Aztec period, metalsmiths had perfected a repertoire of techniques for fashioning copper and bronze objects. Cold hammering, hot hammering, open-mold casting, and lost-wax casting were used to make a variety of products, including both ritual/ elite items such as bells, rings, tweezers, and ornaments, and utilitarian

Figure 4.7   Bronze tools from Aztec houses in Yautepec. There are three sewing needles, an axe, two punches or awls, a bell, and a tweezer (Photograph by Michael E. Smith)

tools such as sewing needles, chisels, awls, axes, and fishhooks (figure 4.7). Some of these techniques originated in South America and others were developed independently by west Mexican peoples.

Experimental research by Dorothy Hosler has shown that Mesoamerican metalsmiths carefully controlled the elemental composition of the two bronzes – copper-arsenic and copper-tin – in order to achieve several ends. To improve the functionality of tools, they added tin or arsenic to copper in low concentrations (2 to 5 percent), which provides the necessary hardness and strength but avoids brittleness. To achieve desired colors in bells and tweezers, artifacts with great symbolic significance, they added tin or arsenic in high concentrations (10 to 20 percent), which alters the colors of the metal to resemble silver and gold. And to make the small bells produce the desired sounds, varying combinations of the elements were used.

Copper and bronze metallurgy was practiced by the Tarascans, enemies of the Aztecs who lived west of central Mexico. Although the Aztecs of the Valley of Mexico did not adopt the technology themselves, it had begun to spread through the Aztec empire in the final century or two before the Spanish conquest. When the Aztecs conquered territory along the Tarascan border, they captured towns with metalsmiths and areas with major copper deposits. An independent metal-producing area recently has been identified in the Huaxtec territory in the eastern empire. Our excavations at Capilco, Cuexcomate, and Yautepec in Morelos yielded surprising numbers of copper and bronze tools. Although these tools were probably manufactured in west Mexico, metallurgical analyses by Hosler indicate that some of them were reworked locally to maintain their shape and hardness. Copper needles, awls, and chisels were sold in the central Tlatelolco market, probably imported from the western frontier of the empire. At the time of the Spanish Conquest, bronze metallurgy was becoming popular in the Aztec empire, and the people of the Valley of Mexico may have been on the verge of developing a more complex metallurgy by adopting copper and bronze smelting from their Tarascan enemies.

Utilitarian crafts and the economy

The makers of the goods described above were not the only artisans who specialized in utilitarian crafts. In addition to obsidian-knappers, potters, weavers, maguey-workers and metalsmiths, ethnohistoric sources mention numerous other artisans, from basketmakers to arrow-makers (table 4.1). Most of these artisans practiced their crafts part-time as a supplement to farming. They sold their goods in the marketplace, which put them at the mercy of economic forces outside of their control. If the demand for their products declined, the families of artisans could devote more effort to farming. Conversely if the demand for craft items increased, or if income from farming decreased, more attention could be given to the household workshop.

At Cuexcomate and Capilco, we found evidence that increasing economic hardship led certain poor peasant households to increase their production of cotton textiles. As standards of living fell in the Late Aztec B period, the houses of the poorest residents had the greatest numbers of spindle whorls and spinning bowls. It appears that part-time cloth production was stepped up by the families who lived in these houses to compensate for hardship due to either declines in agricultural production or increases in their tribute burden.[13]

Full-time producers of utilitarian goods may have practiced their crafts in some Aztec cities (such as Otumba; see below), but many utilitarian craft producers lived in rural areas where they could easily combine their craft with agriculture. The craftsmen described above produced the kinds of goods – pottery, clothing, tools – required by consumers in most preindustrial societies. These petty artisans contrasted greatly with the full-time specialists in luxury goods.

Table 4.1 Types of craft specialists in Late Postclassic Mesoamerica

Specialty	Tenochtitlan	Huexotzinco	Yucatan
Utilitarian Crafts			
Potters	x	x	x
Gourd-workers	x		
Obsidian/flint-knappers	x		x
Rope-makers		x	
Paperworkers	x	x	
Candlemakers	x		x
Woodcarvers	x	x	x
Sandal-makers	x	x	x
Mat-makers	x	x	
Basketmakers	x	x	
Bag-makers	x		
Spinners	x	x	x
Weavers	x		x
Dyers	x		x
Tailors	x		x
Arrow- and shield-makers			x
Carpenters	x	x	x
Masons	x	x	x
Stonecutters	x	x	x
Tanners			x
Burnishers			x
Lime burners	x	x	x
Charcoal burners			x
Luxury Crafts			
Painters and scribes	x	x	x
Lapidaries	x		
Goldsmiths	x		
Silversmiths			x
Copper smelters	x	x	x
Featherworkers	x	x	
Glue-makers	x		
Rubber workers	x		
Flute-makers			x
Tobacco-tube makers		x	
Flower-workers		x	

Sources: Tenochtitlan: Description of occupations in Tenochtitlan (Sahagún 1950–82:bk.100) Huexotzinco: List of occupations in the Matrícula de Huexotzinco (Carrasco 1974); Yucatan: Maya terms for occupations in early dictionaries (Clark and Houston 1998:42–4)

Luxury Crafts

Hernando Cortés and the Spanish conquerors were awed by the exquisite beauty and craftsmanship of Aztec jewelry and ceremonial art. Ornaments of gold and silver, earrings and lip plugs of jade and obsidian, decorative feather art, religious statues of stone, ceremonial knives whose handles were inlaid with shell and turquoise – these and many other luxury goods graced the temples and palaces of the Aztecs. These were not mere baubles, the frivolous playthings of the Aztec nobility. Rather they played a key role in Aztec society, communicating information about status, wealth, etiquette, and belief. Nobles used these goods to show off their position in society. They gave them as gifts to other nobles at important ritual and diplomatic occasions where such gift-giving helped to cement social ties and political alliances (see chapters 6 and 7). Priests used these objects in rituals, and many of these ended up in the ground as buried offerings (see chapter 10).

Ethnohistoric documents provide most of the evidence for luxury goods. Archaeologists have uncovered examples of some of these crafts – particularly stone sculptures and items of jewelry – but to date there is archaeological information on the actual production of only one type of item – obsidian jewelry. Most of our knowledge of these crafts comes from the descriptions in Friar Sahagún's *Florentine Codex*. Information on the styles and uses of luxury goods is discussed in chapter 11.

Featherworking

> *The activity in which they seem to excel over all other human intellects and which makes them appear unique among the nations of the earth is the craft they have perfected of representing with real feathers, in all their natural colors, all the things that they and other excellent painters can paint with brushes. They used to make many things of feathers, including animals, birds, men, cloaks or mantles, apparel for the priests, crowns or miters, shields and flyswatters, and a thousand other things.*
>
> **Bartolomé de las Casas,** Obras escogidas

Feather mosaic was perhaps the most unique art form of the Aztecs. Objects such as fans, shields, warriors' costumes, capes, headdresses, and decorative hangings were made by tying and gluing colorful feathers onto a stiff backing (figure 4.8). These were among the most valuable and esteemed items in Aztec culture. Unfortunately only eight examples survive today. Sahagún's noble informants were very familiar with the

Figure 4.8   Ceremonial featherwork shield (Courtesy Museum für Völkerkunde, Vienna, object no. 43.380)

featherworkers and their products because many of the craftsmen had worked directly for nobles. Most of what we know of featherworking comes from the friar's descriptions.[14]

The great beauty of Aztec feather mosaics derives from the bright colors of the feathers. Often the feathers of readily available local birds such as ducks and turkeys were dyed, but the most striking colors were provided by the natural feathers of lowland tropical birds such as parrots, macaws, and the quetzal. The long tailfeathers of the quetzal in particular were esteemed for their iridescent green color. Quetzal feathers figured prominently in the painted and carved art of earlier Mesoamerican civilizations such as the Classic Maya and Teotihuacan. The name of the Aztec feathered-serpent god, Quetzalcoatl ("quetzal-feathered serpent") is a testimony to the importance of these feathers in ancient Mesoamerica.

Production of a feather mosaic began with the preparation of a stiff backing panel of cotton cloth and maguey fibers, held together and given strength with several layers of glue. The design was carefully drawn on a paper and cotton stencil, then transferred to the backing. The feathers were attached with maguey twine and glue. Modern studies have shown that the featherworkers' glue, made from a species of wild orchid, was quite strong and effective. Inexpensive local feathers were applied first. These were covered with the more attractive, expensive exotic feathers. Finally, ornaments of gold and other materials often were added as parts of the design.

Sahagún describes a division of labor within the households of featherworkers. The master artisan prepared the stencils and backing, and applied the feathers; women of the household dyed and organized the feathers; and children prepared the glue. Like many Aztec crafts, featherworking was a hereditary occupation. Sons of artisans learned the craft by serving as apprentices. The Codex Mendoza shows several master craftsmen, including a featherworker, instructing their sons in their trades (figure 4.9).[15]

Aztec featherworkers lived together in special *calpolli* or neighborhoods (see chapter 6) in the major cities such as Tenochtitlan, Tlatelolco, and Texcoco. The best-known of these *calpolli*, located in Tlatelolco, was called Amantlan, and featherworkers became known as *amanteca*. Within the *calpolli* the featherworkers had their own temple and school, where they joined together to sponsor and participate in public rituals. The exclusivity of the *calpolli* and the hereditary foundation for apprenticeship in the craft made featherworking a restricted occupation, organized much like medieval European guilds.

Most of the feather mosaics were produced for rulers and nobles, who provided the raw materials and supported the artisans with food and other necessities. The nobles used featherwork items for a variety of purposes – for clothing, for gifts to other nobles, for palace decorations, and to adorn images of the gods. The artisans were not members of the noble class, however. They could not wear their products, and if they became wealthy, they were prohibited from openly displaying their wealth. In addition to their work for the ruler and other high nobles, many *amanteca* also produced items for sale in the marketplace. This was an independent operation in which the feathers and other raw materials were purchased in the

Figure 4.9   Master craftsmen instructing their sons in their crafts (Codex Mendoza 1992:v.4:145; f.70r)

market rather than obtained from a noble patron. Although commoners were permitted to buy feather items in the market, most could not afford to do so. The majority of these items probably were purchased by low-ranking nobles, priests, and wealthy merchants.

Goldsmithing

Some of the most beautiful and sophisticated art objects produced by the Aztecs were gold jewelry made with the lost-wax process.[16] In contrast to copper and bronze metallurgy, which had not become fully established in the Valley of Mexico, goldworking had developed into an important luxury craft in Tenochtitlan. The technology of goldsmithing entered Mesoamerica from Central America through systems of overland trade during the Classic period. By the Late Aztec period, the Mixtec peoples of Oaxaca had acquired a reputation as master goldsmiths. Of the pre-Hispanic gold objects still in existence, some of the finest examples come from Mixtec tombs in the Valley of Oaxaca. We know that a number of Mixtec artisans came to live in Tenochtitlan, but it is not clear from the sources whether Aztec gold jewelry was made by resident Mixtecs, native Aztecs, or both.

Sahagún devotes a chapter to goldsmiths, most of which is taken up with a detailed description of lost-wax casting. This was the primary technique for manufacturing lip plugs, bells, pendants and other items of gold jewelry (figure 4.10). A mold was made of clay, sand, and charcoal. First a solid inner section was fashioned and the outer surface modeled to the desired shape. When it had dried and hardened, a thin layer of beeswax and resin was placed over the mold and carefully pressed to cover the contours evenly. The finished gold piece would be an exact replica of this wax layer. The outer surface of the wax was modeled into the form desired for the gold piece, and was then covered with moist clay to form the outer mold. When this section dried and hardened partially, a tube was inserted for the wax to escape. The completed mold was baked, which caused the clay to harden and the wax to melt and run out. The gold ore was heated over a fire in a ceramic vessel, and the liquid metal was poured into the mold to form the object.

As far as we can tell from the limited evidence in Sahagún and other sources, the goldsmiths were organized in a manner similar to the featherworkers. They lived in their own *calpolli* and participated in common rituals in honor of their patron god, Xipe Totec. Most of their work was done for the king and nobles. The depiction in the Codex Mendoza of a goldsmith teaching his apprentice son the trade (figure 4.9) suggests that goldsmithing, like featherworking, was a hereditary occupation. The complexity of the techniques also suggests a hereditary craft with a long period of apprenticeship.

Lapidary production

Aztec lapidary specialists used a variety of precious stones to make jewelry and other valuable objects. As described by Sahagún, "Their creations were lip pendants, lip plugs, and ear plugs, ear plugs of obsidian, rock crystal, and amber; white ear plugs; and all manner of necklaces; bracelets."[17]

Figure 4.10   Gold necklace and pendants made by lost-wax casting (each bead is 3 cm high) (Photograph courtesy of Dumbarton Oaks Research Library and Collections, Washington, DC)

Obsidian ear spools (also called ear plugs) were among the finest objects made by lapidaries (figure 4.11). Great skill and patience were needed to grind the obsidian into the large thin cylinders favored by Aztec nobles. These ear spools were worn in the earlobes like earrings. Ear spools and lip plugs of obsidian are the only Aztec luxury craft items whose manufacture has been thoroughly documented by archaeologists; this information is discussed in the section on Otumba below. Lapidary producers also worked with jade, turquoise, amethyst, chert, and shell. Jade was the single most valuable material to the Aztecs, partly because of its beauty and rarity (it had to be imported from southern Mesoamerica) and partly because of the symbolism of the color green (which stood for water, fertility, and value). Necklaces and bracelets of jade beads were among the most common forms of jewelry.

Mosaics were another lapidary product (figure 4.12).[18] Small tiles of turquoise, imported from outside of Mesoamerica (Arizona and New Mexico) were used in abundance with shell, obsidian, and coral tiles providing color contrast. The most spectacular Aztec mosaics were human skulls covered partially or entirely with stone and shell tiles. Mosaics and inlays were also applied to jewelry, knife handles, stone sculptures, and a variety of other objects.

Figure 4.11   Obsidian ear spools. These examples of fine jewelry took great craftsmanship to manufacture (height 3.5 cm) (Photograph courtesy of the Metropolitan Museum of Art, the Michael C. Rockefeller Memorial Collection, Bequest of Nelson A. Rockefeller, 1979. 1979.206.1088, .1089; all rights reserved, the Metropolitan Museum of Art)

Ethnohistoric information on the organization of lapidary production is similar to that for featherworking and goldsmithing. Lapidary craftsmen probably lived in their own *calpolli*, worshiped their own gods, and had a system of apprenticeship and hereditary recruitment (see figure 4.9). Lapidary products were important enough to the noble class that these artisans were able to influence the course of Aztec imperial expansion. Friar Durán states that lapidary workers convinced Motecuhzoma to conquer certain towns in order to provide them with a more secure source of the special sands and abrasives they needed for their craft. According to ethnohistorical sources, Xochimilco in the southern Valley of Mexico was a center of lapidary production. Archaeological fieldwork has recently identified another city with a significant number of lapidaries – Otumba.

Luxury crafts and the economy

Luxury goods had a far more limited demand than cookpots or obsidian blades because they were expensive and many were used almost exclusively

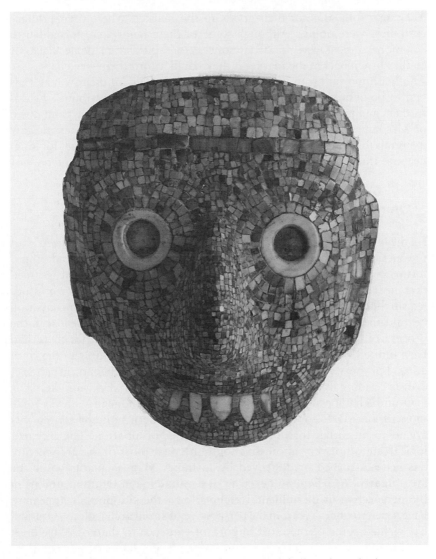

Figure 4.12 Mosaic mask of stone with turquoise, shell, and coral inlay (height 14 cm) (Photograph courtesy of the Saint Louis Art Museum, no. 96:1968)

by nobles and priests. These items required greater skill and effort to produce. As a result, the organization of production for luxury crafts differed greatly from that for utilitarian crafts. Artisans (or artists) were full-time specialists, and much of their work was done directly for noble patrons.

They also sold some of their goods in the market, where their primary customers were nobles. Although some of these items were forbidden to commoners, most were not. Commoners could purchase jade necklaces or feather ornaments in the market if they could afford them (see chapter 5). Another important trait of luxury goods is that many of the raw materials had to be obtained from distant areas, through trade or tribute. Quetzal feathers and jade came from southern Mesoamerica, turquoise from north of Mesoamerica, and coral from the coasts. Obtaining these exotic raw materials to make luxury products was one of the major incentives for long-distance trade in Aztec times, a topic considered in the next chapter.

Otumba: An Aztec Craft Center

IIn the late 1980s, the discovery of abundant evidence for specialized craft production at the site of Otumba took many archaeologists and ethno-historians by surprise. Prior to the Otumba project, scholars had assumed that most craft specialists lived in Tenochtitlan. Archaeologists who studied smaller cities and towns had found little evidence for craft production beyond the ubiquitous spindle whorls that were discarded or lost in the process of domestic textile production. Some suggested that there had been limited, part-time producers of pottery and stone tools in the rural areas, but most agreed that the existence of large numbers of urban specialists residing in towns outside of the imperial capital was unlikely.[19]

Otumba had been a city-state capital in the Teotihuacan Valley. Unlike most former Aztec towns, the colonial and modern Otumba settlements are adjacent, rather than on top of, the Aztec occupation. The archaeological site is not very impressive today because most of the architecture has been disturbed or destroyed by farming. Maguey plants cover the area (figure 4.6). There isn't even a tall pyramid left at Otumba, and from the perspective of monumental archaeology, the site doesn't appear to have much to offer. Yet from the perspective of social archaeology, Otumba has yielded some of the most important evidence to date of Aztec craft production.

The Otumba archaeological project was directed by Thomas H. Charlton, Deborah L. Nichols, and Cynthia Otis Charlton.[20] Thomas Charlton had worked previously on various fieldwork projects in the Otumba area. His observations of certain artifacts on the surface of the Aztec town site (including spindle whorls, obsidian cores, and figurine molds) led him to suspect the existence of numerous specialized craft workshops at Otumba. A fieldwork project was needed to test this hypothesis.

Charlton, Nichols, and Otis Charlton designed a program of systematic surface sampling in which they picked up all artifacts from each of 1,150 5 by 5 m squares. The entire 2 sq km of the Aztec city was divided into a grid of 50 m squares. One 5 by 5 m collection was made in each of these squares, with additional collections taken in those areas with abundant craft production artifacts. These intensive surface collections proved to be very successful in documenting craft production activities at Otumba. Most of the town site has been plowed by farmers in recent times, resulting in the churning up of thousands of previously buried artifacts. The large 5 by 5 m units used for surface collections yielded enough artifacts to reconstruct activities in each area of the site, including both widespread domestic tasks and specialized craft work. By taking at least one surface collection from every 50 m square of the site, the archaeologists were able to trace the spatial distribution of craft production activities across the entire settlement. The surface collections were augmented by test excavations in specific workshop locations.

The Otumba surface collections contained evidence for the manufacture of seven major types of products: obsidian blades, obsidian bifacial tools, basalt tools, lapidary products, ceramic goods, cotton textiles, and maguey textiles. The locations of concentrations of production debris are shown in figure 4.13. Evidence for the manufacture of obsidian prismatic blades consisted of very high concentrations of obsidian in the surface

Figure 4.13 Map of the Aztec city of Otumba showing the locations of areas of craft production (After Otis Charlton 1994, figure 8.1; reproduced with permission)

collections coupled with the presence of debitage (the waste byproducts of chipped-stone toolmaking) and exhausted cores (figure 4.1). These remains were concentrated in several discrete areas of the site (figure 4.13), which suggested a series of small household-based workshops. Evidence for the manufacture of obsidian bifacial tools was also recovered by the Otumba project, but not in the urban center; these items were made at outlying rural villages that had been part of the wider Otumba city-state. Basalt, a hard and porous volcanic rock readily available in the Otumba region, was worked into both domestic implements (such as *manos* and *metates* for grinding corn) and industrial tools (scrapers for loosening the fibers from maguey leaves and polishers for finishing lapidary products). The waste flakes and production tools that indicate basalt working were found at a few scattered locations within the city.

Probably the most spectacular evidence for craft production at Otumba concerned the lapidary industry. From the artifacts recovered in the surface collections and test excavations, Cynthia Otis Charlton reconstructed nearly the entire sequence of steps involved in the manufacture of ear spools, lip plugs, and beads from obsidian and other stones, including chert and rock crystal (figure 4.14). This is the only case where the complete production process of an Aztec luxury craft has been documented archaeologically.

The lapidary workshops at Otumba were identified by the presence of production tools (perforators and polishers of basalt), premanufacture blanks, and partially finished products. Ear spools were made from partially used prismatic blade cores of obsidian, following the technological steps shown in figure 4.14. Because of the brittleness of the volcanic glass, many items broke in the process of manufacture and were discarded. The Otumba artifacts included broken examples from each step of the sequence shown in figure 4.14. Finished pieces were not recovered in the surface collections, however. Most of these had been traded away in Aztec times, and those that ended up on the surface of the site were broken by plowing or picked up by farmers long before the archaeologists arrived. Most lapidary production was carried out in three zones in the southeast portion of the site (figure 4.13). The artifacts were associated with residences, which implies that artisans worked in their homes or else had workshops close to their houses. It is difficult to determine from archaeological evidence whether the artisans were full-time or part-time specialists.

The Otumba ceramic industries used molds to manufacture several types of objects, including incense burners, figurines, and spindle whorls. Evidence for this production consisted of the ceramic molds, production errors and rejects, and large numbers of the finished products. No kilns or firing areas were located, and the type of extensive excavations required to find such features were beyond the scope of the original Otumba project.

Figure 4.14   Technological sequence for the manufacture of obsidian jewelry (Drawing by Cynthia Otis Charlton; reproduced with permission)

Long-handled incense burners, used in both domestic and temple rituals, were manufactured in molds found in the western portion of Otumba. Small ceramic figurines, in the forms of people, animals, and gods, also were produced in large numbers. A large district in the southeast portion of the city contained many molds for figurines (figure 4.15), high concentrations of broken figurine fragments, and instances of duplicate figurines clearly made from the same mold. These workshops also turned out other small mold-made ceramic objects such as clay balls (perhaps used as blowgun pellets), rattle balls, rattles, stamps, and small spindle whorls (see figure 4.3).

Molds for the manufacture of both types of ceramic spindle whorls – the large variety used to spin maguey fiber and the small variety used for cotton – were found at Otumba, but with differing distributions. The

Figure 4.15   Ceramic figurine of a maize ear (right) and a ceramic mold (left) used to form this or other similar figurines. Both artifacts are from Otumba (Scale in cm; photograph by Cynthia Otis Charlton; reproduced with permission)

small cotton whorls were made in small numbers at the figurine workshops, whereas the large maguey whorls were produced in larger numbers in a zone of possible maguey fiber workshops. Cotton whorls were recovered from all parts of the site, pointing to widespread domestic cloth production. Used maguey whorls, on the other hand, were found primarily in the same southeast zone in which they were produced. This concentration of whorls in one area may indicate the existence of workshop areas dedicated to specialized maguey cloth production.

No other Aztec archaeological site has produced this level of evidence for the widespread and concentrated manufacture of so many different craft items. Taken together, the findings of the Otumba project suggest several patterns in the organization of craft production at the city. First, the excavations indicate that production areas or workshops were located within or adjacent to houses rather than in separate workshop buildings. Second, the concentration of several of the industries (particularly the lapidary, figurine, and maguey cloth industries) in their own zones or areas points to specialization on the level of the neighborhood or *calpolli*, as Sahagún described for the luxury artisans. Third, the dating of the collections indicates that the major period of occupation and craft production at Otumba was the Late Aztec period, when both production and exchange in central Mexico reached their maximum development.

Just as any successful research project generates as many new questions as it answers, the results of the Otumba project suggest questions for future research. What, for example, was the role of the elite in sponsoring or controlling craft production? This question is difficult to answer at Otumba because plowing of the site has disturbed clear architectural evidence for elite houses or districts.[21] What were the destinations of the goods produced at Otumba? The archaeologists have determined the places of origin for most of the raw materials used in craft production, but tracing the exchange of the finished products has only begun. Many of these goods must have been intended for export through the markets since the level of production far exceeded the needs of the 10,000 or so residents of Otumba. But did Otumba craftsmen supply only the Otumba city-state, the wider Teotihuacan Valley, the entire Valley of Mexico, or perhaps an even larger area of the Aztec empire? My excavations at Yautepec in Morelos have yielded many prismatic blades made from Otumba obsidian, and a few fragments of Otumba-style obsidian jewelry (see chapter 8), but it is not yet possible to match the finished artifacts with their places of manufacture.

The Otumba project has contributed greatly to our understanding of the techniques and organization of Aztec craft production, providing the first good evidence for the existence of a center of urban craft specialists outside of Tenochtitlan. How did these products move from producer to consumer? The various utilitarian and luxury crafts were part of an economy with quite sophisticated systems of exchange. The size, organization, and ubiquity of Aztec marketplaces greatly impressed the Spanish conquerors. Anyone – commoners or nobles – could obtain virtually any good or service present in Mesoamerica at these markets. Professional merchants were organized into guilds, and both regulated the markets and mounted long trading expeditions to the far corners of Mesoamerica. This was a complex and active economy with several types of currency in circulation, and the Aztec state controlled only a very small part of the overall economy. I now turn from the topic of production to that of exchange.

chapter five
The Commercial Economy

On reaching the market-place . . . we were astounded at the great number of people and the quantities of merchandise, and at the orderliness and good arrangements that prevailed, for we had never seen such a thing before . . . You could see every kind of merchandise to be found anywhere in New Spain.
Bernal Díaz del Castillo, The Conquest of New Spain

The Aztecs, like many other civilizations, relied on markets and merchants to move goods from producer to consumer. By "market," I mean a physical space – a marketplace – where buyers and sellers congregate to exchange goods and services. Markets of this type are still thriving institutions in modern Mesoamerica, and these marketplaces can provide an idea of what their Aztec predecessors may have been like.[1]

Where they still flourish today, markets in cities tend to be held daily, in permanent buildings. Markets in smaller settlements usually are held only once a week, often in an open public plaza. On market day, otherwise sleepy towns and villages became bustling centers of activity. Vendors set up temporary stalls to sell their wares, and buyers arrive early to take care of their weekly purchases. Some of the vendors are professional merchants who travel from market to market; others are farmers or petty artisans, or members of their families, who sell their products as a part-time activity (figure 5.1). In areas with a high population and a complex economy, individual markets are usually linked together into an integrated market system. Such was the case in the Aztec Valley of Mexico, and in many ways the scale and complexity of the Aztec market system surpassed most modern peasant market systems in Mesoamerica.

Figure 5.1 A modern Maya woman selling vegetables in the marketplace, Merida, Yucatan (Photograph by Michael E. Smith)

Marketplaces

Almost every Aztec settlement, from the imperial capital to the smallest villages, had a marketplace that came alive weekly on market day (the Aztec week was five days long). The sheer volume of goods that moved through Aztec markets was enormous, but the efficiency and success of the market system in distributing goods and services relieved the state of the need to manage exchange activities closely. Unlike in the Inca empire and in some other early civilizations, where the central government maintained heavy control over the economy in general, Aztec markets and trade were largely independent of the state.[2]

The Tlatelolco market

The biggest marketplace in the ancient New World was located in Tenochtitlan's twin city Tlatelolco. Hernando Cortés, Bernal Díaz del Castillo, and the other Spanish conquerors were astounded by the great size of the market plaza, the tens of thousands of people, the many hundreds of types of goods for sale, and the orderliness and organization of the market. The best description of the market is that of Cortés himself, and it is worth quoting the conqueror at length to get an idea of the richness of the Tlatelolco market:

> The city has many open squares in which markets are continuously held and the general business of buying and selling proceeds. One square in particular is twice as big as that of Salamanca and completely surrounded by arcades where there are daily more than sixty thousand folk buying and selling. Every kind of merchandise such as may be met with in every land is for sale there, whether of food and victuals, or ornaments of gold and silver, or lead, brass, copper, tin, precious stones, bones, shells, snails and feathers . . .
>
> There is a street of game where they sell . . . rabbits, hares, deer and small dogs which they breed especially for eating. There is a street of herb-sellers where there are all manner of roots and medicinal plants that are found in the land . . . There are barbers' shops where you may have your hair washed and cut. There are other shops where you may obtain food and drink. There are street porters such as we have in Spain to carry packages . . .
>
> All kinds of vegetables may be found there. There are many different sorts of fruits . . . All kinds of cotton thread in various colors may be bought in skeins, very much in the same way as in the great silk exchange of Granada, except that the quantities are far less. They have colors for painting of as good quality as any in Spain, and of as pure shades as may be found anywhere . . .
>
> A great deal of chinaware is sold of very good quality . . . Maize is sold both as grain and in the form of bread . . . Pastries made from game and fish pies may be seen on sale . . .
>
> There is nothing to be found in all the land which is not sold in these markets, for over and above what I have mentioned there are so many and such various other things that on account of their very number and the fact that I do not know their names, I cannot now detail them. Each kind of merchandise is sold in its own particular street and no other kind may be sold there: this rule is very well enforced. All is sold by number and measure, but up till now no weighing by balance has been observed. A very fine building in the great square serves as a kind of audience chamber where ten or a dozen persons are always seated, as judges, who deliberate on all cases arising in the market and pass sentence on evildoers. In the square itself there are officials who continually walk amongst the people inspecting goods exposed for sale and the measures by which they are sold, and on certain occasions I have seen them destroy measures which were false.[3]

The essential features of Cortés's description of the Tlatelolco market – the list of many diverse goods and services, the orderliness of the vendors, and the presence of judges – are repeated in other early accounts. The goods offered for sale included both luxury items and utilitarian goods, plus a wide variety of meat, produce, prepared foods and drink, live animals, and many services. The innumerable tiny stalls selling utilitarian craft goods were operated by the families of the artisans described in chapter 4. Other stalls were operated by full-time or part time merchants of various sorts. The well-known, professional *pochteca* merchants (see below) sold their goods in the market, and also served as the market judges mentioned by Cortés.

The Tlatelolco market was the major marketplace serving both Tenochtitlan and Tlatelolco. It was easily reached from the mainland by either canoe or causeway. Given the limitations on transport in an economy without the wheel or draft animals, the canoe was of paramount importance for moving heavy burdens. Early Spanish observers noted that the lakes around the imperial capital were filled with canoes going and coming from the market. The growth of Tenochtitlan and Tlatelolco from small towns into a single giant metropolis was due in no small part to the success of this market, and the city's island location was an important contributor to that success.

The Valley of Mexico market system

The Tlatelolco market did not operate in isolation. It formed part of a larger regional system of markets that covered the entire Valley of Mexico. The Nahuatl term *tianquiz* was used to refer to any market, large or small. Nearly all cities and towns had marketplaces, but they were considerably smaller than the Tlatelolco market, and they did not excite much comment. One early writer, Friar Torquemada, stated that there were countless markets in central Mexico, but since he did not have enough space to describe them all, he would limit his description to Tlatelolco.[4] Although markets existed in the Early Aztec period, their size and importance increased greatly in Late Aztec times. All of the eyewitness accounts, of course, pertain to the markets of the Late Aztec B period.

Some clues to the nature of markets outside of Tlatelolco are provided by an Early Colonial register of the tax paid by vendors in the market of Coyoacan, a city-state capital in the southern Valley of Mexico. The local *tlatoani* (king) collected the market tax in Spanish money; in pre-Hispanic times the tax would have been paid in cacao beans or cotton *quachtli*, the principal forms of money. Most of the Coyoacan vendors sold utilitarian goods, although some luxury items were mentioned. Vendors included both the artisans who produced the goods and merchants. Among the vendors offering utilitarian wares were specialized potters (both stewpot-makers and griddle-makers), basketmakers, obsidian-blade knappers, maguey-garment makers, broom sellers, lime sellers, medicine sellers, and lake-scum sellers. Merchants selling luxury goods included feather sellers, small-bell makers, and metalworkers. A drawing of an Aztec market from Friar Durán's account (figure 5.2) shows four vendors (on the top and left side) selling to three buyers. Two slaves, with wooden collars, are for sale; the female one demonstrates her skills at spinning cotton. In the center is a round altar where images of the market gods were erected.

Some Aztec markets specialized in particular types of goods. For example, markets in the towns of Azcapotzalco and Itzocan were widely known for the sale of slaves. The holy city of Cholula, in the Puebla Valley east of the Valley of Mexico, had a reputation as a center for trade in luxury items such as jewels, precious stones, and fine featherwork. The market in Acolman, a town in the Teotihuacan Valley, was famous for the sale of dogs. Friar Durán described it as follows:

> It was established that the dogs were to be sold in the periodic market at Acolman and that all those desirous of selling or buying were to go there. Most of the produce, then, which went to this *tianguiz* [market] consisted of small- and medium-sized dogs of all types, and everyone in the land went to buy dogs there – as they do today [ca. 1577], because at this time the same trade is carried on. One day I went to observe the market day there, just to be an eye-witness and discover the truth. I found more than four hundred large and small dogs tied up in crates, some already sold, others still for sale. And there were such piles of ordure that I was overwhelmed.[5]

Only a few Aztec markets were specialized in this fashion. The most important distinctions among markets related less to specialized goods than to hierarchical position. The notion of a hierarchy of marketplaces is crucial for understanding the operation of the Valley of Mexico market system, an example of what economic anthropologists call a complex interlocking market system.[6] In the Valley of Mexico there were four hierarchical levels of markets or central places. The huge Tlatelolco marketplace was the sole example of the top level. The second level consisted of a few cities whose markets were larger or more important than most. Texcoco, the second-largest city, was a second-level market center, as was Xochimilco. The third level comprised markets in city-state centers like Otumba, Coyoacan, and Acolman. Finally, the lowest hierarchical level was filled by the markets of the smaller towns and villages. The levels were distinguished by the numbers of people buying and selling (with greater numbers attending the higher-level markets), the quantity and variety of goods and services offered (with more offered at higher-level markets), and by frequency. The highest-level markets met daily, the city-state markets met once a week (every five days), and the smallest markets met even less frequently.

The periodic schedule of the markets suited the needs of both merchants and consumers.[7] Itinerant merchants traveled from town to town,

Figure 5.2   An Aztec market. The individuals with wooden collars are slaves
(After Durán 1971:pl.29; drawing by Ellen Cesarski)

setting up at each marketplace on market day. This circuit allowed them
to cover a wider area, thereby satisfying a larger demand for their goods
than if they were limited to a single marketplace. Most consumers did not
need to attend the market every day, so the periodic schedule was convenient for them also.

Aztec markets were not just economic institutions; they also served an
important social function. Friar Durán described the social attraction of
Aztec markets as follows:

> The markets were so inviting, pleasurable, appealing, and gratifying to these
> people that great crowds attended, and still attend, them, especially during
> the big fairs, as is well known to all. I suspect that if I said to a market
> woman accustomed to going from market to market: "Look, today is mar-
> ket day in such and such a town. What would you rather do, go from here
> right to Heaven or to the market?" I believe this would be her answer:
> "Allow me to go to the market first, and then I will go to Heaven." She
> would be happier to lose those minutes of glory to visit the marketplace and
> walk about hither and thither without any gain or profit, to satisfy her
> hunger and whim to see the *tianguiz*.[8]

The excursion into town on market day was a social event that provided one of the few opportunities for people who lived in different towns or villages to meet one another. On market day one could learn the latest news or gossip, talk with friends and colleagues, meet potential spouses, and generally keep up with the social life of the community, while also taking care of purchases and seeing the latest goods and styles. Most marketplaces had one or more shrines whose gods watched over the proceedings (figure 5.2), and market day also had its religious functions to complement its economic and social aspects.

Merchants

The occupation of merchant was an important one among the Aztecs. From written sources we know of at least two types of professional merchant: the *pochteca* or guild-merchants of the Valley of Mexico who traded on an international scale, and regional merchants whose activities were confined to smaller areas. In the *Florentine Codex* Friar Sahagún devoted all of book 9 to the *pochteca*, and as a result we have considerable information on their activities and lifestyle; in contrast, there are only scattered references to Aztec regional merchants.

The *pochteca* were full-time professionals who occupied a special status within Aztec society that was lower than the nobility but higher than most commoners. Their activities included trade expeditions both within and outside of the empire, oversight of marketplaces in the Valley of Mexico, and foreign service for the emperor in the form of spying and fighting with enemy states. Although some of the *pochteca* trade was carried out directly for the state, the bulk of their transactions were privately motivated and financed. Most of the abundant luxury goods that Aztec nobles used to display their wealth and status – items such as jewelry, stone carvings, and fancy clothing – were either purchased from *pochteca* or made from materials brought by *pochteca*, who had obtained them from foreign or local sources.

Some *pochteca* became quite wealthy to the point where their riches surpassed those of many nobles. Since merchants were not part of the noble class, however, they could not display their wealth openly in public. Much of their trade was carried out in secret to hide the extent of their success. When a group of *pochteca* returned home from a lengthy expedition, they arranged to enter the city under the cover of darkness:

> Not by day but by night they swiftly entered by boat. And as to their goods, no one could see how much there was; perhaps they carefully hid – covered up – all the boats . . . And when he had quickly come to unload what he had

acquired, then swiftly he took away his boat. When it dawned, nothing remained.[9]

The *pochteca* were organized into guilds with closely controlled, hereditary membership. These guilds existed in only 12 cities: Tenochtitlan, Tlatelolco, Azcapotzalco, Cuauhtitlan, Huitzilopochco, Chalco, Coatlinchan, Huexotla, Mixcoac, Otumba, Texcoco, and Xochimilco. These cities, all located in the Valley of Mexico, included the major political capitals (Tenochtitlan and Texcoco), the most active economic centers (Tlatelolco, Otumba, and Xochimilco), and other important city-state capitals. Merchants were hierarchically ranked; among the categories were "principal merchants" at the top, followed by slave dealers, disguised and spying merchants, and ordinary *pochteca* who were called *oztomeca*. At the bottom of the order were apprentice merchants who were in the process of learning the trade. The *pochteca* guilds had their own laws of conduct, which they enforced in their own courts, distinct from the regular legal system.

The *pochteca* organized large expeditions lasting many months to conduct their trade with distant areas. Each expedition would involve several merchants and apprentices as well as a crew of professional carriers or *tlameme* to bear the loads of goods in large backpacks (figure 5.3A). Friar Sahagún noted that the merchants were trained soldiers and carried weapons for protection: "As they traveled the road, they went girt for war. They bore their shields, their obsidian-bladed swords, [and] their devices, because they passed through the enemy's land, where they might die [and] where they took captives."[10]

The merchants would plan their itinerary carefully with stops at a succession of marketplaces in order to obtain the best bargains possible. In Mesoamerica, these merchants were permitted to cross foreign borders, even those between hostile enemies. When *pochteca* traded in markets outside of the empire, they often served as spies for the Mexica, gathering information on resources, armies, and defenses. A portion of their trade was conducted directly for the emperor. For example, the emperor Ahuitzotl (r. 1486–1502) gave the *pochteca* 1,600 cotton cloths, which they traded for such luxury items as jade, shell, and feathers for the ruler. He also provided an armed guard for the expedition, which passed through or near enemy territory.

Most of the goods traded by the *pochteca* were luxury items of high value but low bulk that could be transported easily by human carrier.[11] As described by Friar Durán, the profession of merchant involved

buying and selling, going forth to all the markets of the land, bartering cloth for jewels, jewels for feathers, feathers for stones, and stones for slaves,

Figure 5.3 *Pochteca* merchants. (A) merchants following a trail with loads of merchandise on their backs (After Sahagún 1950–82:bk.9:fig.13); (B) merchants in a market with some of their wares: gold finger rings, gold lip plugs, obsidian lip plugs, a jaguar skin, a necklace of jade and turquoise, and a pendant of gold (After Sahagún 1950–82:bk.9:fig.3) (Drawings by Ellen Cesarski)

always dealing in things of importance, of renown, and of high value. These [men] strengthened their social position with their wealth.[12]

Among the trade goods of the *pochteca*, listed by Sahagún, were elaborately decorated capes and skirts, colorful tropical bird feathers, numerous objects of gold, necklaces, spinning bowls, earspools, obsidian blades and knives, shells, coral, needles, animal fur and skins, various herbs and dyes, slaves, and jewelry of jade, jadeite and turquoise (figure 5.3B). The *pochteca* worshiped a number of gods, and it is not surprising that these included gods who presided over space and the cosmos, warrior gods, and gods who could provide humans with riches.[13]

Far less information exists about the regional merchants, called *tlanecuilo*, who were not part of *pochteca* guilds. We do know that these middlemen were common participants in Aztec markets. They tended to trade in a smaller range of goods than the *pochteca*, and most of their goods were foodstuffs and utilitarian items, not luxuries. These included cacao, maize, amaranth, chia, chili, tortillas, turkeys, fish, salt, sandals, cotton, gourd bowls, baskets, and wood. Many of the *tlanecuilo* specialized in a particular type of good, for example salt was a common specialty. The division of labor among merchants, with *pochteca* trading primarily in luxuries and *tlanecuilo* in food and utilitarian goods, ensured that markets throughout the empire were well supplied with all types of goods.[14] How did consumers buy these goods?

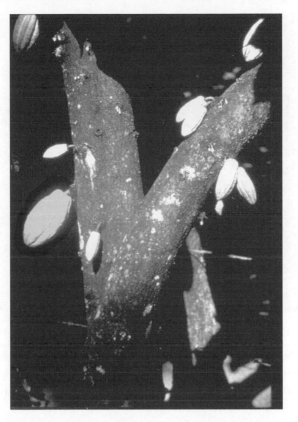

Figure 5.4 Cacao pods. The cacao beans are removed from large pods that grow directly out of the trunk of the cacao tree (Photograph by Janine Gasco; reproduced with permission)

Money

Some marketplace exchanges may have been carried out by bartering one good for another, but the Aztecs also used at least two forms of money: cacao beans and cotton textiles.[15] Cacao beans grow in large pods on domesticated cacao trees in the southern tropics of Mesoamerica (figure 5.4). People removed the pods and separated the large beans from a white pulp and then dried the beans (figure 5.5). Cacao beans were valuable because they had to be brought to central Mexico from distant lowland areas, of which the southernmost imperial province of Xoconochco was the primary source. Although the Aztecs made a form of hot chocolate beverage, only nobles could afford to drink it. Most people used cacao as currency.[16]

Cacao beans were used for small purchases. For example, one obsidian

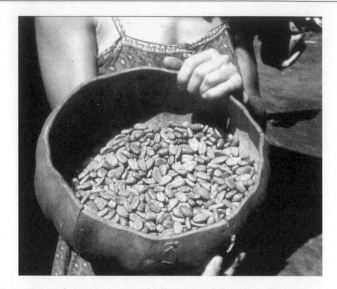

Figure 5.5   Cacao beans in a gourd (Photograph by Janine Gasco; reproduced with permission)

blade was worth 5 cacao beans. An Early Colonial list of market prices from 1545 gives an idea of the worth of various goods as expressed in cacao beans, assuming that prices had not changed too radically in the 25 years following the Spanish Conquest:

- One good turkey hen is worth 100 full cacao beans, or 120 shrunken cacao beans . . .
- A hare or forest rabbit is worth 100 cacao beans each.
- A small rabbit is worth 30.
- One turkey egg is worth 3 cacao beans.
- An avocado newly picked is worth 3 cacao beans . . .
- One large tomato will be equivalent to a cacao bean . . .
- A long narrow green chile, 5 (for a cacao bean) . . .
- A newly picked prickly pear cactus fruit is equivalent to 1 cacao bean, when fully ripe two cactus fruit (for a cacao bean) . . .
- Chopped firewood [a bundle or log] is equivalent to 1 cacao bean . . .
- A tamale is exchanged for a cacao bean . . .
- Fish wrapped in maize husks is worth 3 cacao beans.[17]

The use of cacao for currency was so widespread and economically important that counterfeiting and deceptions were serious problems. Unscrupulous vendors would remove the outer skin from a bean and stuff it with dirt or sawdust. The doctored "beans" were then mixed with a batch of real beans to be passed off on naive customers. That this practice was commonplace is implied by a Nahuatl-language Christian confessional manual recorded by Friar Alonso de Molina in 1569. The priests would ask merchants:

> And when you sold cacao beans, perhaps you mixed your bad cacao beans with the good ones to merchandise them all together, whereby you deceive the people? . . . And perhaps you toast the small, the shrunken cacao beans, whereby you enlarge them so they will appear plump?[18]

There were even specific laws to punish cacao counterfeiters.

For larger purchases, the Aztecs used *quachtli*, cotton capes of standardized sizes. Any family, noble or commoner, could weave *quachtli* as part of normal domestic cloth production (see chapter 4). Nobles, city-states, and temples also received them through tribute payments. There were different sizes and grades of *quachtli* with corresponding levels of value. Three common grades were worth 65, 80, and 100 cacao beans each, and some highly valuable examples were worth up to 300 cacao beans. It was said that 20 *quachtli* could support a commoner for a year in Tenochtitlan. Among the expensive items that could be purchased with this money were gold lip plugs (25 *quachtli* each) and necklaces of fine jade beads (600 *quachtli*).

Cacao and cotton textiles were used as currency not only in Aztec central Mexico, but throughout Mesoamerica in the Late Postclassic period. In addition to these two products, a number of other commodities served as more limited media of exchange or money in various regions and contexts. Among these goods were T-shaped bronze "axes," bronze bells, feather quills filled with gold dust, salt, Pacific seashells of the genus *Spondylus*, and precious stones.[19]

Material Evidence for Aztec Commerce

The ethnohistoric accounts of markets and merchants reviewed above provide a good overview of the forms and organization of Aztec commerce, but they are short on concrete information about the movements of the specific goods that were exchanged. Archaeology has begun to fill in this missing information. In some cases, the mere presence of distinctive foreign goods at a site provides evidence for trade. For example, when Aztec III Black-on-Orange ceramics, manufactured in the Valley of Mexico, turn up at distant sites, we know that some sort of exchange must have taken place. In other cases, the origins of artifacts cannot be determined easily, but sophisticated techniques of chemical analysis can reveal the place of origin for some of the raw materials used in their manufacture. These techniques, which have been applied primarily to obsidian and pottery, allow archaeologists to trace exchange routes and trade connections with great precision. Other trade goods that have been documented archaeologically include turquoise, jadeite, rock crystal, and other precious stones, bronze, shell, and even painted codices. Here I focus on the more extensively studied obsidian and ceramics.

Obsidian exchange

Obsidian, because of its superior cutting abilities and the large numbers of finished blades that could be produced from a single core, was one of the most widely traded goods in ancient Mesoamerica. The volcanic glass occurs in a limited number of natural deposits (all in highland areas), and obsidian from each geological source has a slightly different chemical composition. When an obsidian artifact is analyzed by one of several chemical techniques, its composition can be compared to samples taken from the various source areas to determine the geological location from which the obsidian originated.[20] Unfortunately we cannot always determine the places where the material may have been worked between the quarry and the final location of the artifact at a site.

Fortunately for archaeologists, obsidian from the Pachuca source area has a distinctive green tint that easily distinguishes it from most other Mesoamerican obsidians without the need for expensive chemical analyses. Pachuca was the major source of obsidian for the Aztecs, and artifacts made of the distinctive green material are common at virtually every known Aztec site. Even at Otumba, whose city-state territory included a major obsidian source, obsidian from Pachuca was imported for its superior qualities of prismatic blade manufacture. Sites like Cuexcomate and Yautepec in Morelos have yielded large quantities of obsidian, which was much preferred for tools over chert, an abundant, locally available stone. Of the tens of thousands of obsidian artifacts I have excavated at these sites, over 90 percent are of the green Pachuca variety.

Friar Sahagún lists obsidian blades among the goods traded by the *pochteca*, and Pachuca obsidian has been found at Late Aztec sites throughout much of Mesoamerica, including Yucatan and other Maya-speaking areas far beyond the borders of the Aztec empire. Pachuca obsidian even found its way to sites in the enemy Tarascan empire, and obsidian from Tarascan-controlled sources has been found at Aztec sites in Morelos. Native historical accounts give the impression that the Aztecs and Tarascans had little to do with each other beyond their battles and imperial activities (see chapter 7). The archaeological record, on the other hand, provides direct evidence for the concrete actions of people. Whatever Aztec and Tarascan nobles may have said about each other, merchants crossed imperial borders, and commoners bought and used obsidian tools that originated in enemy territory.

Ceramic exchange

The use of chemical analysis to study exchange is much more difficult for ceramic artifacts than for those of obsidian, partly because the raw material – clay – is far more widely distributed. In most cases, the fired clay cannot be traced to a specific point of origin. Nevertheless, from patterns in the chemical composition of potsherds, the archaeologist often can infer the number of different ceramic production centers represented in a collection of artifacts, and sometimes the region of origin of imported objects. A recent study of the chemical composition of the most abundant type of Aztec decorated ceramic (Aztec III Black-on-Orange) by Mary Hodge, Leah Minc, Hector Neff, and James Blackman has overturned prior models of Aztec ceramic exchange and revealed that the system of production and exchange was more complex than previously thought.[21]

Fine-paste, orange ceramic bowls and plates painted with black designs were in use throughout the time of Aztec occupation of the Valley of Mexico. During the Early Aztec period, there were several distinct painting styles, each with limited spatial distributions (these styles are variants of the types Aztec I and Aztec II Black-on-Orange). This suggested to scholars that three to five regional production-exchange systems had operated in the valley. Chemical analyses of sherds from the different styles confirmed this interpretation and revealed the operation of several different local market systems with little exchange of ceramics between them.

In the Late Aztec period, a single style of painted ceramic, called Aztec III Black-on-Orange, came to dominate the inventories of households in the Valley of Mexico. The painted designs on these ceramics are simple and busy, with many thin parallel lines combined with other motifs (figure 5.6). These ceramics give the impression of being mass produced. In comparison with the Early Aztec types, Aztec III ceramics show a high degree of stylistic uniformity throughout the Valley of Mexico and in the foreign areas to which they were traded (the sherds in figure 5.6 were imports I excavated at the provincial town of Cuexcomate in Morelos). Most archaeologists had assumed that this uniformity of style resulted from the operation of a single workshop or cluster of workshops, which

Figure 5.6   Sherds from imported Aztec III Black-on-Orange ceramic plates excavated at Cuexcomate (Photograph by Michael E. Smith)

supplied the entire Valley of Mexico with these pots through the market system.

The chemical analyses indicated a different situation, however. There were in fact at least four production zones for Aztec III ceramics, located in or near the cities of Tenochtitlan, Texcoco, Chalco, and Ixtapalapa. The workshops in each zone used local clays from around the lakes, shaped the clay into the same forms, and painted the vessels using a single, Valley-wide style. Although Mary Hodge and Leah Minc have been able to identify a few painted motifs whose use was largely limited to a single production area, most of the painted decorations are virtually identical in the four zones. These findings show that ceramic production was more decentralized than previously thought, and they imply a high level of exchange and stylistic interaction within the Valley of Mexico that led to a single popular style being produced in several different areas. This study also illustrates the pitfalls of studying ancient artifact exchange and interaction on the basis of style alone, without the benefit of chemical analysis.

During the Early and Late Aztec periods, the potters of each region of central Mexico developed their own distinctive ware of painted ceramics. Various styles of polychrome painting, with red, black, and orange designs on a white background, were applied to serving vessels in the valleys

Figure 5.7   Cholula Polychrome ceramic tripod plate (diameter 23 cm)
(Photograph courtesy of the Saint Louis Art Museum, no. 85-1950)

to the east, south, and west of the Valley of Mexico. These painted bowls
were widely traded among regions, and many Aztec families, commoners
and nobles alike, owned and used vessels from several different areas. The
most elaborate polychrome ceramics were produced in Cholula (figure
5.7) and were among the most widely traded wares in central Mexico. It
was said that Motecuhzoma II would only eat off plates and dishes from
Cholula, the finest in the empire.[22]

The simpler Aztec III Black-on-Orange pottery was also popular outside of its zone of origin in the Valley of Mexico. Examples imported
from the valley are found at Late Aztec archaeological sites throughout
central Mexico. But it was not the only pottery from the Valley of Mexico
that was exported to other areas. Excavations in Morelos typically uncover several decorated types imported from the Valley of Mexico (figure
5.8). One of these ceramic imports, called Texcoco Fabric-Marked, was a
basin for salt transport (see figure 4.2).

The Aztecs produced salt by boiling and evaporating the salt water
from the Valley of Mexico lakes in large crude ceramic basins. The salt
was packed into the same basins for transport.[23] Broken sherds from these
salt vessels are easy to identify because their surfaces bear the impressions
of coarse, burlap-like, maguey cloth that was applied to the vessels before
firing to give them texture (figure 5.8). Salt vessels are found in large

Figure 5.8   Imported Valley of Mexico ceramic sherds excavated at Cuexcomate and Capilco in Morelos. Upper left: Aztec III Black-on-Orange; upper right: Texcoco Fabric-Marked salt vessels; lower row: Xochimilco Polychrome (Photograph by Michael E. Smith)

quantities at most Aztec archaeological sites in central Mexico. Every Aztec-period house I have excavated in Morelos yielded numerous sherds of this type – further evidence for extensive trading relations between the Valley of Mexico and surrounding areas. Major salt works were present in several of the outer provinces of the Aztec empire, but within 100 km or so of the Valley, most households obtained their salt through trade with producers from around the Valley of Mexico lakes.

A complex economy

The various economic institutions and practices described in chapters 3, 4, and 5 all worked together in a dynamic and complex economy that bound the various parts of the Aztec empire into a single economic, social, and cultural unit. The growing populations required increased production of food and tools; the craftsmen who manufactured obsidian tools or ceramic vessels required merchants to sell their goods and to obtain raw materials; the merchants required money to facilitate their transactions; the use of money required additional production (for cloth) and trade (for lowland cacao); and the overall dynamism and prosperity of the economy encouraged further population growth. These trends are evident in the results of archaeological studies that have focused on the transition from the Early Aztec to the Late Aztec periods. Late Aztec occupations yield many more imported artifacts, have more evidence for craft production activities, and show signs of heavier reliance on intensive farming methods (see chapter 12).

This dynamic economy, with a significant commercial component, was not limited to the Aztec empire. The Aztec economy was closely linked to other regional economies in Late Postclassic Mesoamerica through processes of commercial trade and the exchange of information; this wider Mesoamerican context will be explored more fully in chapter 12. One component of the expanding Aztec economy was a major increase in the trade of commodities. A commodity is simply a good that is bought and sold. In earlier periods, many Mesoamerican trade goods were not commodities; they were gifts between nobles, tribute items, objects distributed by leaders to their subjects, or other politically controlled goods not traded through market systems. Of the hundreds of commodities in the

Table 5.1   Key trade commodities in Late Postclassic Mesoamerica

Commodity	Place of origin	Images
Utilitarian Goods		
Obsidian and obsidian tools	Central Mexico	Fig. 4.1
Raw cotton	Lowlands	
Polychrome pottery	(widespread)	Figs. 5.7, 5.8, 9.6
Salt	(widespread)	
Slaves	(widespread)	Fig. 5.2
Plain textiles	(widespread)	Figs. 4.4, 7.4
Luxury Goods		
Cacao (as money and beverage)	Southern Mesoamerica	Figs. 5.4, 5.5
Greenstone jewelry	Southern Mesoamerica	Fig. 5.3
Copper axe-money	Tarascan empire	
Copper/bronze bells	Tarascan empre	Fig. 4.7
Feathers and feather ornaments	Tropical lowlands	Figs. 4.8, 7.4
Gold jewelry	Oaxaca and Tenochtitlan	Figs. 4.10, 5.3
Turquoise jewelry	Southwestern US	Figs. 4.12, 5.3
Obsidian jewelry	Central Mexico	Figs. 4.11, 4.14, 5.3
Painted manuscripts	(widespread)	Fig. 11.1
Decorated textiles	(widespread)	Fig. 7.4

Source: Smith and Berdan 2002

Late Aztec economy, the most important ones are listed in table 5.1. This list shows clearly the links between the Aztec economy and other areas of Mesoamerica and beyond. The example of polychrome pottery illustrates the importance of commodities in the Aztec economy. In the earlier Teotihuacan and Classic Maya economies, polychrome pottery was a luxury good strongly controlled by elites. But in Aztec central Mexico, polychrome pottery was sold in markets, and even peasant farmers purchased some vessels, whose broken fragments we excavate today.[24]

The market system was the institution that linked the various sectors and regions within this dynamic economy. Marketing, using one or more of the forms of currency discussed above, was also the one activity that allowed the average person to get ahead economically. As might be expected, some people tried to profit through deception. This concerned the first Spanish priests in central Mexico, and Friar Molina's confessional manual contains the following entries for petty traders:

> And when you sell chilis, perhaps you mix the small ones, the damaged ones with the large ones, whereby you deceive the people?
> And when you bought good capes, perhaps you inserted them among the poor ones? And when you filled in the holes of the holey capes, perhaps you did not show your customer that the capes were holey, damaged, whereby you made sport of him?[25]

The fact that such practices were singled out by Friar Molina shows how important marketing was and how far some people would go to gain from their commercial dealings (see also Friar Molina's admonition about counterfeit cacao beans on page 117 above).

Clearly the Aztec economy was highly commercialized and dynamic, but it was not a capitalist economy. There was no wage labor, land was not a commodity to be bought and sold (except under certain limited circumstances), and opportunities for investment were limited to *pochteca* expeditions. Marketplace trade gave the Aztec commoners and merchants a chance to advance themselves, but only up to a point.[26] Aztec markets and the overall economy were embedded in a rigid system of social classes, and no amount of economic success would enable one to cross class barriers.

chapter six
Family and Social Class

> *Seventh house. Here is the home of some people none of whom is baptized. Here is the home of one named Yaotl. His wife is named Mocel. He has one child named Huitzitl, now twenty years old. Here is Yaotl's younger sibling, who is married, named Huelitl. . . . Yaotl works 20 [matl], 10 matl wide, and his younger sibling works 7 matl by 6 matl wide. Here is his tribute: every 80 days he delivers one quarter-length of a Cuernavaca cloak and one quarter-length of a doubled cloak. They do it jointly, so that in one year [they deliver] one Cuernavaca cloak and one tribute cloak. This is all; no narrow cloaks, no turkey hens, no turkey eggs. That is all. Five are included in one house.*
>
> **S. L. Cline, The Book of Tributes** *(entry for a commoner household in a Nahuatl-language census from the town of Quauhchichinollan, Morelos, ca. 1540)*

The family or household was the basic social unit in Aztec society, but only in the past two decades have we begun to learn much about Aztec families. Thanks to translations of Nahuatl documents, such as the one quoted above, and archaeological excavations of houses, we are now gaining an appreciation for patterns of family life, household organization, and gender roles. One of the important new findings is the great influence that social classes played in structuring Aztec life and society. There were two social classes, nobles and commoners, separated by a wide and unpassable chasm.[1]

Nobles or lords ran the government, owned the land, commanded the army, and lived a more luxurious lifestyle than commoners. Although commoners greatly outnumbered nobles, they were obliged to serve these lords and pay them tribute. These great inequities might suggest that

Aztec commoners were oppressed serfs leading bleak lives of servitude. This was not the case, however. Commoners had considerable control over their own destinies, and most managed to meet their basic needs and even provide themselves with some level of economic comfort in spite of their duties to lords and kings. Much of the evidence for this observation comes from recent excavations of houses and villages, where the hidden lives of anonymous peasants and artisans are being revealed for the first time.

Growing up Aztec

In spite of the importance of social classes, there were many similarities in the ways noble and commoner children were raised. Basic notions of Aztec culture on children's behavior and gender roles cut across the class divide. The Codex Mendoza provides the most vivid and complete description of the Aztec life cycle.[2]

Birth and childhood

As in all cultures, childbirth was an important event among the Aztecs. Women were aided by a midwife, whose duties went beyond simply helping with the birth process. Midwives also supervised the rituals that accompanied birth and named the newborn child. The Codex Mendoza describes the midwife's duties after birth as follows (see figure 6.1):

> At the end of four days after the infant's birth, the midwife carried the infant, naked, and took it to the courtyard of the house of the one who has given birth. And in the courtyard they had placed a small earthen tub of water on rushes or reeds [as a mat] called tule, where the said midwife bathed the said infant . . . And after the said bath, the said midwife ordered [three] boys to call out loudly the new name of the infant . . . And the name they gave it was that which the midwife wished. And at the beginning, when the infant was taken to be bathed, if it was a boy, they carried him with his symbol in his hand, and the symbol was the tool used by the boy's father, whether of the military or professions like metalworker, woodcarrier, or whatever other profession [figure 6.1, top right] . . . And if the infant was a girl, the symbol they gave her for bathing was a distaff with its spindle and its basket and a broom, which were the things she would use when she grew up [figure 6.1, bottom right]. And they offered the male infant's umbilical cord, along with the little shield and arrows symbolized in bathing, in the place where they warred with their enemies, where they buried it under the ground. And likewise for the girl, they buried her umbilical cord under the metate, a stone for grinding tortillas.[3]

The midwife

The symbols

The three boys who call out the
name of the recently-born infant

The rushes with their little
earthen pan of water

The broom, distaff and spindle,
and little basket

Figure 6.1   Aztec childbirth customs. The midwife is about to bathe the newborn (Codex Mendoza 1992:v.4:119; f.57r)

This presentation of symbols to the newborn established the child's gender identity early in life. Boys were expected to grow up to be warriors and to have an occupation like their father's, and girls were expected to grow up to manage the household, where cooking, weaving, cleaning, domestic offerings, and child-rearing were their major activities. The descriptions of Aztec childhood in the Codex Mendoza show the differential training of boys and girls. By five years of age, boys were already "toting light loads of firewood and carrying light bundles to the tiangues, or market place. And they [mothers] taught the girls of this age how they had to hold the spindle and distaff in order to spin."[4]

By the age of seven, boys had learned to use nets to catch fish, and girls were spinning cotton (see figure 4.4). To the Aztecs, gender identities were not natural or inherent; rather they had to be achieved or produced through key ceremonies – such as the presentation of symbols by the midwife – and through the encouragement of tasks appropriate to each gender – such as fishing and spinning (see below).

The young were kept in line by a combination of threats of corporal punishment and speeches that stressed correct behavior. Parents "gave them good advice so they would always apply themselves and spend their time in something to avoid all idleness."[5] Aztec punishments were severe, as these examples from the Codex Mendoza show:

> An 8-year old boy is being warned by his father not to be deceitful, or he will be punished by being pierced in the body with maguey spikes.
>   Likewise they punished them [10-year olds] for being rebellious, beating them with sticks and offering other threats.
>   They punished the 11-year-old boy or girl who disregarded verbal correction by making them inhale chile smoke, which was a serious and even cruel torment.[6]

Until the age of 15, nearly all training was carried out in the home by the parents. The Codex Mendoza shows women teaching their daughters to spin, to weave, to sweep, and to cook and prepare food (see figures 3.2, 4.3). Fathers are depicted instructing their sons in a variety of tasks including fishing, carrying, and marketing. In another part of the Codex, skilled craftsmen instruct their sons in their work (see figure 4.9).

School

All boys and girls attended school at some point between 10 and 20 years of age. There were two types of school: the *telpochcalli* ("youth's house") for commoners and the *calmecac* for nobles and exceptional commoners.[7] A *telpochcalli* was located in every town, and large cities had many, one in every *calpolli* (neighborhood). All commoner boys attended these schools, where they lived under spartan conditions. Girls also attended, but we do not know whether they lived on the premises. Instruction was carried out separately for boys and girls. All of the students received training in singing, dancing, and musical instruments, mostly for rituals.

Young men worked on civic projects, from carrying firewood for the temples to repairing temples, roads, and bridges. The major focus of male education in the *telpochcalli*, however, was military training. Seasoned warriors instructed the youths in martial arts, and then the students went off to war for practical training. At first they assisted by carrying baggage and arms for soldiers; later the novices carried their own arms. Eventually, they were allowed to participate fully in battle and to attempt to capture enemy prisoners for sacrifice.

The *calmecac*, a more exclusive school, was attended by nobles and the most promising commoner youths. These schools, each associated with a major temple, provided training for future leaders in government, the priesthood, and the military. Self-control, discipline, and obedience were stressed in the live-in *calmecac*. According to Friar Durán, instruction covered a wide variety of subjects: "all the arts: military, religious, mechanical, and astrological, which gave them knowledge of the stars. For this they possessed large, beautiful books, painted in hieroglyphics, dealing with all these arts [and these books] were used for teaching."[8]

Military and religious arts were the most important subjects at the *calmecac*. The younger students trained as novice priests, and their duties included sweeping, gathering decorative boughs and sacrificial maguey thorns, and helping the head priests with offerings of incense, sacrifices, musical performances, and astronomical observations. As students advanced, they also trained for battle, much like the students in the *telpochcalli*, and they eventually advanced to the level of full warriors.

Adult Life and Social Roles

Marriage

Young men married in the late teens or early twenties, but young women married much younger – often as early as 10 or 12 years old. When a young man's parents decided that he was ready to marry, they consulted with his teachers and with relatives to select an appropriate bride.[9] An elderly female matchmaker approached the young woman's parents. If the negotiations were successful, the groom's family consulted soothsayers to determine an appropriate day for the ceremony. It was thought that a marriage celebrated on an unlucky day would not succeed.

Wedding ceremonies took place in two parts, beginning with an elaborate all-day feast at the bride's house. Her mother and female relatives worked for days to prepare *tamales* (steamed food – see chapter 3) to feed the many people who would attend. The guests were served in a particular order, and each was given food, flowers, tobacco, and drink (cacao and *pulque*). At sunset the bride was bathed and clothed in a special outfit. She then received a lecture from the elders of the groom's family: "Forever now leave childishness, girlishness; no longer art thou to be like a child . . . Be most considerate of one; regard one with respect, speak well, greet one well. By night look to, take care of the sweeping, the laying of fire. Arise in the deep of night [to begin domestic tasks]."[10]

Following the speeches, the bride was carried by the groom's relatives to his house. Relatives of the couple accompanied the bride in a procession with torches. The second part of the wedding ceremony, at the groom's house, is described in the Codex Mendoza (see figure 6.2) as follows:

Figure 6.2 Aztec wedding ceremony. The bride and groom have tied their capes together to signal their union. Below them a feast is waiting, and on the sides older relatives are giving the young couple advice (Codex Mendoza 1992:v.4:127; f.61r)

And when they arrived at the groom's house, the groom's parents led her to the patio of the house to receive her, and they put her in a room or house where the groom was waiting. And the bride and bridegroom sat on a mat with its seats, next to a burning hearth, and they tied their clothes together, and offered copal incense to their gods. And then two old men and two old women, who were present as witnesses, gave food to the bride and bridegroom, and then the elders ate.[11]

The elders then gave advice to the newlyweds; this is shown by the speech scrolls in figure 6.2. After four days, another feast was held with food and drink, dancing, and exchanges of gifts between the new in-laws. Once married, young people assumed adult roles and responsibilities, and these varied tremendously depending upon one's social class, occupation, place of residence, and gender.

Gender roles

In daily life men typically worked outside the home, whereas the house was the domain of women. Most men were farmers who spent the day in their fields during the agricultural season (May through November, the central Mexican rainy season). During the rest of the year men were often away from home, fulfilling their service obligations, either as warriors (chapter 7) or as laborers. Artisans worked closer to home, in their house, yard, or a nearby workshop, often assisted by their families.

Women spent most of their time in and around the home. Their major activities were childrearing, cooking, housekeeping, domestic ritual, weaving and marketing.[12] A woman's contributions to the household economy were considerable. Her textiles were needed to pay tribute, and any extra cloth a woman made could be exchanged for other goods. She did the marketing for the family, buying the weekly necessities and selling the family's surplus food or craft products. Even noblewomen, who did not have to produce tribute cloth or worry about bargains in the marketplace, spent much of their time spinning and weaving, for this was an important part of gender identity regardless of social class.

Commoner women spent much of their work time cooking and preparing food. Grinding corn for tortillas and *tamales* was the single biggest task. Before the advent of mechanical mills, modern Mesoamerican peasant women would spend five or six hours each day grinding corn for the family's meals. Aztec women must have spent a similar amount of time at the *metate* (grinding-stone). A woman's cooking duties often went beyond the needs of her immediate family. Her *tamales* and sauces were left as offerings at the temples (where they were eaten by the priests). She sometimes was required to provide food for the local lord, and she could be called upon to make tortillas and other provisions when her city-state's armies marched off to war.

Women had a more important role in domestic ritual than men. When a woman swept her house and yard with a broom every morning, she was doing more than simply cleaning her home. She was setting the world straight by purifying the domestic realm. Sweeping was also a crucial part of the rituals that priests carried out at the temples and the *calmecac*. The power of brooms thus linked women and priests in a common battle against the forces of disorder and darkness. Women also carried out other domestic rituals such as burning incense and maintaining the household altar.[13]

Social Classes

Nobles or lords composed only about 5 percent of the total Aztec population, but they were firmly in control of society.[14] Unlike elites in more open societies, the position and privileges of the Aztec nobility were rigidly specified by law (an example is the reforms of Motecuhzoma I, p. 48 above). Such laws limited the use or consumption of key goods, such as decorated capes, fancy jewelry, or two-story houses, to the nobility. Lords were further distinguished from commoners by birth, for membership in the nobility was strictly hereditary.

In practical terms, the power and wealth of the Aztec nobility rested on their control of land, labor, and tribute. All of the land in a city-state belonged ultimately to the *tlatoani*, but he granted estates to high lords called *tetecuhtin* (sing. *tecuhtli*) and to important temples. These estates were passed on to the descendants of the *tecuhtli*, or maintained in perpetuity by the temples. Below the rank of *tecuhtli* were the regular nobles, or *pipiltin* (sing. *pilli*). Most *pipiltin* served a *tecuhtli* or *tlatoani*, often residing in or around his palace.

To Aztec nobles, peasants and other commoners existed to serve them. *Macehualli* (pl. *macehualtin*), the term for commoner, means "subject," but commoners varied in their degree of subjugation, from the heavy burdens of slaves to the relative freedom of the *pochteca* merchants. Most commoners, however, had a number of typical obligations to their lord, first and foremost of which was to provide him with regular payments of tribute in goods. These payments were assessed by family and consisted of cotton *quachtli*, food items, or specific goods produced by the family. Commoners also provided their lord with regular labor service. Men cultivated the lord's land, women spun and wove for him, and both sexes worked as domestic servants. Such duties typically rotated among the lord's subjects, with each family contributing several weeks of work each year. These payments of goods and labor, called *tequitl*, were the basic duties of nearly all commoners.

In addition to *tequitl*, commoners were called upon to serve nobles for various special activities. The Aztecs did not have a standing army, and troops were conscripted for each campaign. When a large project was carried out, such as the construction of a temple or canal system, commoners were called up in a labor draft for the occasion. Just how heavy were the obligations of commoners? The paucity of numerical data in documentary sources makes this a difficult question. We don't know how many days of labor were required each year, how many *quachtli* were owed, or how much time it took to produce them.[15]

Commoners

Peasants and the calpolli

Peasants, like most other commoners, were organized in wards and *calpolli* groups. A *calpolli* was a group of families who lived near one another, were subject to a single lord, controlled a block of land, and often shared a common occupation.[16] In urban settings, *calpolli* comprised neighborhoods, and many economic specialists such as merchants and artisans lived together in their own *calpolli*. In rural areas, Nahuatl-language written records used the term to describe two different sizes of settlement. A small *calpolli*, or ward, comprised a cluster of 10 to 20 houses, the families who lived in them, and their assigned agricultural land. The village of Capilco in Morelos, with its 21 simple houses (figure 3.7), was probably such a ward. The term *calpolli* was also used to denote a much larger grouping composed of several wards under a common *tecuhtli* lord. In some rural *calpolli*, the wards were spread widely over the landscape; in others they were clustered together to form a rural town. These settlements typically had a *telpochcalli* school for their youth, and many also had a temple, a market, and perhaps a ballcourt. Many *calpolli* included wards in both urban and rural settings. The urban wards typically included the residences of the leading nobles and other *calpolli* officials, while the rural wards consisted primarily of peasants.

Calpolli lands were farmed by the member households. In theory the governing council of the *calpolli* divided the land among the constituent families. In practice, however, individual plots were inherited informally from one generation to the next. If new land opened up, or if an existing plot was left abandoned, the *calpolli* council would reallocate the land. Rights of use for an individual plot could be sold, but the land remained under the general jurisdiction of the *calpolli* and *altepetl* (city-state). Ethnohistorian James Lockhart describes the situation as follows:

> A land sale, then, was openly brought before the authorities, and a feast-like ritual accompanied the transfer like any other. Indeed, one way of looking at a transaction of this type is that the seller for a consideration relinquished his allocation from the *altepetl/calpolli* and permitted the authorities to reallocate it in the usual way to the buyer.[17]

The relationship between *calpolli* and the nobility varied by region. In the Valley of Mexico, Morelos and the Toluca area, many or most *calpolli* were under the jurisdiction of a noble, who held ultimate control of the *calpolli* land. Nobles lived in *calpolli* towns (see discussion of Cuexcomate below), and the resident commoners paid tribute to their local noble (see discussion of the noble Molotecatl below). Nobles also held lands apart from *calpolli*, and peasants who worked these lands typically did not belong to a *calpolli*. These commoners were considered dependent upon their lord, perhaps in a fashion analogous to medieval European serfs. These dependent workers may not have had the same degree of control over their farm plots as *calpolli* members, although the situation is far from clear in the sources. In the eastern Nahua area of Puebla and Tlaxcala,

Figure 6.3   Wall foundations and floor of a peasant house excavated at Capilco (Photograph by Michael E. Smith)

the *calpolli* was not as important in rural social organization. Nobles in this area headed large *teccalli*, or noble houses, to which commoners were attached by obligations of service and tribute. The nature of peasant life in this area is not as well understood.[18]

Rural life

The site of Cuexcomate, with 135 simple houses, was probably a rural *calpolli* town.[19] In addition to the peasant houses, Cuexcomate also had a small palace, a temple, a public plaza, and a special civil building that may have been a *telpochcalli* (figure 3.7). The Cuexcomate *calpolli* comprised three or four wards. Families at Cuexcomate and the nearby single-ward village of Capilco lived in small one-room houses with sun-dried mud-brick (adobe) walls and thatched roofs. All that remains of their houses today are the wall foundations and floors that were constructed of stone (figure 6.3). When in use, these houses probably looked much like modern adobe peasant houses (figure 6.4).

Nahuatl census records tell us that small houses such as these were home to either nuclear families or joint families that consisted of more

Figure 6.4   Modern adobe peasant house in the village of Tetlama, not far from Capilco (Photograph by Michael E. Smith)

than one married couple.[20] In many areas, the average household size was five to six members, although, in some communities, the average size exceeded eight persons per household. Sometimes servants or other unrelated persons lived with a family. Many houses were arranged in small patio groups with two to five houses built around a common open courtyard (figure 3.7). Although the residents of a patio group often were related, perhaps as a multigeneration extended family, in other cases unrelated families lived together. The Nahuatl term for these units is *cemithualtin*, meaning "those in one yard."

The houses at Capilco and Cuexcomate were so small that most domestic activity probably took place in the patio outside, which was kept clear of debris. People threw their trash to the sides and rear of the house, and the study of artifacts from these locations provides information about the activities and social conditions of the families who lived in each house. Broken potsherds from ceramic cookpots, storage jars, serving bowls, and tortilla griddles give abundant evidence for the preparation of meals by the women of Capilco and Cuexcomate. When pots broke, sherds accumulated around the house and yard. Friar Sahagún noted that Aztec babies "spend their time piling up earth and potsherds, those on the ground."[21] In addition to the tens of thousands of such sherds excavated from each house, obsidian blades and basalt grinding tools, such as the *metate* for maize, provide additional evidence for kitchen activities (obsidian and basalt tools were also used for other domestic activities, and in some cases were used for craft production). Every house excavated at these sites also yielded ceramic spindle whorls and spinning bowls, and many had bronze sewing needles. Several types of ritual artifacts were found at all houses, including figurines and incense burners.

Whereas women's activities – food preparation, textile manufacture, and domestic offerings – left abundant material evidence for archaeologists to find, men's work is almost invisible at these sites. Most of the men were probably farmers, but farm tools or other evidence of farming are not found in domestic contexts. Family members in some houses worked part-time making paper from tree bark (see chapter 10). This paper, used for both writing and rituals, was a major tribute good paid by the inhabitants of Morelos to the Aztec empire.

To judge from the nature of the artifacts found around each house, the peasants of Capilco and Cuexcomate were quite well-off economically. They were able to obtain trade goods from all over central Mexico, including obsidian from Pachuca and Otumba, salt from the Valley of Mexico, bronze goods from western Mexico, and ceramic serving bowls from the Valley of Mexico, Cholula, Toluca, Cuernavaca, and Yautepec (figure 5.8). These imported bowls, many with elaborate polychrome decoration, were found in nearly all houses. The large number of imported goods suggests that the inhabitants of Capilco and Cuexcomate were able to produce sufficient crops, textiles, paper, and other goods beyond their domestic needs and tribute quotas to enter the markets as participants.

The presence of a noble's palace at Cuexcomate does not appear to have had much effect on the economic conditions of peasants since the artifacts from commoner houses at Cuexcomate were almost identical to those from houses at Capilco, where there were no nobles. If peasants had been severely exploited to the point where they spent all of their time meeting household and tribute needs, we would not have recovered such a rich and varied domestic artifact inventory at every house. Nevertheless, there were signs of social and economic stress just before the Spanish Conquest. In the Late Aztec B period (AD 1430–1550) the standard of living of both commoners and nobles at these sites declined. Demographic, economic, and political expansion had apparently reached the point of diminishing returns. An increasing burden of tribute (both local and imperial) and declining agricultural yields probably combined to lower the standards of living of most families.[22]

Urban commoners

In many ways the lives of urban commoners were not very different from the lives of rural peasants. Both were *macehualtin*, subject to nobles, and both lived as members of *calpolli*. Most Aztec cities were small settlements, and many urban residents were farmers or part-time craftspersons whose domestic conditions resembled those of peasant families in rural villages. On the other hand, cities were the place of residence and seat of government for the *tlatoani*, and urban commoners were more likely than their rural cousins to be subject directly to the royal palace. Also, because cities were the locations of major markets and concentrations of nobles, urbanites were more likely to be craft specialists. Specialists in the luxury crafts, in particular, would have benefited by living and working near the king and other noble patrons.

In our excavations at the urban center of Yautepec in Morelos, we found that the houses of commoners were only slightly larger and fancier than those at Capilco and Cuexcomate (figure 6.5).[23] They were far more similar to rural peasant houses than to noble residences. Their domestic artifacts were nearly identical to those excavated at the rural sites, with one major difference: evidence for part-time domestic craft production was much more abundant and widespread among Yautepec houses than at their rural counterparts. Some Yautepec households were involved in producing blades and other tools of obsidian, and the manufacture of ceramic figurines was also a common domestic activity (as evidenced by molds similar to those found at Otumba).

Slaves

At the bottom of the social scale were the slaves, *tlacotin* (sing. *tlacotli*). People became slaves through debt or punishment, but not through birth; slavery was not hereditary. Slaves could marry, have children (who were free), and even own property. Anyone could own a slave, but most slave-owners were nobles. The owner was responsible for feeding and housing the slave and had control over the slave's labor.

People sold themselves into slavery when they could not support themselves. During the great famine of the 1450s, for example, many Aztecs sold themselves to people of the Gulf Coast where economic conditions were better. Slaves used the purchase amount (said to be 20 *quachtli* in Tenochtitlan) to support themselves for a year or so, after which time they would begin their servitude. Some people incurred such large debts through gambling on the game *patolli* or the ballgame that selling themselves as slaves was the only way out. Failure to pay tribute was another

Figure 6.5 Wall foundations of urban commoner houses excavated at Yautepec (Houses 1, 2 and 3; see map, figure 8.6) (Photograph by Michael E. Smith)

way to become a slave, with the purchase price going to cover the tribute debt. Some other crimes were also punishable in this way.

The change in status from free citizen to slave was an official act that had to be witnessed formally by four officials. Slaves then either began work for their master or were sold in the market. Some *pochteca* merchants specialized in trading slaves, and several markets were known as centers for the slave trade. Slaves for sale were identified by large wooden collars (figure 5.2). Although slaves could in theory be used for any type of work, in practice most worked as servants in the palaces of lords. Female slaves were particularly valued for their spinning and weaving skills and were put to work making *quachtli* for their owners (the slave for sale in figure 5.2 shows off her spinning abilities for prospective buyers). The Aztecs did not use large gangs of slaves to perform heavy labor for farming or public works projects, and the overall economic contribution of slaves was quite modest.

Social mobility

Two avenues by which commoners could raise their position were success at warfare and the priesthood. Warriors were ranked by the number of enemy soldiers they had captured, and a highly successful commoner soldier could reach a status far above his compatriots. In the middle years of the Aztec empire, Motecuhzoma I created a special title, *quauhpilli*, for the most accomplished warriors. They were given some of the privileges and responsibilities of nobles. This category of "nobles by achievement" was later abolished by Motecuhzoma II, who insisted that only true, hereditary nobles could enjoy the privileges of the elite stratum. Successful warriors still gained prestige, but remained firmly within the commoner class. Success in the ranks of the priesthood (chapter 10) could also elevate the status of a commoner, but again they could not cross the threshold into the nobility.

The great wealth of the *pochteca* merchants and luxury artisans suggests that they may have formed an emerging Aztec middle class. Nobles had gained their wealth and position through control of land and the labor of commoners, the traditional bases of power in ancient Mesoamerica. One of the changes of the Late Postclassic period was an explosion of commerce throughout Mesoamerica, not just within the Aztec empire. Long-distance trade and local marketplaces thrived, which gave merchants and artisans new opportunities to gain wealth and influence. By tapping this new source of wealth that was outside of the nobility's traditional power base, many merchants and artists rose above the mass of commoners. Not being nobles, however, they had to hide their wealth and present a modest appearance.[24]

Nobles and their Palaces

Nobles lived and worked in large sumptuous compounds or palaces. These served as residences and as administrative buildings where the lord attended to the affairs of whatever social or political institution (such as *calpolli* or city-state) was under his direction. Although there was enormous variation in the size and elegance of palaces, related to their inhabitant's position within society, Aztec palaces shared a common layout of rooms and platforms surrounding a central courtyard with a single entrance from outside.[25] In this section I examine the palaces of four nobles to illustrate the range of variation and to give an idea of the activities that took place in the residences of lords. These four nobles range from a lowly provincial *pilli* to one of the imperial kings of the Aztec empire.

A rural pilli at Cuexcomate

The town of Cuexcomate was laid out around a central public plaza. On the east side was a small temple-pyramid probably dedicated to the town's patron deity. The north and west sides of the plaza were occupied by compounds consisting of interconnected mounds. We excavated several mounds and patios in these compounds and came to the conclusion that they were elite residences. Group 6 on the west was occupied during the Late Aztec A period and was the larger and better preserved of the two compounds. Group 7 on the north was occupied only during the following Late Aztec B period. Here, I focus attention on group 6 as an example of the palace of a low-ranking provincial noble.[26]

Group 6 at Cuexcomate was not a very imposing sight prior to excavation, appearing as several low mounds arranged around a patio. These mounds turned out to be the ruins of a noble's palace, whose size and architectural quality set it far above the predominant commoner houses at the site. Our crew cleared off the top layers of rubble on these mounds to uncover the architectural plan of the final construction stage. We also excavated into the mounds and located the remains of three earlier construction stages. Figure 6.6A is an artist's reconstruction of how group 6 may have looked in the early 1400s, shortly before its abandonment. At that time, it consisted of a series of connected low platforms around a patio with rooms, passages, and shrines built on top of the platforms. The platforms were built of stone and covered with a layer of red-painted lime plaster.

Our hypothesis that group 6 was the palace of a noble is based upon both the architecture and the artifacts. With a surface area of 540 sq m, this compound is much larger than the typical commoner house at the site (commoner houses averaged around 20 sq m). The manner of its construction and the materials used were far superior to those of the commoner houses. The elevation of rooms on platforms also set group 6 apart from commoner houses, most of which were built at ground level. The artifacts found in the trash deposits adjacent to the compound were typical domestic wares (cooking pots, serving bowls, obsidian blades, and the like), but with a greater proportion of fancy imported items than in deposits from commoner houses.

This arrangement of rooms elevated on platforms that surround a central patio is consistent with ethnohistoric descriptions and maps of Aztec palaces in the Valley of Mexico. This compound was probably the residence of a low-ranking provincial *pilli* to whom the 250 or so inhabitants of the Late Aztec A *calpolli* of Cuexcomate paid tribute. Nobles often were polygamous, and the individual room blocks may have been separate apartments for the lord's wives. Servants or artisans in the service of the lord probably lived in neighboring commoner houses. For example, houses in a nearby commoner patio group had very high frequencies of paint pigments and bark beaters, which suggests that their residents were artisans who made paper and paints. These items would have been used by the nobles of group 6 or their scribes to produce historical and reli-

Figure 6.6   Artist's reconstruction of the Cuexcomate palace (A) in comparison with a commoner house (B) (Drawing by Rachel Sader)

gious painted books. Group 6 was abandoned in the 1430s or 1440s, at which time a second and far more modest elite compound, group 7, was built on the empty north side of the plaza. We don't know why group 6 was abandoned, but conquest by outsiders may have had something to do with it. From historic documents, we know the area was conquered twice at about that time: once in the 1420s by the expanding Cuauhnahuac state and again around 1440 by the Aztec empire under Itzcoatl.

Molotecatl, a tecuhtli lord in Molotlan

Molotlan was a *calpolli* that comprised an urban neighborhood, probably in the city of Yautepec. Molotecatl, a *tecuhtli* lord in charge of Molotlan, was almost certainly of higher rank than the *pilli* who lived in group 6 at Cuexcomate. We know Molotecatl's name and something about his social position from a Nahuatl-language census compiled very shortly after the Spanish Conquest.[27] The document called him "Molotecatl tecuhtli" and listed the inhabitants of his palace, along with the other members of the Molotlan *calpolli*. Figure 6.7 shows the genealogy of Molotecatl's extended family, who inhabited three structures that probably were raised on platforms and arranged around a patio. Molotecatl lived in house 1 with his five wives and children, the children and grandchild of a deceased wife, and a sister. House 2 contained three family

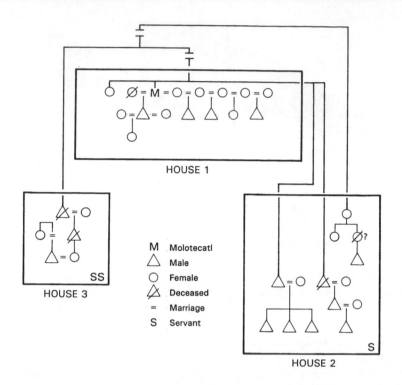

Figure 6.7 Genealogy of the inhabitants of the palace of Molotecatl tecuhtli showing the residents of the three structures (Based upon Carrasco 1972; drawing by Ellen Cesarski)

units, headed by a great aunt and two of Molotecatl's brothers, and a kitchen servant (perhaps originally a slave). House 3 was inhabited by the extended family of Molotecatl's deceased uncle as well as two servants, one of whom was a messenger and the other a woman who spun and wove. These three houses and the patio constituted Molotecatl's palace, which was probably a larger version of the Cuexcomate palace pictured in figure 6.6.

Molotecatl was in charge of the *calpolli* of Molotlan, a large neighborhood that comprised 128 households, divided into nine wards ranging from 1 to 32 households in each. Molotecatl owned the land of the entire *calpolli*, much of it valuable irrigated farmland. The commoner members paid him tribute in order to farm individual plots. The tribute of the *calpolli* members consisted of cotton cloth, farm produce, and labor service. To fulfill their labor service, commoner women came to the palace to spin and weave, which furnished Molotecatl with a large supply of cloth that contributed greatly to his wealth. *Tecuhtli* lords such as Molotecatl used part of their cloth income to pay their own tribute to their king.[28] In the case of Molotecatl, archaeologists have excavated the palace where his king lived.

The tlatoani of Yautepec

For many years archaeologists were aware of a large Aztec-period mound at the edge of the modern town of Yautepec in Morelos, but none of us had any idea of the importance of this structure. When the mound was threatened by urban expansion in the 1980s, a local citizen's group organized to help save it. A team of Mexican government archaeologists began excavations at the mound in 1989, under the direction of Hortensia de Vega Nova, and fieldwork continued through 1996. The excavators discovered an enormous stone platform some 6,000 sq m in area (0.6 ha, or about 1.5 acres) that had been the royal palace of the *tlatoani* of Yautepec. This is one of the few Aztec royal palaces to be excavated by archaeologists.[29]

Yautepec was a powerful polity whose *tlatoani* ruled over four or five lesser city-states in the Yautepec river valley. The Aztec city of Yautepec, located under and adjacent to modern Yautepec, was the largest city in the area, and the sumptuous royal palace was of a size befitting the power of the city's king. The outer walls of the structure were sloping panels of stone 4 m high that presented an imposing image to the people of Yautepec. Entrance was by a single stairway up the west side of the building, which led to a passageway into the heart of the palace. Excavations on top of the platform have uncovered numerous courtyards, rooms, and passages, all constructed of stone covered with layers of lime plaster (figure 6.8). Unlike the Cuexcomate palace, whose walls were painted with a simple coat of red, the Yautepec palace walls were covered with elaborate polychrome murals. There is evidence for several stages of construction at this structure. To date, archaeologists have cleared only about one-quarter of the palace. If there was a large central patio or courtyard, it has not been found yet. Another royal palace, at Calixtlahuaca is described in chapter 8 (see figure 8.3). Some idea of the nature of activities at royal palaces can be learned from ethnohistoric description of one of the largest and most sumptuous palaces in the entire Aztec empire, that of Nezahualcoyotl, king of Texcoco.

Nezahualcoyotl, imperial ruler of Texcoco

Nezahualcoyotl became ruler of Texcoco and the Acolhua peoples during the final years of Tepanec dominance. He helped the Mexica king Itzcoatl

Figure 6.8   Rooms and passages in the palace of the *tlatoani* of Yautepec
(Photograph by Michael E. Smith)

defeat the Tepanecs in 1428 and was one of the founding kings of the
Triple Alliance empire. He went on to become one of the most respected
and renowned of the Aztec rulers with a reputation as a statesman, soldier, builder, poet, and lawgiver. The story of Nezahualcoyotl's life was
recorded in the early 1600s by the chronicler Fernando de Alva Ixtlilxochitl,
a direct descendant of the Acolhua king. Alva Ixtlilxochitl devoted two
chapters of his work to a description of Nezahualcoyotl's palace.[30] His
information came from an earlier drawing of the palace, oral histories,
and his own observations of the ruins of the palace.

Nezahualcoyotl's compound in Texcoco measured 1,032 by 817 m, an
area of 84.3 ha (over 200 acres). It consisted of numerous buildings, gardens, temples, a ballcourt, a zoo, and a market, all surrounded by massive
adobe-brick walls. The many sections of the palace building described by
Alva Ixtlilxochitl included living quarters for the king; living quarters for
the queen and attendants; servant's quarters; a throne room; many chambers and halls for judges, councilors, officials, and ambassadors; a hall for
warriors; a science and music hall; a section for poets, philosophers, and
historians; an archive room; storehouses for weapons; and storehouses
for tribute from subject kings. Although we do not know the size of the

main palace building itself, it may have been comparable to that of Motecuhzoma II in Tenochtitlan, which measured 2.4 ha.[31]

Part of the palace compound was a religious sector with over 40 temples and other structures, among them a tall twin-temple pyramid dedicated to the deities Tlaloc and Huitzilopochtli, a round pyramid for Quetzalcoatl, sacrificial stones, priests' residences, and a special *calmecac* for the education of royal youth. In all there were over 300 rooms in the palace compound. This was the central administrative center of the Acolhua domain where much of the business of state was carried out. The city of Texcoco covered about 4.5 sq km, and the palace compound occupied much of the city center.

Apart from his achievements as king of the second most powerful state in the Aztec empire, Nezahualcoyotl was famous as an intellectual, poet, and philosopher. He was an expert architect and builder, who designed the dikes that regulated the waters of Lake Texcoco and kept Tenochtitlan from flooding. Nezahualcoyotl had a number of smaller palaces scattered around his kingdom, the best known of which was Texcotzinco. Here, on a hilltop above Texcoco, he built a center for ritual and relaxation that included a residence, a bath complex, and a botanical garden.[32] The canals, aqueducts, and pools at Texcotzinco have delighted visitors from Aztec times to the present day.

Relations among nobles

All nobles regardless of rank, from lowly *pipiltin* to the high kings, shared an interest in maintaining and protecting their privileged positions and lifestyles. This gave the nobility a common interest that cut across the political divisions of city-states and the empire. Nobles promoted this common interest in several ways. First, they encouraged the adoption of a set of ideas – an ideology – that justified their privileged position of the nobility. This ideology, present in myths, rituals, and formal orations, consisted of themes such as "human fate is in the hands of the gods," "everyone has duties to perform," and "hard work and suffering is the normal condition of humankind." Thus commoners should accept their lot in life and should not question the position of the nobility. Although this ideology helped nobles maintain control over commoners, it took more than ideas to uphold a very unequal social order.[33] The second way that nobles promoted their common interest and maintained their privileged positions was through coercion. City-states and institutions like the *calpolli* and *teccalli* were organized in part to maintain the control of commoners by the nobility. Political institutions are discussed in the next chapter.

The third method used by the nobility to pursue their common interests was to develop an extensive network of social, economic and stylistic interaction that promoted a strong sense of group solidarity and accentuated their separation from commoners. Nobles could only marry other nobles, and used marriage alliances to link separate families and dynasties into a single, interlocking kinship network.[34] The practice of a low-ranking ruler or noble marrying the daughter of a more powerful ruler was widespread in Mesoamerica, and the Aztec kings used it extensively (see the discussion of the third Mexica *tlatoani*, Huitzilihuitl, in chapter 2).

The exchange of luxury goods among nobles reinforced their interaction network. Nobles presented their peers with gifts of cloth, feathers, jewelry, and the like on many occasions. A major setting for such gift-giving was the state ceremony. These occasions were held for coronations, funerals, temple dedications, and victory celebrations. Typically the host city invited nobles from all over, including foreign and enemy lords. Large-scale theatrical presentations were staged for commoners and nobles alike, and then the nobles withdrew for more exclusive festivities. They ate and drank together, exchanged gifts, listened to speeches, participated in dances, and generally enjoyed themselves away from the eyes of the commoners. The bonds forged and maintained among the nobles were so strong that they crossed political borders and even bound enemy nobles together. Tlacaelel, advisor to the Mexica kings, articulated this principle in a speech reported by Friar Durán:

> It seems to me that it would not be unreasonable to invite them again [nobles and rulers of the enemy states of Tlaxcalla and Metztitlan] to this solemn occasion because, even though we are enemies in the wars that we wage, in our festivities we should rejoice together. There is no reason why they should be excluded since we are all one, and in these times it is reasonable that there be a truce and sociable communication among the rulers.[35]

This "truce and sociable communication among the rulers" was a primary form of diplomacy between politically independent city-states, and reveals the close connections between social class and the state. We now turn to Aztec political organization.

chapter seven
City-State and Empire

All the different things the ruler attended to:

- That cities be destroyed.
- War.
- Death.
- Singing, dancing.
- Guarding.
- The ball court; the rubber ball.
- The market.
- The *patolli* game.
- The installing of a ruler.
- The installing of lords.
- If there is a famine.
- If there is a plague.
- That payment to the gods be made.
- That copal [incense] be offered.
- The guarding of the city.
- Removing filth from the roads.
- Sweeping.
- The assembling of the seasoned warriors.

Bernardino de Sahagún, Primeros Memoriales

This list shows the wide range of activities that engaged Aztec kings. From warfare to dancing, from cleaning the city to offering incense, from installing officials to supervising the ballgame; an Aztec king was responsible for almost everything that happened in his kingdom. Aztec kings (*tlatoque*; sing. *tlatoani*) ruled city-states, and by the time the Spaniards arrived in 1519, nearly all of these city-states were under the control of the Aztec empire. Most of the surviving ethnohistoric information about politics and kings comes from Tenochtitlan, the imperial capital, and not surprisingly the available written documents emphasize the power and glory of Tenochtitlan and its empire. Although the empire was certainly a rich and mighty institution, the city-state was actually more influential in

Aztec life and politics. Most people gave political allegiance to their local city-state, not to the empire, and the city-state formed the social and economic universe within which they lived out their lives. The Aztec empire was built on a foundation of city-states, and these units retained their identity and many social and political functions even under imperial control.

City-States

Altepetl

Altepetl is the Nahuatl term usually translated as "city-state" or "kingdom."[1] For the Aztecs, an *altepetl* was a community with laws, boundaries, a central town with surrounding farmland, and a *tlatoani* or king. There were about 50 of these city-states in the Valley of Mexico in 1519, and the Aztec empire ruled over an additional 450 subject city-states. Native histories often describe city-states as founded by immigrant peoples, the early Nahuatl migrants from Aztlan or later migrating groups.

The founding of a new *altepetl* was heralded by the construction of a royal palace, a temple-pyramid, and a market. These three structures both practically and symbolically established the city-state as the pre-eminent political, religious, and economic unit in the lives of its inhabitants. The royal palace was the heart of the city-state. It served not only as the residence of the *tlatoani*, but also as the center of administrative and social activity. The temple housed the image of a patron god who watched over the citizens of the *altepetl*. The size and luxury of the central temple communicated the importance and success of the city-state. When a city-state was conquered in warfare, its defeat was symbolized by a burning temple (see chapter 11). The market provided an economic focus for exchanges that helped bind the city-state together.

The royal palace, temple, and market were normally located near one another and formed the nucleus for a town or small city. This urban center contained wards of the more important *calpolli* in the city-state. Labor obligations in the city-state, such as service at the palace or public works projects, rotated among the constituent *calpolli*. In some respects the *altepetl* can be considered a *calpolli* writ large. Sometimes the *calpolli* were composed of peoples from different ethnic groups, including both Nahuatl speakers (such as Mexica, Acolhua, Chalca, or Tlahuica) and others (such as Otomi, Matlatzinca, or Mixtec). As a result, Aztec city-states were often multiethnic, with political boundaries cutting across ethnic divisions.

The tlatoani

Friar Sahagún provides us with the Aztec nobles' view of a good *tlatoani*:

> The good ruler (is) a protector; one who carries (his subjects) in his arms,
> who unites them, who brings them together. He rules, takes responsibili-
> ties, assumes burdens. He carries (his subjects) in his cape; he bears them in
> his arms. He governs; he is obeyed. (To him) as shelter, as refuge, there is
> recourse.[2]

Tlatoque were selected by a high council of *tetecuhtin* nobles, male kin of
the deceased ruler. Usually a brother or a son succeeded to the office, but
sometimes a nephew or grandson of the previous ruler was chosen (see
the genealogy of the Mexica *tlatoque* in figure 2.9). The council deliber-
ated to find the appropriate successor, who was viewed as the god
Tezcatlipoca's selection to the post. Tezcatlipoca, sometimes known as
"We his slaves," was the most powerful Aztec deity. Among the Mexica
many *tlatoque* had been successful war leaders under earlier rulers.

The installation of a new Mexica *tlatoani* involved a series of elaborate
ceremonies and activities – a rite of passage through which the chosen
noble was transformed into a being worthy of speaking in the voice of
Tezcatlipoca. First, the candidate stood naked before the image of the god
Huitzilopochtli to present offerings. He then went into retreat with his
tetecuhtin for four days of fasting and penance. Upon emergence, he was
required to lead a brief military excursion to gather captives for sacrifice
at his installation ceremony. An all-night prayer vigil to Tezcatlipoca pre-
ceded the formal installation ceremony. The entire kingdom and *tlatoque*
and nobles from other city-states were invited to witness the pageants,
theatrical presentations, dances, musical performances, and human sacrifices that accompanied the ruler's installation. These ceremonies were intended to impress upon the citizens the link between the new king and the
god Tezcatlipoca, the supernatural basis for political authority.

Tlatoque were also concerned with the dynastic basis of their authority. Political legitimacy for the Aztec kings was derived from their genealogical connections with the earlier Toltec dynasty of Tula. The Aztec
concept for legitimate rulership, *tlatocayotl*, depended upon this appar-
ent lineage. Each local Aztec city-state dynasty could trace its ancestry
back to Tula, although in many cases the genealogies were fictional. When
the Mexica, newly settled at Tenochtitlan, wished to establish a *tlatocayotl*
for the first time, their ruler, not yet a *tlatoani*, married a princess from
Culhuacan whose pedigree provided a direct link to the Toltec kings that
the subsequent Mexica dynasty would follow.

The *tlatoani* owned or controlled the land within his city-state, and received the tribute of both his direct commoner subjects and his subordinate lords. He served as the military leader of the polity by organizing campaigns, overseeing the defense of the city-state, and sometimes leading his troops into battle. In addition to being the voice of Tezcatlipoca, the *tlatoani* sponsored religious celebrations and led many of the state rituals. Finally, as protector of his people, he settled disputes that could not be resolved through the normal process of judicial hearings.

The power and exalted position of the *tlatoani* led to a luxurious lifestyle. He wore the costliest clothing, ate the most exotic delicacies, had access to the greatest number of servants, aides, and entertainers, and lived in the most sumptuous palace in the kingdom. Many nobles and commoners served in the royal court. In painted manuscripts a king was depicted wearing a pointed crown and seated on an elevated platform (figure 2.11). This platform or throne was covered with one or both of the ancient Mesoamerican symbols of royalty: a reed mat or a jaguar pelt.

The *tlatoani* was assisted by a council of nobles and a series of lower-ranking bureaucrats. Other lords served as judges to hear suits, and in some city-states there was a group of superior or appeals judges. An early Spanish governor of New Spain, Alonso de Zorita, described Aztec judges as follows:

> The Indian judges of whom I spoke would seat themselves at daybreak on their mat dais, and immediately begin to hear pleas. The judges' meals were brought to them at an early hour from the royal palace. After eating, they rested for a while, then returned to hear the remaining suitors, staying until two hours before sundown. Appeals from these judges were heard by twelve superior judges, who passed sentence in consultation with the ruler.[3]

The political landscape

Recently, ethnohistorians and archaeologists have joined forces to reconstruct the Aztec political landscape for the first time.[4] This effort to map the boundaries and settlements of Aztec city-states has been facilitated by the new focus on administrative documents as a major source of data. The first step in this procedure is to review the documents from a region to determine which cities or towns had a *tlatoani*. Then it is often a simple matter to locate these on a map. Aztec Texcoco, Chalco, Otumba, Yautepec, or Calixtlahuaca were located precisely where the modern cities of these names are located today. Some place names were changed. For example, the Spaniards had trouble pronouncing Cuauhnahuac and the city's name became Cuernavaca ("cow horn"). In other cases, towns were moved forcibly by the Spaniards, and some Aztec towns were abandoned completely, which makes it difficult to impossible to locate the original Aztec *tlatoani* center.

The second step is to reconstruct the territories of these capitals. Luckily many of the early Spanish documents – particularly those known as the *Relaciones Geográficas* – list the names of villages and hamlets that were subject to each *tlatoani* or to the capital town. In some areas these small, subject settlements survive today and can be located on detailed modern maps; in other areas the smaller settlements have disappeared, making it difficult or even impossible to map the territories of Aztec city-states. Scholars have found in some cases that the small settlements subject to nearby city-state centers lay interspersed with one another so that it is not possible to draw clear boundaries around the territories of the polities. Although this appears confusing to us today, in fact it reveals a crucial point about political organization in ancient Mesoamerica. Polities were defined not in terms of territory or space – as they are in the modern world – but in terms of personal obligations. The city-state of Tepexpan, for example, consisted of all of the people who owed allegiance to the *tlatoani* of Tepexpan. The fact that some of those people lived closer to the city-state centers of Acolman or Teotihuacan than to the center of Tepexpan did not matter. Research has identified similar ruler-centered conceptions of polities among other Mesoamerican cultures, including the Mixtecs and the Classic Maya.[5]

A number of ethnohistoric studies have followed these methods to reconstruct the regional political landscape in various parts of the Aztec empire. The research of the late Mary G. Hodge went beyond this by correlating city-state territories with known Late Aztec archaeological sites.[6] The 1579 *Relación Geográfica* from Coatepec, for example, not only lists subjects of the town but also provides a map. Using this document and other sixteenth-century reports and lawsuits Hodge was able to map the extent of Coatepec and nearby city-states as they existed in 1519. She then compared her ethnohistoric map of this area with the results of the Valley of Mexico Archaeological Survey Project and was able to assign the many small- and medium-sized sites to their appropriate city-state (figure 7.1). Hodge has produced the most accurate and complete political map of the Aztec Valley of Mexico to date, and the application of her procedures to other areas promises to yield additional insights.

Relations among City-States

Aztec city-states did not exist in isolation. They formed large, regional groups whose member states were in constant communication and interaction with

Figure 7.1 Map of city-state territories in the southeastern Valley of Mexico (not all of the Aztec sites in this region are depicted on the map) (From Hodge 1994:56; reproduced with permission)

one another. Somewhat paradoxically, nearby city-states engaged simultaneously in both peaceful interactions – trade, political alliances, and visits among lords – and relations of warfare and domination. These regional groups or systems of city-states were quite volatile and alternated between periods of stability and episodes of unrest and rapid change. In this sense, the Aztec political landscape resembled other historically known city-state systems such as those of Archaic and Classical Greece, Early Dynastic Sumeria, Medieval Italy, and nineteenth-century west Africa. In all of these cases, nearby city-states were linked by a similar language and culture but maintained their political autonomy and distinctiveness.[7] Competition among sister city-states is endemic in these settings. In the Aztec case, this competition frequently led to conquest and political domination, culminating in the formation and expansion of the Triple Alliance empire.

Peaceful relations

Nearby city-states maintained three main types of peaceful relations: trade, elite networks, and political alliances. Aztec city-states were small in size, and very few could afford to be economically self-sufficient. Political borders did not stop either merchants or consumers from traveling to markets in foreign city-states. Specialized markets attracted customers from large areas. For example, people from city-states all over the northeast Valley of Mexico traveled to Acolman to shop at its famous dog market. When people needed a costly or specialized item not available at their local city-state market, they could travel to the nearest large market to make their purchase. Nobles from Acolman, for example, might go to Texcoco or Tenochtitlan to buy jewelry and feathers.

As discussed in chapter 6, royal families and other nobles were heavily involved in many activities that transcended the borders of individual city-states. Nobles often married across city-state lines, partly to forge political alliances and partly for the simple reason that in many small city-states there were not enough potential spouses who were nobles. Lords commonly visited their peers in other city-states to participate in ceremonies, festivals, and political summits. Friar Durán describes many of these events. When Nezahualpilli, king of Texcoco, died in 1515, nobles from all over central Mexico attended his funeral:

> Then the other leading men of Tenochtitlan, one after another, made sorrowful speeches to the body of the Texcoco king, expressing condolences for his death but speaking to him as if he were still alive. Each one presented jewels and other gifts, according to his possibilities. The king of Tacuba also sent slaves and gifts of royal mantles and jewels, as did the ruler of Chalco and the lords of Xochimilco and of the Marquesado [i.e., Cuauhnahuac]. Noblemen of all the land came with quantities of jewels and gifts and with many slaves.[8]

The economic and social ties among city-states did not prevent them from fighting one another in an attempt to achieve political domination, however.

Warfare and domination

The goal of warfare among the Aztecs was to conquer other city-states in order to force them to pay tribute.[9] Warfare was not used to expand the territory of a state since the losing city-state typically maintained its *tlatoani*, government, and lands intact. The losing king simply had to acknowledge the dominance of the victorious king and agree to pay him a specified amount of tribute each year. A secondary goal of warfare was to capture enemy soldiers for sacrifice. Human sacrifice was a fundamental part of Aztec religion, and most victims were soldiers captured in battle.

War and battle were dominant themes running throughout Aztec culture. There were no permanent standing armies, and military service was required of all males. Success in warfare was an important part of male identity (see chapter 6). Birth was compared to combat, and women who died in childbirth were likened to warriors. All boys were taught military skills and values at the *telpochcalli* and *calpolli* schools.

The public status of a young man was determined by the number of enemy captives he had taken in battle. Various ranks of warriors were proclaimed publicly by dress and jewelry. New soldiers with no captives could wear only plain capes and not jewelry. Upon taking his first captive, a soldier became a "leading youth" and was allowed to wear special face paint and a decorated cape in public; he also became eligible for marriage. With each additional captive, a man gained new privileges. For example, a four-captive warrior could dance at important public ceremonies and wear fine lip plugs and a headband with eagle-feather tassels. The most successful warriors joined elite military orders known as eagle warriors, jaguar warriors, Otomi warriors, and shorn warriors. These exalted soldiers were the commanders and leaders in battle, and enjoyed many privileges back home. Eagle and jaguar warriors, for example, could dine at the royal palace, drink *pulque*, and keep concubines. The advancement of a young man up the military ladder was a source of great pride for his family and *calpolli*.

Aztec warfare was ritualized and followed a distinct protocol, although actual battles were fierce and serious. The ruler of a city-state bent upon expansion first sent ambassadors to request the surrender of the targeted town. Gifts were offered to the local lord and the consequences of refusal were described. These threats included military conquest, the possible destruction of the town, and the imposition of a heavy burden of tribute. Sometimes a local *tlatoani* submitted willingly, assuming a lower rate of tribute; in other cases, he sent the ambassadors home with scorn, and war soon followed. The king of the aggressor state could raise an army quickly from among the eligible youths and experienced soldiers, and the women provided food and supplies for the campaign. Although these procedures did not lead to surprise attacks, they did not prevent the use of ambush and trickery on the battlefield.

Forces were led into battle by the most experienced warriors, with the sounds of drums and trumpets urging on the attack. Once battle was joined, soldiers fought with determination and vigor. The primary offensive weapons were thrusting spears and swords. The Aztec sword (*maquahuitl*) consisted of a long, flat wooden handle into which were fitted rows of obsidian blades (figure 7.2). The extreme sharpness of the obsidian blades made these swords highly effective weapons. The Spaniards described several instances in which Aztec soldiers cut off the heads of horses with a single blow. The bow and arrow was used as an offensive weapon also, and some groups made use of clubs and slings.

Soldiers normally carried shields into battle. These were made of wood covered with elaborate decorations, often of feathers (figures 7.2, 7.4). The Spaniards described Aztec shields as quite good at stopping arrows and swords. Soldiers wore body armor of thick, quilted cotton cloth that could stop arrows and darts. War leaders adorned themselves with feather tunics, headdresses, armbands, and other decorative clothing.

The need to capture enemies for sacrifice greatly influenced the nature of fighting in Aztec wars. At one level, armies sought to kill numerous opponents to gain victory. On another level, however, soldiers tried to injure or cripple enemy fighters in order to capture them alive. Captures made by a group of soldiers brought far less status than solo seizures, so most soldiers fought individually, one on one, each opponent seeking to subdue the other for capture.

Victory on the battlefield came when one army succeeded in killing and capturing enough enemy soldiers to subdue and demoralize its opponent. Sometimes victory required the conquest and partial destruction of a city, as indicated in the burning temple glyph for a conquered city (figure 11.3). Each army returned to its capital, one with rejoicing and celebration, the other with tears and sorrow. The victorious king set the tribute quota for the conquered city-state, and the losing monarch was forced to pay tribute while acknowledging the superiority of his conqueror. In most cases, the victor did not depose the conquered king nor attempt to administer directly the territory of his new domain. So long as the tribute continued to flow to the victors he and his successors usually avoided meddling in the internal affairs of subject states. This form of indirect rule was put to use when the Triple Alliance began its program of imperial expansion after 1428, and explains many characteristics of that empire as the Spaniards encountered it in 1519.

Figure 7.2   Soldiers carrying *maquahuitl* swords into battle (After Sahagún 1950–82:bk.8:fig.78; drawing by Ellen Cesarski)

The Empire of the Triple Alliance

What kind of empire?

The principles of warfare, tribute payment, and indirect rule outlined above were worked out among the Aztec city-states during the twelfth through fourteenth centuries. When the Triple Alliance of Tenochtitlan, Texcoco, and Tlacopan was formed in 1428, the rulers put these practices to work to build their empire. Together, these states easily achieved military and political control of the Valley of Mexico. Once they had consolidated the economic and demographic power of the Valley of Mexico, they set out to dominate an ever-increasing area. By 1519, the alliance controlled an area greater than any previous Mesoamerican realm. But was this loosely organized group of city-states an empire? Some scholars state that because of major deficiencies, "this was not an empire at all."[10] The Aztecs had no standing armies; they left conquered kings in office instead of sending governors or administrators to the provinces; they did not build an infrastructure of roads, cities, or warehouses throughout their realm; and fortresses and garrisons were few and far between. Ethnohistorian Ross Hassig counters this argument by analyzing the Aztec empire from a comparative perspective. He shows that the Triple Alliance was in fact typical of a certain kind of ancient empire.

Historians and political scientists divide empires into two basic types: territorial or direct, and hegemonic or indirect.[11] The popular image of an ancient empire is represented by large territorial domains such as the Roman, Assyrian, or Inca empires. All of these had standing armies, direct political control of the provinces, and major construction programs. Their rulers attempted to incorporate subject peoples into the culture of the dominant power. Hegemonic empires, by contrast, are ruled through indirect control, using a combination of force and persuasion to gain compliance by client kings. Far less effort is devoted to managing the affairs of subject peoples. Examples of ancient hegemonic empires include Athens during the Classical period, the eastern portion of the Roman empire, and the Aztec Triple Alliance. The alliance's Mexica rulers, however, did not lack deliberate strategies and plans for imperial expansion and administration; in fact they employed several distinct strategies to create and exploit the empire for their own ends.

Imperial control in the Valley of Mexico

The first goal of the newly formed Triple Alliance was to gain control over the city-states of the Valley of Mexico.[12] Once these had been conquered or otherwise incorporated into the empire, the imperial rulers initiated a series of political reforms designed to tighten their control and to prevent nearby city-states from rebelling or resisting. These reforms went beyond the heretofore accepted pattern of city-state expansion discussed above and signaled the beginnings of a new, higher level of political and social control and integration. Unfriendly *tlatoque* were removed from office and replaced by nobles sympathetic to the empire. A system of tributary provinces was established that was separate from the preexisting city-state governments. Tribute was collected directly by imperial tribute-collectors, thereby keeping it out of the hands of local city-state rulers. Under this system the imperial kings could deal with subject rulers as allies and colleagues, not tribute-payers, at the same time that they were assessing heavy tribute payments from their colleagues' commoner subjects.

As the empire expanded outside the Valley of Mexico, two factors shaped the continuing development of city-states within the Valley. First, the final conquest of Chalco in 1465 brought an end to the warfare that had been endemic among the Valley of Mexico city-states. Under the resulting Pax Azteca of the Late Aztec B period, the market system flourished, and the entire valley became more tightly integrated economically and socially. Second, the growth of the empire in the outer provinces produced a great influx of riches into the valley in the forms of tribute and trade goods. The imperial rulers strengthened their bonds with other dynasties by sharing some of this wealth as gifts to nobles at increasingly frequent and sumptuous gatherings and ceremonies. Marriage alliances among the Valley of Mexico nobility also strengthened regional ties.

Imperial Strategies and Control

Tribute and warfare in the outer provinces

Aztec imperial expansion was motivated by economic interests: the Triple Alliance wanted access to a regular supply of wealth and riches from foreign lands.[13] The growing numbers of commoners in Tenochtitlan and the other imperial capitals required ever-increasing amounts of food, cloth, and other necessities, and the nobles required exotic luxury goods to maintain their lifestyles and social positions. To obtain these goods, the Mexica kings and their Acolhua allies devised two fundamental strategies. The economic strategy involved the conquest of rich areas and the establishment of a program of regular tribute payments as well as the encouragement of trade and markets throughout the empire. The Aztecs were not the only imperialists in Late Postclassic Mesoamerica, however. When their expansion brought them into conflict with other powerful enemies, the Triple Alliance devised a second strategy. This frontier strategy involved the creation of client states along enemy frontiers to shoulder much of the burden of protecting the empire so that tribute and trade could flourish in the inner provinces.

These two strategies led to the creation of two distinct types of imperial provinces in the outer empire. Tributary provinces included city-states well under imperial control that could provide the regular tribute and trade required by the economic strategy. These provinces tended to comprise the city-states with the longest history of imperial control and those distant from major Aztec enemies such as the Tarascan empire or Tlaxcalla. Strategic provinces on the other hand were established to help maintain the imperial borders and frontiers without massive investment by the Triple Alliance. A map of the empire (figure 7.3) shows the locations of the tributary and strategic provinces as they existed in 1519. These 55 provinces contained some 450 city-states, all subject to the Triple Alliance in some manner (table 7.1).

The economic strategy

Groups of adjacent conquered city-states were organized into tributary provinces. A prominent town was selected to head each province, and

Figure 7.3   Map of the provinces of the Aztec empire. See table 7.1 for the names of the provinces (After Berdan et al. 1996; drawing by Pam Headrick)

Table 7.1   Provinces of the Triple Alliance empire

No.	Province	Type
1	Axocopan	Tributary
2	Atotonilco (de Pedraza)	Tributary
3	Xilotepec	Tributary
4	Chiapan	Strategic
5	Xocotitlan	Tributary
6	Ixtlahuaca	Strategic
7	Cuahuacan	Tributary
8	Tollocan	Tributary
9	Ocuilan	Tributary
10	Malinalco	Tributary
11	Temazcaltepec	Strategic
12	Tlachco	Tributary
13	Cuauhnahuac	Tributary
14	Huaxtepec	Tributary
15	Ocuituco	Strategic
16	Chiauhtlan	Strategic

17	Quiauhteopan	Tributary
18	Tlacozauhtitlan	Tributary
19	Tepequacuilco	Tributary
20	Zompanco	Strategic
21	Tetellan	Strategic
22	Tlapan	Tributary
23	Cihuatlan	Tributary
24	Tecpantepec	Strategic
25	Ayotlan	Strategic
26	Ometepec	Strategic
27	Xoconochco	Tributary
28	Miahuatlan	Strategic
29	Teozacualco	Strategic
30	Teozapotlan	Strategic
31	Ixtepexi	Strategic
32	Coyolapan	Tributary
33	Coayxtlahuacan	Tributary
34	Tlachquiauhco	Tributary
35	Yoaltepec	Tributary
36	Tecomaixtlahuacan	Strategic
37	Acatlan	Strategic
38	Ahuatlan	Strategic
39	Tepeacac	Tributary
40	Tochtepec	Tributary
41	Cuetlaxtlan	Tributary
42	Cempoallan	Strategic
43	Quauhtochco	Tributary
44	Xalapa	Strategic
45	Misantla	Strategic
46	Tlatlauhquitepec	Tributary
47	Tetela	Strategic
48	Tlapacoyan	Tributary
49	Cuauhchinanco	Strategic
50	Atotonilco (el Grande)	Tributary
51	Atlan	Tributary
52	Tochpan	Tributary
53	Tzicoac	Tributary
54	Huexotla	Strategic
55	Oxitipan	Tributary

See Figure 7.3 for the locations of provinces by number.
Source: Berdan et al. 1996

those towns gave the provinces their names. In some cases the head town was the capital of the most powerful city-state in the province, while in others a less prominent town was selected. The Triple Alliance assessed each province an annual tribute quota. This information was recorded in manuscripts stored in the imperial capitals. The second part of the Codex Mendoza is an Early Colonial copy of one such imperial tribute roll. Each province was allotted one or two pages in the codex. The province of Coayxtlahuacan, located in the modern state of Oaxaca and inhabited by Mixtec speakers, provides an example (figure 7.4; see figure 7.3, province no. 33).

Coayxtlahuacan was the head town of the province, so its glyph was painted at the top of the page. Other towns in the province, most of them capitals of city-states, are listed under the head town. The remainder of the page lists the imperial tribute goods and the quantities to be paid. A feather attached to the top of an item indicates the quantity 400; a flag stands for 20. The five symbols along the top of the page represent capes and other textiles, totaling 2,000 items. Another page of the codex states that these textiles were delivered semiannually, so the province of Coayxtlahuacan paid a total of 4,000 textiles each year. Other tribute items paid annually were 2 feathered warrior costumes with shields; 2 strings of jade beads; 800 quetzal feathers; 40 bags of cochineal dye; 20 gourd bowls of gold dust, and a royal feather headpiece. These goods were assembled and sent to Tenochtitlan by an imperial tribute collector called a *calpixqui*. Unfortunately we know almost nothing about the actual collection of tribute in the outer provinces. Did each town contribute a small portion of the whole range of a province's tribute, or did towns specialize in the type of tribute they paid? Did a province's tribute collector have underlings in each town? To what extent did imperial tribute collectors rely upon local kings and officials to help gather the goods? This is one of the major gaps in our knowledge of the operation of the Aztec empire.

When all of the imperial tribute in the Codex Mendoza is added up, the quantity and diversity of goods are impressive (table 7.2). The most common items, paid by almost every province, were capes of cotton or maguey. As easily transportable items of money and wealth, it is not surprising that textiles were the principal tribute goods of the empire. Nearly all provinces also provided warrior costumes and shields, tribute that symbolized the military domination of the empire over the provinces. Luxury goods, particularly tropical feathers, were also major tribute items, as were many specialized goods such as copal incense, paper, and liquidambar. Foodstuffs, animal products, and building materials were minor items of imperial tribute.

In many cases, the empire used the tribute system to obtain local specialties from the provinces. For example, cochineal dye, made from an insect that lives on the prickly-pear cactus, was produced in many towns in the Coayxtlahuacan region (figure 7.4); bark paper was a major item

Figure 7.4   The tribute of the imperial province of Coayxtlahuacan as depicted in the Codex Mendoza (1992:v.4:91; f.43r)

of tribute from towns in Morelos, where it was produced in quantity; and the Pacific coastal province of Cihuatlan paid in seashells, cacao, and other local products. On the other hand, many tribute goods were not native to the provinces that had to pay them. Of the tribute demanded of Coayxtlahuacan, the tropical feathers were not available in highland Oaxaca, nor were the jade beads or gold dust. In order to obtain these exotic goods, the people of Coayxtlahuacan had to engage in commerce with other areas. At first glance, it may seem that the Aztecs demanded

Table 7.2 Imperial tribute as recorded in the Codex Mendoza

Category	Item	Total annual amount[a]
Textiles and clothing	Quachtli and other capes	128,000 items
	Garments	19,200 items
	Raw cotton	4,400 loads
	Cochineal dye	65 bags
Military supplies	Warrior costumes with shields	665 sets
	Canes for arrows	32,000 items
Jewelry and luxuries	Colorful feathers	29,680 items
	Feather products	7 items
	Feather down	20 bags
	Lip plugs	82 items
	Amber	2 large pieces
	Turquoise masks	10 items
	Other turquoise items	5 items
	Jade beads and stones	22 strings
	Gold objects	65 items
	Gold dust	60 bowls
	Gold bars	10 items
	Copper/bronze bells	80 items
	Copper/bronze axes	560 items
Foodstuffs	Maize and other staples	88 large bins
	Chiles	1,600 loads
	Honey	3,800 jars
	Salt	4,000 loaves
	Ground grain	320 baskets
	Cacao beans	680 loads
Animal products	Live eagles	2 or more
	Deer skins	3,200 items
	Jaguar skins	40 items
	Bird skins	160 items
	Seashells	1,600 items
Building materials	Lime for construction	4,400 loads
	Wood beams and planks	14,400 pieces
Miscellaneous products	Copal incense	64,000 balls
	"	3,200 baskets
	Balls of rubber	16,000 items

(*Table 7.2 contd.*)

Category	Item	Total annual amount[a]
	Paper	32,000 sheets
	Reed mats and seats	16,000 items
	Canes	48,000 items
	Gourd bowls	17,600 items
	Pottery bowls	2,400 items
	Yellow ocher	40 pans
	Liquidambar	16,000 cakes
	„	100 jars
	Carrying frames	800 items
	Firewood	4,800 loads

[a] I use Frances Berdan's calculations of the annual quantities of tribute (Codex Mendoza 1992:v.1:154–6). The organization by category is my own.
Source: Codex Mendoza 1992:f.18v–55r

this nonlocal tribute merely to save themselves the trouble of obtaining distant goods, such as feathers, gold, or jade, directly. But Aztec merchants also supplied these and other exotic goods to Tenochtitlan independently of the tribute system. Another explanation for the prevalence of nonlocal tribute is that it was part of a deliberate effort to stimulate trade and commerce throughout the empire.

This forcing of provincial peoples to engage in long-distance trade to obtain tribute goods was part of the economic strategy of the Triple Alliance. In addition to demanding tribute payments, imperial rulers took a number of steps to promote and encourage trade and markets. For example, the *pochteca* and other merchants were encouraged and backed by the empire, and key market towns in the provinces were protected from foreign interference. The empire thus employed two tactics to implement its economic strategy: direct state control through regular tribute payments, and indirect promotion of commerce, whose benefits were felt throughout Mesoamerica.

The frontier strategy

The expanding Aztec empire soon ran up against powerful enemy states that could not be subdued. Its two most intractable enemies were Tlaxcalla and the Tarascan empire.[14] Tlaxcalla included several Aztec city-states that banded together to successfully resist conquest by the Triple Alliance. Although surrounded by the empire and under siege, the Tlaxcallans were still holding out when the Spaniards arrived in 1519. The Tarascan polity was a powerful, non-Aztec empire whose size and influence matched that of the Triple Alliance. When direct warfare failed to subdue these states, the Aztec rulers devised a frontier strategy to keep them at bay. City-states located along the enemy frontiers were brought into the empire through conquest or threat, but were treated more as allies than as subjects. In lieu of regular tribute payments these client states were asked to maintain the borders and to give occasional "gifts" to the empire; they were not listed in the Codex Mendoza or other imperial tribute rolls. This situation was described in the *Relación Geográfica* from the town of Totoltepec, a client state on the Tarascan border:

> The Mexican king Axayacatl made war [on the people of Totoltepec] until he subjugated them. They did not bring him tribute because they were on the Tarascan frontier; they supplied the Mexica soldiers that were stationed there and at the fortress of Oztuma [see below]. A few times each year they sent presents to Mexico consisting of capes, green stones, and copper.[15]

Some of these client states engaged in low-intensity warfare with the enemies, others manned fortresses, and some supplied garrisons (as in the case of Totoltepec above). The direct economic benefit of these city-states to the empire was minimal, although most did engage in some form of trade with Aztec merchants. Rather, their role in the empire was strategic: they helped to protect the borders so that imperial tribute and trade activities in the inner tributary provinces could proceed unimpeded in a safe, peaceful climate.

Imperial fortresses and cities

Unlike more territorially organized empires like the Roman or Inca polities, the indirect nature of Aztec imperial rule did not lead to the widespread construction of administrative centers, storehouses, roads, or other types of imperial infrastructure in conquered areas. Nevertheless, the Aztecs did build or support a number of fortresses and cities in their outer provinces. The best-known examples are the fortresses of Oztuma and Cuauhtochco, and the ceremonial precinct of Malinalco.

Oztuma was a major fortress along the Tarascan frontier, which was supported by nearby client states like Totoltepec (see the quotation above).[16] It was located in an area rich in mineral resources, close to Alahuistlan, one of the major salt-production centers in central Mexico. The Tarascan king was very interested in this region (province 19 in figure 7.3), and it was the scene of nearly continuous warfare throughout

MALINALCO

Temples Cut Into Rock

0 _____ 20
meters

Eagle-Warrior
Temple

Edge of Cliff

Figure 7.5   Map of the hilltop ceremonial precinct of Malinalco (After Marquina 1964:206)

the Late Postclassic period. When the Aztec imperial armies moved into this area, they had to overcome a mountaintop fortress of the local Chontal people at a place called Ixtepec, near Oztuma. Many people were killed or fled in the Aztec conquest of the region, and king Ahuitzotl built a new fortress at Oztuma and sent families of Nahua immigrants from the Valley of Mexico to populate the fortress and other nearby towns.[17]

The Oztuma fortress, which came to mark the western frontier of the

Aztec empire, was attacked repeatedly – but unsuccessfully – by Tarascan armies. Traces of impressive walls and other fortifications survive at Oztuma, but so far very little fieldwork has been done. Surface surveys along the Aztec side of the Aztec/Tarascan frontier have located many smaller hilltop fortresses that were built and maintained by local client states (like that at Ixtepec), but none of these has been excavated. These sites – particularly Oztuma – are a high priority for archaeological research on the Aztec empire.

Another imperial site in the western provinces is the hilltop ceremonial precinct of *Malinalco* (figure 7.5).[18] Located high on a cliff overlooking the fertile Malinalco Valley (province 10 in figure 7.3), this site was built by the Mexica emperor Ahuitzotl. It consists of three temples carved into the bedrock of the mountain plus a series of small shrines and ceremonial platforms. The most impressive feature is Structure 1, often referred to as the Eagle-Warrior Temple (figure 7.6). This circular shrine was entered by 13 steps guarded by two sculptures of jaguars. The stairs lead to an outer platform with two other sculptures (now destroyed). The face of an earth monster is carved in relief around the doorway to the inner chamber so that entrance to the shrine was through the earth monster's mouth. The inner chamber has a bench around half of its circumference. Carvings of two eagles and a jaguar are incorporated into the bench, and a carved eagle occupies the center of the floor, probably serving as a throne or altar. The entire structure, including the sculptures, was carved from bedrock, quite an impressive feat from both an engineering and an aesthetic perspective.

One of the other rock-cut chambers at Malinalco had a painted mural depicting a procession of warriors. Excavations at Malinalco uncovered an elaborately carved wood drum, one of the finest examples of Aztec woodcarving known today; it depicts images of dancing jaguars and eagles. Also recovered at the site were numerous portable stone sculptures, abundant jewelry, copper bells, and other valuable items. The symbolism and function of the Malinalco compound have been much debated. Warfare and the associated solar cult are prominent iconographic themes at the site. The dominant interpretation of Structure 1, based on the abundant depictions of eagles and jaguars, is that it served as a precinct for rituals and gatherings of elite Mexica eagle warriors. An alternative hypothesis is that Malinalco was built as a monument to Mexica imperial power, and that the iconography related more to coronation and rulership than to eagle warriors. These two views are not mutually exclusive, however, and both probably have some validity.

Another Aztec fortress in the outer provinces was the town of *Quauhtochco*, capital of a major tributary province in the eastern empire along the Gulf of Mexico (province 43 in figure 7.3).[19] A large pyramid at the site attracted the attention of early archaeological travelers in Mexico

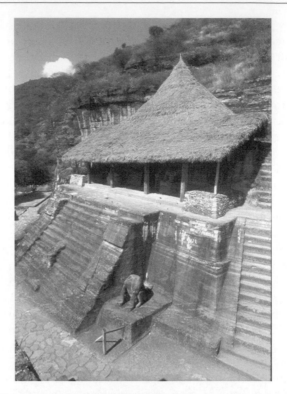

Figure 7.6   Entrance to the Eagle-Warrior Temple, a rock-cut circular structure at Malinalco (Photograph by Robert Frerck, Odyssey Productions, Chicago)

(figure 7.7). This temple was built in the Mexica style, quite different from other Postclassic temples along the Gulf coast. Alfonso Medellín Zeñil excavated the hilltop site in the 1950s and found remains of a defensive wall surrounding a small town with the pyramid and various other buildings. He recovered an abundance of Aztec ceramic vessels imported from the Valley of Mexico, particularly decorated serving plates and incense burners. It appears that there was a group of Mexica soldiers, or perhaps others, living at Quauhtochco. Because Quauhtochco was a provincial capital in 1519, far from any hostile imperial frontiers at that time, it must have functioned as a fortress at an earlier period, probably during the reign of Motecuhzoma I (1440–68) who conquered many of the Gulf Coast provinces.

Whereas Quauhtochco – with its Mexica-style temple and abundant Aztec imports – stands out as an unusual site in the eastern Aztec empire, the Totonac city *Zempoala* illustrates a more common type of regional

Figure 7.7   Mexica-style temple at the fortress of Quauhtochco in Veracruz as it appeared in 1805. The illustration was made by artist José Luciano Castañeda, who accompanied Captain Guillermo Dupaix on an archaeological tour of Mexico between 1805 and 1808 (Dupaix 1834:pl.9, see also Castañeda 1978:no.6116)

urban center.[20] The architecture follows local Totonac styles, including an abundance of circular temples dedicated to the wind god (figure 7.8). Although a few Valley of Mexico imports were recovered, the bulk of the artifacts are local Totonac types. The city, which covers about 1.5 sq km, was laid out around 12 large, irregularly shaped walled compounds that contained the main public architecture – temples, shrines, palaces, and open plazas. Figure 7.8 shows part of one of the compounds ("Walled System 4") with the Great Temple on the left and a variety of circular and rectangular shrines. The compound walls were not very high; they served a symbolic function of delineating public space in a large urban center rather than a defensive function. Although Zempoala was part of the Aztec empire, it shows few direct influences from Tenochtitlan. It was a regional city that served regional functions. In this respect Zempoala was

Figure 7.8   The City of Zempoala, a major urban center in the eastern Aztec empire (Photograph by Christopher Pool, reproduced with permission)

far more typical of cities throughout the empire than were Quauhtochco, Oztuma, or Malinalco (see further discussion in chapter 12). Nevertheless, these sites do reveal that even hegemonic empires like the Aztec empire did build some fortresses, temples, and other structures in their outer provinces.

Mexica Propaganda and the Limits of Empire

Ethnohistoric sources that derive from statements of the Mexica nobility do not always mesh with the view of the Aztec empire I have presented above. The Mexica were reluctant to admit their failed efforts to conquer Tlaxcalla, the Tarascans, and some other states. Their own accounts of the empire in the chronicles gloss over these shortcomings. For example, Friar Durán gives the following description of a state ceremony in Tenochtitlan that involved the display and exchange of lavish gifts among Mexica nobles and their guests from other states: "They saw that [the Mexica] were masters of the world, their empire so wide and abundant that they had conquered all the nations and that all were their vassals. The guests, seeing such wealth and opulence and such authority and power, were filled with terror."[21] This account is clearly a statement of propaganda, not fact, since the Mexica had not by any means "conquered all the nations." In their public statements the Mexica conveniently forgot Axayacatl's devastating defeat at the hands of the Tarascans.

Tlaxcalla, the independent eastern Aztec state surrounded by the empire, is another case in point. When some Spanish soldiers asked Motecuhzoma and his generals why they did not complete their conquest of this renegade area, they received the following excuse: "We could easily do so; but then there would remain nowhere for the young men to train [militarily], except far from here; and, also, we wanted there to always be [nearby] people to sacrifice to our gods."[22]

In other words, they claimed that the Triple Alliance was not really trying to conquer Tlaxcalla but preferred to engage in "practice" wars. The Mexica called these battles "flowery wars" (*xochiyaoyotl*) to distinguish them from wars of conquest. The Tlaxcallan rulers, however, responded to this question quite differently. They told the Spaniards that the Aztecs had them surrounded, had cut off their foreign trade in luxuries and salt, and were trying hard to defeat them, but had yet to succeed. Again, the Mexica words ring more of propaganda than of truth.[23] The Tlaxcallans were formidable foes indeed, and the Triple Alliance simply was not powerful enough to defeat them. The Tlaxcallans later delivered a fatal blow to their enemy when they allied themselves with Hernando Cortés and participated in the conquest of Tenochtitlan in 1521.

The Triple Alliance may not have managed to "conquer all the nations," but the "wealth and opulence" that so impressed visitors to Tenochtitlan were real enough. When one considers the imperial tribute pouring into the capital two to four times a year together with the trade goods imported by Aztec merchants, the volume of incoming wealth was immense. This imperial wealth was instrumental in the growth of Tenochtitlan, and the size and grandeur of the capital city were concrete manifestations of the economic success of the empire.

chapter eight
Cities and Urban Planning

> As long as the world will endure, the fame and glory of Mexico-
> Tenochtitlan will never perish.
>
> **Chimalpahin**

Tenochtitlan, the Aztec imperial capital, was the largest city ever built in the ancient New World. Founded in AD 1325, Tenochtitlan grew into an island metropolis of 200,000 inhabitants. Until recently, almost all surviving information on Aztec urbanism concerned this great metropolis, and next to nothing was known about other Aztec cities. Most had been destroyed or buried under Spanish and, later, modern communities. Once Spain took control over Mesoamerica in 1521, Spanish colonists moved into many Aztec cities and immediately began to refashion them into European-style urban centers. These settlers rarely left descriptions of the earlier communities. Yet other cities and towns were abandoned soon after the Spanish conquest.

Today the few surviving Aztec urban settlements have become rather unassuming archaeological sites. Because they lack the huge pyramids and other grandiose architecture that for so long attracted archaeologists, these sites were ignored by early investigators. Many modern writers have assumed that other Aztec cities were simply small versions of Tenochtitlan, but recent archaeological work has shown this to be false. When fieldworkers following the "social archaeology" approach turned their attention to urban centers such as Otumba, Huexotla, Xaltocan, and Yautepec, they discovered a very different type of settlement from the imperial capital.

Outside of Tenochtitlan, urban settlements were small in size and today would be considered quite rural in appearance. Houses were small and widely spaced, with orchards and gardens filling the area in between them. Yet these towns and cities functioned as urban centers. People from the entire polity depended upon the city-state's central settlement. It contained markets, temples, and administrative buildings that served a wider hinterland, and these institutions, not size or population density, made a community urban.[1] In this chapter I review the new evidence concerning smaller Aztec cities and then discuss the more traditional information on the imperial capital.

City-State Capitals

Fictional visit to Amecameca, an Aztec city

The following fictional vignette gives an idea of how a typical Aztec city-state capital in the Valley of Mexico might have appeared to a visitor.[2]

Opan, whose name means "On the road," is an itinerant merchant approaching the city-state capital of Amecameca in the southeast Valley of Mexico. He is a young *pochteca* merchant from the Acolhua capital Texcoco, and his small party of five *tlamamah* (carriers) are bringing obsidian tools and jade jewelry from Otumba to exchange for various local and imported goods at the Amecameca market. Situated near the major pass between the Valley of Mexico and Morelos, Amecameca lies along an ancient trade route, and its markets offer imported goods from lowland areas to the south.

The edge of the city is demarcated by low, stone field walls that separate the surrounding cornfields from urban houselots. The walled houselots are fairly large, and include gardens, turkey pens, trash heaps, and open yard areas in addition to the adobe-walled houses and storehouses. Opan notices that houses in Amecameca are somewhat smaller than those in his native Texcoco but their construction and form are quite similar. In some cases, two or three houses are arranged around a small patio (much like the rural town of Cuexcomate described in chapters 3 and 6); in other cases, a single house occupies a lot. Although most houses are within shouting distance of one or more neighbors, privacy is maintained by the large size of the houselots and the dense foliage of the many fruit trees and other garden crops tended by each family.

After a short walk past the green gardens of the outer city, the travelers pass a small market plaza next to a modest temple-pyramid. There are a few other unassuming stone buildings nearby. A number of people look with interest on the merchant's party. This plaza must be the center of one of the *calpolli* of Amecameca, he thinks. Opan wonders how many of these neighborhoods make up the city of Amecameca, certainly far fewer than in Texcoco. Nevertheless, Amecameca is a good-sized city for one so far from the central lakes of the Valley. A vendor beckons from under her awning, but her wares hold no allure for Opan. What a change from Otumba, he muses. There, many of the neighborhoods specialize in one or more crafts, and good bargains can be found in the small *calpolli* markets; in fact several bundles of the obsidian blades Opan carries were purchased at such a neighborhood market in Otumba. But this *calpolli* market in Amecameca offers only some corn, beans, and ceramic cookpots. Opan becomes anxious. Will the central market have the cotton, paper, feathers, and other goods he is seeking?

The group moves on toward the city's center, and Opan continues to silently compare Amecameca to other settlements they have just passed through. The residential areas of this urban center, an important city-state capital with more than one *tlatoani*, so far look identical to the small villages along the Chalco–Amecameca road. The large houselots and gardens with ample greenery make all of these hinterland cities and towns appear rural to an urbanite from Texcoco, the second-largest Aztec city. How do these provincials react when they visit a real city like the imposing imperial capital Tenochtitlan, which dwarfs even the great ancient city of Texcoco? Opan's thoughts are interrupted when the group at last reaches the center of town and the features that distinguish Amecameca from a village appear.

Their first glimpse of the city's center is the temple-pyramid, which towers over all other structures. The road they have followed ends at the back of the royal palace, a complex of stone buildings built on a large, low platform. It is still early, and several peasants from the countryside wait listlessly in the shade for a palace official to assign them tasks for the day. The palace and temple, the largest buildings in the city-state, both face onto an open plaza, where many people mill around, perhaps waiting for a ceremony to begin. The market is on the opposite, southern side of the plaza, so the group must go around the central area. Opan turns right, along the west side, passing to avoid the crowd gathering near the pyramid. Here, on the west side of the plaza, a game is in progress in the ballcourt, and the bearers slow down to catch a glimpse of the action. Opan hurries them on, however, since his destination is now in view.

It is market day in Amecameca, and the market plaza is filled with throngs of buyers amid the many stalls and booths. Opan notes with satisfaction that only a few vendors offer obsidian blades or jewelry. A local associate of Opan's guild has already paid the market tax and saved a choice stall, so after a brief conversation with the market judge, Opan unpacks his wares. These are what separate cities from villages, he thinks – the market, the pyramid, the palace, the plaza, and the throngs of people who gather around them to take care of their personal and professional needs. What would a merchant do without cities and towns?

Urban planning and layout

Most Aztec cities and towns were founded by Aztlan immigrants in the twelfth and thirteenth centuries. The layout of the capital cities followed a plan with a long heritage in Mesoamerica. In this tradition, cities were arranged around a sacred central zone that comprised a rectangular public plaza bordered by the important civic and religious buildings. The orientation and placement of the central buildings were carefully planned, often following the dictates of astronomical principles. Outside of the central precinct, however, formal planning was abandoned. Houses, workshops, markets, schools, and neighborhood temples were dispersed throughout the city, separated by gardens and open lots. This ancient pattern of urban layout was used by most Mesoamerican civilizations of the Classic and Postclassic epochs, including the lowland Classic Maya and the Zapotecs of the Valley of Oaxaca, and it was natural for the early Aztecs to draw on this tradition when they designed their first cities.[3]

Aztec city-state capitals – such as Amecameca, Otumba, and Yautepec – played a more important role in the daily lives of most people than did the distant imperial metropolis. Peasants came to town to attend the market, to participate in religious ceremonies, to pay their tribute, and to take care of innumerable other social and administrative obligations. A large, open public plaza formed the heart of the city, with the *tlatoani's* palace, a temple, and other civic structures arranged along its four sides (figure 8.1). The temple-pyramid always occupied the east side, probably because east was the direction of the sunrise. A single or double stairway led up the west or front side of the pyramid to the platform on top. Roofed temple rooms that housed the idols of the city-state's patron gods crowned the pyramid. This structure was the central focus of supernatural power in the city and polity. Many cities had a ballcourt along the plaza, where the Mesoamerican ballgame was played (see chapter 10). Other civic buildings that faced the plaza could include a *telpochcalli* school or various smaller temples or shrines.

These stone buildings and the plaza itself were laid out with a common orientation, usually close to the cardinal directions. The consistency of this pattern among surviving city centers suggests that urban central zones were carefully planned in accordance with basic principles of political and religious cosmology. The close proximity of the palace and temple would have reinforced the link between the earthly realm of the *tlatoani* and the sacred realm of the gods. The king ruled for the gods, and his

Figure 8.1   Plans of the central precincts of four Aztec urban centers in Morelos (Drawing by Michael E. Smith)

political power had supernatural backing. The layout and orientation of these central precincts is consistent with the Aztecs' preoccupation with the east–west passage of the sun and a four-directional cosmology.

Outside of the sacred central zone, Aztec cities showed little evidence for planning or controlled growth. Houses and house groups were scattered here and there, buildings did not follow a common orientation, and formal streets or avenues were absent. Nobles and commoners lived in wards and *calpolli*. At least some of these urban *calpolli* were specialized economically.[4] Houses in most Aztec cities were small, simple structures built of adobe bricks. Cuexcomate, a rural town, not a city-state capital, is the only center whose housing pattern has been mapped completely (figure 3.7). The houses and patio groups of its 800 residents were distributed across an area of 14.6 ha with considerable open area within the town that was probably devoted to farming. Most Aztec cities were larger than Cuexcomate; the average city-state capital in the Valley of Mexico had 9,000 inhabitants in an area of 200 ha (2 sq km). The population densities of the larger urban settlements, however, were similar to that of Cuexcomate (the city-state capitals averaged 45 persons per hectare, whereas the density at Cuexcomate was 55 persons per hectare). This suggests that Cuexcomate's pattern of scattered houses separated by large open lots may also have characterized other Aztec urban centers.

Only a few cities managed to grow beyond the modest size of their contemporaries, usually when a polity experienced great political and economic success as capital of a large domain or empire. Apart from the obvious case of Tenochtitlan, examples include Azcapotzalco (the Tepanec capital before 1428) and Texcoco (Tenochtitlan's partner in the Triple

Alliance) in the Valley of Mexico, and Cuauhnahuac in Morelos. Little survives of these cities archaeologically, and only Texcoco has any useful ethnohistoric descriptions.[5] These cities all had more than 20,000 inhabitants, and their central precincts were probably larger and more impressive than most cities.

Provincial Cities and Towns

The general urban patterns reviewed above are best illustrated with concrete examples. The archaeological sites of Coatetelco and Calixtlahuaca were provincial Aztec cities whose public architecture has been excavated and restored. Yautepec is a site where fieldwork has concentrated on houses rather than large buildings. These three sites provide a cross-section of the available information about Aztec cities in central Mexico outside of the Valley of Mexico.

Monumental archaeology: Coatetelco and Calixtlahuaca

Coatetelco was a medium-sized urban site in the Late Aztec period.[6] The central part of the city was excavated and restored by Raúl Arana Alvarez in the 1970s, revealing a ballcourt (figure 10.12), a small temple-pyramid (figure 10.8), and several other structures, all grouped around a public plaza (figure 8.2). The residential areas of the site are buried today under the modern town of Coatetelco. The Coatetelco ballcourt is one of the few Aztec ballcourts to be excavated. Under the main stairway of the west ballcourt platform, Arana encountered elite burials with hundreds of grave goods, including ceramic vessels, obsidian, jade, and copper-bronze objects. An unusual carefully stacked pile of *manos* (basalt tools for grinding maize on a *metate*) was found adjacent to the ballcourt; this is still visible at the site today.

Coatetelco is important because it is one of the few Aztec cities whose central precinct has been excavated extensively. The numerous small platforms in the plaza adjacent to the ballcourt are an unusual feature. Several of these contained buried offerings, including a collection of long-handled incense burners similar to the one shown in figure 10.2. The rather modest temple-pyramid at Coatetelco shows that not all Aztec cities had large imposing pyramids like those at Tenochtitlan, Tenayuca, or Teopanzolco. Unfortunately the Coatetelco excavations did not target the likely palace nor any of the residential zones.

Calixtlahuaca was a major political capital in the Toluca Valley prior to the conquest of that area by Axayacatl around 1474.[7] José García Payón

Figure 8.2 Drawing of the main plaza at Coatetelco, Morelos, as excavated by Raúl Arana Alvarez (After Konieczna Z. 1992; drawing by Michael E. Smith)

Figure 8.3 Palace at Calixtlahuaca in the Toluca Valley (After García Payón 1981:fig.8)

excavated and restored a series of large buildings in the 1930s (figure 8.3), but unfortunately never published his fieldwork in full. Calixtlahuaca covered more than a square kilometer along the sides and at the base of a hill. The best-known building is a large circular pyramid dedicated to Ehecatl, the wind god (figure 10.10). This structure was built in four stages. A series of rich burials were placed in front of the stairs, and two stone sculptures were excavated adjacent to the pyramid – a life-size image of a man wearing an Ehecatl mask, and a cylindrical sacrificial stone covered with relief carvings of symbols of human blood. Also noteworthy is the large palace compound (figure 8.3), and several groups of temples arranged around small plazas (figure 8.4). At 3,500 sq m (not including the open courtyard) the Calixtlahuaca palace is the second largest Aztec palace (after Yautepec) to be excavated.

The layout and planning of Calixtlahuaca remain somewhat of a mystery. There does not appear to be a central public plaza flanked by a large pyramid and palace. The palace sits alone at the base of the hill, not far from a large, low platform that has not been excavated yet. The circular pyramid – like circular temples at other Aztec sites – does not seem to lie in the urban core district, but rather sits by itself at some distance from the palace. None of the other temple groups (e.g., figure 8.4) are large enough to have served as the central temples of the city. Because García Payón focused his excavations on the major architecture, he uncovered numerous elite or other special burials and offerings at Calixtlahuaca, and these proved to be quite rich. They included hundreds of ceramic vessels; numerous objects of copper and gold; much jewelry of obsidian, rock crystal, and other precious stones; and hundreds of human bones that had been cut with parallel notches (figure 9.10).

Figure 8.4   Temple group at Calixtlahuaca in the Toluca Valley (Photograph by Michael E. Smith)

Social archaeology: Yautepec

Sites like Coatetelco and Calixtlahuaca, excavated following the "monumental archaeology" approach (see chapter 1), provide important information on urban public architecture and the layout of urban core districts, but reveal little of the nature of life in Aztec cities. To gain an idea of the kinds of people who lived in cities and towns, their activities and ways of life, it is necessary to excavate residential structures. This was the goal of the Albany Yautepec project.

Yautepec was an important capital city in Morelos with several nearby city-states subject to its *tlatoani*. As discussed in chapter 6, Yautepec has the largest surviving Aztec royal palace. After the success of the initial seasons of Hortensia de Vega Nova's excavations at the palace, my wife and I were invited by the Mexican government to work at Yautepec. The palace was on the edge of the modern town with Aztec residential areas extending into agricultural fields to the west and south. This left major areas of Aztec Yautepec open for fieldwork. De Vega Nova continued her work at the palace and we concentrated on excavating houses and other features in other parts of the site. Although fieldwork at the palace is still not completed, and our analyses of artifacts are still in progress, the two complementary projects have already uncovered much new information on Aztec urban life.[8]

In our first season of fieldwork, we used surface concentrations of artifacts to trace the size and shape of the Aztec city. This was easy in the plowed fields, but required patience and perseverance within town. Our field crews spent a lot of time knocking on doors and explaining our purpose to the people of Yautepec so that they would let us root around in their yards for potsherds, obsidian, and other traces of Aztec occupation. I was surprised at how well we were able to find artifacts in and around modern Yautepec, and the goodwill of the citizens contributed greatly to our success. We made several hundred collections of artifacts from 2 by 2 m squares (figure 1.9) and used computer-generated maps of artifact density to help draw the borders of Aztec Yautepec. The city reached its maximum extent, 210 ha (2.1 sq km), in the Late Aztec B period, just prior to the Spanish Conquest. Although there were some earlier villages at the site, the major occupation began in the Early Aztec period, which suggests that Yautepec, like other Aztec cities, was founded by Aztlan immigrants.

Our second season was devoted to excavations of houses, garbage middens, and other key areas in and around Aztec Yautepec.[9] We placed excavations in various parts of the modern town, including schoolyards, vacant lots, residential neighborhoods, churchyards, plowed fields, and even a street. In all we placed excavations in 17 different areas of Yautepec. Twelve of these 17 excavations were undertaken specifically to find buried houses. We located and excavated seven Aztec houses (figure 8.5; see also figure 6.5 and accompanying discussion) as well as numerous other domestic deposits.

The locations of the excavations and houses are shown superimposed on our map of Yautepec in figure 8.6. We dug one elite residence (structure 6), five commoner dwellings (structures 1–4 and 7), and one intermediate structure (no. 5). These are among the first urban Aztec houses excavated in central Mexico. We were somewhat surprised that the urban houses (see chapter 6) were quite similar in size and construction to the rural houses we had excavated previously at Cuexcomate and Capilco (chapter 3). The population density of Yautepec was not much higher than the rural sites,[10] and this implies that this city had considerable open space for gardens and fields within its borders.

Preliminary results indicate that there may have been a zone of wealthy residents to the west of the royal palace, perhaps a *calpolli* with primarily nobles and/or wealthy commoners. Although the houses we excavated in other parts of the city were smaller than those in this one neighborhood, we think that most Yautepec residents were fairly prosperous. The artifact assemblages from all of the excavated houses included many imported goods (such as obsidian from Pachuca, salt from the Valley of Mexico lakes, pottery from many parts of central Mexico, and copper and bronze from the Tarascan territory) in addition to local items. In domestic contexts throughout Yautepec, we uncovered considerable evidence for the production of goods such as obsidian tools and jewelry, ceramic figurines, bark paper,

Figure 8.5 Excavation of an urban commoner house in Yautepec. This house was first discovered by a public works crew while grading the street (House 7; see map, figure 8.6) (Photograph by Michael E. Smith)

Figure 8.6   Map of Aztec Yautepec showing the locations of our excavation zones and the houses excavated in 1993. The houses are drawn to a common scale; the largest, House 6, measures 23 by 18.5 m (Drawing by Ellen Cesarski)

and cotton textiles. None of these artifact deposits, however, was heavy enough to suggest that they were the remains of workshops. Unfortunately, we cannot tell from our scattered excavations whether Yautepec had economically specialized *calpolli* similar to those at Otumba.

The locations of the colonial and modern Yautepec settlements, just to the north of Aztec Yautepec, contributed enormously to the success of our fieldwork. In most central Mexican towns the Spanish settlement was constructed directly on top of the Aztec settlement. The Spaniards typically tore down the Aztec pyramid to make a base for construction of a Catholic church. We tested this notion by excavating in and around Yautepec's sixteenth-century church and convent but found no evidence for a temple or other Aztec structure beneath. We do not know why the early Spanish settlers of Yautepec founded their town to the north of the Aztec city, but as archaeologists we are grateful for this turn of events.

Rural and urban

Rural and urban contexts were not as sharply differentiated as they are in modern societies. Most Aztec cities were quite "rural" in appearance, owing to their unplanned residential districts, farming within the urban site, the presence of large houselots, and an overall low population density. Outside of the downtown area, cities did not look much different from towns and villages. A similar comparison can be made in the opposite direction: there was much of the "urban" in the countryside. Nobles lived in rural areas as well as in the city. Many crafts were produced in the countryside, and peasant families were remarkably well connected to central Mexican market networks. Aztec peasants were not impoverished, isolated serfs but rather prosperous and sophisticated producers and consumers.

The explanation for this similarity between the rural and the urban lies in the nature of Aztec economic and political organization. Economic and demographic expansion in the Early Aztec period set the scene for prosperity in both urban and rural areas. In Late Aztec times, the growth of stable city-states made the countryside a safe place to live and work. The ensuing expansion of merchant activity and marketplace trade linked all parts of central Mexico – rural and urban – together into a single economic network. Peasants did not have to move to the city to prosper, and urbanites did not have to give up the farming life or differentiate themselves socially from their country cousins. Tenochtitlan, however, did not fit this pattern of rural-looking cities. The Mexica capital was a settlement of a different order than other Aztec cities.

Tenochtitlan

> *Proud of itself*
> *is the city of Mexico-Tenochtitlan.*
> *Here no one fears to die in war.*
> *This is our glory.*
> *This is Your Command,*
> *oh Giver of Life!*
> *Have this in mind, oh princes,*
> *do not forget it.*
> *Who could conquer Tenochtitlan?*
> *Who could shake the foundation of heaven?*
> **Cantares Mexicanos**

Tenochtitlan was a city built to impress visitors, both human and divine. Just as the city awed the first Spaniards who saw it (see chapter 1) Tenochtitlan also overwhelmed Aztecs visiting from the provinces (figure 8.7).[11] Part of Tenochtitlan's grandeur derived from its sheer size (200,000 inhabitants on an island of 13.5 sq km) and part reflected the deliberate planning and layout of the city. This was not just a political capital and market center. Tenochtitlan was forged into a sacred imperial city whose size and layout proclaimed the Mexica view of their destiny as rulers of the empire.

Urban planning and layout

Tenochtitlan was the last of the city-state centers to be founded by the Aztlan migrants.[12] The Mexica began by constructing a shrine to their god Huitzilopochtli at the place where they had seen the omen of the eagle perched on a cactus. The name Tenochtitlan means "Among the Stone-Cactus Fruit"; its glyph is a fruited nopal cactus growing out of a stone. The town was laid out around the shrine, which was soon enlarged into a stone

Figure 8.7   Reconstruction of the city of Tenochtitlan (looking east) on the eve of Spanish conquest (detail from a painting by Miguel Covarrubias in the Museo Nacional de Antropología e Historia, Mexico City) (Photo: Robert Frerck, Odyssey Productions, Chicago)

pyramid. This structure, with twin stairways leading to two temples, was the earliest stage of the Templo Mayor. In its early days, Tenochtitlan probably resembled the city-state capitals described above, with a formally planned city center surrounded by unplanned residential quarters.

The Mexica's growth in power and influence during the Late Aztec A period (AD 1350–1430) was mirrored by explosive growth in the size and prosperity of Tenochtitlan. In the Late Aztec B period, following the Tepanec war of 1428, Tenochtitlan became capital of the empire and the Mexica set out to redesign the city to differentiate it from other Aztec cities and towns. The Mexica saw themselves as heirs to the powerful ancient empires of Teotihuacan and Tula, and they deliberately appropriated principles and concepts from the ruins of those abandoned capitals in order to refashion Tenochtitlan in their image. First, they used a grid layout, similar to that at Teotihuacan, to establish a common alignment for all buildings. Second, they effected a radical change in the layout of the downtown area by walling off a sacred religious precinct from the rest of the city. Third, they deliberately copied architectural and sculptural styles from Teotihuacan and Tula in their rebuilt downtown area.[13] They also drew on a more recent – but still ancient – tradition when they used the Early Aztec twin-stair style of pyramid for their Templo Mayor. This may have been done in homage to Early Aztec cities rich in historical tradition like Tenayuca.

Unlike the haphazard layouts of most towns and cities, the entire urban area of Tenochtitlan was carefully planned and rebuilt according to fundamental political, religious, and practical principles. The regular grid pattern demonstrated the power of the Mexica rulers. In ancient civilizations around the world, only strong kings were capable of impressing their will on a city by designing the whole settlement sufficiently in advance to produce a grid layout. The application of the grid plan to Tenochtitlan was a public statement about the grandeur and power of the island city and its links to ancient Teotihuacan.

The influence of religion was also felt in the planning and layout of Tenochtitlan. The city's grid was established close to the cardinal directions (the orientation of streets and buildings was 6.5 degrees east of true north). In Mesoamerican cosmology, the four cardinal directions had important symbolic significance, each with its own gods, rituals, and colors. This religious cosmology, which normally found expression only in the central precincts of city-state capitals, was extended to the entire city of Tenochtitlan. Major avenues extended out from the sacred precinct along the cardinal directions, dividing the city into four major quarters (figure 8.8). Because it monitored the path of the sun, the east–west axis was the more important one, and this was reflected in the placement and orientation of the Templo Mayor and other shrines in the sacred precinct.

Figure 8.8   Map of Tenochtitlan and Tlatelolco (After Calnek 1972:108; drawing by Ellen Cesarski)

In addition to these political and religious influences, practical consid-erations also contributed to the adoption of a grid plan at Tenochtitlan. A rectilinear grid is the easiest layout to use in a rapidly expanding city. As rocks and fill were brought from the shore to reclaim land for *chinampas* and houses, it was convenient to lay out canals and roads at right angles, following a single orientation for the entire city.

The Mexica drew upon their knowledge of the central ceremonial zone at Tula (figure 2.3) to redesign their downtown area. In place of the open public plaza bordered by religious and civic buildings that was standard at other Aztec cities, the Mexica created a walled sacred precinct whose buildings were arranged in a pattern similar to that used at Tula, Limiting public access to the precinct was part of a Mexica plan to elevate their religion to a mystical state cult (see chapter 9). In a further break with prior Aztec practice, each Mexica king constructed his own palace rather than reusing a single palace as at smaller Aztec cities. These palaces were built next to, but outside of, the sacred precinct. The Mexica kings further emphasized their associations with Teotihuacan and Tula by erecting buildings in the styles of these ancient capitals; archaeologists have excavated at least one structure in each style near the central Templo Mayor in the sacred precinct. The kings also had sculptures carved in the ancient Teotihuacan and Toltec styles and displayed these in and around the precinct. By the late 1400s the architectural transformation of Tenochtitlan was complete, and the city was one of the largest and most impressive urban centers in the world.

Tlatelolco

A major contribution to the great size and prosperity of Tenochtitlan was its annexation of the adjacent city of Tlatelolco.[14] Tlatelolco had begun as an independent Mexica city-state located on an island just north of Tenochtitlan. During the fifteenth century Tlatelolco developed into the major commercial city of central Mexico. The *pochteca* merchants established Tlatelolco as their base of operations, and its market grew into the largest and richest in the Valley of Mexico. It was perhaps inevitable that the two adjacent city-states would come into conflict with one another, and in 1473 the Mexica emperor Axayacatl conquered Tlatelolco and incorporated the city into the polity of Tenochtitlan. By that time the two cities had expanded into one another, and together they formed a single large urban center (figure 8.8). When we refer to Tenochtitlan after 1473, what is usually meant is the combined twin cities of Tenochtitlan and Tlatelolco.

A large part of the central ceremonial precinct of Tlatelolco has been excavated, providing important information on Aztec urban architecture (figure 8.9). The double-stair main pyramid of Tlatelolco was quite similar to the Templo Mayor of Tenochtitlan in size and plan (see chapter 10).

Associated with the central pyramid are numerous smaller temples and shrines. A circular temple dedicated to Ehecatl was the setting for some of the richest burials and offerings excavated at any Aztec site outside the Templo Mayor of Tenochtitlan (figure 8.9, lower right). Northeast of this was a "calendar temple" decorated with carved day name glyphs. A skull rack platform (small rectangular platform at the top of figure 8.9) had an adjacent burial of human skulls, arranged in neat rows and each perforated on the sides for hanging on poles (see chapter 10). In addition the Tlatelolco ceremonial precinct included an unusual sunken patio and numerous rectangular and circular altars and platforms.

The central precinct of Tlatelolco was almost as luxurious and impressive as that of Tenochtitlan itself, and by the late 1400s the combined urban center of Tenochtitlan/Tlatelolco was the largest and richest city in the New World. What did it look like to visitors?

Fictional visit to the imperial capital

This fictional vignette describes Tenochtitlan from the perspective of a visitor from the provinces.

The young provincial lord Mihua ("Possessor of arrows") has been invited to attend his first state ceremony at the imperial capital. He is the eldest son of the *tlatoani* of Yautepec, who cannot attend because of other commitments. Mihua crosses the mountains on foot with his personal servant, and they pass through several settlements on their way to one of the causeways that lead to Tenochtitlan. These cities and towns are larger and busier than those of his valley at home, he notes. As they start across the western causeway toward the capital, the young noble is greatly impressed at the huge city spread out before him (figures 8.7 and 8.8). He has never seen a road as wide or straight as this causeway, nor an aqueduct as large and well made as the one that runs along the road carrying fresh water to the city from springs at Chapultepec on the shore.[15]

While on the causeway, Mihua marvels at the drawbridges that can be raised to let canoes pass through. He realizes that these could also be pulled up for defense in case of attack. But then who would ever attack this enormous and powerful city? The lake surrounding Tenochtitlan seems full of boats, particularly in the northern area around Tlatelolco, home of the central market. There are the small canoes of individual farmers or craftsmen bringing their goods to market, and the larger vessels with shaded seats carrying fancily dressed lords on their way to the capital.

At the outskirts of the island city Mihua sees miles and miles of greenery from the maize and vegetables that grow year-round in the *chinampa* plots. His servant comments that these densely planted fields make the

TLATELOLCO

Figure 8.9   Map of the ceremonial zone at Tlatelolco; see also figure 12.11 (The arms of the scale are 20 m long. Author: Salvador Guilliem Arroyo; drawing: Fernando Botas; surveyor: Carlos González. Proyecto Tlatelolco 1987–2001, Instituto Nacional de Antropología e Historia. From Guilliem Arroyo [1999:277]. Reproduced with permission)

farms back in Yautepec look pretty scraggly. The Yautepec countryside is known far and wide in the provinces for its highly fertile irrigated croplands, but even the most productive plot cannot match the exuberant maize, beans, and amaranth of the *chinampas*. Long straight canals run everywhere, including both thoroughfares for large boats carrying people and goods, and small canals for farmers moving among their fields. The visitors notice the small, flat-roofed houses of farmers built on solid land in the midst of their family plots.

The provincial lord marvels at a high and mighty Mexica noble, who, dressed in incredible finery, rides in a flat-bottomed barge with a decorated awning for shade. Mihua complains to his servant about the luxurious treatment afforded the Mexica lord while nobles visiting from important cities like Yautepec have to fight their way along the causeway through crowds of merchants, servants, and other commoners.

The visitors come to the end of the *chinampa* area, and the causeway widens into a road traversing the main residential zone of the city. Like the canals and *chinampas*, the roads and houses are all aligned along the same north–south and east–west grid that covers the city. Nonfarming commoners live in small houses similar to their farming cousins, but the houses are packed much closer together than anything back in Yautepec. Several generations of an extended family emerge from a modest house along the avenue, and Mihua is secretly pleased that even in the great Tenochtitlan commoners live crowded together in small houses, just like back home. The travelers come upon a sumptuous two-story house surrounded by well-tended gardens, obviously the palace of a noble. These luxurious buildings become more common along the avenue as the two proceed toward the city center, but smaller commoners' houses can be seen back behind the palaces, off the central thoroughfare.

At the intersection with another wide straight avenue, Mihua glances down to the left and sees towering pyramids and crowds of people. The ceremonial precinct dwarfs any that he has seen before, but he remembers his father's instruction not to be fooled by the district precincts in Tenochtitlan. This is only the center of one of the four great quarters of the city, not the heart of the city that is his destination. Crossing the street, servant and master enter what appears to be a new *calpolli*. Mihua had noticed professional carriers hauling heavy loads of copper and gold to workshops in the last neighborhood. A glimpse of the end of a procession in honor of the god Xipe Totec, patron of metalworkers, confirms his opinion that they had just passed a metalworker's *calpolli*. In this new neighborhood, yards are surrounded by high walls. Some men emerge from a doorway, and Mihua looks in and sees a large, well-built house of a single story. The men are well dressed and prosperous-looking, but they wear the clothing of commoners, not nobles. These must be the famous *pochteca*. Mihua has heard that the city also contains neighborhoods composed entirely of foreigners where people speak strange languages and dress oddly, but he has yet to see any of these people along the main west avenue.

The approach to the center of Tenochtitlan is signaled by larger crowds of people in the streets and plazas and by the increasingly grandiose architecture of nobles' palaces, temple-pyramids, and other government buildings. The huge Templo Mayor looms over the center of the city, the blood on its stairs visible from a great distance. The travelers have arrived at the wall of the sacred precinct and the end of the avenue. Just outside the precinct are several palaces of the Mexica *tlatoque*. Mihua is awed not only at the size and luxury of these compounds (far larger than his father's royal palace back home), but also at their number. Each Mexica *tlatoani* has built his own palace, leaving the homes of his predecessors as monuments to the greatness of the dynasty. Mihua has heard rumors of this practice, which is contrary to the usual Aztec custom of using the same palace for successive kings. He locates the correct palace from his father's instructions and enters the outer courtyard, where he asks directions of an important-looking official. Just then his second cousin, a low-ranking member of the Mexica royal family, arrives and the two young lords head for the sacred precinct to witness a gladiator sacrifice. Mihua's servant stays at the palace to help with various tasks until his lord returns.

The sacred precinct of Tenochtitlan, larger than some provincial towns, greatly impresses Mihua. The walled compound measures about 500 m on a side.[16] Inside he can see numerous temples, altars, shrines, schools, and assembly halls, dominated by the towering twin-stair Templo Mayor pyramid (figure 1.1). He knows that at any time of day, some ceremony is taking place, either a public spectacle such as a sacrifice or procession, or a private ritual by priests, warriors, or other important persons. The size and grandeur of this inner sacred city overwhelms the provincial visitor, who stops to stare. His cousin is amused at this typical newcomer's reaction to the sacred precinct. In Yautepec and other provincial capitals, the state religion is served by a single, modest temple-pyramid located on the central public plaza; here in Tenochtitlan religion occupies its own inner city, closed off from public view and even separated by a wall from the palace of the emperor. These Mexica gods must be powerful indeed, Mihua thinks.

chapter nine
Creation, Death, and the Gods

> *How the gods had their beginning and where they began is not well known. But this is plain, [that] there at Teotihuacan . . . when yet there was darkness, there all the gods gathered themselves together, and they debated who would bear the burden, who would carry on his back – would become – the sun. And when the sun came to arise, then all [the gods] died that the sun might come unto being . . . And thus the ancient ones thought it to be.*
>
> *Bernardino de Sahagún,* Florentine Codex

A fundamental idea of Aztec religion was that the gods sacrificed themselves in order to benefit humankind. In one myth the gods threw themselves into a huge fire to create the sun; in another they spilled their own blood in order to create people. These myths established a debtor relationship between humankind and the gods – a debt that could be repaid only through offerings of human blood and life. Human sacrifice and bloodletting, also known as autosacrifice, were primary forms of ritual in Aztec society.

The earliest Mesoamerican religions focused on agricultural fertility and worship of the sun. The great Classic-period civilizations of the Maya and Teotihuacan harnessed these themes to the goals of the state through selective use of human sacrifice and bloodletting. The Aztecs borrowed much of their religion from their predecessors at Teotihuacan and Tula, but the Aztlan migrants also brought their own gods and rituals with them. Aztec religion was a complex blend of these two traditions, unified by emphases on blood, sacrifice, and debt payment. With their rise to power following the Tepanec war, the Mexica rulers and priests began a deliberate program of transformation of their religion to link the gods, myths, and ceremonies even more strongly to the interests of the state and empire.

Myths of creation provide a gateway into the complexities of Aztec religion. The Aztecs had numerous diverse, even contradictory, myths describing the creation of the world, the gods, people, and things. Four of these myths are presented here to illustrate some of the fundamental concepts of Aztec ritual and belief.[1]

Myths of Creation

The four suns

At the beginning of creation there was an original high god, Ometeotl ("Two Deity"), who existed in both a male form, Ometecuhtli ("Two-Lord"), and a female form, Omecihuatl ("Two-Lady").[2] This couple produced four sons: Tezcatlipoca, Xipe Totec, Quetzalcoatl, and Huitzilopochtli. The latter two were given the task of creating the earth, other gods, and people. With the births of these four gods, a cycle of creation and destruction began that continues to the present day.

There have been four previous ages or "suns," each controlled by a different god and peopled by a distinctive race. Each sun was destroyed by a different cataclysm. The god Tezcatlipoca presided over the first sun, when a race of giants roamed the earth. This sun was destroyed by jaguars who ate the giants and destroyed the earth. During the second sun, presided over by Quetzalcoatl, humans who lived on acorns populated the earth. This sun was destroyed by hurricanes, and the people were transformed into monkeys. People of the third sun, under the god Tlaloc, ate aquatic seeds. The world was destroyed by a fiery rain, and humans were turned into dogs, turkeys, and butterflies. The fourth sun, presided over by Chalchiuhtlicue, was a time of gatherers who ate wild seeds. They were turned into fish in a great flood.

The fifth sun is the age we still live in today. Its presiding deity is Tonatiuh, the sun god, and its people are maize-eaters. According to Aztec myth, this world too will be destroyed, by earthquakes, and its people will be devoured by sky monsters. The destruction of a world age or sun can only come at the end of a 52-year cycle known as the calendar round (see chapter 10), but the number of cycles that will pass before the cataclysm is unknown. Therefore, when a cycle was completed, and the sun began to rise on the first day of a new calendar round, the Aztecs celebrated a ritual known as the New Fire ceremony to give thanks for another cycle of existence. The last New Fire ceremony was conducted in 1507. If the Aztec calendar is projected forward, nine cycles have been completed since that date, and our current cycle will end in AD 2027.

Quetzalcoatl and the bones of the ancestors

The creation of the fifth sun, the current age, fell to Quetzalcoatl and Tezcatlipoca. In one version of this myth, the two gods found the earth completely covered with water from the flood that ended the fourth sun. The giant earth monster Tlaltecuhtli ("Earth Lord"), a crocodile-like creature, swam in the sea searching for flesh to eat. The gods turned themselves into serpents, entered the sea, and tore Tlaltecuhtli in half. The upper part of her body became the land, and the lower part was thrown into the sky to become the stars and heavens. Plants and animals grow from the back of Tlaltecuhtli and rivers pour from her body.

With the land and sky in place, the gods were ready to create people. They sent Quetzalcoatl to the underworld, Mictlan ("Place of the dead"), to retrieve the bones of the people from the fourth sun:

> And then Quetzalcoatl went to Mictlan. He approached Mictlantecuhtli and Mictlancihuatl [Lord and Lady of the underworld]; at once he spoke to them:
>   "I come in search of the precious bones in your possession. I have come for them."
>   And Mictlantecuhtli asked of him, "What shall you do with them, Quetzalcoatl?"
>   And once again Quetzalcoatl said, "The gods are anxious that someone should inhabit the earth."
>   And Mictlantecuhtli replied, "Very well, sound my shell horn and go around my circular realm four times."
>   But his shell horn had no holes.[3]

The false conch horn was the first of several tricks that Mictlantecuhtli used to block Quetzalcoatl's mission. Quetzalcoatl called upon worms to drill a hole in the shell, and bees to make the horn play. When Mictlantecuhtli heard the horn, he at first allowed Quetzalcoatl to gather the bones, but later changed his mind. His helper spirits dug a hole, and a quail appeared and startled Quetzalcoatl, who tripped and lost consciousness. The bones were scattered and broken, and the quail chewed on them. Quetzalcoatl finally rose, gathered up the bones, and escaped from Mictlan.

Quetzalcoatl carried the bones to Tamoanchan, a place of paradise. The old goddess Cihuacoatl ("Woman Serpent") ground them on the *metate* and placed the powder in a jade bowl. Quetzalcoatl and the other gods gathered around and shed their blood upon the ground bones, and the first people of the fifth sun were made.

The birth of the sun at Teotihuacan

Once the earth, people, and maize had been created, the gods gathered in the darkness at Teotihuacan to bring forth the sun. Two gods were chosen for the task: Tecciztecatl, a rich, powerful, and haughty lord, and Nanahuatzin, a weak, poor, scab-covered god. A huge pyre was built for a fire sacrifice. The gods called upon Tecciztecatl to throw himself into the fire. Four times he attempted to do their bidding, only to stop short. Then Nanahuatzin gathered his resolve, ran, and leaped into the flames, where his body was quickly burned up. Shamed at his earlier timidity, Tecciztecatl also jumped into the fire, followed by an eagle and a jaguar. For their bravery, these two animals became warriors, patrons of the two great Aztec military orders.

A great light appeared as Nanahuatzin rose in the east as Tonatiuh, the sun god. Then Tecciztecatl also rose as a second sun. The gods worried that the world would be too bright, so they threw a rabbit at Tecciztecatl to dim his light. He became the moon, on whose surface a rabbit can still be seen today. But the sun did not move in the sky. The gods sent a falcon to ask Tonatiuh why he did not move. He replied, "Why? Because I'm asking for their blood, their color, their precious substance."[4] The gods realized they must sacrifice themselves to make the sun move across the sky. Quetzalcoatl performed the deed, cutting open the chests of the gods and removing their hearts to offer up to Tonatiuh. And so the sun assumed its correct path across the sky. The Aztecs believed that just as these gods sacrificed themselves for the sun, so too people had to provide blood and hearts to keep the sun going.

The heroic birth of Huitzilopochtli

The goddess Coatlicue ("Serpent Skirt") was doing penance and sweeping at Coatepec ("Serpent Hill") when she saw a ball of feathers float down from the sky. She took the feathers and placed them inside her shirt. When she finished sweeping, Coatlicue went to remove the feathers, but they were gone. In fact, they had impregnated the goddess. Her children, the Centzon Huitznahua ("The Four Hundred Southerners") became aware of her pregnancy:

> And when the Centzon Huitznahua saw that their mother was already with child, they were very wrathful. They said, "Who brought this about? Who hath made her heavy with child? She hath dishonored and shamed us!"
> And their elder sister, Coyolxauhqui, said to them, "My elder brothers, she hath affronted us; we must slay our mother, the wicked one who is already with child . . ."

And when Coatlicue learned of this, she was sorely afraid and deeply saddened. And her child, who was in her womb, comforted her. He spoke and said to her: "Have no fear; already I know [what I must do]."[5]

Coyolxauhqui and her siblings dressed for war and climbed the hill of Coatepec toward Coatlicue. Just as they reached the summit, Coatlicue gave birth to Huitzilopochtli. The newborn god was fully mature and ready for battle with his shield, darts, war paint, and Xiuhcoatl (fire-serpent weapon).

Then with it [the Xiuhcoatl] he pierced Coyolxauhqui, and then he quickly struck off her head. It came to rest there on the slope of Coatepec. And her body went falling below; it went crashing in pieces; in various places her arms, her legs, and her body kept falling.[6]

Huitzilopochtli then chased the Centzon Huitznahua and killed most of them.

This mythological event was commemorated on a large carved stone, which depicts Coyolxauhqui's dismembered body (figure 9.1). The Coyolxauhqui stone was part of a buried offering placed in front of the stairway to Huitzilopochtli's shrine on the Templo Mayor. The pyramid itself was referred to as Coatepec, and the human sacrifices that occurred on its summit reenacted Huitzilopochtli's victory over Coyolxauhqui.

Aztec Religion: Historical Background

There is a discrepancy between two of the myths recounted above: in the first myth, Huitzilopochtli is said to have been created by Ometecuhtli and Omecihuatl; in the last, he was born from the womb of Coatlicue. Was Huitzilopochtli a high creator god, or just another patron deity? This is only one example of the numerous inconsistencies and contradictions found in the corpus of Aztec myths and religious accounts. Aztec religion appears to us today as a highly complex and confusing system of gods, myths, rituals, and beliefs. Part of this complexity originated in the incomplete fusion of different historical religious traditions and in the incomplete processes of imperial manipulation and transformation promoted by the Mexica kings. But another source of confusion about Aztec religion derives from the accounts of the sixteenth-century chroniclers who may not have fully understood all of the beliefs and practices that they recorded. Unfortunately their information on religion came not from the experts – Aztec priests – but from laymen. In fact, no Aztec priest ever explained his or her religion to a Spanish chronicler. For these and other reasons the religion of the Aztecs was complex, dynamic, and confusing,

Figure 9.1   Drawing of large stone disk showing Coyolxauhqui's dismembered body (diameter 3.25 m) (Drawing by Emily Umberger; reproduced with permission)

and today we can only claim a very partial and incomplete understanding of it.[7]

The major inspirations for the development of the Aztec gods, myths, and rituals were the traditions of earlier central Mexican civilizations (particularly Teotihuacan), the Aztlan migrants from northern Mexico, and the peoples conquered by the expanding Aztec empire. A number of Aztec gods can be traced back to Classic-period Teotihuacan. Carvings on the Pyramid of the Feathered Serpent, for example, depict two of these deities (figure 9.2). The feathered serpent was either Quetzalcoatl or an earlier

Figure 9.2   Classic-period antecedents of the Aztec gods Tlaloc and
Quetzalcoatl from the Pyramid of the Feathered Serpent at Teotihuacan
(Photograph by Michael E. Smith)

form of this god, and the goggle-eyed figure, known as the storm god at
Teotihuacan, may have been an early form of the Aztec rain god Tlaloc,
or perhaps Xiuhcoatl.[8]

Other gods were brought to central Mexico by the Aztlan migrants.
Huitzilopochtli, whose primary associations were with blood and warfare, had been the patron deity of the Mexica from the time of their migration from Aztlan. The ascension of the Mexica to power was
accompanied by the elevation of Huitzilopochtli from a simple patron
god to a powerful high god. Tlacaelel, advisor to the Mexica kings, "went
about persuading the people that their supreme god was Huitzilopochtli."[9]
The two temples atop the Templo Mayor pyramid were dedicated to Tlaloc
and Huitzilopochtli. These central temples of the Aztec empire symbolized the social and cultural blend that made up the Aztec world: Tlaloc,
the ancient central Mexican god of rain and fertility, sat next to
Huitzilopochtli, the newly arrived Mexica god of warfare and sacrifice.
Some gods also were adopted from conquered peoples and integrated into
the imperial pantheon of Tenochtitlan. The idols of these gods were removed from their home temples and set up in the Coacalco, a special
temple that was a kind of prison for foreign gods.

The Gods

The teotl concept

The Nahuatl term *teotl* means "deity" or "sacred power." This is a complex and multifaceted concept that does not fit well with modern preconceptions of ancient polytheistic religion. We tend to think of ancient gods in terms of the Greek pantheon. Zeus, Athena, Poseidon, and the other Greek gods were very human-like with their own unique personalities, powers, and domains. They often took human form and entered society undetected. Aztec gods, on the other hand, are better viewed as invisible spirits or forces whose roles, natures, and forms blended together. Each deity had certain characteristic attributes or insignia. Many of these, such as hats, pendants, clothing, and jewelry, were shared by more than one god. As a result scholars often disagree over the correct identification of gods in the codices or sculptures. Gods were sometimes depicted in human form, and on ritual occasions, people impersonated deities by dressing in their insignia. One would never have mistaken a god for a person, however.

Many gods had special roles as patrons of particular social or ethnic groups. Just as Huitzilopochtli was the patron of the Mexica people, many cities and *calpolli* had their own patron gods. Occupational groups also had their own gods: Tezcatlipoca was the patron of kings, Quetzalcoatl of priests, Teteoinnan of midwives, and Xipe Totec of goldsmiths.

Written sources contain names for as many as 200 distinct gods and goddesses, several of whom were closely related to one another, sometimes as transformations of a single deity. One such common transformation involved the concept of duality. Ometeotl (god of duality, literally "Two-Deity"), for example, contained male and female transformations, Ometecuhtli ("Two-Lord") and Omecihuatl ("Two-Lady"). Sometimes Quetzalcoatl was a priestly creator god, but at other times he donned special insignia to become Ehecatl, god of wind.

It is difficult to keep track of Aztec deities with all of their transformations and blending. Ethnohistorian H. B. Nicholson has superimposed an order upon this pantheon by classifying the gods into 14 complexes of closely related deities. He groups these complexes into three overarching themes: celestial creativity and divine paternalism; rain, moisture, and agricultural fertility; and war, sacrifice, blood, and death (table 9.1). Each of the deities in the table is at the head of a complex or group of gods and goddesses who are related in their themes and roles. These 14 complexes encompass 129 deities as listed by Nicholson. An

Table 9.1   The principal Aztec deities

Deity	Meaning	Themes and roles
Deities of celestial creativity and divine paternalism		
Ometeotl	Two-god	Original creator of the gods
Tezcatlipoca	Smoking mirror	Omnipotent power, patron of kings
Xiuhtecuhtli	Turquoise lord	Hearth and fire
Deities of rain, moisture, and agricultural fertility		
Tlaloc	(uncertain)	Rain, water, agricultural fertility
Centeotl	Maize god	Maize
Ometochtli	Two rabbit	*Pulque*, maguey, fertility
Teteoinnan	Mother of gods	Earth and fertility; patroness of curers and midwives
Xipe Totec	Our lord with the flayed skin	Agricultural fertility; patron goldsmiths
Deities of war, sacrifice, blood, and death		
Tonatiuh	He goes forth shining	Sun
Huitzilopochtli	Hummingbird of the left or south	War, sacrifice, sun; patron of the Mexica
Mixcoatl	Cloud-serpent	War, sacrifice, hunting
Mictlantecuhtli	Lord of the place of death	Death, underworld, darkness
Other deities		
Quetzalcoatl	Quetzal-feathered serpent	Creation, fertility, Venus, wind; patron of priesthood
Yacatecuhtli	Nose-lord	Commerce; patron of merchants

Each of these deities heads a deity complex of closely related gods and goddesses.
Source: Nicholson 1971:table 3

example of a deity complex, the Tezcatlipoca complex, is shown in table 9.2. Tezcatlipoca ("Smoking Mirror"), was the most powerful god in terms of influence on people's lives. Four gods in this complex – Moyocoyani, Telpochtli, Titlacahuan, and Yaotl – are versions of Tezcatlipoca himself, and the others are deities closely related to the smoking mirror. I have used Nicholson's system to structure the following descriptions of the gods.[10]

Table 9.2   Gods of the Tezcatlipoca complex

Deity	Meaning	Themes and roles
Tezcatlipoca	Smoking mirror	Omnipotent universal power
Chalchiuhtotolin	Jade turkey	Penitence
Itztli	Obsidian blade	Justice, punishment
Ixquimilli	Eye-bundle	Justice, punishment
Metztli	Moon	Moon
Moyocoyani	Maker of himself	Universal power
Omacatl	Two reed	Feasting, revelry
Tecciztecatl	Person from the place of conch-shells	Moon
Telpochtli	Male youth	Patron of *telpochcalli* school
Tepeyollotl	Heart of the hill	Caves, darkness, jaguars
Titlacahuan	We his slaves	Universal power
Yaotl	Enemy	Universal power

It is not clear whether all of these were separate deities or alternative names for Tezcatlipoca.
Source: Nicholson 1971:table 3

Deities of celestial creativity and divine paternalism

Nicholson's first theme, celestial creativity and divine paternalism, covers the original creation of the world and the ultimate source of life.[11]

Ometeotl. In his guise as the couple Ometecuhtli and Omecihuatl, Ometeotl was the original creator of the gods and the world. These abstract celestial deities were invoked in sacred poetry and philosophical works, but had no formal cult dedicated to their worship.

Tezcatlipoca. Tezcatlipoca is often described as the Aztec high god (figure 9.3). In his obsidian mirror, "Tezcatlipoca could see all that took place in the world,"[12] and he carried arrows to inflict punishment on wrongdoers. People were filled with fear and dread before the awesome power of Tezcatlipoca:

> Thus I fall before thee, I throw myself before thee; I cast myself into the place whence none rise, whence none leave, the place of terror, of fear. May I not have aroused thy annoyance; may I not have walked upon thy fury. O master, O precious nobleman, O our lord, perform thy office, do thy work![13]

It is fitting that this most powerful god was the patron of kings.

QUETZALCOATL   TEZCATLIPOCA   MICTLANTECUHTLI

XOCHIQUETZAL   TLALOC

Figure 9.3 Five Aztec gods. Quetzalcoatl and Tezcatlipoca (Codex Borbonicus 1974:22); Mictlantecuhtli (Codex Borbonicus 1974:10); Xochiquetzal (Codex Telleriano-Remensis; Quiñones Keber 1995:f.22v); Tlaloc (Codex Borgia 1976:pl.20) (Drawing by Ellen Cesarski)

Xiuhtecuhtli. Xiuhtecuhtli was associated with fire and life. Fire figured prominently in many rituals and a sacred fire was always kept burning at the temples. In his manifestations as Huehueteotl ("Old God"), this god presided over the domestic hearth fire, where household rituals were performed. Two goddesses in this complex were Chantico ("In the House") and Coyolxauhqui ("Painted with Bells"), the unlucky rebellious sister of Huitzilopochtli (figure 9.1).

Deities of rain, moisture, and agricultural fertility

The gods of rain, moisture, and agricultural fertility were among the most worshiped of Aztec deities, by both priests and lay persons. Nicholson groups the many fertility gods into five complexes.[14]

Tlaloc. The ancient storm god of Teotihuacan (figure 9.2) is a possible ancestor of Tlaloc, the principal rain god among the Aztecs. One of the major earth deities, Tlaloc's main purpose was to send rain to nourish maize and other crops. In figure 9.3 he is shown using a digging stick to cultivate maize in an irrigated field. Tlaloc had four or five versions or transformations, the Tlaloque, who assisted him. They brewed the rain in huge vats in caves on mountaintops, from whence they also sent out thunder and lightening.

Centeotl. The cult of the maize god Centeotl overlapped the cult of the Tlaloc complex. The cult included various deities of solar warmth, flowers, feasting, and pleasure, such as Xochipilli ("Flower Prince") and Macuilxochitl ("Five Flower"), the patron of the game *patolli*.

Ometochtli. Ometochtli was one of a group of 400 rabbits, the Centzon totochtin, who were deities of the alcoholic beverage *pulque*. The goddess Mayahuel was a fertility figure who personified the maguey plant itself.

Teteoinnan. Teteoinnan represented a complex of many female earth deities that were associated with agricultural and sexual fertility. An important member of this group was Xochiquetzal ("Flower-Quetzal Feather"; see figure 9.3), a young and attractive goddess of sexual desire, flowers, feasting, and pleasure. She was the female counterpart of Xochipilli and Macuilxochitl and had jurisdiction over pregnancy and childbirth. Xochiquetzal was also the patroness of spinning and weaving. Tlazolteotl ("Filth Goddess"), another earth mother figure, was associated with sexual excess and childbirth (figure 9.4). Just as the earth was the place of birth, it was also the place of death. Several goddesses in this complex have affiliations with death, among them Cihuacoatl ("Serpent Woman"), Coatlicue ("Serpent Skirt," the mother of Huitzilopochtli) and the Tzitzimime, poorly understood female spirits or deities.

Xipe Totec. Xipe Totec was a powerful fertility god and the object of a gruesome ritual of sacrifice. After the victim was killed, his skin was removed to be worn by a priest or by a deity impersonator who symbolically became the god. Carved and painted images of Xipe Totec can be identified by the flayed skin that covers the wearer inside; the sculpture in figure 9.5 is a particularly graphic example.

Deities of war, sacrifice, blood, and death

Deities of war, sacrifice, blood, and death required human blood in order to maintain the earth, the sun, and life itself. This blood was

Figure 9.4   The goddess Tlazolteotl giving birth (height 20 cm) (Photograph courtesy of Dumbarton Oaks Research Library and Collections, Washington, DC)

provided through either autosacrifice – personal bloodletting as a form of worship – or human sacrifice. Because most sacrificial victims were obtained in battle, these deities encouraged warfare and, hence, imperial expansion.

Tonatiuh. Tonatiuh, the sun god, overlapped considerably with Ometeotl and represented a kind of high creator god. Whereas the benign, fertility related aspects of the sun were represented in the Centeotl complex, Tonatiuh was more involved in the militaristic and sacrificial aspects of the sun. He was the patron god of warriors, who fulfilled their duty to the sun by capturing prisoners to sacrifice on the pyramid.[15]

Huitzilopochtli. With strong solar associations, the powerful war god Huitzilopochtli required a constant supply of sacrificial victims.

Figure 9.5   The god Xipe Totec. The deity wears the flayed skin of a sacrificial victim, tied across his back (height 77 cm) (Photograph courtesy of the National Museum of the American Indian, Smithsonian Institution, 16/3261)

Mixcoatl. Mixcoatl and the closely related Camaxtli were gods of warfare and hunting. Originally associated with northern Chichimec groups, these deities became patrons of the Tlaxcalteca, Huexotzinca, and other enemy Aztec groups east of the Valley of Mexico. Another god in this complex was Tlahuizcalpantecuhtli, a god of stars and the sky closely connected to the planet Venus.

Mictlantecuhtli. There were many gods and goddesses of death and the underworld, of whom Mictlantecuhtli (figure 9.3) was the most prominent. Tlaltecuhtli ("Earth Lord"), who was torn in half to form the earth and the sky, also belonged to this complex. These and other death deities had strong symbolic links to health and fertility (see below).

Other deities

Two deities do not fit easily into the three themes described above: Quetzalcoatl and Yacatecuhtli.[16]

Quetzalcoatl. Quetzalcoatl, the feathered serpent (figure 9.3), was one of the most important gods of ancient Mesoamerica. His attributes cut across all of the above themes. As a prime creator, he was associated with Ometeotl and Tezcatlipoca, and in his guise as Ehecatl, god of the wind, he belonged with Tlaloc. Temples dedicated to Ehecatl were circular in shape so that the wind could blow easily around them (see chapter 10). The patron of the *calmecac* school and of the priesthood, Quetzalcoatl was a god of learning and knowledge. The high priests of Tenochtitlan were given the title "Quetzalcoatl."

Yacatecuhtli. Yacatecuhtli was the patron god of the *pochteca* merchants.

Death, Burial, and the Afterlife

The prominence of sacrifice, blood, death and the underworld in Aztec mythology was matched by an abundance of death symbols in everyday life. Mictlantecuhtli (figures 9.3, 10.11) was not the only deity with skeletal attributes; numerous other gods and goddesses had skulls for their heads, or else wore clothing decorated with skulls or crossed long bones. The motif of a skull with crossed bones was a common theme in Aztec iconography. It occurred on ceramic vessels used in royal feasts and rituals (figure 9.6) and was carved or painted on low stone ceremonial platforms or altars at numerous Aztec cities. To our modern, western way of thinking this looks like a gruesome symbol of death and terror; indeed, the skull and crossbones was the element of the "Jolly Roger" flag of the feared Caribbean pirates.[17] But in the Aztec world skeletal imagery, particularly the skull and crossbones motif, were symbols of fertility, health, and abundance. There was a close symbolic link between death and fertility, between the bones of the dead and the health of the living. The gods and goddesses of death were in fact deities of fertility with powers to help people.[18]

Figure 9.6   Serving bowl decorated with skull and crossbones (diameter 15.5 cm) (Photograph courtesy of the Milwaukee Public Museum; catalog no. 54467)

Aztec attitudes toward death were quite complex and multifaceted. Important aspects of these beliefs were expressed in funerals, burial practices, and myths about the underworld. The Aztecs believed in several distinct afterworlds, and one's fate depended upon one's status in life and upon the manner of one's death.[19] Soldiers who died in battle and sacrificial victims went to an eastern solar realm to accompany the sun during its rise to zenith. Women who died in childbirth went to a western solar realm where they accompanied the sun during its setting. People who died by drowning or other causes related to the rain god (such as lightning or certain diseases) went to the earthly paradise of Tlalocan. Most people, however went to one of the nine levels of *Mictlan*, the underground realm of death.

Friar Durán gives information on Aztec funerals and burial:

> Some people were buried in the fields; others, in the courtyards of their own homes; others were taken to shrines in the wood; others were cremated and their ashes buried in the temples. No one was interred without being dressed in his mantles, loincloths, and fine stones. In sum, none of his possessions

Figure 9.7   Remains of a commoner child buried next to his family's house at Capilco (Photograph by Michael E. Smith)

were left behind; and if he was cremated, the jar which received his ashes was filled with his jewelry and stones, no matter how costly. Dirges similar to our responses were chanted, and [the dead] were mourned, great ceremonies taking place in their honor. At these funerals [people] ate and drank; and if [the deceased] had been a person of quality, lengths of cloth were presented to those who had attended the funeral. [The dead man] was laid out in a room for four days until [mourners] arrived from the places where he had friends. Gifts were brought to the dead man; and if the deceased was a king or chieftain of a town, slaves were killed in his honor to serve him in the afterlife . . . The funeral rites lasted for ten days filled with sorrowful, tearful chants.[20]

Some of these practices are evident in a series of commoner burials I excavated at Cuexcomate, Capilco, and Yautepec. All of the skeletons at the first two sites were children or infants. They were buried under the housefloor or in the yard next to the house. Most were placed in an upright sitting position, which coincides with images of mummy bundles in Aztec pictorial sources. Some individuals were buried with ceramic bowls as offerings, whereas others were buried without any goods (figure 9.7). At Yautepec we found both infant burials and adults (figure 9.8). The placement of burials in and around the house gives clues to Aztec

Figure 9.8 Remains of commoner adults buried next to House 4 at Yautepec (Photograph by Lisa Montiel)

Figure 9.9 Burial of a king. The corpse is wrapped in a shroud and wears a necklace and feather headdress. The man and woman with offerings (including a cup of cacao, a tripod bowl with meat, and *tamales* in a basket) are servants who will be buried alive with the king "in order to prepare food, for it was not known where they were going" (Códice Tudela 1980:288) (After Códice Tudela 1980:f.58r)

attitudes toward death. The dead were still considered part of the family, and they took their place within the domestic compound. It is likely that families conducted rituals or made offerings to their deceased members, much as modern Mesoamerican peoples do in the Day of the Dead ceremonies on November 2.[21]

Burials of kings and nobles were much richer and more elaborate than the simple commoner burials I have excavated. Apart from two funerary urns recovered at the Templo Mayor – which may contain the ashes of Mexica kings – no true royal burials have been excavated at Aztec sites. An image from the Códice (Codex) Tudela (figure 9.9) shows the funeral of a king. The body is being presented with food and cotton capes by servants who are both chanting and crying. The cremated burial of a noble or important warrior was excavated at the Eagle-Warrior Hall near the Templo Mayor of Tenochtitlan, and this gives an idea of the nature of noble burials. The remains were accompanied by decorated textiles, gold jewelry, bronze objects, jaguar claws, and fancy heirloom ceramic vessels from Classic-period Teotihuacan and Toltec-period Tula.[22]

At Calixtlahuaca, José García Payón excavated a series of secondary burials in ceremonial locations that may pertain to nobles or other important persons (figure 9.10). Secondary burials result from a two-stage process of interment. First the body is left to decay naturally, perhaps in a tomb. Then the bones are gathered and reburied in their final resting place, often with offerings. The Calixtlahuaca burials were interred adjacent to and in front of temples, and had rich offerings of ceramic vessels, bronze objects, jewelry, and other items. They are unusual in that the femurs and other long bones were cut with parallel notches prior to final burial

A.   B.

Figure 9.10   Drawing of two ceremonial secondary burials with offerings at Calixtlahuaca; note the notched femurs. (A) Burial 1 from the circular pyramid (see figure 10.10), associated with a buried sculpture of Ehecatl. (B) Burial from Structure 5 (García Payón 1941:66, 67).

(figure 9.10). These cut bones are not uncommon at Aztec sites and are another example of the prevalence of death and skeletal imagery in Aztec society.[23] There may have been a specific symbolic association between the cut bones and the practice of human sacrifice; in many cases a femur from a sacrificed victim was preserved and displayed by the person who sponsored a sacrificial ceremony. It is to the practice and significance of Aztec human sacrifice that we now turn.

chapter ten
Temples and Ceremonies

The most important and solemn feast, in which the most splendid ceremonies took place, was that of the god known as Tezcatlipoca. These superstitious people commemorated it with such varied rites and sacrifices that it was a wondrous thing . . . The temple in which the idol of Tezcatlipoca stood was lofty and magnificently built. Eight steps led to a landing twelve or fourteen feet wide. Beyond it stood a wide, long chamber the size of a great hall . . . No one dared enter this place, with the sole exception of the priests appointed to serve in the cult of the god.

Diego Durán, Book of the Gods and Rites
and the Ancient Calendar

Aztec pyramid-temples were imposing buildings, "lofty and magnificently built" in Friar Durán's terms. Their vivid impact on people – Aztecs as well as the conquering Spaniards – derived not only from their architecture, but also from the bloody sacrificial ceremonies that occurred at the top of the stairs. The stairs of pyramids were stained red-brown with the dried blood of sacrificial victims. This chapter explores rituals like human sacrifice and the temples where they took place. But first we need to consider the priests who supervised these ceremonies.

Priests

Each of the gods had one or more temples where its idol was kept, and each had a group of full-time priests dedicated to its worship.[1] Most priests were men who had begun their training early, in the *calmecac*. Noble youths who showed ability and inclination were joined by promising commoner boys whose parents had dedicated them to the priesthood. These young men carried the title *tlamacazton* ("little priest") and spent about a year learning the rudiments of priestly lore and duties. The most accomplished of them were chosen to become full priests, or *tlamacazqui* ("giver of things"). Female priests, *cihuatlamacazqui* or "female giver of things," were less common than males. Also trained at the *calmecac*, most of these women served for only a short while and then left the priesthood to marry.

Priests had three main types of duties. Most important was the performance of rituals. Priests kept the sacred fires burning in large braziers, played music at ceremonies, and made numerous offerings to the gods. They left food for idols, offered their own blood by autosacrifice, and burned incense. Incense made from the sap of the copal tree was offered at nearly all ritual occasions. Priests used long-handled "frying-pan" incense burners. At one end was a shallow dish where the copal incense was burned, and the other end of the long handle was shaped like a serpent head. Inside the hollow handle were small clay pellets that produced a rattling sound like a rattlesnake's tail. These censers, with their serpent symbolism, were often depicted in drawings of priests and ceremonies (figure 10.1). Whole censers have been excavated from offerings at temples (figure 10.2), and I found numerous broken fragments in a trash deposit behind the temple at Cuexcomate. But priests were not the only ones to use the long-handled censers. Sahagún shows a woman using such a censer to offer incense around her hearth (figure 10.1E), and archaeologists have excavated countless fragments in domestic deposits at Aztec sites. The same kinds of censers used by priests at temples were also used for domestic rituals in the home (see below).

A second type of priestly duty was administration and caretaking. Priests managed the economy of the temples, including construction, personnel, and provisions. They took care of the idols and sacred objects, and were constantly sweeping for cleanliness and symbolic purification. The third priestly duty was in the realm of education and learning. Priests ran the *calmecac*, supervised the *tlamacazton* and lay personnel, and kept the sacred books. Priests were literate, and were the repositories of Aztec learning and knowledge concerning the gods and rituals, the calendar, and astronomy.

Above the *tlamacazqui* was a smaller group of elite priests called fire priests, *tlenamacac* or "fireseller." These priests were responsible for the performance of the highest ritual – human sacrifice. Regular priests assisted at the stone of sacrifice, but only a fire priest could wield the lethal flint knife. At the top of the priestly hierarchy were two high priests with the title *quetzalcoatl*. The holiest and most devout of all priests, one presided over each temple at the top of the Templo Mayor pyramid – the Tlaloc temple and the Huitzilopochtli temple.

Figure 10.1 The use of long-handled censers as depicted in the codices. (A) Priest with censer and maguey thorn for autosacrifice (Codex Magliabechiano 1983:f.87); (B) The deity Cipactonal with priestly paraphernalia, including a censer (Codex Borbonicus 1974:21) (C) Priest using censer in a Tlaloc ceremony (Sahagún 1950–82:bk.6:fig.10); (D) Novice priest with paraphernalia (Codex Mendoza 1992:f. 63r); (E) Woman offering incense at home (Sahagún 1950–82:bk.7:fig.18) (Tracings by Benjamin Karis)

Figure 10.2 Long-handled censer decorated with small circular reliefs; the end of the handle is a serpent head (length 70 cm) (Photograph courtesy of the Saint Louis Art Museum, no. 257-1978)

Priests must have presented a terrible picture to outsiders. Their faces and bodies were dyed black. Much of their body was scarred and mutilated from constant bloodletting. Their unwashed hair, worn long, became matted with dried blood from their ears and tongue. The fire priests and their assistants were also covered with blood from sacrifices. Why so much blood?

Human Blood Offerings

The myths recounted in chapter 9 established the rationale for human blood offerings. The gods sacrificed themselves to create the world and sun, and offered their own blood to create people. Humankind owed a tremendous debt to the gods, and this debt could only be discharged through frequent offerings of human blood. The Aztecs accomplished this duty through two practices: autosacrifice and human sacrifice.

Autosacrifice

The god Quetzalcoatl performed the first act of autosacrifice when he bled himself to give life to the bones of the ancients. Other gods also bled themselves, as shown in a carved stone relief from Tenochtitlan (figure 10.3A) in which Tezcatlipoca and Huitzilopochtli pierce their ears. All people engaged in autosacrifice at some point in their lives, usually to petition the gods for agricultural or human fertility. Human blood was linked to fertility in all Mesoamerican religions, and blood was the most valuable substance one could offer to the gods.

The most common act of autosacrifice was to pierce one's earlobes or upper ear with pointed maguey thorns. Sometimes other parts of the body were pierced, including the tongue, thigh, upper arm, chest, and genitals. The most devout practitioners (priests, for the most part) would pierce their flesh and then pull hollow straws or reeds through the hole. Priests engaged in autosacrifice nightly. They bathed and purified themselves, burnt incense, and proceeded to a secluded spot where they carried out the ritual. Friar Sahagún listed four different kinds of bloodletting practiced by the priests: "the drawing of straws," "the offering of thorns," "the bloodying," and "the cutting of ears"[2] (figure 10.3B).

Although autosacrifice was an important and prevalent ritual, it was only a substitute for the more powerful human sacrifice. In the words of art historian Cecilia Klein, "autosacrifice from the beginning was viewed as a symbolic death substituted for the real thing and, as such, as a debt payment made in return for continued life."[3]

Figure 10.3　Rituals of autosacrifice. (A) The gods Tezcatlipoca and Huitzilopochtli pierce their ears with pointed bones (from a carved stone; image after Nicholson and Quiñones Keber 1983:31); (B) Two priests pierce their tongue and ear with maguey thorns (After Codex Magliabechiano 1983:f.79r) (Drawings by Ellen Cesarski)

Heart sacrifice

Friar Sahagún's Nahua informants described a heart sacrifice as follows:

> Thus was performed the sacrificial slaying of men, when captives and slaves died, who were called "Those who have died for the god."
> Thus they took [the captive] up [to the pyramid temple] before the devil,[4] [the priests] going holding him by his hands. And he who was known as the arranger [of captives], this one laid him out upon the sacrificial stone.
> And when he had laid him upon it, four men stretched him out, [grasping] his arms and legs. And already in the hand of the fire priest lay the [sacrificial] knife, with which he was to slash open the breast of the ceremonially bathed [captive].
> And then, when he had split open his breast, he at once seized his heart. And he whose breast he laid open was quite alive. And when [the priest] had seized his heart, he dedicated it to the sun.[5]

After the heart was removed, the victims "were sent rolling down the steps of the temple, and the steps were bathed in blood."[6] A priest then cut off the head for mounting on a skull rack next to the pyramid. Such a sacrifice is illustrated in the Codex Magliabechiano (figure 10.4).

The victims of this ritual were not considered ordinary mortals. They

Figure 10.4   A heart sacrifice on a temple-pyramid. Next to the feather banner the heart is offered up to the sun. The body of the victim of a previous sacrifice rests at the base of the stairs, which are covered with blood (After Codex Magliabechiano 1983:f.70r; drawing by Ellen Cesarski)

were viewed as deities whose deaths repeated the original sacrificial deaths of gods described in myth. The key Aztec concept here was *ixiptla*, often translated as "deity impersonator." The preparations for a sacrifice began long before the actual cut of the knife, sometimes as much as a year in advance. A victim was chosen to become the god on a set date some time in the future. Through a series of rites, the human victim was transformed into the embodiment of the god on earth. The greatly respected *ixiptla* spent his last days or months living as a god, and when the day of sacrifice arrived, he went with honor to meet his fate.

Most victims for sacrifice were enemy warriors captured in battle. The captor sponsored the sacrifice, thereby gaining prestige. The higher the rank of the victim, the greater the honor. Captives were brought back from the battleground and housed until the time for their ceremony of transformation. Victims were carefully chosen to match the requirements of the god to be honored. Most gods required warriors for their *ixiptla* although some were satisfied with slaves purchased for the occasion. Tlaloc required children for his *ixiptla*, either purchased as slaves or the secondary offspring of nobles. Women were sometimes sacrificed as *ixiptla* for female deities. The most stringent requirements were those of Tezcatlipoca for the sacrifice in the ceremony of Toxcatl. His *ixiptla*, selected a full year in advance, had to be a handsome, well-bred youth with no bodily imperfections.

The transformation from human to *ixiptla* began with a physical and ritual cleansing. Slaves purchased for sacrifice in particular had to be bathed carefully to erase all traces of impurity. The cleansed victim was then dressed in the clothing and insignia of the god. Once fully attired, he became the god and was addressed and worshiped accordingly. The *ixiptla* carried out the rituals specified for that god, such as dancing, singing, and making special ceremonial processions through the city. He was attended by priests and given many luxuries, including delicacies to eat and women for sexual pleasure.

To be chosen as an *ixiptla* was considered a great honor. Warriors were prepared to die proudly and honorably if they were captured. The respect and admiration granted an *ixiptla* must have affected the victim greatly. According to the nobles who gave Friars Sahagún and Durán their information, sacrificial victims mounted the bloody steps of the pyramid with dignity and pride.

Not all sacrifices took place on top of a pyramid. The cult of Xipe Totec, whose priests dressed in the flayed skin of sacrificial victims (figure 9.5), included two spectacular forms of sacrifice. In the so-called "gladiator sacrifice" an especially brave captive warrior was tied to a large, carved, circular stone and forced to fight a mock battle with an experienced Mexica soldier. The victim was given a sword whose obsidian blades had been replaced by feathers, but his adversary was fully armed and dressed for battle. In the "arrow sacrifice" the victim was tied spread-eagled to a wooden frame and shot full of arrows so that his blood dripped on the ground. In addition to these sacrifices to Xipe Totec, some victims were sacrificed by burning in a large fire pit, and others simply had their necks slit.

Many sacrifices were followed by a ceremonial meal at the home of the family of the captor or sponsor. Often the femur of the victim was hung up and displayed publicly at this occasion; perhaps the notched femurs excavated at Calixtlahuaca and elsewhere (figure 9.10) had once been displayed this way. At the special meal the family ate a portion of the victim's body. This was a highly religious occasion designed to honor the victim's memory. The victim was viewed as a symbolic kin relation of his captor, and this act of cannibalism was a sacred part of the whole ritual of sacrifice. Only a portion of the body was eaten, for this meal had a symbolic not a nutritional significance.[7] The gods also partook of the blood of the victims. After some sacrifices, the sponsor gathered up the blood in a bowl and "placed upon the lips of all [the images of] the devils the blood of him who had died for the gods."[8]

Explaining Aztec sacrifice

Many ancient peoples around the world practiced human sacrifice, from the Greeks and Hebrews to the Inca and Maya. But few cultures made sacrifice such a central part of their religion as the Aztecs, and few cultures carried out human sacrifice on the same scale as the Aztecs.[9] Over the years anthropologists have attempted to account for the importance and prevalence of human sacrifice in Aztec religion. Some very different hypotheses have been proposed to explain this phenomenon. The most obvious explanation, one that would have been given by the Aztecs themselves, is that the gods required human sacrifices. Aztec religion held that sacrifices were needed to keep the universe going, and this theme is prominent in mythology (chapter 9). Furthermore, human sacrifice was seen as a primary means of atonement or expiation for moral transgressions.[10] Most Aztecs were deeply religious people, and they believed their myths and religious precepts. Simply put, priests practiced sacrifice, and people put up with sacrifice because they believed that it was necessary for the continued existence of the universe.

This religious explanation for human sacrifice is fine as far as it goes. One cannot understand the existence or nature of such practices without reference to the beliefs behind them. Nevertheless, anthropologists know that a people's own rationalization for their behavior often provides only a partial explanation for their actions. Aztec myths may explain why people practiced human sacrifice, but not why they practiced it so frequently. Nor do they explain why sacrifice was so common among the many widely dispersed ethnic groups who made up Aztec civilization. Could not the Aztecs have held fast to their myths and paid their debt to the gods with only a few sacrifices a year and with far less elaboration in the means of killing victims? To understand the pervasive nature of Aztec human sacrifice, one must consider not only religious belief, but also the other purposes human sacrifice may have served in Aztec society.

In the 1970s anthropologist Michael Harner gained media attention for his suggestion that the prevalence of sacrifice among the Aztecs could be explained by a lack of protein in their diet. Compared to most cultures around the world, the Aztec diet contained very little meat. Certainly, the rapidly growing population had depleted the game resources of most areas and the Aztecs did not have large, domesticated herd animals on which they could rely for meat. Therefore, Harner argued, sacrifice was stepped up to provide meat in the diet. This theory is more noteworthy for its media attention than for its scholarly rigor.[11] As I discussed in chapter 3, the relatively small contribution of meat to the Aztec diet did not prevent people from getting adequate protein. Processed maize was complemented by beans to provide a complete protein source. Intensification of agricultural practices gave larger crop yields. The Aztecs did not need to resort to cannibalism to meet their protein needs.

A third explanation for the extent of Aztec human sacrifice, the explanation most commonly accepted today, stresses political factors. Aztec politics and religion were closely entwined. Kings ruled with the blessing of the gods, and the priests and temples were under the protection of the state. Human sacrifices were carried out in the service of politics. They were used as a form of external propaganda to demonstrate to other kingdoms the awesome power of the gods and the state. Extensive sacrifices at major public ceremonies advertised this power to subjects, allies, and enemies alike. Enemy rulers who attended the coronation of a Mexica king, for example, and were forced to witness the sacrifice of their own captured soldiers received a potent message about the superiority and might of the Aztec empire.

Propaganda by terror also was directed toward commoner subjects. Sacrifices were public spectacles that took place in highly visible settings – on top of the pyramid and in the open city plaza. Witnessing the gruesome deaths of not only enemy soldiers but also local slaves, infants, and the occasional free commoner must have made most people think twice before engaging in any form of resistance against their king or local noble. Just as commoners paid tribute in goods and services to nobles, so humans paid sacred tribute in blood to the gods. Both practices were obligatory debt payments, and the analogy between tribute and sacrifice was not lost on the Aztec people. This political use of human sacrifice was a feature of all Aztec city-states, not just Tenochtitlan. The Mexica of Tenochtitlan, however, carried sacrifice to great lengths, particularly at the great central temple-pyramid, the Templo Mayor.

The Templo Mayor

The primary site of human sacrifices in Tenochtitlan was the huge temple-pyramid known as the Templo Mayor. This massive stone monument was located in the sacred precinct, a walled holy city that covered 25 ha (about 35 acres) in the heart of Tenochtitlan.

The sacred precinct of Tenochtitlan

Most Aztec cities had a central religious area whose pyramids and other monuments faced a public plaza where crowds gathered to witness ceremonies (chapter 8). At Tenochtitlan the Mexica walled off this central sacred zone, which became an inner city of its own (figure 1.1). Priests and nobles could enter the sacred precinct, and commoners were probably invited in to attend key ceremonies. Friar Sahagún included only the most prominent temples, shrines, and halls in his illustration of the precinct (figure 10.5); Spanish eyewitness descriptions listed over 70 individual structures.[12]

The Templo Mayor, with its bloodstained twin stairways, dominated the precinct (figure 10.5, no. 1). The artist who painted Sahagún's illustration wanted to make sure that he portrayed the Huitzilopochtli temple in sufficient detail, so he added an enlargement above the main temple (no. 2). Huitzilopochtli (or his *ixiptla*) is shown wearing the god's characteristic feathered headdress and carrying his fire-serpent weapon. Standard-bearers (probably stone statues) flank the Templo Mayor. Just in front of the central temple is a low, circular platform dedicated to the wind god Ehecatl (no. 3). A priest with an incense burner and incense bag stands on the platform. Below the platform is the skull rack (*tzompantli*), with two skulls shown (no. 4). One of Cortés's soldiers reported that the great skull rack in the sacred precinct held 136,000 skulls; this estimate is probably exaggerated. Below the *tzompantli* is a ballcourt (no. 5).

To the right of the Ehecatl shrine, another low platform supports the circular stone used in the gladiator sacrifice ritual dedicated to Xipe Totec (no. 6); notice the ropes used to tether the victim during his fatal battle, and the blood on the steps of the platform. Below the gladiator stone sits Xipe Totec's temple (no. 7), complete with bloody stairs. Xipe Totec himself (or his *ixiptla*) is drawn upside down, adjacent to the gladiator stone. The two buildings in the lower left are an Eagle Warriors Hall for the jaguar and eagle warriors (no. 8), and a *calmecac* school (no. 9). The priest offering incense to Ehecatl has just come from the *calmecac*, as shown by the series of footprints. Among the temples in the sacred precinct that were not depicted in the Sahagún drawing were several dedicated to Tezcatlipoca; shrines to Tonatiuh and other gods; and the Coacalco temple, which housed foreign gods taken from conquered peoples. The captivity of foreign gods in the Coacalco "prison" symbolized both the subjugation of foreign peoples to the Aztec empire and the Aztecs' respect for the gods and beliefs of their subjects. This use of religious buildings as symbols of the empire's greatness was even more pronounced at the Templo Mayor itself.

The Templo Mayor

The heart of modern Mexico City was built over the ruins of the sacred precinct. Mexican archaeologist and architect Ignacio Marquina long ago

Figure 10.5   Early Spanish drawing of the sacred precinct of Tenochtitlan (after Sahagún 1905–7:v.6:39). Likely interpretations of the buildings are (1) the Templo Mayor with Tlaloc and Huitzilopochtli temples, (2) magnification of the Huitzilopochtli temple, (3) circular shrine to Ehecatl, (4) skull rack, (5) ballcourt, (6) stone for the gladiator sacrifice, (7) temple of Xipe Totec, (8) Eagle Warriors Hall, (9) *calmecac* school. The two figures flanking the Templo Mayor are stone standard bearers and the upside-down figure on the right is probably Xipe Totec or his *ixiptla* (Drawing by Ellen Cesarski)

determined where the Templo Mayor and other major structures were located in relation to modern streets and buildings, but no one suspected that the foundations of these buildings were still intact, nearly five centuries after their destruction. The chance find of the huge, carved Coyolxauhqui stone (figure 9.1) by power-company workers digging a trench in 1978 set off one of the largest excavation projects ever under-taken in Mexico. This project was directed by archaeologist Eduardo Matos Moctezuma. The Coyolxauhqui stone had been placed in front of the pyramid stairs as an offering, and Matos knew from Marquina's maps that the Templo Mayor was located immediately east of the find. When archaeologists extended the power-company's trench to the west, they came upon the lower steps of the pyramid. The combination of an undis-turbed major offering and the intact stairs suggested that the Templo Mayor was in better condition than anyone had expected.[13]

Unfortunately, in order to excavate the Templo Mayor, a number of sixteenth-century Spanish buildings had to be torn down. When the exca-vations were completed, however, the lowest levels of the Templo Mayor were open for all to see (figure 10.6). Like nearly all Mesoamerican pyra-mids, this structure was enlarged and rebuilt numerous times. The initial shrine, which probably dates to Tenochtitlan's early years, is located be-low the modern water table and could not be excavated. The second stage of construction consisted of a low platform with two temples and two stairways. The platform and the lower courses of the temple walls remain today. Up to five additional stages of enlargement were carried out, but only the lowest sections of the outer walls and the lowest steps for each stage remain today. It seems logical to assume that each Mexica *tlatoani* undertook a program to enlarge and improve the central temple, but it has proven difficult to correlate the construction stages with the reigns of individual kings.[14]

In addition to the foundations of the Templo Mayor itself, some of the pavements and floors from various stages of construction have survived, and parts of several additional buildings have been excavated. One of the most interesting is the Eagle-Warrior Hall located just north of the Templo Mayor; this is probably the building shown in Sahagún's map of the sa-cred precinct (figure 10.5, no. 8). In a separate but related project, deep shafts were dug under the Mexico City Cathedral, which covers much of the sacred precinct, just west of the Templo Mayor. These excavations were made as part of a program to shore up the foundations of the Cathe-dral, which has been slowly sinking in the soft soil for four centuries. But before the engineers finished with the shafts, archaeologists were able to recover the traces of numerous buildings, shrines, and offerings.[15]

At the Templo Mayor offerings were placed under floors and below stairs at each stage of construction (figure 10.7). These are interesting both for the fine objects they contain and for the symbolism of the ob-jects, which helps us understand the meaning that the Templo Mayor held for the Mexica.[16] The main temple was often referred to by the Az-tecs as Coatepec ("Serpent Hill"), the place where Huitzilopochtli was born and later killed his sister Coyolxauhqui. The 1978 find of the

Figure 10.6   The Templo Mayor today. Stairways from several construction stages are visible. The temples of the earliest excavated stage are under the roof at right. The Coyolxauhqui stone (figure 9.1) is visible under the scaffold in front of the stairs (Photograph courtesy of Eduardo Matos Moctezuma; reproduced with permission of the Instituto Nacional de Antropología e Historia)

Coyolxauhqui stone as a temple offering dramatically confirmed this mythological association. Many of the human sacrifices carried out at the Templo Mayor were reenactments of Huitzilopochtli's victory over Coyolxauhqui.

Strangely enough, the Coyolxauhqui stone turned out to be one of only a few overt references to Huitzilopochtli that were uncovered by the Templo Mayor excavations. On the other hand, Huitzilopochtli's pyramid partner Tlaloc – the rain god – was glorified numerous times in the nearly 100 buried offerings that were excavated (figure 10.7). Most goods in these offerings were symbolically related to water and fertility. For example the organic remains of coral, seashells, and alligators were frequently included with offerings in the small stone subfloor chambers, as were stone and ceramic depictions of seashells and other symbols of water and fertility.

Many of the offerings from the Templo Mayor contained other objects

Figure 10.7   Offering 61 excavated in front of the Templo Mayor. Among the contents of this buried chamber are stone deity sculptures, incense burners, and diverse symbols of water and fertility including a crocodile skull, coral, and seashells (Photograph courtesy of Eduardo Matos Moctezuma; reproduced with permission of the Instituto Nacional de Antropología e Historia)

that served to glorify the Aztec empire and Tenochtitlan's role as its capital. From historical documents, we know that the Mexica were aware they were the heirs to a tradition of central Mexican empires that stretched back to Teotihuacan and that they deliberately stressed their connections and continuity with these earlier cultures as a source of legitimacy for their own place as overlords of an expanding empire.[17] The offerings are archaeological confirmation of the importance the Mexica placed on this heritage. Fine objects from earlier Mesoamerican cultures were carefully guarded, and some of these, such as Teotihuacan masks, were placed in the Templo Mayor offerings. Other objects, including stone sculptures and ceramic vessels, were deliberately fashioned in the styles of Tula and

Xochicalco. In addition to offering something valuable to the gods, the Mexica of Tenochtitlan once again appear to be proclaiming themselves worthy of the mantle of Teotihuacan and Tula, powerful religious and political cities that ruled over large domains.

Another aspect of imperial symbolism in the Templo Mayor offerings was the predominantly foreign origin of the goods. Most of the objects in these offerings came from areas under Aztec control. The shells, alligators, and other maritime objects were from imperial provinces along the Pacific and Gulf of Mexico coasts. The numerous, fine-carved masks in the ancient Mezcala style originated in the Balsas River Valley of Guerrero, included in the southwestern provinces of the empire. Most of these items were probably received by the Mexica as tribute. Their burial in and around the Templo Mayor may have symbolized the subordination of their makers to the power of the mighty Tenochtitlan.

Other pyramids, other sacrifices

Every city-state capital had its own major temple-pyramid facing the central plaza (chapter 8). The few of these that have survived are similar to the Templo Mayor in both form and function. The pyramids at Teopanzolco (figure 2.5), Tenayuca (figures 2.7, 2.8), and Tlatelolco (figure 8.9, center) are the primary examples of the twin-stair temple-

Figure 10.8   Partially restored small temple-pyramid at Coatetelco, an Aztec city in Morelos (Photograph by Michael E. Smith)

Figure 10.9   Small circular pyramid from Tenochtitlan. Three of the five construction stages are visible today. This structure was uncovered during the excavation of the Mexico City metro, and today it sits in the middle of the busy Pino Suárez metro station (Photograph by Michael E. Smith)

pyramid style that was popular during the Early Aztec period (see chapter 2). During Late Aztec times, many or most pyramids – outside of Tenochtitlan and Tlatelolco – were built with a single stairway. Pyramids at Coatetelco (figures 8.2, 10.8), Calixtlahuaca (figure 8.4), and Cuexcomate (figure 8.1) are good examples.

During the Postclassic period, another type of pyramid-temple became popular throughout Mesoamerica, from central Mexico to Yucatan: the circular temple. Many excavated Aztec sites have one or more of these temples. A nice example was encountered during work on the Mexico City metro (figure 10.9), and it now sits in the middle of the busy Pino Suárez metro station. One of the largest examples was excavated at Calixtlahuaca (figure 10.10). Circular temples were dedicated to Quetzalcoatl in his guise as Ehecatl, the god of wind: "This Quetzalcoatl was the one they say (made the world). And thus they call him lord of the wind because they say that this Tonacatecuhtli, when it seemed right to him, blew and engendered this Quetzalcoatl, to whom they made round temples without any corners."[18]

Excavations of these "round temples without any corners" (shown in figures 10.9 and 10.10) have turned up offerings of large stone sculptures of Ehecatl buried under the walls. In front of the circular temple in the

Figure 10.10   Circular pyramid at Calixtlahuaca (Photograph by Michael E. Smith)

ceremonial precinct at Tlatelolco (figure 8.9, lower right) archaeologists found a series of rich burials and offerings, many showing the symbolism of Quetzalcoatl and Ehecatl.[19]

Although direct evidence is sparse, most of these pyramids outside of Tenochtitlan probably were settings for rituals of human sacrifice. The Spanish conquerors noted sacrifices in many of the cities they encountered en route to Tenochtitlan, and local documents from throughout the Aztec empire mention extensive human sacrifices before 1519. At Teopanzolco, a small platform across the plaza from the twin-stair pyramid (figure 2.6) contained a burial chamber with many decapitated human skulls, the remains of a large sacrificial ritual. Other evidence of sacrificial rituals is provided by skull racks. Clear identifications of skull racks at Aztec sites are rare, but this may be due to the architectural emphasis of most excavations at urban sites. The architectural remains of one of the few clearly identified skull racks – at Tlatelolco – consist of an unremarkable low rectangular platform (figure 8.9), a kind of feature common at nearly all excavated urban sites. Adjacent to the Tlatelolco platform was a burial with numerous severed skulls perforated with holes in their sides for mounting on the wooden beams of the skull rack. It appears that after skulls had sat on the rack for some time they were buried adjacent to the platform to make way for new, fresher human heads. Aztec skull racks thus consisted of a wooden frame for the skulls, erected on top of a regular low stone altar or platform. It is likely that if areas around low platforms and altars were excavated more fully, additional offerings of skulls at other sites would be found.[20]

Other rituals in addition to sacrifice took place at smaller temple-pyramids. At Cuexcomate, priests discarded ritual objects and other materials in a heap behind the pyramid. When we excavated this refuse pile, we found large numbers of long-handled incense burners and many broken ceramic bowls and plates, probably from offerings of food.[21] Such offerings were made during both private rituals of the priests and public ceremonies that involved the entire community.

Public Ceremonies

The sacred precinct was the stage for some of the most important rituals for the well-being of the empire and the city of Tenochtitlan. These included private rituals of penance and bloodletting by the many priests who lived in the precinct, public sacrifices and pageants attended by priests and nobles, and the occasional major public spectacle attended by a wider audience. Most people, however, were more intimately involved in other types of ceremonies and rituals. First I discuss rituals of a public nature – those that occurred in open, public settings and permitted the participation of large numbers of people. Then I discuss rituals of a more private nature that were conducted within the confines of the home.

The monthly ceremonies

Each of the 18 Aztec months had a distinctive series of ceremonies, which involved priests, rulers, nobles, and commoners alike. These ceremonies were devoted to particular religious themes, especially agricultural fertility. Many of the human sacrifices took place as parts of these monthly celebrations. Friars Durán and Sahagún left detailed records of the individual rituals carried out at each monthly ceremony.[22] I have drawn from their descriptions for the following example of the public ceremonies during the month of Toxcatl.

Toxcatl, May 4–23, fell at the height of the dry season.[23] The days were hot and dusty; many streambeds were dry. Stores from the fall's harvest were running low, and farmers were anxiously awaiting rain so that new crops could be planted. The ceremonies of Toxcatl were dedicated to Tezcatlipoca in supplication for the start of the coming rainy season. The culminating event of the Toxcatl ceremonies was the sacrifice of

Tezcatlipoca's *ixiptla* at the end of the month. This impersonator, selected by the priests a year in advance, had to be a young man of physical perfection: "For he who was chosen was of fair countenance, of good understanding and quick, of clean body – slender like a reed; long and thin like a stout cane; well-built."[24] The impersonator was trained in flute-playing, speech, and flower-carrying, and spent most of the year roaming the streets of Tenochtitlan with an entourage.

At the start of his last month, the *ixiptla* went to the *tlatoani*, who adorned him in the insignia and regalia of Tezcatlipoca. He was given four young women, who symbolized fertility goddesses, as wives. The entire group visited all parts of the city during this final month, leading up to the sacrifice at the Templo Mayor. The "marriage" between Tezcatlipoca and the four goddesses occurred after nearly a year of abstinence and symbolized the coming of fertility following a long period of sterility or drought. The sacrifice itself symbolically marked the end of the dry period.

The theme of fertility after drought was also portrayed in the other rituals of Toxcatl. A large image of Huitzilopochtli was covered with amaranth dough, dressed in the god's insignia, and carried in procession to a temple where it was set up to receive offerings. Priests stoked the temple braziers into towering fires and offered incense. Quail were sacrificed to Huitzilopochtli's flames and later eaten by the king and nobles. The women of the city performed leaping dances to the music of drums and turtle-shell rattles. Warriors participated in an undulating "serpent dance," and young women performed a "popcorn dance" in which they were adorned with strings of popcorn that symbolized food and fertility. Toward the end of the feast, priests practiced bloodletting on all of the children, while other priests went around to people's homes, spreading incense.

Everyone, from the lowest commoner to the highest priests and king, was involved in some aspect of the Toxcatl ceremonies. Although the Toxcatl ceremony was "one of the most ostentatious and imposing known to the Indians,"[25] similar sets of rituals involving all ranks of society took place in each of the 18 months.

The New Fire ceremony

The New Fire ceremony, also known as the "binding of the years," was carried out upon the completion of each 52-year calendar cycle. The myth of the five suns predicted the destruction of the world by earthquakes at the end of a calendar cycle, but it was not known which cycle would be the last one. Preparation for the possible end of the world began with major housecleaning: all household idols, cooking implements, clothing, and mats were discarded, and houses and yards were carefully swept and cleaned. During the last five unlucky days of the last year of the cycle, fires were extinguished, and the people climbed up on their roofs to await the fate of the world.

After dark on the final day of the calendar cycle, priests climbed the mountain Citlaltepec near Tenochtitlan to observe the heavens. Today Citlaltepec is called Cerro de la Estrella; both names mean "Star Mountain." The Pleiades constellation was the augury of the sunrise of the new cycle. The priest-astronomers anxiously followed this cluster of stars as it rose in the sky. If the constellation crossed the zenith as it normally does, they knew that the sun would rise again and the world would be spared for at least another 52 years. One hurdle remained, however. A new fire had to be kindled there on the mountaintop by a fire drill placed on the chest of a sacrificial victim: "all were frightened and filled with dread . . . it was claimed that if fire could not be drawn, then [the sun] would be destroyed forever; all would be ended; there would evermore be night."[26]

Once a flame was lit, the victim was sacrificed and his heart was thrown into the fire. The fire was carried to a temple in Tenochtitlan, where it was used to light many carefully made torches. Warriors, messengers, and other swift runners took up the torches to carry the flame to all parts of the empire. Eventually, everyone's hearth was relit from the new fire. People everywhere rejoiced at the start of a new 52-year cycle, and they obtained new household goods to begin again. I suspect that the New Fire ritual was particularly appreciated by potters, obsidian knappers, mat makers, idol makers, and other artisans, although Sahagún and the other sources are silent on this issue.

We excavated two ritual dumps at Cuexcomate that contained the remains of household goods, most likely broken and discarded in a New Fire ceremony.[27] Unlike usual domestic refuse, which was spread around people's back yards and built up over a period of time, the materials in the ritual dumps were placed into shallow pits in residential courtyards and covered with a layer of rocks. We know that these deposits were not simple trash pits because many pottery vessels could be pieced back together, indicating that they were deliberately broken at the pit. Vessels from ordinary trash deposits at this site could almost never be reassembled because the pieces were so widely scattered. These ritual dumps, and others at sites in the Valley of Mexico, support Sahagún's descriptions of such practices and confirm that celebrations like the New Fire Ceremony took place in rural areas far from Tenochtitlan.

Figure 10.11   An Aztec ballcourt with a game in progress (After Codex Magliabechiano 1983:f.80r; drawing by Ellen Cesarski)

The ballgame

The Aztec ballgame *tlachtli* was a public ceremony with ancient roots that combined ritual, sport, and entertainment.[28] The ballgame was played with a hard rubber ball on a large I-shaped court (figures 10.11, 10.12). Carved stone rings were mounted vertically in the center of the walls, often at the top of a sloping ramp. Players could only hit the ball with hips or knees, and wore protective suits of deerskin. If a player hit the ball through a ring, his team won the game. Goals were rare occurrences, however, and most games were probably won and lost on points gained for various maneuvers and skills. Sometimes the game was played between teams of players; at other times, individuals faced off against each other (figure 10.11).

The ballgame was a sacred event charged with religious meaning. The ball was viewed as the sun that passed through the dark underworld (represented by the court) each night. The ballgame was a holy battle between the sun and the moon, between the sun and the planet Venus, or between the gods of youth and those of old age. The ballgame also had sacrificial connotations, and the ball was likened to a severed human head. In the ballcourt in figure 10.11, death is indicated by four human skulls and three death-heads, symbols of the god Mictlantecuhtli. Priests used the ballgame as a form of divination to predict the future and to help guide the actions of kings. A game would be commissioned and a possible

Figure 10.12   Aztec ballcourt at Coatetelco (Photograph by Michael E. Smith)

future course of events assigned to each team. The results of the game were seen as an omen of the future.

The ballgame was significant not only as a religious event but also as one of the few organized athletic events in Aztec culture. The teams of neighboring cities played each other. Nobles both played the game and attended as spectators, gambling feathers and jade on the outcome. Some nobles could afford to gamble large sums at the ballcourt, but poorer nobles or commoners could find themselves in trouble. Of these latter individuals, Friar Durán said with scorn:

> These wretches played [the ballgame] for stakes of little value or worth, and since the pauper loses quickly what he has, they were forced to gamble their homes, their fields, their corn granaries, their maguey plants. They sold their children in order to bet and even staked themselves and became slaves.[29]

Private Rituals

Domestic ritual

Not all ritual was carried out in public ceremonies. Every Aztec home was also a setting for worship, much of which paralleled the actions that took place in temples and processions. Friar Durán described this domestic worship:

> All this food and drink was offered up in the temples, and each person offered the same in his domestic shrine . . . People made little hills of

amaranth dough within their homes [and placed them] in shrines or special niches where the idols were kept, just as today they keep the (Christian) images.[30]

Most domestic rituals were carried out by women, who used sweeping and petitions to the gods to keep the spiritual world of the home and family in balance. Excavations of Aztec houses have turned up considerable evidence for domestic rituals that are barely suggested in the ethnohistoric sources.[31] Although no shrines like those mentioned by Durán have been found, domestic trash deposits do contain abundant, broken ritual objects, the most common of which are clay figurines (figure 10.13). Many figurines represent deities, and others depict people (women more commonly than men), animals, and other natural objects. When archaeologists find figurines, the heads are rarely connected to bodies, which suggests that they may have been broken deliberately before they were discarded. Figurines were most likely used in curing and other domestic rituals by women of the family or by other women, who, as professional curers or midwives, came into the home.

Remains of long-handled frying-pan incense burners or censers of the sort used by priests (figures 10.1, 10.2) are also common in Aztec domestic trash deposits. Ethnohistoric sources described several occasions on which priests purified houses with the censers, but the large numbers of fragments of such vessels suggest that the commoners also must have used them in their homes to burn incense. These domestic incense burners were identical to those found at temples. Excavated deposits from temples, however, have several times as many of these artifacts as the average house. Other domestic rituals included rites associated with childbirth, weddings, and burial after death.

Magic, astrology and divination

The Aztecs practiced a variety of forms of magic and divination.[32] Most of these acts were performed by specialists of several types, including fortune-tellers, physicians, and magicians. These specialists included both men and women. The names of the different types of fortune-telling gives an idea of the nature of these practices: "Casting kernels of maize," "Tying of knots," "Looking into the water." The first type was probably the most prevalent, and indeed this kind of divination is still practiced today by some Mesoamerican native peoples. The best description is by the friar Hernando Ruiz de Alarcón, who traveled through rural Nahuatl-speaking areas of Guerrero and Morelos in the early 1600s stamping out idolatry. He found a flourishing culture of rural fortune-tellers and

Figure 10.13   Ceramic figurines used in domestic rituals at Yautepec
(Photograph by Michael E. Smith)

physicians (he called them "sorcerers") who were practicing their craft
invoking the ancient Aztec gods in Nahuatl. As part of Ruiz de Alarcón's
efforts to put an end to these pagan practices, he recorded the chants and
actions of the rituals. Here is an example:

> The sorcery with the maize . . . they pretend it to be a general remedy for
> stolen things; for absent persons; for illnesses and their cause, and for their
> cures . . . After arranging the kernels on the cloth, he [the sorcerer] begins
> his charm with those remaining in his hand, shaking them, tossing them in
> the air, and returning often to pick them up. Then he begins the following
> invocation: "Please bring yourself forth, / Precious prince 7 Serpent. / Please
> come forth, / Those of the Five Signs, / Those of one courtyard. / . . . / I shall
> see / In my book, / In my mirror, / What is causing trouble / For the unfor-
> tunate person, / The child of the gods.[33]

In this spell, recorded in Nahuatl, "Precious prince 7 Serpent" refers to
the maize kernels that will answer the question, and "Those of the Five
Signs, Those of one courtyard" refers to the sorcerer's fingers.

Another form of magic and divination was based on the 260-day ritual
calendar, the *tonalpohualli*. This calendar, described in more detail in the

next chapter, was used to predict the fate of individuals (based upon their birth date), and to determine days to hold important events, both ritual and practical. Individual days were considered to be either lucky, unlucky, or neutral, as were particular groups of 5 or 13 days. Days and groups of days were ruled by particular deities; figure 1.6, for example, shows a group of 13 days (a *trecena*) over which Quetzalcoatl presided. Much of this system resembles modern astrology.

Important ceremonies were tied to specific days in the 260-day calendar, and people arranged their affairs around the lucky and unlucky associations of particular days. For example the *pochteca* merchants made sure that the day they set out on a long journey was a lucky day. Much of the complex, esoteric meaning of this calendar and its symbolism have been lost, and the content of the ritual books based upon it, such as the

Figure 10.14   Portion of an astrological table showing predictions for specific days of the 260-day ritual calendar (After Seler 1963)

Codex Borgia (figures 1.6, 11.1), are only partially understood today. Near the start of the Codex Borgia, for example, is a table that links groups of five days to specific symbols (figure 10.14). Some of these appear to be good omens (e.g., birth from a shell) but the majority (capture in war, strangling, plagues, and the like) are negative. Others (e.g., the owl) remain inscrutable to us today.

The Christian friars, who worked hard to convert indigenous peoples following the Spanish Conquest, were favorably impressed with the religiosity and devotion of the Nahua people, even though they objected to much of the content of native religion. Religious worship was well integrated into daily life at all levels of society. Beyond myths and rituals, religion was the context for the development of many of the intellectual and aesthetic accomplishments of the Aztecs, to which we now turn.

chapter eleven
Science and Art

The philosophers and wise men had charge of recording all the sciences of which they had knowledge and of which they had achieved understanding, and of teaching from memory all the songs that preserved their sciences and histories.

Fernando de Alva Ixtlilxochitl, Obras históricas

The scientific and artistic achievements of the Aztec peoples were considerable. I have already touched upon many of these in the preceding chapters, for science and art were inextricably bound up with other aspects of Aztec culture. The Aztecs, like most ancient peoples, did not distinguish categories of "science" and "art" in the manner we do today. Many scientific ideas were applied toward practical ends in areas such as agriculture, architecture, craft production, and medicine. Others were applied toward religion and ritual, as in the cases of astronomy and calendrics. Aztec art, too, was integrated into religion, politics, and society. The Aztecs did not appear to have had a concept of "art for art's sake," although they clearly valued technical ability and aesthetic balance in many diverse artistic media. Sculptures and paintings depicted gods and rituals, poetry dealt with humankind's place in the cosmos, and dance and music were part of state ceremonies. Since religion and politics were closely bound, much Aztec art also served overt political ends. Monumental sculptures and large buildings proclaimed the glory of the city-state, and painted books and wall murals recorded the great deeds of current and past dynastic rulers. In this chapter I examine several aspects of Aztec science and art that have not been treated in detail in previous chapters: writing, calendars and astronomy, technology, medicine, and art.

Writing

Paper

The Aztecs wrote on many media – stone sculptures, ceramic vessels, and other objects – but the most common medium was painted manuscripts. Most manuscripts consisted of long strips of paper folded accordion-style and painted on both sides (figure 11.1). Only a few of these books, or codices, survived the Spanish Conquest, but they continued to be painted in much the same manner into the Colonial period. Quite a few of these Aztec-style colonial documents have been preserved.

Some manuscripts were painted on deerskin and others on cloth, but most used paper made from the inner bark of the wild fig tree.[1] These trees were abundant in the Morelos area, where many towns specialized in papermaking. The Spanish botanist Francisco Hernández observed

Figure 11.1   Modern reproduction of an Aztec folded book, the Codex Borgia (1976) (Photograph by Mark Schmidt. Codex Borgia [Codex Vaticanus mess. 1] Facsimile-Edition by Akademische Drück u. Verlagsanstalt, Graz Austria, 1976)

papermaking in the Morelos town of Tepoztlan in the mid-sixteenth century and wrote a detailed description of the process. The papermaker first stripped the bark off the tree with a stone knife, then soaked it in running water to coagulate the sap. The sap was scraped off, and the bark boiled in an alkaline solution to loosen and separate the fibers. The wet fibers were arranged in layers on a wooden drying board and pounded with a hammer made from a flat, grooved pounder of basalt stone that was bound to a wooden handle. These basalt tools, called bark-beaters, are a commonly found artifact at Aztec sites in Morelos (figure 11.2). Beating the fibers rendered them pliable and fused them together into paper. The papermaker trimmed these sheets to the size and shape desired and polished them with a stone. Finally, a coating of white lime was applied to stiffen the paper and produce a surface for painting. Contemporary Otomi, who live north of the Valley of Mexico, still make paper this way for rituals, and their methods have been adopted by peasants in the state of Guerrero, who make paper for the colorful paintings they sell to tourists and collectors.[2]

Books and scribes

The Aztecs produced codices and other manuscripts or books for a variety of purposes.[3] Religious books such as the Codex Borgia (figure 1.6) and the Codex Fejérváry-Mayer (figure 11.5) contained depictions of gods and rituals, along with much information on the 260-day ritual calendar. These books were used by priests for divination and to keep track of rituals. Historical books typically consisted of a list of years in the year-count calendar accompanied by representations of key events in the history of a dynasty. Section one of the Codex Mendoza, the *Tira de la Peregrinación* (figure 2.4) and the *Tira de Tepechpan* (figure 2.11) are important examples of historical books. There were several types of administrative books, including tribute lists such as section two of the Codex Mendoza (figure 7.4), maps of city-state territories, and records of landholdings. The conqueror Bernal Díaz del Castillo made a note of Motecuhzoma's tribute books: "he [Motecuhzoma's steward] kept an account of all the revenue that was brought to Montezuma in his books, which were made of paper – their name for which is amal [amate] – and he had a great house full of these books."[4]

Books and manuscripts were painted by trained scribes, *tlacuilo*, who were themselves nobles, or commoners in the service of nobles and priests. Priests and philosophers also learned to write. Friar Sahagún described the scribe as follows:

Figure 11.2 Stone bark-beaters from Yautepec used to pound bark fibers into paper (Photograph by Michael E. Smith)

> The scribe: writings, ink [are] his special skills. [He is] a craftsman, an artist, a user of charcoal, a drawer with charcoal; a painter who dissolves colors, grinds pigments, uses colors.
>
> The good scribe is honest, circumspect, far-sighted, pensive; a judge of colors, an applier of the colors, who makes shadows, forms feet, face, hair. He paints, applies colors, makes shadows, draws gardens, paints flowers, creates works of art.[5]

Professional scribes often specialized in one of the various types of books. The occupation of scribe was hereditary, and the Codex Mendoza illustrates a scribe (painter) teaching his trade to his son (figure 4.9). The central symbol in the figure, two diagonal scrolls within a rectangular frame, is the Aztec glyph that signifies writing or scribal activity.

Mesoamerican background to Aztec writing

The Aztec writing system was one of five distinct writing systems developed in ancient Mesoamerica; the others are the Maya, Mixtec, Zapotec, and Epi-Olmec.[6] Although each of these scripts expressed a different language and had its own patterns of writing, they shared common pre-occupations with ruling dynasties, elite affairs, ritual, and calendrics. During the Classic period (AD 150–900) the Maya carved inscriptions on buildings, stelae, and other stone monuments, many of which still survive today. Classic Maya writing was the most complete of the Mesoamerican scripts, capable of recording anything that could be said in the Maya languages. A pre-Maya writing system, the Epi-Olmec script, recently was discovered in the Olmec area of the Mexican Gulf Coast. Although only a limited number of carved inscriptions have been found, linguists John Justeson and Terence Kaufman already have deciphered many of the glyphs.

Two different writing systems were developed by the ancient cultures of Oaxaca. Toward the end of the Formative period (around the time of Christ) Zapotec speakers in the Valley of Oaxaca invented a script that today is known through carved stone inscriptions at Monte Alban and other sites in that area. During the early part of the Postclassic period (ca. AD 900–1200), Mixtec speakers in the mountainous zone north of the Valley of Oaxaca worked out a pictographic writing system that survives in a number of painted pre-Hispanic manuscripts such as the Codex Nuttall. Most existing Mixtec books are historical accounts of the ruling dynasties of the Mixtec city-states. Compared with Classic Maya writing, Mixtec writing was limited in scope, capable of expressing only a narrow range of historical and ritual events. The origins of Aztec writing may reach back to early systems of signs and symbols at Teotihuacan and Xochicalco, but the many stylistic and iconographic similarities between Mixtec and Aztec writing suggest that the Mixtec script, too, played an important role in the development of Aztec writing.

The Aztec writing system

Aztec manuscripts usually included two types of elements – pictures and glyphs – blended together so that it is sometimes difficult to separate them. Many events, places, people, and things were depicted by straightforward pictures that could be interpreted easily by the reader. With a little practice scholars today can "read" many of these pictures without any knowledge of Nahuatl. This very generalized form of communication had the advantage of not being tied to a particular language. Speakers of Nahuatl, Otomi, Tarascan, or Maya could all have read the pictorial parts of Aztec written texts.

Aztec hieroglyphs, on the other hand, were far more precise in their meanings. A hieroglyph, or glyph, is a sign that stands for a word, sound, or concept in a specific language. Aztec writing made use of several hundred glyphs.[7] The calendrical date was a common type of glyph, and historical accounts were based upon the year-count. According to the *Tira de Tepechpan*, for example, the reign of the Mexica king Motecuhzoma II began in the year 10 Tochtli or AD 1502 (figure 2.11). Ritual books most frequently used day names from the 260-day ritual calendar (see below). Numerical glyphs were also common. In Aztec writing, a dot stood for 1; a flag meant 20; a feather meant 400; and a priestly incense bag indicated 8,000 (figure 7.4 shows the flag and feather glyphs).

Personal names and titles were another category of glyph. Glyphs for actions and events were less frequent, but examples do exist. Place-names were the most common type of Aztec glyph, and several hundred were included in the first two sections of the Codex Mendoza – the conquest list and the tribute list. Hundreds of objects also were depicted in the Codex Mendoza, as well as other sources, but these illustrations are better described as pictorial representations, not glyphs.

This rather small repertoire of hieroglyphs limited the scope of what Aztec writing by itself could express. As I discuss in chapter 1, however, written texts were not meant to be used alone; they were mnemonic devices that listed important people, events, or places, the remaining information to be filled in from the memory of the reader. The telling of history, for example, was primarily oral in format, with books serving only to outline the main events. Nevertheless, the principles of Aztec hieroglyphic writing were sophisticated, and the glyphs were much more than simple pictures of people and things.

Types of hieroglyphs

Aztec writing employed three types of signs or hieroglyphs of increasing complexity and abstraction: pictographs, ideographs, and phonetic elements.

Pictographs are straightforward depictions of objects and people. In Aztec writing, a picture of a rabbit on a hill meant Tochtepec ("on the hill of the rabbit"). Tzonpanco ("on the skull rack") was represented by a drawing of a skull rack (see figure 11.3 and box). Pictographs were the most common type of Aztec glyph.

Ideographs are conventionalized representations of ideas or meanings. Their interpretation depends upon a certain level of cultural understanding, since the way in which a concept is depicted is usually culturally specific. The burning temple ideograph (figure 11.3, "Conquest"), for example, meant military conquest. In the glyph for Cuicatlan ("place of song"), the song was represented by a flowery speech scroll, a common Nahuatl metaphor for song. The Yopico glyph ("in the place of the Yopes")

Figure 11.3 Place-name glyphs from the Codex Mendoza illustrating the principles of Aztec writing; see box for explanation (Drawing by Ellen Cesarski)

Glyphs from the Codex Mendoza

1 Pictographic Glyphs

Tochtepec, "on the hill of the rabbit" (Codex Mendoza 1992:v.4:97; f.46r)

toch(tli):	rabbit
tepe(tl):	hill, or place of
c:	on, or in

Tzonpanco, "on the skull rack" (Codex Mendoza 1992:v.4:40; f.17v)

tzonpan(tli):	skull rack
co:	on, or in

Ychcateopan, "on the temple of cotton" (Codex Mendoza 1992:v.4:79, 83; f.37r, 39r)

ichca(tl):	cotton
teopan(tli):	temple
pan:	on

2   **Ideographic Glyphs**

Military conquest (Codex Mendoza 1992:v.4:26; f.10v) (depiction of a burning temple)

Cuicatlan, "place of song," or "place of the Cuicateca" (Codex Mendoza 1992:v.4:91; f.43r)

cuica(tl):	song
tlan:	abundance of, or place of

Yopico, "in the place of the Yopes" (Codex Mendoza 1992:v.4:45; f.20r)

yopi(tzontli):	Xipe Totec's cap
Yopi(me):	a group living on the southwest edge of the Aztec empire

3   **Glyphs with Phonetic Elements**

Coatlan, "where there are many snakes" (Codex Mendoza 1992:v.4:51; f.23r)

coa(tl):	snake
tlan:	where there is an abundance of
tlan(tli):	teeth (phonetic)

Coatzinco, "on the small snake" (Codex Mendoza 1992:v.4:89; f.42r)

coa(tl):	snake
tzin:	small
tzin(tli):	rump (phonetic)
co:	on, or in

Itzamatitlan, "near the Ceiba trees" (Codex Mendoza 1992:v.4:54; f.24v)

itzama(tl):	ceiba tree
titlan:	near or among
itz(tli):	obsidian (phonetic)
ama(tl):	paper (phonetic)

NOTE: These etymologies are from Berdan (1992b).

was a depiction of Xipe Totec's peaked cap, an association based upon the importance of this god to the Yope people.

Phoneticism is the use of signs to represent words, syllables, or sounds. Phonetic glyphs were the most complex type of Aztec sign. Many examples of Aztec phonetic writing employed the "rebus principle," in which a word difficult to depict in writing was replaced by a word or words with the same sound (homonyms) that were easier to depict.[8] In figure 11.3 the glyph for Coatlan ("where there are many snakes") uses a pictograph for the snake (*coatl*), but the sound "tlan" is depicted by teeth, *tlantli*; in the case of Coatzinco ("on the small snake"), the "tzinco" sound is signaled by a pictograph for rump (*tzintli*); Itzamatitlan ("near the Ceiba tree") is written with two phonetic parts – *itztli* (obsidian) and *amatl* (paper).

Calendars and Astronomy

Calendars and timekeeping were a major concern of most Mesoamerican civilizations, which used several distinct calendrical systems for different purposes. The most widespread of these systems was a 260-day ritual calendar used for divination, astrology, and religious record-keeping. Annual calendars were used to keep track of events within the solar year, and various larger cycles of time were developed to keep track of events across the years. Use of these calendars hinged on careful observations of the stars and planets, so astronomy was a well-developed science. The Aztecs inherited a rich tradition of calendrics and astronomy from earlier Mesoamerican cultures, and from this tradition they focused their attention on three types of calendar: the ritual calendar, the annual calendar, and the 52-year calendar round.[9]

The 260-day ritual calendar

Mesoamerican peoples used a cycle of 260 days to keep track of rituals, to forecast the future, and to determine which days would be lucky or unlucky for the outcome of various events and actions. This calendar comprised two repeating, meshed cycles: a cycle of 20 day names and a cycle of 13 numbers. The 20 day names are listed in table 11.1; their glyphs are depicted in figure 11.4. The cycle of day names begins at the top with Cipactli (Alligator) and runs through Xochitl (Flower); it then returns to Cipactli to repeat again. The cycle of numbers similarly repeats itself, running from 1 to 13 over and over. Each day in this calendar is identified by a number and a day name. Given 20 day names and 13 numbers, there are 260 unique combinations.

Table 11.1 The 20 day names

Day name	Meaning	Associated numbers in the 260-day ritual calendar				
Cipactli	Alligator	1	8	2	9	etc.
Ehecatl	Wind	2	9	3	10	
Calli	House	3	10	4	11	
Cuetzpallin	Lizard	4	11	5	12	
Coatl	Snake	5	12	6	13	
Miquiztli	Death	6	13	7	1	
Mazatl	Deer	7	1	8	2	
Tochtli	Rabbit	8	2	9	3	
Atl	Water	9	3	10	4	
Itzcuintli	Dog	10	4	11	5	
Ozomatli	Monkey	11	5	12	6	
Malinalli	Grass	12	6	13	7	
Acatl	Reed	13	7	1	8	
Ocelotl	Jaguar	1	8	2	9	
Cuauhtli	Eagle	2	9	3	10	
Cozcacuauhtli	Vulture	3	10	4	11	
Ollin	Movement	4	11	5	12	
Tecpatl	Flint knife	5	12	6	13	
Quiahuitl	Rain	6	13	7	1	
Xochitl	Flower	7	1	8	2	

Glyphs for the day names are portrayed in figure 11.4

Table 11.1 shows the first few cycles of the 260-day ritual calendar (*tonalpohualli*). The first three days, for example, are 1 Cipactli, 2 Ehecatl, and 3 Calli. When the first cycle of 13 numbers is completed, the number 1 is paired with the fourteenth day name (1 Ocelotl), which is followed by 2 Cuauhtli, and so forth. When the final, twentieth day name, is reached (7 Xochitl), the day name cycle starts over with the next number in sequence, 8 Cipactli, 9 Ehecatl, and so on. After 260 days, 13 cycles of day names have been coupled with 20 cycles of numbers, and the final, unique, combination (13 Xochitl) is reached. The calendar then comes back to its starting point, 1 Cipactli, and a new cycle begins. Figure 1.6 shows a 13-day section of the *tonalpohualli* running from 1 Ocelotl to 13 Miquiztli. The 260-day calendar is probably the calendrical form with the greatest antiquity in Mesoamerica. No one, however, is sure just how a period of 260 days was selected for this important ritual cycle.

In Aztec culture this simple calendrical cycle was the foundation for a

Figure 11.4   Model showing the operation of the 260-day ritual calendar, the *tonalpohualli*. The numbers 1–13 are combined with the 20 day names (From *Mexico*, by Michael D. Coe, 4th edn, Coe 1994, Thames and Hudson, p. 180; reproduced courtesy of Michael D. Coe)

complex series of ritual associations. For example, each group of 13 days was a unit named by its first day (1 Cipactli, 1 Ocelotl, 1 Mazatl, and so on). These groups, known today by the Spanish term *trecenas*, were thought to have special symbolic significance, and each was presided over by a different deity. In figure 1.6, for example, the *trecena* starting with 1 Ocelotl is ruled by Quetzalcoatl. The 260-day calendar also included 13 deities known as the "Lords of the Day," 13 holy birds, and 9 "Lords of the Night" deities. In addition, each of the 20 day names had its own patron deity and a complex symbolism and cultic significance that are not well understood (figure 11.5).

The annual calendar

The annual solar calendar consisted of 365 days arranged into 18 months of 20 days, with 5 unlucky days to finish out the year. The actual solar year is closer to 365.25 days long, and earlier Mesoamerican peoples had calculated its precise length. The Aztecs had this knowledge, but we do not know how they resolved the discrepancy, whether they added days (as in our leap years) or used some other means to keep the calendar in tune with the seasons.

Figure 11.5   Passage from the Codex Fejérváry-Mayer, a ritual book of the
Borgia group of codices. On the right is the god Ehecatl-Quetzalcoatl carrying a
fan and copal incense. On the left a goddess – perhaps Tlazolteotl – walks along
a road. Her path is blocked by a serpent and by a censer with copal incense.
These deities or their actions are somehow associated with the five day names
depicted at the base (Codex Fejérváry-Mayer 1971:35; see discussion in Berger
1998:100–1)

The annual calendar was used for both practical and religious purposes.
It kept track of the seasons and the monthly public ceremonies, and it
may have had a role in agriculture.[10] Each 20-day month was divided into
4 weeks of 5 days, and this period structured everyday life much as the 7-
day week organizes our lives today. Weekly markets, for example, were
held every 5 days, and smaller markets convened every 20 days.

The calendar round and year-count

When the 260-day ritual calendar was combined with the 365-day annual
calendar the result was a major cycle of 18,980 days, or 52 years. Each
day in this cycle, called the "calendar round", had a unique combination
of entries in the two calendars. For example, the Spaniards first entered
Tenochtitlan on November 8, 1519. This was the ninth day of the month
Quecholli in the annual calendar, and the day 8 Ehecatl in the ritual calendar. This same designation (9 Quecholli, 8 Ehecatl) reappeared every
52 years.

The year-count, a simplified version of the calendar round, was used to
keep track of the years. Each year within the 52-year calendar round was
assigned its own designation of a name with numeral. Four of the day

names were used for this purpose, and they were referred to as the year bearers Calli, Tochtli, Acatl, and Tecpatl. They were combined with the numbers 1 through 13 following the same principle of repeating cycles as the 260-day calendar. The combination of 4 day names with 13 numbers produced a 52-year cycle that matched the cycle of the calendar round.

The events recorded in Aztec native historical accounts were dated using the year-count. Since we know that the Spaniards entered Tenochtitlan in the year 1 Acatl, or AD 1519, we can correlate the European and Aztec calendars to assign European dates to the events of Aztec history. Table 11.2 lists the years from 1 Tochtli (1506) to 5 Acatl (1523) in the year-count (see also figure 2.11). Each year name reoccurs every 52 years, however, which causes great problems for the reconstruction of Aztec history from native historical sources. It is impossible to tell from the year name alone which cycle an event belongs to. According to the sources, for example, Tenochtitlan was founded in the year 2 Calli, but 2 Calli could be AD 1273, 1325, 1377, 1429, or 1481 (to name only five possibilities). We have ascertained that 1325 is the correct date only by carefully cross-checking with other events.

Astronomy

The Aztecs, like all peoples of ancient Mesoamerica, were avid astronomers who carefully tracked the stars and planets at night. Most observa-

Table 11.2 The year-count calendar and its correlation with the European calendar

Aztec year	European year	Aztec year	European year
1 Tochtli	1506	10 Acatl	1515
2 Acatl	1507 (new fire celebrated)	11 Tecpatl	1516
3 Tecpatl	1508	12 Calli	1517
4 Calli	1509	13 Tochtli	1518
5 Tochtli	1510	1 Acatl	1519 (arrival of Cortés)
6 Acatl	1511	2 Tecpatl	1520
7 Tecpatl	1512	3 Calli	1521 (fall of Tenochtitlan)
8 Calli	1513	4 Tochtli	1522
9 Tochtli	1514	5 Acatl	1523

Source: Caso 1971

tions and calculations were made by priests and nobles. In the Codex Mendoza, for example, a priest was depicted observing the stars in order to keep track of the schedule for nightly rituals (figure 11.6). Friar Torquemada described king Nezahualpilli of Texcoco as a great astronomer:

> It is said that he was a great astrologer; that he was much concerned with understanding the movement of the celestial bodies. Inclined to the study of these things, he would seek in his kingdom for those who knew of such things, and he would bring them to his court. He would communicate to them all that he knew. And at night he would study the stars, and he would go on the roof of his palace, and from there he would watch the stars, and he would discuss problems with them.[11]

The archaeoastronomer Anthony F. Aveni has worked out many of the details of Aztec astronomy.[12] Mesoamerican astronomers typically used fixed locations in temples and other buildings to observe the heavens. They tracked the rising and setting of the sun, moon, planets, and stars at the horizon by placing sets of crossed sticks along the line of sight. The precise direction of the sun at sunrise was a particularly important orientation in Mesoamerican cosmology. The position where the sun rises in the east varies throughout the year. The sun rises at its northernmost point

This drawing with eyes means night

Head priest who is looking at the stars in the night sky to ascertain the time for services[1] and duties

Figure 11.6   A priest tracks the stars at night (Codex Mendoza 1992:v.4:131; f.63r)

on the summer solstice (June 21) and at its southernmost point on the winter solstice (December 21). In valleys surrounded by high mountains, such as the Valley of Mexico, astronomers tracked the direction of the sunrise by noting the point of the sun's appearance over specific mountain peaks and other features on the eastern horizon. The length of the solar year was easily calculated by noting the direction where the sun rose on a solstice and counting the number of days until it returned to the same position.

Important astronomical alignments and orientations were recorded and used by surveyors and architects to lay out cities and buildings. For example, the Templo Mayor was designed so that on the spring equinox (March 21) the sun rose directly between the Huitzilopochtli and Tlaloc temples. The monthly ceremony of Tlacaxipehualiztli, dedicated to Xipe Totec, a god with solar associations, was held at this time. Friar Motolinía noted that the ceremony took place "when the sun was in the middle of [the temple of] Huitzilopochtli, which was the equinox, and because this was a little twisted, Motecuhzoma wished it torn down and straightened."[13] Aveni measured the alignment of the Templo Mayor and found that its orientation, 7 degrees south of east, matched precisely the direction of the sun when it rose over the massive platform in the notch between the two temples on March 21 in Late Aztec times.

Aztec astronomers tracked many other celestial bodies in addition to the sun. The New Fire ceremony, which celebrated the start of a new 52-year calendar round was signaled not by sunrise but by the passage of the Pleiades constellation across the zenith of the midnight sky. Astronomers calculated to great accuracy the length of the solar year, the lunar month, the period of revolution of the planet Venus (584 days), and other celestial cycles. They noted and predicted solar and lunar eclipses and paid close attention to comets and shooting stars. Although some of this great body of astronomical knowledge was put to practical use in the calibration of calendars, most functioned more in the realm of divination and ritual. The emphasis on astronomical alignment was related to the important role of the cardinal directions in Aztec symbolism; rituals were choreographed to conform to key alignments and directions, and heavenly bodies from the stars and planets to comets were thought to have religious significance.

Cyclical time and linear time

The Aztecs, like other ancient Mesoamerican peoples, were clearly fascinated by repeating cycles of time. Their calendars were cyclical in form, and many consisted of the intersection of two or more cycles. The natural cycles of the seasons, the sun, the stars and the planets were all tracked carefully by priests and astronomers. Repeating cycles were also prominent in Aztec mythology; the myth of multiple creations and destructions – the five suns – is a good example. But there was simultaneously a strong conception of linear time in Aztec society. This is shown most clearly by the continuous year-count annal form of historical codex (figure 2.11).[14]

The continuous year-count annal was a relatively late innovation of the Mexica and other Aztec groups. Earlier central Mexican and Mixtec pictorial histories took one of two forms: depictions of the deeds of rulers and important persons organized by event, and maps of territories upon which historical persons and actions were placed. These two forms of historical codex continued to be used through the Late Aztec period, but the Aztecs favored the innovative continuous year-count annal for the depiction of dynastic histories. Although the year-count repeated every 52 years, the sequence of year glyphs continued uninterrupted for the entire length of the historical narrative. The very nature of this arrangement of glyphs shows the linear conception of dynastic time and history that was encoded in these codices. This form of historical document was designed to show off the continuous line of rulers, establishing the legitimacy of the ruling dynasty. Historical narrative, like so many aspects of Aztec religion and knowledge, was closely tied to city-state politics, and its form and function served the interests of rulers and nobles.

Technology

The most impressive examples of Aztec technology were in the realms of agriculture (chapter 3) and crafts (chapter 4).[15] The Aztecs were not great innovators in these areas; for the most part they took advantage of the advances made by earlier Mesoamerican peoples. Intensive agricultural methods like irrigation, terracing, and raised fields had been around since the Classic period at least, but the Aztecs were the first to put all of these methods to use on a massive scale. Their transformation of the central Mexican landscape to feed the growing population was a real technological achievement.

In the category of craft technology, the examples of obsidian and bronze stand out. The ancient Mesoamerican technique of prismatic blade production – yielding the sharpest edges known to modern science – is one of the premiere achievements of ancient technology anywhere in the world. The Aztecs made some minor modifications to the process of blade production, but for the most part they employed methods that had been practiced for millennia. The technology of bronze production – actually a Tarascan, not Aztec, craft – was quite sophisticated, and Tarascan metallurgists were highly skilled in achieving desired concentrations of copper, tin, and arsenic for specific tools and other objects. Other Aztec crafts with complex technologies include rubber production, textiles, ceramics, lapidary production, and featherworking.

The technology involved in Aztec architecture and construction was also impressive. The lime plaster used for floors and walls was a form of concrete whose production made use of several separate chemical reactions, and some examples remain as hard as modern concrete even after 500 years. Irrigation canals were able to cross rivers and ravines on tall aqueducts, and this technology was used on the canal that brought drinking water across the lake to Tenochtitlan from springs at Chapultepec on the lake shore.[16] Architecture and engineering require a system of workable mathematics, and the Aztecs used a base-20 number system for arithmetic, calendrics, and land measurement.[17] This numbering system was also crucial for commerce and tribute since goods were measured by counts and volume, not by weight. As shown above, there were glyphs for quantities of 1, 20, 400, and 8,000. In general, science and technology were practical and empirical, even when applied to religious phenomena. Another area of practical science and technology was medicine.

Medicine

The Aztecs had an extensive body of knowledge and belief concerning health and sickness. Their overall level of health was quite good for a preindustrial population, but many illnesses and injuries were common.[18] The Aztecs attributed illnesses to one of three types of causes: supernatural, magical, or natural. Supernatural ailments were sent by the gods as punishment for various transgressions. They were treated by making religious offerings and undergoing confession to a priest. Magical illnesses were caused by a sorcerer known as a *tlacatecolotl*, literally "owl man." These malevolent individuals cast spells on others, causing them to become ill or even die. Such spells were diagnosed through divination, often using the method of casting maize kernels (chapter 10). Treatment of magical ailments involved the use of precious stones (e.g., jade, quartz crystals), and often the consumption of exotic substances (e.g., worms, skunk blood, and skunk spray).

More practical diagnoses and cures were carried out by physicians, who treated naturally caused illnesses and injuries. Physicians were learned and experienced men and women. Female curers worked mostly within people's homes, and the chroniclers, who were mostly males and priests, unfortunately provide little information on these important women. Friar

Sahagún's Nahua informants described the qualities of a good physician as follows:

> The true doctor.
> He is a wise man [tlamatini];
> he imparts life.
> A tried specialist,
> he has worked with herbs, stones, trees, and roots.
> His remedies have been tested;
> he examines, he experiments,
> he alleviates sickness.
> He massages aches and sets broken bones.
> He administers purges and potions;
> he bleeds his patients;
> he cuts and he sews the wound;
> he brings about reactions;
> he stanches the bleeding with ashes.[19]

This description probably applied equally well to male and female physicians.

In the realm of naturally caused ailments and injuries, Aztec medicine was highly empirical and practical. Snakebites were treated by cutting the wound and sucking out the poison. Fractured bones were set successfully, and cures for wounds were very effective. Sahagún described in detail the treatment for a head wound.[20] The blood was washed away and the wound cleansed, first with urine, then with maguey sap (known for its curative properties). Next, an ointment of maguey sap and herbs was applied, and the wound bound tightly to keep out the air. If inflammation (infection) occurred, the medicine was applied several times; if not, the wound was kept bandaged until it healed.

The Aztecs used hundreds of medicinal herbs, and modern studies have shown that these had true pharmaceutical value in curing ailments and injuries. Many Aztec medical practices were more effective than those used by early Spanish doctors, and the Spanish emperor soon sent physicians and other scientists to study Aztec medicine and herbs. The priest Motolinía was quite impressed with Aztec physicians: "They have their own skilled doctors who know how to use many herbs and medicines which suffices for them. Some of them have so much experience that they were able to heal Spaniards, who had long suffered from chronic and serious diseases."[21]

Fractured bones were healed by setting the limb with a plaster cast strengthened by a splint. Although fractures were known to be caused by simple injuries, on a symbolic level they were attributed to the mythological quail who caused Quetzalcoatl to drop and break the bones of the ancestors in Mictlan (chapter 9). As a physician set a fracture, he recited a chant acknowledging this mythological association:

> Well now,
> O Quail,
> O One from the Place of Disturbance,
> What harm are you doing
> To the bone from the Land of the Dead [Mictlan],
> Which you have broken,
> Which you have smashed? . . .
> I am the Priest,
> I am the Plumed Serpent [Quetzalcoatl]
> I go to the Land of the Dead . . .
> There I shall snatch up
> The bone of the Land of the Dead.
> They have sinned –
> The priests,
> The dust-birds;
> They have shattered something,
> They have broken something.
> But now we shall glue it,
> We shall heal it.[22]

Art

The Mixteca-Puebla style

Aztec paintings and sculptures were executed in a distinctive style that was one expression of a more widespread phenomenon scholars call the "Mixteca-Puebla style." The Mixteca-Puebla style evolved out of an earlier tradition of painted pottery produced in coastal Mesoamerica from the Epiclassic through the Early Postclassic periods (AD 750–1150). At that time, standardized religious symbols, such as feathered-serpent designs and the step-fret motif, were painted on ceramic vessels in many areas of Mesoamerica outside of central Mexico. In the Early Aztec period, peoples of the "Mixteca-Puebla region" – southern Puebla and northwestern Oaxaca – adopted many of these symbols and created a painting style that used vivid colors and a standardized, precise, geometric depiction of images. H. B. Nicholson and Eloise Quiñones Keber describe several characteristics of the style: "Imaginative exaggeration of prominent features, strong black outlines, and bright, flat colors, resulted in images of striking boldness and visual impact."[23] Even without the use of color, as in sculptural reliefs or tracings from painted manuscripts, the vivid Mixteca-Puebla images stand out (see figures 9.3, 9.6, 10.3).

Artists in the city of Cholula, in the heart of the Mixteca-Puebla region, probably participated in the creation and elaboration of the Mixteca-Puebla style during the Early Aztec period. Cholula had long been a holy city and pilgrimage center (its central pyramid was the largest in Mesoamerica), and its renowned Cholula Polychrome ceramics (figure 5.7) were painted in the Mixteca-Puebla style. Other examples of the style include Postclassic polychrome ceramics from Puebla, Tlaxcalla, the Mixtec region, and the southern Valley of Mexico (figure 9.6); mural paintings from the Mixteca-Puebla area; and the Mixtec codices. In the Late Aztec period, Artists throughout central Mexico adopted the Mixteca-Puebla style for their painted manuscripts, such as the Codex Borgia (figure 1.6), and sculptural reliefs (figures 9.1, 11.10–11.12).

Aztec manuscripts and sculptures in the Mixteca-Puebla style were produced by scribes and artists for the use of the nobility. The widespread adoption of this style throughout central Mexico was facilitated by the network of interaction within the Aztec noble class described in chapter 6. The use and enjoyment of objects decorated with the Mixteca-Puebla style was not limited to the nobility, however. Commoners had ready access to the polychrome ceramics of Cholula and other areas through the market system, and fragments of these vessels are not uncommon in commoner contexts at Aztec sites. This style was so popular in Late Aztec Mesoamerica that it spread far beyond the central Mexican highlands. Manuscripts and murals painted in the Mixteca-Puebla style have been found in several of the distant, outer provinces of the Aztec empire. Similar murals were also painted on the Caribbean coast of Yucatan and in highland western Guatemala, Maya-speaking areas outside of the empire. The Aztecs were part of the Mesoamerican world system, a social universe far more extensive than the territory of their empire. The distribution of the Mixteca-Puebla style is graphic evidence for the economic and cultural integration of Postclassic Mesoamerica.[24]

The art and politics of imperial sculpture

Stone sculpture was a major medium of Aztec art,[25] and Aztec sculptors far surpassed their earlier Mesoamerican ancestors in technical and aesthetic abilities. A sculpture of the goddess Tlazolteotl giving birth (figure 9.4) shows the realism of many Aztec pieces, as does a depiction of a man carrying a cacao pod (figure 11.7). Animals were frequent subjects of the sculptors, and snakes were the most often portrayed. Some snakes were carved naturalistically (figure 11.8); others were stylized representations of Quetzalcoatl, the feathered-serpent god. Jaguars were the next most commonly carved animal, and many of these images convey a sense of

Figure 11.7   Sculpture of a man holding a cacao pod (height 35 cm) (Photograph courtesy of the Brooklyn Museum, 40.16, Museum Collection Fund)

power (figure 11.9) befitting the importance of the jaguar in Aztec thought. Jaguar warriors were the elite troops, Tezcatlipoca had jaguar associations, and kings sat on jaguar skin thrones. Deities were another popular subject of sculptors, and ritual objects such as stone boxes, bowls, and panels were also common. These small- and medium-size sculptures of humans, animals, deities, and ritual objects, were carved in many city-states throughout the Aztec heartland. We found numerous small stone sculptures at Cuexcomate, which shows that their use was not limited to cities. After the Triple Alliance empire came to power a new school of monumental imperial stonecarving developed in Tenochtitlan.

Figure 11.8   Sculpture of a snake (diameter 61 cm) (Photograph courtesy of Dumbarton Oaks Research Library and Collections, Washington, DC)

Figure 11.9   Sculpture of a jaguar (length 28 cm) (Photograph courtesy of The Brooklyn Museum, 38.45, Carl de Silver Fund)

Mexica sculptors drew on the stylistic elements and iconography of the Mixteca-Puebla style to create huge, relief-covered, stone monuments that glorified the state and empire. Teams of carvers, who worked for the king and other state officials, created some of the most dramatic monuments of the ancient New World. Through their size, composition, and iconography, these huge sculptures were intended to communicate deliberate messages about the might and legitimacy of the empire. The basic themes or messages of Mexica imperial sculpture were that the Mexica possessed the religious and political right to rule the world, that they had inherited this right from the ancient civilizations of Teotihuacan and the Toltecs, and that the empire enjoyed a cosmic significance beyond mere politics.

Imperial stone monuments portrayed the cosmic structure of the universe and associated the empire with cosmic principles in order to legitimize the actions of its imperial leaders. The "Temple of Sacred Warfare" was a powerfully symbolic monument that brought the political content of Aztec sculpture to the forefront (figure 11.10). A massive model of a temple-pyramid, it was decorated with relief carvings on all sides that illustrated the themes of warfare, human sacrifice and death, autosacrifice, the sun, and the founding of Tenochtitlan. The overarching message portrayed on this sculpture was that war was a sacred obligation because it was waged to capture victims for sacrifice and that just as human sacrifice and autosacrifice were carried out for the sun to ensure that it would rise, so too were they required for the continuing glory of the imperial capital Tenochtitlan.

The so-called "Aztec calendar stone," the best-known Aztec monument, was another imperial sculpture that proclaimed the glory and legitimacy of Mexica rule (figures 11.11, 11.12). Research by art historian Richard Townsend suggests that this colossal monument (3.6 m in diameter and 25.4 tons in weight) was originally set horizontally, not vertically as it now stands in the Museo Nacional de Antropología in Mexico City. The central figure, the sun god Tonatiuh, was a death god in the Mictlantecuhtli complex.[26] The creation of the earth was symbolized by glyphs for the four previous suns or creations. The date 13 Acatl, prominently displayed at the top of the disk, was the year of the creation of the present sun, and it also marked the year of the accession of Itzcoatl, the Mexica king who created the Aztec empire. This correspondence of dates was significant, for it gave the temporal political event a cosmic importance.

The 20 day names arranged in a circle around the central figures account for the popular name of the monument, but it did not function as a calendar. The day names merely indicated the passage of time and the link between time and power. Around the perimeter of the disk were carved two fire-serpents, *xiuhcoatl*, that related to Huitzilopochtli and sacred warfare. The eight triangular pointers were both solar rays and directional indicators. The four larger pointers indicated the four cardinal directions and served as a symbol for the entire earth. In short, the "Aztec calendar stone" conveyed the message that the Aztec empire covered the whole earth (territory in all four directions), and that it was founded upon

Figure 11.10 "Temple of Sacred Warfare" sculpture (height 1.22 m) (Photograph by Michael E. Smith; reproduced with permission of the Instituto Nacional de Antropología e Historia)

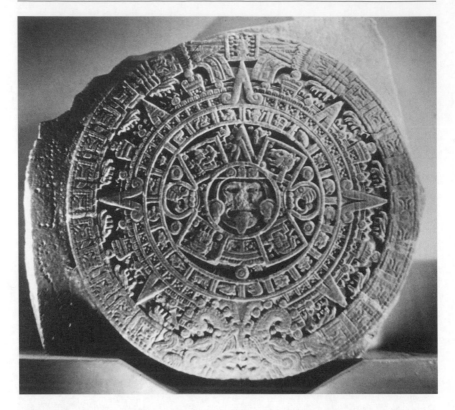

Figure 11.11   The so-called "Aztec calendar stone" (diameter 3.58 m) (Photograph by Michael E. Smith; reproduced with permission of the Instituto Nacional de Antropología e Historia)

the sacred principles of time, directionality, divine warfare, and the sanction of the gods.

Literature and Poetry

Literature and poetry were oral arts practiced by priests and members of the nobility.[27] The Aztecs greatly valued oratorical skill, and fine speakers and poets had high reputations. The Acolhua king Nezahualcoyotl, for example, was widely revered as a great poet. The Nahua informants of Friar Sahagún had this to say about orators:

Figure 11.12   The so-called "Aztec calendar stone" (Drawing by Emily Umberger; reproduced with permission)

> The good narrator:
> pleasing words, joyful words,
> he has flowers on his lips.
> His speech overflows with advice,
> flowers come from his mouth.
> His speech, pleasing and joyful as flowers;
> from him come noble language
> and careful sentences.[28]

Fortunately, many poems, histories, and formal speeches by such narrators were recorded in Nahuatl soon after the Spanish Conquest. Ethnohistorian Miguel León-Portilla divides Aztec literature into four categories: myths, sacred hymns, lyric poetry, and histories. I explore myths in chapter 9 and histories in chapter 1; here my discussion focuses on sacred hymns and poetry.

Sacred hymns

Sacred hymns were chanted at ceremonies to honor the gods. Most were exhortations to the highest and most powerful deities, such as Ometeotl, Tlaloc, and Huitzilopochtli. The majority of hymns were dedicated to Tezcatlipoca, who was often addressed as "Giver of Life." In the following hymn, the Giver of Life is invoked in his roles as both the creator and destroyer of the world:

> With flowers you write,
> Oh Giver of Life!
> With songs you give color,
> with songs you shade
> those who must live on the earth.
> Later you will destroy
> eagles and tigers [jaguars];
> we live only in your painting
> here, on the earth.
> With black ink you will blot out
> all that was friendship,
> brotherhood, nobility.
> You give shading
> to those who must live on the earth.
> Later You will destroy
> eagles and tigers [jaguars];
> we live only in your painting
> here, on the earth.[29]

Tezcatlipoca, the Giver of Life, is described here as both a poet ("With flowers you write"; see below) and a scribe (the black ink, colors, and painting).

Lyric poetry

The Nahuatl phrase for poetry was *in xochitl, in cuicatl*, which translates as "flower and song." Flowers and the beauty of the world were important themes of lyric poetry, as was the celebration of the singer or poet:

> The flowers sprout, they are fresh, they grow;
> they open their blossoms,
> and from within emerge the flowers of song;
> among men You scatter them, You send them.
> You are the singer![30]

Many poems dealt with the transience of life and the ability of poetry to transcend mortal limitations. The great Acolhua king Nezahualcoyotl expressed these ideas as follows:

> My flowers shall not cease to live;
> my songs shall never end:
> I, a singer, intone them;
> they become scattered, they are spread about.[31]

This concern for life's impermanence and the inevitability of death was a major preoccupation of Aztec literature and poetry. Nezahualcoyotl's poem quoted in chapter 1 is a good example: "Not forever on earth, only a little while." But if our lives arc short, we should enjoy them while we can:

> One day we must go,
> one night we will descend into the region of mystery.
> Here, we only come to know ourselves;
> only in passing are we here on earth.
> In peace and pleasure let us spend our lives; come let
> us enjoy ourselves.
> Let not the angry do so; the earth is vast indeed!
> Would that one lived forever; would that one were
> not to die![32]

Music and Dance

Music and dance were holy arts, performed mainly at rituals and ceremonies.[33] Drums were the instruments most commonly mentioned in written sources and most often depicted in drawings. In figure 11.13 the instrument on the right is a large upright wooden drum known as a *huehuetl* that was played with the hands. On the left is a horizontal "slit gong" (*teponaztli*) made of a single piece of wood that produced two tones when struck in different places with mallets. Below these, men are playing pottery flutes. Other instruments included trumpets of cut conch shells, pottery whistles, and rattles of various types.

These instruments were used to accompany the ritual dances at public ceremonies. One such dance is illustrated in figure 11.13. The dancers carry feather bundles and elaborate rattles. Many dances included both men and women, and the participants often moved in a circular pattern around the musicians in the center. Friar Durán was fascinated by Aztec dance and song, although he was scandalized by some of the dances of young people:

Figure 11.13   Ritual dance accompanied by drums (left, *teponaztli*; right, *huehuetl*) and flutes. The dancers, holding rattles and feathers, circle around an image of the god Macuilxochitl in the center (After Códice Tudela 1980:f.66r)

Young people took great pride in their ability to dance, sing, and guide the others in the dances. They were proud of being able to move their feet to the rhythm and of following the time with their bodies in the movements the natives used, and with their voice the tempo. The dances of these people are governed not only by the rhythm but by the high and the low notes in the chant, singing and dancing at the same time.

Thus these differences in songs and dances existed: some were sung slowly and seriously; these were sung and danced by the lords on solemn and important occasions and were intoned, some with moderation and calm, [while] others [were] less sober and more lively. These were dances and songs of pleasure known as "dances of youth," during which they sang songs of love and flirtation, similar to those sung today on joyful occasions. There was also another dance so roguish that it can almost be compared to our own Spanish dance the saraband, with all its wriggling and grimacing and immodest mimicry. It is not difficult to see that it was the dance of immoral women and fickle men . . . it is highly improper.[34]

chapter twelve
Final Glory, Conquest, and Legacy

Nothing but flowers and songs of sorrow
are left in Mexico and Tlatelolco,
where once we saw warriors and wise men.
We wander here and there
in our desolate poverty.
We are mortal men.
We have seen bloodshed and pain
where once we saw beauty and valor.
We are crushed to the ground;
we lie in ruins.
There is nothing but grief and suffering
in Mexico and Tlatelolco,
where once we saw beauty and valor.
Have you grown weary of your servants?
Are you angry with your servants,
O Giver of Life?

Cantares Mexicanos

Aztec civilization reached the height of its development in the years following AD 1500, only to be cut short by a band of Spanish conquerors between 1519 and 1521. The coming of the Europeans in the aftermath of Christopher Columbus's voyages spelled doom for many hundreds of native cultures in North and South America. Some peoples, including the Aztecs, were conquered by force, others submitted peacefully, and still others resisted European advances for centuries. Some were wiped out by epidemic disease before they were able to choose resistance or submission. The Aztecs were the first state-level society encountered by the European invaders, and the means of their conquest – military defeat combined with decimation by epidemics – were to be repeated many times across the New World.

There are no full-blooded Aztecs still alive, and nowhere are there any villages that preserve Aztec culture unchanged. Yet Nahuatl does survive as a living language for over one million people, and modern Nahua culture includes many traits preserved from the distant, pre-Spanish past. Beyond the boundaries of contemporary Nahua villages, Aztec traits have been interwoven into modern Mexican culture. Many Mexicans look to the Aztecs for the origin of their cultural heritage and take pride in the achievements of Aztec civilization. The Aztec heritage belongs to us all, however, and the Aztecs can teach us much about human society and its diversity of lifeways and practices.

The Final Century: 1428–1519

Most of this book describes Aztec civilization during the 91 years between the formation of the Triple Alliance empire in 1428 and the arrival of the Spaniards in 1519. In many ways this interval, the Late Aztec B period, represented the pinnacle of cultural development in ancient Mesoamerica. The expansion of the empire brought peace and order to central Mexico. The explosive growth of markets and craft production joined diverse regions and sectors together in a burgeoning economy that brought prosperity and opportunity to many people. Cities flourished and rural pioneers opened up new land to cultivation to feed a growing population. Political and economic successes were aided by a vigorous state religion, which in turn allowed learning and the arts to thrive. Important intellectual advances were made in the diverse fields of history, poetry, philosophy, medicine, astronomy, and engineering. Painting, sculpture, and other visual arts were elevated to new aesthetic heights under the patronage of the state and religion. These developments came at a cost, however.

Aztec society was sharply divided by class. Economic and cultural rewards were not evenly distributed. Human sacrifice was used by the state to terrorize commoners, who had no voice in the arena of politics. Nobles controlled most of the wealth and had more freedom than did commoners. Prosperity benefited all classes in some way (except perhaps the slaves), but ultimately, the economy rested upon the backs of the peasants in the field. As the empire expanded, some of this burden was shifted from the Valley of Mexico to more distant provinces through the system of imperial tribute. Nevertheless, the tribute system was not productive enough to fully compensate for the rapid growth of the Aztec population.

Population growth stimulated the growth of markets, commerce, and craft production, but economic prosperity, in turn, may have encouraged people to have larger families. Demographic growth was a major factor pushing the expansion of cities, city-states, and the empire, which furthered the evolution of religion and intellectual life. The most immediate and direct effect of the Aztec population explosion was the intensification of agriculture. During the Late Aztec B period, however, society began to show signs of stress. Feeding the three million Aztecs was increasingly difficult, and famines occurred with more frequency. Archaeological reconstructions of life at rural sites point to sharp declines in the standard of living of Aztec peasants under the empire, owing most likely to declining agricultural productivity and increased tributary exploitation by city-states and the empire.

These processes of change and growth were not limited to central Mexico. In fact they were occurring throughout Mesoamerica in the Late Postclassic period. Populations increased, agriculture intensified, local dynasties consolidated their power, and cities and towns flourished. One of the largest and most powerful cities outside the empire was Tzintzuntzan, capital of the Tarascan empire (see chapter 7).[1] The main state temple complex in Tzintzuntzan consisted of a huge platform upon which rested five large keyhole-shaped temples called *yacatas* (figure 12.1). In terms of its horizontal extent, this structure dwarfed the Templo Mayor of Tenochtitlan. The development of Tarascan civilization paralleled Aztec growth in many ways, and this is just one example of the widespread growth and dynamism in Late Postclassic Mesoamerica.

The Late Postclassic period was remarkable for the high levels of communication and interaction that linked polities and peoples in all corners of Mesoamerica.[2] Long-distance commercial exchange reached the highest level of the Mesoamerican past in Late Postclassic times; areas outside central Mexico had professional merchants similar to the Aztec *pochteca* and *tlanecuilo*, other towns had markets and craft specialists, and money in the form of cacao beans and cotton *quachtli* were ubiquitous from the Maya realm to the Tarascan empire. The commodities discussed in chapter 5 (table 5.1) were traded throughout all of Mesoamerica, and a common set of luxury goods were used by local elites in virtually every city and town. But economic exchange was not the only type of long-distance contact binding Mesoamerica into a single unit, or world-system, in Postclassic ties.

This period also witnessed an unprecedented level of stylistic communication and sharing. Murals in the International Style (part of the Mixteca-Puebla style; see chapter 11) were painted in all areas, and elites throughout Mesoamerica exchanged painted codices whose calendrical, ritual, and historical content – in addition to their styles and iconography – were widely shared. For example, the highland Maya city of Iximche', capital

TZINTZUNTZAN

Figure 12.1 Reconstruction drawing of the religious center of the Tarascan capital Tzintzuntzan. Five circular temples – called *yacatas* – sit on top of a massive platform (After Marquina 1964:256)

of the Kaqchikel peoples, was in many ways a typical Late Postclassic Maya city (figure 12.2).[3] Nearly all of the artifacts and architecture con-form to local highland Maya patterns, but two temples have attached low platforms decorated with skulls and crossbones that would be right at home in Tenochtitlan. Although some archaeologists have suggested that Mexica peoples moved to Guatemala and brought such symbols with them, a much more likely explanation is that the local Kaqchikel king knew about the skull-and-crossbone symbol, and its use on low platforms (chap-ter 9), from a traded codex or from a visiting ambassador or merchant. Symbols like this were well traveled in Postclassic Mesoamerica, provid-ing visual evidence for the high level of communication and integration – both commercial and stylistic – that linked the entire area into a single social and cultural network.

Aztec civilization was just one culture among many in Late Postclassic Mesoamerica. But it is the culture that we know the most about today. Its pathway of development illustrates the two-headed results of demographic, economic, and political expansion: prosperity and cultural florescence coupled with growing hardship for the commoner class, and impending crises for society as a whole. This was the situation that Hernando Cortés and his army encountered in 1519.

Figure 12.2   Palace and temples at the highland Maya city of Iximche'
(Photograph by Timothy Smith; reproduced with permission)

Conquest by Spain

Cortés and Motecuhzoma

In the decades after Columbus's first voyage of 1492, the Spaniards colo-
nized the Caribbean islands and set up a base in Cuba.[4] Several expeditions
explored parts of the Mexican and Central American coasts, where the
Spaniards heard rumors of a rich and powerful kingdom in Mexico. In
February of 1519, Hernando Cortés set sail from Cuba with 11 ships and
500 men to explore the Mexican coast. Funding for the expedition was
split between the Spanish crown, represented by governor Diego de Velásquez
in Cuba, and Cortés himself. At the last minute, Velásquez had second
thoughts about the ambitious Cortés and withdrew permission for the trip,
but Cortés sailed anyway. Later the governor tried unsuccessfully to recall
and imprison Cortés. On the island of Cozumel, off the east coast of the
Yucatan Peninsula, Cortés came upon Gerónimo de Aguilar, a Spaniard
who had survived shipwreck several years earlier. Aguilar had learned to
speak Yucatec Maya, and he joined the expedition as an interpreter.

The group then rounded the peninsula and stopped at Potonchan on
the Gulf Coast. A local army came out to meet the Spaniards, but after
a brief battle, the natives withdrew. Their leaders offered Cortés gifts,

including several young women. Among the women was Malintzin, a noblewoman, bilingual in Nahuatl and Maya, who had been sold into slavery. The combined linguistic abilities of Malintzin and Aguilar enabled Cortés to communicate with the Aztecs. Malintzin (also called Marina or Malinche) proved to be a useful assistant to the Spaniards. She later became Cortés's mistress and bore him a son, Martín.

When the Spaniards landed in the territory of the Totonac peoples, near what is today the city of Veracruz, they were greeted by messengers from Motecuhzoma. The Mexica king had been following their progress, and he sent Cortés gifts of precious feathers and gold. This offering was made in part to ascertain who these strange foreigners were. Some thought that the Spaniards could be gods, and their reactions to the gifts would help to clarify their nature. But the Spaniards did not respond like gods. In the words of Friar Sahagún's Nahua informants:

> They laid before them golden streamers, quetzal feather streamers, and golden necklaces.
> And when they have given them the gift, they appeared to smile, to rejoice exceedingly, and to take great pleasure. Like monkeys they seized upon the gold. It was as if then they were satisfied, sated, and gladdened. For in truth they thirsted mightily for gold; they stuffed themselves with it, and starved and lusted for it like pigs.[5]

Cortés imprisoned the messengers and forced them to witness the firing of a cannon, which terrified them. He then released them to return to Motecuhzoma with a frightening account of the strangers. The Mexica king was perplexed. He summoned his wise men and magicians, but they, too, were unable to fathom the nature of the Spaniards. Cortés and his army did not behave like gods, nor did they behave like a Mesoamerican invading army. Motecuhzoma chose to wait before taking any action against the strangers. His hesitation contributed to the rapid Spanish victory.

Hernando Cortés set up camp and spent several months exploring the area in the vicinity of his landfall. He engaged the local Totonac rulers in skirmishes and negotiations. The Totonacs soon came to respect the military abilities of the Spaniards, whose swords, guns, armor, horses, fighting dogs, and military tactics held great advantage over Mexican obsidian swords and the one-on-one fighting style of Mesoamerican armies. Local rulers complained bitterly about the heavy burden of imperial tribute, and Cortés responded by taking some haughty Mexica tribute-collectors prisoner. The audacity of this action astonished the Totonac nobles, who quickly came over to the side of the Spaniards when Cortés offered to free them of Mexica domination.

By this time, Cortés had heard descriptions of the great imperial capital Tenochtitlan and its incredible riches. His army set out for central

Mexico accompanied by hundreds of allied Totonac troops. The Spaniards did not head directly for the Valley of Mexico, however. Cortés had learned that Motecuhzoma could field armies of many thousands of soldiers, and his small group of Spaniards and Totonacs was no match for such forces. Instead, the expedition headed for Tlaxcalla, the powerful Aztec state that still resisted conquest by the Triple Alliance. At first Cortés's soldiers were challenged by the Tlaxcallan armies, but Cortés soon convinced the rulers to join him in his march to Tenochtitlan. Motecuhzoma was increasingly worried about the Spaniards' intentions. Several times he sent precious gifts (including objects of gold) to Cortés, accompanied by the suggestion that there was no need for Cortés to visit the capital city. His troops were welcome to take the gifts and simply return across the water. The gold, of course, made the Spaniards more anxious than ever to see the city. Gold was what they sought.

The Spaniards and their Totonac allies left Tlaxcalla with several thousand additional soldiers. The party first visited the nearby holy city of Cholula. There they were welcomed by the nobles. Cortés, however, fearing an ambush, ordered his armies to massacre thousands of unarmed Cholulan warriors. Then, the people of Cholula were compelled to declare their loyalty to Spain. Cortés and his forces now struck out for Tenochtitlan. Motecuhzoma continued to send gifts and messages urging Cortés to head back to Spain, but the Spaniards and their allies pressed on. At last they entered the Valley of Mexico and approached the lake. The Spaniards were awed by the sight of the great cities with their monumental buildings (see the quotation that begins chapter 1).

Cortés proceeded along the causeway toward Tenochtitlan, and Motecuhzoma went to greet him. In the words of Friar Durán:

> When Motecuhzoma heard that the Spanish captain was approaching, he again ascended his litter and then, carried on the noblemen's shoulders in the same way he had come, he went out to meet him. On seeing Cortés, he descended. When Cortés saw this, he climbed down from his horse and went to embrace the Aztec sovereign, treating him with much reverence. Motecuhzoma did the same, paying homage to the other with humility and words of welcome. From one of his noblemen he took a splendid necklace of gold, inlaid with precious stones, and placed it around Cortés's neck.[6]

Great crowds had gathered to witness the meeting and gawk at the Spaniards. The soldier Bernal Díaz later recalled:

> Who could now count the multitude of men, women, and boys in the streets, on the roof-tops and in canoes on the waterways, who had come out to see us? . . . So, with luck on our side, we boldly entered the city of Tenochtitlan or Mexico on 8 November in the year of our Lord 1519.[7]

Motecuhzoma made the Spaniards welcome and put them up in the sumptuous palace compound of his father, the great Mexica *tlatoani* Axayacatl.
Cortés repaid this courtesy by taking Motecuhzoma prisoner on the pre-
text that a group of Spaniards on the coast had been attacked by native
warriors. Cortés began to govern Tenochtitlan through the fiction that
Motecuhzoma was still in authority. The Spaniards tried to suppress sacrificial rituals, with only partial success. This tense situation continued
for several months. Then, in April of 1520, Cortés received news that an
expedition had landed on the coast with orders from Velásquez to arrest
him. He set off at once with half of his forces, leaving Pedro de Alvarado
in charge of the capital.

Cortés managed to defeat the newly arrived Spanish force and won
them over to his side. Meanwhile, Alvarado was having serious difficul-
ties in Tenochtitlan. When he heard that human sacrifices were to be performed at a ceremony honoring Huitzilopochtli, Alvarado had the
defenseless participants massacred in the temple courtyard. Outraged by
the slaughter, the Mexica armies attacked the Axayacatl palace. At this
point Cortés returned with his troops and new recruits, who managed to
fight their way back into the palace. The ruling council of Tenochtitlan
had long opposed Motecuhzoma's cooperation with the Spaniards and
voted to depose the king. They elected his brother, Cuitlahuac, to replace
Motecuhzoma as *tlatoani*. Hostilities continued, and at some point
Motecuhzoma was killed. Spanish sources stated that he was killed by a
stone thrown by one of his own people, whereas native accounts related
that he was murdered by the Spaniards.

Cortés and his group were besieged. Amidst the fighting they made
plans to flee the city (figure 12.3). On the night of June 30, 1520, they
attempted to slip out of Tenochtitlan. Many of the Spaniards had laden
themselves with heavy loads of gold, which slowed down their escape.
This night has since been called the *noche triste* (night of sorrows) due
to the heavy casualties of the bloody battles that took place. Eventually Cortés and his army made it across the causeway and retreated
over the mountains to regroup in Tlaxcalla. Additional Spanish soldiers arrived to fortify the positions on the coast and to reinforce
Cortés's army. The general kept busy recruiting new native allies and
organizing his troops.

Several months later, Cortés set off for Tenochtitlan once again. This
time he was supported by over 700 Spaniards and close to 70,000 native
troops. The army split into two parts, and each fought its way to the edge
of the lakes by a different route. The combined Spanish and Tlaxcallan
armies successfully defeated many local city-states that had been fortified
with Mexica soldiers (figure 12.4). Numerous *tlatoque* declared their allegiance to Spain. When the armies met up, they laid siege to the island

Figure 12.3   Aztec warriors attack the Spaniards, who try to flee Tenochtitlan (After Durán 1994:pl.60; drawing by Ellen Cesarski)

capital. The fighting was fierce, with many casualties on both sides, but the invaders wreaked the greatest devastation with an unintentional weapon: disease. Friar Sahagún's native informants described the situation as follows:

> While the Spaniards were in Tlaxcala, a great plague broke out here in Tenochtitlan. It began to spread during the thirteenth month [the month of Tepeilhuitl, October 11–30] and lasted for seventy days, striking everywhere in the city and killing a vast number of our people. Sores erupted on our faces, our breasts, our bellies; we were covered with agonizing sores from head to foot.
>
> The illness was so dreadful that no one could walk or move. The sick were so utterly helpless that they could only lie on the beds like corpses . . . If they did move their bodies, they screamed with pain.
>
> A great many died from this plague, and many others died of hunger. They could not get up to search for food, and everyone else was too sick to care for them, so they starved to death in their beds.[8]

The siege of Tenochtitlan went on for several months, during which time many who were not injured became seriously ill. At some point before or during the siege, Cuitlahuac died of smallpox. He was replaced by Cuauhtemoc, a nephew of Motecuhzoma and a fierce warrior. The Spaniards blocked shipments of food into the city and cut off the fresh water supply by destroying the aqueduct from Chapultepec. The Mexica warriors fought bravely, but the outcome of the siege was inevitable. On August 13, 1521, Cuauhtemoc was captured and the Spaniards claimed victory over the Mexica. The Tlaxcallan soldiers,

Figure 12.4   Battle between the Mexica and Spaniards (with their Tlaxcallan allies) (After Muñoz Camargo 1981:f.277r; drawing by Ellen Cesarski)

however, went on to massacre many of the remaining inhabitants of Tenochtitlan. The defeat and destruction of the city was remembered in the following elegy:

> Broken spears lie in the roads;
> we have torn our hair in grief.
> The houses are roofless now, and their walls
> are red with blood.
> We have pounded our hands in despair
> against the adobe walls,
> for our inheritance, our city, is lost and dead.
> The shields of our warriors were its defense,
> but they could not save it.[9]

Perspective

The question is sometimes asked, "How did 500 Spaniards manage to defeat the Aztec empire whose armies had tens of thousands of warriors?" As the above account should make clear, this question is not well phrased. The Aztec empire was defeated by 500 Spaniards, aided by tens of thousands of native allies and a disease epidemic of proportions never before seen in the New World. Much of the Spanish success was owed to the political astuteness of Hernando Cortés, who quickly divined the disaffection towards the Mexica that prevailed in the eastern empire. He turned that desire for rebellion to his own benefit through strategic alliances with the Totonacs and other Mexica subjects as well as with their traditional enemies, the Tlaxcallans. These indigenous troops deserve credit for a major part of the Spanish victory. The superior weapons of the Spaniards – particularly guns and swords – are another reason for their success.

Motecuhzoma's hesitancy to attack the initial Spanish forces also contributed to the Aztec's defeat. Had the Mexica *tlatoani* challenged the Spaniards before they reached the Valley of Mexico, he might have prevailed.[10] Motecuhzoma's actions so puzzled and troubled the Nahua nobility that, after the conquest, they contrived a story to account for them. First, they concocted an "ancient" prophecy which stated that the god-king Quetzalcoatl would return from across the eastern sea to rule Mexico in the year 1 Acatl, or 1519. Next, they invented a series of omens and signs that pointed to the coming of Quetzalcoatl. Finally, they claimed that Motecuhzoma truly believed Cortés to have been the deity himself. In the context of this story, Motecuhzoma's hesitation made sense; he thought that the arrival of the Spaniards was the second coming of Quetzalcoatl, not an invasion of strange foreigners.[11]

Ethnohistorians Ross Hassig and Michel Graulich have suggested more reasonable explanations for Motecuhzoma's indecision. Hassig argues that at first Motecuhzoma was unafraid of the Spaniards since the power of the Triple Alliance empire was great enough to awe most potential enemies. Nor did Cortés and the Spaniards behave like a Mesoamerican invading army. Their behavior was puzzling to the Mexica, but not initially threatening. In Mesoamerican warfare, invading forces did not arrive unannounced. Intentions were clearly broadcast in advance of actual hostilities, but Cortés professed friendly intentions. Furthermore, following his defeat of the Mexica's enemies, Tlaxcalla and Cholula, Cortés might have been approaching Tenochtitlan to propose an alliance. In Hassig's words, "So instead of meeting the Spaniards at some distance from Tenochtitlan and fighting them as they would have met an enemy force, the Aztecs permitted them to enter their capital, as they would have if they were peaceful."[12]

Graulich notes that in Mesoamerican warfare, defeated kings who did not resist their conquerors were left in power and assessed a lower tribute quota than kings who put up a fight. He suggests that Motecuhzoma's hesitation can be explained in part by his use of this principle. The Mexica king may have thought that his armies stood little chance against the Spaniards, and therefore a policy of limited resistance was more likely to leave him in power and to obtain a less severe burden of tribute for his people. By the time the Spaniards were expelled from Tenochtitlan, and Motecuhzoma was replaced by more aggressive rulers, first Cuitlahuac and then Cuauhtemoc, it was too late for the Aztecs. The invading force had been heavily reinforced by both Spanish and native soldiers, and the dreaded smallpox virus had begun to decimate the population. Ultimately, this microorganism proved far more deadly than either Cortés's political shrewdness or Motecuhzoma's failure to attack.

The smallpox virus that devastated Tenochtitlan has been traced to a single soldier who arrived in Mexico in 1520 while Cortés was in Tlaxcalla preparing for his final assault.[13] Because many communicable diseases, such as smallpox, measles, and typhus, were absent in the New World, the Aztecs and other native peoples did not have any resistance to them. The situation was different in Europe (and in most of the world today), where a long history of exposure to these diseases had lessened their impact on the population. The first appearance of a contagious disease in an area always sets off the most devastating epidemic. When a disease such as one of these is unleashed on a new population, the resulting "virgin-soil epidemic" is usually catastrophic. The smallpox epidemic of 1520–1 was the first of many such virgin-soil epidemics to sweep through the New World in the centuries following European contact. According to one estimate, the population of the Valley of Mexico was reduced from 1.6 million in 1519 to 900,000 in 1521 as a result of this epidemic alone.[14]

The Nahuas under Spanish Rule

The Spanish conquest of the Aztecs and other Mesoamerican peoples was carried out for both economic and religious objectives. The conquerors initially sought gold (they "lusted for it like pigs"[15]), and later the colonists and the crown exploited Indian labor in silver mines and in agricultural endeavors. The Conquest was also conducted in the name of God, with missionizing and conversion as major goals. Consequently the two institutions with the greatest immediate effect on people were the *encomienda* (a grant of land and native labor made to an influential

Spaniard), which organized Indian labor for economic gain, and the church. I am switching here to the term "Nahuas" to describe the Aztecs and their descendants after the Spanish Conquest, following the suggestion of ethnohistorian James Lockhart.[16] Central Mexican civilization as described in chapters 1 through 11 was greatly transformed after 1521, and I hesitate to use the term "Aztec" for the modified Colonial-period culture. This should not obscure the great continuity in many aspects of culture, particularly those related to the Nahuatl language. I use the term "Indian" to refer to native peoples after 1521, both Nahuas and others.

After 1521, boatloads of colonists began to arrive from Spain. Mesoamerica became a Spanish colony known as Nueva España, or New Spain, and its capital, Mexico City, was built over the ruins of Tenochtitlan. New Spanish towns and cities were founded throughout central Mexico, usually on the sites of existing Aztec towns. Some Spaniards moved to rural estates to become holders of *encomiendas*, but most remained in urban areas. As mining and sugarcane cultivation were established, the colonial economy of New Spain boomed, attracting ever more colonists. A few of the Nahua nobility learned Spanish and became involved in the colonial economy, but most of the Nahua people who were not killed off by disease remained in their native communities and continued to speak Nahuatl. They were now subjects of the Spanish empire, which replaced the Aztec empire, and were rapidly adopting the Christian religion of their conquerors. Nevertheless, in many respects, life continued much as it had before the Spanish Conquest.

The encomienda

By 1521 the dust had settled on the ruins of the Aztec empire and the remaining Nahuas began a process of accommodation to new masters. The *encomienda* was a key institution of the Early Colonial period.[17] The Spanish crown had experienced earlier problems with *encomiendas* in the Caribbean, with the *encomenderos* assuming too much power and independence from the crown. Fearing that this would happen in New Spain as well, the crown forbade the establishment of the *encomienda* system there. But just as he had ignored Velásquez's order to halt his initial expedition, Hernando Cortés ignored the crown's wishes and proceeded to distribute *encomiendas* as rewards to his soldiers and associates. Once started, the institution received the support of the crown and soon spread throughout Spanish areas of Mesoamerica.

The Indians assigned to an *encomienda* were required to provide tribute goods and labor service to the *encomendero*, whose responsibility it was to protect them and to see to their religious conversion. The tribute goods paid to the *encomendero* usually consisted of daily necessities. For example, in the 1540s one Spaniard was provided daily with the following goods: 3 chickens, a load and a half of maize, 200 chilis, a loaf of salt, 12 loads of fodder, pine pitch, a load of charcoal, 12 loads of firewood, and the labor of 8 Nahua servants. The Indians' obligations went far beyond supplying provisions, however. Their heaviest burden was labor, either on agricultural estates or in mines.

Although the *encomienda* system was a highly exploitative means of controlling Indian labor, it had the effect of permitting Nahua local government and customs to continue under Spanish rule. *Encomiendas* were almost always allocated along the lines of preexisting political units. In most cases, an entire *altepetl* (city-state) was given to an *encomendero*, and many aspects of the pre-Hispanic *altepetl* organization (such as the office of *tlatoani* and the *calpolli* system) continued to operate for more than a century after the Spanish Conquest. These Colonial-period *altepetl* did not fight wars nor sponsor sacrificial ceremonies, but regulated land allocations and mobilized tribute much as they had done in earlier times.[18]

As the sixteenth century wore on, waves of epidemics continued to wash over Mesoamerica. In 1531 measles swept through the land, followed by an unidentified disease in 1532, and yet another smallpox epidemic in 1538. The deadliest epidemic hit in the years 1545–8, when typhus wiped out 60 percent or more of the Nahua inhabitants of central Mexico. It was followed by a mumps epidemic in 1550, another unknown disease in 1559–60, a second round of measles in 1563–4, and typhus once again in 1576–80. By that time the Nahua population in the Valley of Mexico numbered only 200,000 people, a reduction of 88 percent from the size of the 1519 population. The decline in the Nahua population had reached its nadir.

The church

The conversion of native peoples to Christianity was a fundamental goal of Spain's conquest and colonization of Mesoamerica.[19] Well-educated Spanish friars of the mendicant orders (Franciscans, Dominicans, and Augustinians) were soon sent from Spain to attend to the religious conversion and welfare of the Nahuas and other peoples. Mass baptisms of thousands of individuals were carried out, and within a few decades of the Conquest, most Nahuas had been converted. The friars quickly realized that their preaching would be far more effective if delivered in Nahuatl (and other native languages), and so they learned the language and trained Nahua assistants and scribes to help them. Friars Sahagún, Durán, and others began the systematic study of Aztec religion in order to better

Figure 12.5   Sixteenth-century Christian church and convent at Xochimilco
(Photograph by Louise Burkhart; reproduced with permission)

understand people's beliefs and to enable the priests to convert the Nahuas
and to save their souls more successfully. Priests became the partisans and
protectors of the Indians against their overexploitation by Spanish
*encomendero*s and crown officials, and the Nahuas welcomed priests into
their communities.

Churches were built throughout central Mexico, many associated
with large convents and monasteries (figure 12.5). Like the great
temple-pyramids of the Aztecs, these massive structures served not only
as places of worship but also as symbols of the power and glory of
God, deliberately built to impress the Indians.[20] A typical pattern in
Nahua towns was to tear down the pyramid and erect a church on the
elevated platform made by the rubble. This practice sent a strong message that the Christian God was supreme and was to be worshiped in
place of Huitzilopochtli, Tezcatlipoca, and the rest. From the perspective of the Nahuas, the placement of the church on top of the former
pyramid created continuity in the location and significance of sacred
space. Indian communities took pride in their churches, which became
symbols of local identity in New Spain. The Spaniards even built a
church on top of the largest pyramid of ancient Mesoamerica, the arti-

Figure 12.6   Church built on top of the abandoned Cholula pyramid, an artificial mountain (Photograph by Michael E. Smith)

ficial mountain of Cholula (figure 12.6). This pre-Aztec pyramid had been abandoned several centuries before the Spanish Conquest, but Cholula had remained a holy city, and the friars were particularly concerned to make it a Christian city.

The friars encouraged the policy of *congregación*, designed by the Spanish colonial administration to gather together scattered Nahua settlements into new, larger towns with churches. The resulting *congregaciones* were partly a response to the continuing Nahua population decline of the sixteenth century. Gathering the Indians together in one place made it easier to preach to them, easier to protect them from overexploitation, and to the colonial officials, easier to collect imperial and *encomienda* taxes.

The Nahuas were quickly to become nominal Christians, but did not entirely abandon the ways of their former religion:

> they did not undergo a conversion experience, in the sense of responding to a personal spiritual crisis by consciously and intentionally replacing one entire belief system with another . . . [Aztec religion] was more a matter of collective, community rites and celebrations than of an individualized, personal faith . . . The native people interpreted Christianity in terms that were more or less compatible with their own cultures.[21]

The Nahuas did not have the concept of a "faith" or "religion" as a domain separable from the rest of culture, and their new religion is best seen as a syncretism or blend of Aztec beliefs and Christian beliefs. Conversion involved the adoption of essential Christian rites and practices, while the basic mind-set remained that of traditional Nahua culture. Rather than passively accepting a completely new and foreign religion, people created their own adaptation of Christianity, compatible with their colonial situation and with many of their traditional beliefs and values. Some of the early priests recognized the partial nature of these conversions, lamenting that in place of a thousand gods, the Indians now had a thousand and one. The pervasive influence of Nahua beliefs on central Mexican Christianity continues today and many aspects of modern folk Catholicism can be traced back to the Aztec past.[22] The syncretism of the Nahua and Spanish religions received concrete expression in the incorporation of Aztec religious symbols and objects into sixteenth-century churches and convents (figures 12.7, 12.8).

Acolman, cloister detail

Figure 12.7   Carving in the Augustinian convent at Acolman, ca. 1550 (Drawing by Richard Perry; reprinted with permission from *Mexico's Fortress Monasteries* by Richard Perry, 1992, p. 45)

Figure 12.8   Aztec sacred stone box set into the wall of the Dominican convent at Yautepec, ca. 1550. This box is used for holy water today (Photograph by Michael E. Smith)

Continuity and Change

What were the effects of the Spanish Conquest on Aztec civilization? Clearly some things, such as human sacrifice, were eliminated immediately, whereas others, such as the Nahuatl language, have survived to the present day. Aztec imperial institutions and practices were the first to go. The Aztec empire ceased to exist in 1521, native warfare came to an end, the imperial trade and tribute systems closed down, and the outward signs of state religion were quickly suppressed.

Traditional patterns of community life, on the other hand, endured for several centuries in many rural areas. James Lockhart's research with Nahuatl-language documents shows that the *altepetl* was allowed to carry on within the framework of the *encomienda* and colony, serving as a powerful force for the preservation of Nahua culture and practices. Within the Colonial-period *altepetl*, Nahuatl was still spoken and the *calpolli* remained the dominant unit of settlement.[23] Change came only gradually, with many practices continuing through the seventeenth and eighteenth centuries.

For the peasants in the field it may have made little difference whether they were subjects of the Aztec empire or the Spanish empire. Men and women still produced goods for their family, for their *altepetl*, and for a distant foreign overlord. They remained tied to the land, rarely venturing far from their village, and social life revolved around the *calpolli* and *altepetl*, not some distant imperial city. These peasants were the carriers of the Mesoamerican cultural tradition. It was through their lives and actions, not the lives of nobles or priests, that many aspects of Aztec culture were maintained despite the great upheaval of the Spanish Conquest.

This basic continuity in peasant life explains the seemingly odd situation found by archaeologists at rural Nahua sites of the Early Colonial period. Although the Spanish Conquest initiated the most dramatic and catastrophic cultural changes ever to occur in Mesoamerica, there is little direct evidence of it at rural sites. People continued to build the same types of houses, and continued to make and use traditional household goods, such as unglazed Aztec orange pottery and obsidian tools, for more than a century after 1521. Goods from Europe, or whose manufacture used new European technologies, such as glazed ceramics and iron nails, do not appear at rural sites until after 1650. This situation contrasts sharply with that of urban areas where the introduction of Spanish material items was rapid.[24]

At first, new Spanish traits were simply incorporated into preexisting Nahua cultural patterns. In the words of James Lockhart:

> In the economic realm as in the others, a strong indigenous base continued to provide the framework while Spanish items and modes quickly entered everywhere, not so much displacing as infiltrating, interpenetrating, and being assigned to niches already existing in the indigenous cultural scheme.[25]

Change eventually did come to peasant villages, however. Spanish replaced Nahuatl as the dominant language in most areas, although in isolated communities Nahuatl has survived. Spanish practices and culture gradually infiltrated Nahua villages, while Nahua practices had their own impact on the new Colonial culture of New Spain. Considerable intermarriage between Indians and Spaniards took place and, by the time of the Mexican Revolution of 1910, most if not all Nahuas were of partial Spanish ancestry. Today Mexican culture is a true blend of Aztec traits, Spanish traits, and traits developed during the four and a half centuries of colonial and national rule. Similarly, the Mexican people are mestizos, their genetic heritage a combination of Indian and Spanish traits, with some African, Asian, and other European genes contributed as well. The Spanish Conquest may have put an end to the Aztec empire and it may have brought about the deaths of millions of people, but it did not extinguish Nahua culture. Today there are over one million Nahua Indians who speak Nahuatl, and Mexican national culture owes much of its distinctiveness and heritage to the contributions of Aztec civilization.

The Aztec Legacy: Modern Nahua Indian Culture

The category "Indian" in Mexico was invented with the arrival of Hernando Cortés in 1519. At first, the term was used to refer to the natives: Aztecs, Mayas, Zapotecs, and many other peoples who were culturally and biologically distinct from the invading Spaniards. As the Colonial period proceeded with its extensive genetic and cultural mixing, "Indian" came to be a social rather than a racial category. Today in Mexico, an "Indian" is someone who speaks a native language and lives in rural poverty.[26] Anthropologist Judith Friedlander has lived in the traditional Nahua village of Hueyapan, Morelos, and describes the nature of Indian identity as follows:

> Contemporary [Nahua] Indians have been placed in a contradictory position: while being preserved as living tribute to Mexico's noble indigenous past, they are also being discriminated against for being Indians in a Mestizo-oriented society . . . To be Indian in Hueyapan is to have a primarily negative identity. Indian-ness is more a measure of what the villagers are not or do not have vis-à-vis the hispanic elite than it is of what they are or have . . . [To the villagers of Hueyapan], to be Indian, in other words, signified primarily that you were poor.[27]

Although characterized by the preservation of the Nahuatl language and rural poverty, Nahua Indian villages today also conserve many traditional practices that can be traced back to the Aztecs, most prominently in the sphere of domestic material culture. For example, when peasants construct traditional adobe-brick houses today, they often employ techniques and materials identical to those used by their Aztec ancestors five centuries ago (figure 12.9).[28] Traditional diet and food in modern Nahua villages exhibit many continuities with Aztec times. Maize and beans are still the mainstay of the diet, with tomatoes, avocados, chili peppers, and squash as important supplements. Today most villagers buy their tortillas ready-made from a special bakery called a *tortillería*, although on special occasions women still take out the *metate* and *comalli* to make tortillas by hand.[29]

Even in the most conservative Indian household, however, European-derived foods play a major role. Rice, onions, beef, pork, and chicken have become deeply embedded parts of traditional cuisine. The principle feast dish today, *mole*, can be traced back to the Aztecs (the name is from

Figure 12.9   A farmer in the village of Tetlama, Morelos, builds the stone foundation for a traditional-style house of adobe bricks. The resulting foundation walls are almost indistinguishable from nearby Aztec peasant house foundations; see figure 6.3 (Photograph by Michael E. Smith)

molli, which means "sauce" in Nahuatl), but many of the ingredients of modern *mole* are derived from European cuisine, not Aztec. The example of diet is illustrative of the general situation in which Indian culture is an intermingling of Aztec and European traits. Cultural features or customs that are viewed as "traditionally Indian" today cannot necessarily be traced back to the pre-Hispanic past.[30]

Handwoven textiles are another example of a modern Indian tradition derived from both Aztec and Spanish origins. In Hueyapan, for example, women still spin thread by hand and weave cloth with a backstrap loom (figure 12.10) virtually identical to that used by the Aztecs (see figure 4.4). Although the technology is pre-Hispanic, the fiber they work is wool, not cotton or maguey, and the clothing they make conforms to Spanish, not indigenous, traditions.[31]

The modern Nahua Indian peoples of Mexico are not Aztecs living in the twentieth century. The blending of Aztec and Spanish cultures was a process in which people adopted some new traits and rejected others, just as they maintained some ancient practices and abandoned others. Mod-

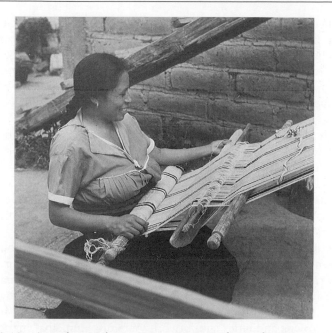

Figure 12.10   A modern Nahua woman, Doña Epifania of Hueyapan, Morelos, weaves cloth on a traditional backstrap loom. She is dressed in the traditional skirt and blouse of Hueyapan women (Photograph by Judith Friedlander; reproduced with permission from *Being Indian in Hueyanan* by Judith Friedlander. Copyright (c) 1975; St. Martin's Press, Inc.)

ern village culture is not merely a static mixture of Aztec and medieval Spanish traits, however; it too has been evolving for several hundred years. The Nahua peoples have created their own dynamic, unique culture, and continue to create it today, by meeting new challenges with the resources and knowledge available to them, of whatever origin. Some Nahuas have become completely integrated into the national culture, and others have kept to themselves in isolated villages. But in both Indian villages and Mexico City, much of the distinctive flavor of modern Mexican culture derives from the Aztec past.

The Aztec Past and the Mexican Present

Mexican national culture today owes much of its heritage to the Aztecs and other ancient Mesoamerican peoples. This is perhaps most obvious in the realms of food and economics. The maize and bean duo is ubiquitous in the diet of urban Mexicans, if not as prominent as it is in that of rural Indians. The maize tortilla is the national staple, and *tortillerías* are found in just about every rural village and urban neighborhood today.[32] Many popular foods, from *tacos* and *tamales* to chili peppers and *pulque*, can be traced directly to the Aztecs. Today, families most often make *mole* and other sauces in an electric blender, but almost every central Mexican household also owns a stone mortar and pestle with the same form and called by nearly the same names as their Aztec predecessors (the modern term for mortar in Mexican Spanish, *molcajete*, derives from the ancient Nahuatl term *molcaxitl*). The Spanish language as spoken in Mexico has been influenced by Nahuatl in several ways. Many Nahuatl terms have been incorporated into Spanish, and the characteristic lilting cadence that distinguishes the Spanish spoken in central Mexico from that of other areas can be attributed to Nahuatl influence.

Aztec markets continued to flourish after the Spanish Conquest, and periodic markets are still a vibrant part of modern Mexican culture. Found in both rural and urban areas, the weekly market remains a major provider of food and other goods and has yet to be superseded by the expanding numbers of discount stores and supermarket chains. Most large Mexican towns and cities support one or more municipal marketplaces that are open daily, with the weekly markets serving individual neighborhoods. Traditional craft items, such as textiles, pottery, and carved wood, are widely used not only in Indian villages but also in many middle-class Mexican homes. Furthermore, they are also popular with the many tourists who visit Mexico each year. These craft items are rarely found in the chain stores but are commonplace in the municipal and periodic markets, as well as in special tourist markets.

In the middle of Mexico City, where the central precinct of Tlatelolco once stood, is the Plaza of the Three Cultures. These three cultures – Aztec, Spanish, and modern Mexican – together symbolize the Mexican nation and its heritage. In Tlatelolco all three are physically present in close juxtaposition: Aztec pyramids from the Tlatelolco sacred precinct, the Early Colonial church of Santiago Tlatelolco, and modern high-rise apartment buildings (figure 12.11). The symbolism of the Plaza of the Three Cultures is important for modern Mexicans, and in 1964, President Alfredo López Mateos dedicated a plaque in Tlatelolco that reads, "On 13 August, 1521, Tlatelolco, heroically defended by Cuauhtemoc, fell into the power of Hernando Cortés. It was neither a triumph nor a defeat, but the painful birth of the Mestizo nation that is Mexico today."

The Mexican people have always looked back to the Aztecs with pride and admiration. Just as the Aztec dynasties used their Toltec heritage to establish their legitimacy, the Mexican government today turns to Aztec civilization as a source of authenticity and continuity with the past. The

Figure 12.11   Plaza of the Three Cultures in Tlatelolco: Aztec, Colonial Spanish, and modern Mexican; see also figure 8.9 (Photograph by Louise Burkhart; reproduced with permission)

national symbol of Mexico is taken directly from Aztec history: the eagle holding a snake, perched on a cactus (figure 12.12). In the fourteenth century this symbol marked the sacred place where Huitzilopochtli told the Mexica to build Tenochtitlan, and as the national capital, Mexico City remains a sacred place today.

One aspect of Mexico's veneration of the Aztec past is the attention given to archaeology by the national government. In Mexico archaeologists do not just study ancient cultures; rather they uncover the national heritage for the benefit of the entire nation. Most archaeological research in Mexico is conducted by the federal government, through the Instituto Nacional de Antropología e Historia. The enormous resources poured into the Templo Mayor excavations in the 1970s and 1980s show the level of government commitment to documenting the Aztec past. As the central monument of Tenochtitlan, the Templo Mayor today symbolizes the grandeur of Aztec civilization. The results of these and other excavations, and the results of ethnohistoric research, have worth for people worldwide, however, not just for Mexicans. This information occupies a prominent place in the collective human story.

Figure 12.12   The national symbol of Mexico, from the Mexican flag. This image is taken from the Mexica account of the founding of Tenochtitlan (Image by Robesus.com; reproduced with permission)

A Wider Perspective

Modern technology and communication have made the world seem smaller and have greatly reduced the variety of cultures on our planet. We seem to be moving toward a single, homogeneous, global commercial culture. This process began with the European age of exploration, and it continues at a rapid pace today. In order to comprehend the nature of our species, our strengths and weaknesses, it is essential to understand the great diversity of peoples and cultures that once lived on earth. The evolution from egalitarian farmers to state-level societies was perhaps the most momentous social transformation in human history. The appearance of kings, laws, writing, money, and unequal social classes marked a watershed in human affairs. Once this threshold was reached, at different times in different regions, there was no turning back.

We still live in states, the kind of society that first appeared with the Sumerians, Egyptians, Mayas, and Teotihuacan. We can learn much about ourselves by studying how institutions of government and social classes first arose, what life was like under the early states, how these civilizations adapted (or not) to their surroundings, and how they interacted with other peoples.[33] With growing problems of ethnic conflict in the world today, the Aztecs provide an example of how states have dealt with issues of economic and political domination and ethnic interaction.

The Aztecs are a prime example of an early complex society. They forged a way of life suited to their conditions independently of Old World cultures, and gained economic and political success through their own unique accomplishments. Study of the Aztecs provides us a glimpse of the past of all humanity and helps us to view the present and the past from a broader perspective. This wider perspective is the goal of modern anthropology, and it is no surprise that Aztec studies today form a crucial part of the discipline of anthropology.

The Nahua historian Fernando de Alvarado Tezozomoc was concerned that the history of the Aztecs never be forgotten. In Nahuatl he recorded the following passage shortly after AD 1600:

> Thus they have come to tell it,
> thus they have come to record it in their narration,
> and for us they have painted it in their codices,
> the ancient men, the ancient women.
> Thus in the future
>
> never will it perish, never will it be forgotten,
> always we will treasure it,
> we, their children, their grandchildren,
> brothers, great-grandchildren,
> great-great-grandchildren, descendants,
> we who carry their blood and their color,
> we will tell it, we will pass it on
> to those who do not yet live, who are yet to be born,
> the children of the Mexicans, the children of the Tenochcans.[34]

After nearly five centuries we can answer Alvarado Tezozomoc confidently that the story of the Aztecs will never be forgotten. It lives on in their painted codices and the many other objects that survive; it lives on in the written descriptions of Spaniards and Nahuas; it lives on in the Mexican people today; it lives on in the ruins of Aztec houses and temples; and it lives on in the world of modern archaeological and historical scholarship.

Notes

1   The Aztecs of Mesoamerica

1   *Cantares Mexicanos* 1985:f.17r (translated from the Nahuatl by León-Portilla 1963:72).
2   Some scholars object strongly to using the term "Aztec" at all. López Austin (2001:68), for example, states that "The use of the term 'Aztec' to denote the Mexica people is incorrect" and an "erroneous designation." Given the lack of a native term for the Nahuatl-speaking peoples of central Mexico (Mexicas and others), I feel justified in using the word "Aztec" for this purpose. See discussion of the use of the term Aztec in Barlow (1945) and Berdan et al. (1996:4).
3   Lockhart 1992.
4   The social archaeology approach, which originated in the 1970s and 1980s, is described most explicitly by Renfrew and Bahn (2000). Influential applications to Mesoamerica include Blanton et al. (1993), Flannery (1976), and Marcus and Flannery (1996). Hodge (1998) reviews recent Aztec archaeological research from this perspective.
5   For an overview of Mesoamerican cultures from ancient times to the present, see Carmack et al. (1996).
6   Kirchoff (1943) published the first list of Mesoamerican traits; see Weaver (1993) for a more recent example. The more common modern interaction approach is exemplified by Blanton and Feinman (1984) and Smith and Berdan (2002).
7   The best treatment of Mesoamerican environments in historical and modern times is West and Augelli (1989). Paleoenvironmental research directed at reconstructing climate, land forms, and other features for the prehistoric past has only just begun in central Mexico; see O'Hara et al. (1994), O'Hara and Metcalfe (1997), or Caballero and Ortega (1998).
8   See the glossary at the back of the book for definitions of key Aztec terms.
9   In an influential article, Sanders (1956) first pointed out these unique features of central Mexico, which he called the "central Mexican symbiotic region." See also Sanders et al. (1979).

10   Not all scholars believe that the past can be studied objectively and scientifi-
cally. Those who follow the "construction" model of scholarship assert that
the past is unknowable and the evidence vague. The researcher is free to
construct any interpretation that cannot be contradicted logically. Any interpretation of the past is as good as any other in this view. This model is un-
duly pessimistic. There are agreed-upon methods of scientific investigation
and historical research that give us powerful means to demonstrate that some
interpretations of the past are in fact far more reasonable and likely than
others. On the other hand, an opposing "discovery" model of scholarship
errs in the opposite direction by suggesting that researchers simply discover
an objective and fixed truth that exists independent of a scholar's procedures
or ideas.

11   *Anales de Cuauhtitlan*, f.57 (Bierhorst 1992:116). I have modified the spell-
ings of the Mexica kings to conform to the standard versions used in this
book. Boone (2000c) is the most complete modern study of Aztec historical
codices.

12   The standard scholarly edition of the Codex Mendoza is that of Francis F.
Berdan and Patricia Rieff Anawalt; see Codex Mendoza (1992); this is available in an excellent paperback edition (Berdan and Anawalt 1997).

13   Cortés 1962; Díaz del Castillo 1963.

14   Durán 1971:79–80. This volume contains Durán's descriptions of religion
and daily life and another book (Durán 1994), based on pictorial histories
and interviews with Aztec historians, is the most complete historical account
of the Mexica people. These two books are English translations of vols. 1
and 2 of the original Spanish publication (Durán 1967).

15   The English edition of the *Florentine Codex* was translated and edited by
Arthur J. O. Anderson and Charles E. Dibble (Sahagún 1950–82). An earlier
version of Sahagún's work, the *Primeros Memoriales*, is also important
(Sahagún 1993; 1997). There is a large body of scholarship on Sahagún and
his work; two useful collections are Edmonson (1974) and Klor de Alva (1988).

16   Alva Ixtlilxochitl (1975) is the major edition of this chronicler, whose work
has not been translated into English. No complete edition of Chimalpahin's
works exists, although Susan Schroeder is working toward this goal
(Chimalpahin Cuauhtlehuanitzin 1965; 1997; Schroeder 1991). Keen
(1971:196–201) provides useful information on Alva Ixtlilxochitl and
Chimalpahin.

17   Gerhard (1993), Gibson (1964), Kellogg (1995), and Lockhart (1992) review many of these documents. English translations of key administrative
documents may be found in Anderson et al. (1976), S. L. Cline (1993), and
Lockhart et al. (1986).

18   Acuña 1984–7. Central Mexico is covered in vols. 6–9. H. F. Cline's (1972)
discussion of the *Relaciones Geográficas* includes an English translation of
the original questionnaire.

19   Acuña 1984–7:v.6:201–2 (author's translation).

20   The results of the overall survey project are described in Sanders et al. (1979),
who provide references to the individual survey reports; see also Sanders
(1999) and Nichols (1996).

21   Intensive site surface research at Aztec sites is described in Brumfiel (1980; 1986; 1992), Charlton et al. (1991), and Smith et al. (1994). See discussion in chapters 4 and 8.
22   The Templo Mayor project is described in chapter 10. Other excavations of monumental architecture are discussed at greater length in chapters 2, 7, and 8. Marquina (1964) describes most of these sites.
23   See Evans (1988), M. E. Smith (1992a; 1993), Smith et al. (1999), and de Vega and Mayer (1991).
24   These projects are described in Brumfiel (1992), Charlton et al. (2000), Parsons et al. (1982a), and Smith et al. (1994); see also Hodge (1998).
25   Aztec cotton spinning is discussed in chapter 4. For the functional interpretation of spinning bowls, see Fauman-Fichman (1999) and Smith and Hirth (1988).
26   Quiñones Keber (1996) provides a perspective on the early development of Aztec art history. Florescano (1993), McVicker (1989), and Walsh (1997) discuss nineteenth-century collecting of Aztec art. Recent important publications by art historians include Baird (1993), Boone (2000a; 2000b; 2000c), Klein (2000), Leibsohn (1994), Milbrath (2000), Pasztory (1983), Quiñones Keber (1995), Townsend (2000), and Umberger and Klein (1993).

2   The Rise of Aztec Civilization

1   For general treatment of Mesoamerican archaeology, see Blanton et al. (1993), M. D. Coe (1994; 1999), Smith and Masson (2000), and Weaver (1993). For central Mexico before the Aztecs, Sanders et al. (1979) is the best single source.
2   The central Mexican Postclassic chronology is discussed in the papers in Fowler (1996); see also M. E. Smith (1992b) and Sanders et al. (1979). Division of the Late Postclassic period into two phases is described by Smith and Doershuk (1991) and Hare and Smith (1996).
3   There are numerous excellent publications on Teotihuacan. Some important works are Berlo (1992), Berrin and Pasztory (1994), Carrasco, et al. (2000), Cowgill (1997; 2000), McClung de Tapia and Rattray (1987), Millon (1973), Pasztory (1997), and Taube (2000b).
4   Teotihuacan–Aztec continuities and disjunctions are discussed in the papers in Carrasco et al. (2000) and Diehl and Berlo (1989); see also López Luján et al. (2000) and Umberger (1981; 1996).
5   Epiclassic sites are discussed in Diehl and Berlo (1989) and Hirth (2000).
6   The Aztec native historical accounts of Tollan and the Toltecs are discussed by Davies (1977) and Nicholson (2001), and archaeological research at Tula is discussed by Cobean (1990), Diehl (1983), Healan (1989), L. Jones (1995), Mastache et al. (2002), and Smith and Montiel (2001).
7   Archaeologists have found Toltec ceramic vessels alongside Teotihuacan pots in burials at Tenochtitlan (López Luján et al. 2000), and Mexica artists copied Toltec styles just as they copied Teotihuacan and Early Aztec styles (Umberger 1981; 1996).
8   The Aztlan migrations, mentioned in most surviving native histories, are dis-

cussed by Davies (1973:3–22), M. E. Smith (1984), and van Zantwijk (1985:22–36).

9   Mesoamerican languages and their historical development are discussed in Suárez (1983) and Kaufman (1976). For Nahuatl historical linguistics, see Kaufman (1976) and M. E. Smith (1984).

10   This avoidance is reflected in archaeological settlement patterns, where there is little continuity of occupation between sites of the Early Postclassic (AD 950–1150) and Early Aztec (AD 1150–1350) periods. Most Early Aztec sites were new foundations, although some of the small Early Postclassic sites continued to be occupied into the Aztec period.

11   Early Aztec city-states are discussed by Brumfiel (1983), Calnek (1978; 1982), Hodge (1984), and M. E. Smith (2000).

12   There is no full excavation report on Teopanzolco. Angulo Villaseñor (1976) and Marquina (1964) provide some information. The sacrificial burial is described in Lagunas and Serrano (1972), and ceramics from the site are described in M. E. Smith (2002). The site is open to the public today; some of the finds are on display at the Museo Regional de Cuauhnahuac in downtown Cuernavaca. The Museo Regional was built by the conqueror Hernando Cortés over the ruins of the Late Aztec royal palace of Cuauhnahuac, and some of the palace ruins can be seen today at the museum.

13   The basic report on Tenayuca is Anonymous (1935); information can also be found in Marquina (1964). Limón Boyce (1997) describes some of the more recent excavations. Tenayuca is open daily to the public; there is a nice museum displaying some of the finds.

14   The main prose native accounts of Mexica history are found in Alvarado Tezozomoc (1975a; 1975b), the Codex Chimalpopoca (Bierhorst 1992), Durán (1994), and Torquemada (1975–83). The best synthesis and presentation of these accounts is Davies (1973).

15   Alvarado Tezozomoc 1975a:49–51 (translated by Davies 1973:31).

16   Many scholars accept 1325 as a reasonable date for the founding of Tenochtitlan. Nevertheless, excavations near the Templo Mayor in Mexico City located Early Aztec deposits in the lowest levels (Matos Moctezuma 1999; Vega Sosa 1979), leading some scholars to suggest that there may have been an earlier settlement on the site that is not mentioned in the historical accounts (e.g., Graulich 1992b; M. E. Smith 1992b).

17   This story is recounted in Alvarado Tezozomoc (1975a:94–5). Marriage alliances as a form of diplomacy are described by P. Carrasco (1984).

18   León-Portilla 1963:155. According to Michel Graulich (1992b:25–6), Itzcoatl rewrote the histories in part to promote the rags-to-riches view of the Mexica past. He wanted to denigrate the achievements of the pre-Mexica peoples of the Valley of Mexico and to deny that Tenochtitlan existed as a settlement prior to its "founding" by the Mexica in 1325 (see chapter 8). P. Carrasco (1999) is the definitive study of the organization of the Triple Alliance.

19   Durán 1994:209–10. Not all of the laws are listed here.

20   See Pollard (1993) on Tarascan civilization.

21   Graulich (1992b) points out that most of the towns depicted on the Tizoc stone were conquered by his predecessors. This is another example of the

Mexica kings rewriting history to glorify their dynasty and rulership.
22   These "rebellions" are described by Hassig (1988) and Davies (1973; 1987).
23   This is the view of Davies (1973:216) and Graulich (1994).

3   People on the Landscape

1   The climate patterns are revealed by geophysical studies of changing lake
    levels in central Mexico. The start of dry conditions around AD 600 coincided
    with the fall of Classic-period Teotihuacan, and their end coincided with the
    Aztec population explosion. This temporal pattern is nearly the opposite of
    older views based upon poor data (e.g., Armillas 1969) that posited a change
    to drier conditions in the eleventh and twelfth centuries. The new
    paleoenvironmental data are reported in Caballero and Ortega (1998),
    Metcalfe et al. (1989), O'Hara et al. (1994), and O'Hara and Metcalfe (1997).
2   Larger families became economically beneficial to most people. Extra chil-
    dren contributed in the fields or the workshops to help meet increasing trib-
    ute demands, and to help families get ahead economically. City-state rulers
    had two good reasons to encourage larger families: more tribute-payers, and
    more males to serve in the army. The relationship between population growth
    and socioeconomic change was one of mutual encouragement or, in the lan-
    guage of systems theory, positive feedback. Population growth stimulated
    social changes, some of which in turn encouraged further population growth.
    Unfortunately, there are no detailed studies of Aztec demography; see the
    limited discussion in Brumfiel (1983), Sanders et al. (1979), Smith and Heath-
    Smith (1994), Whitmore and Williams (1998), and Williams (1989).
3   The literature on population pressure, agriculture intensification, and their
    relationships in ancient Mesoamerica and elsewhere is large. See Morrison
    (1996), Netting (1993), Sanders et al. (1979), and Wilk and Stone (1998).
4   The various Spanish estimates of the size of Aztec armies are discussed by
    Sanders (1970:403–4) and Hassig (1988; 1994).
5   See Borah and Cook (1963), Henige (1998), Sanders (1970), and Whitmore
    (1992).
6   The results are described in Sanders et al. (1979:216–19), and their methods
    are discussed in Sanders et al. (1979:34–52). Charlton (1970) is one of the
    studies of modern settlements in the Valley of Mexico used for population
    estimates. The methods of archaeological demography are far from foolproof,
    but comparisons with historical sources show that the archaeological popu-
    lation estimates are at least roughly correct. Similar patterns of rapid Late
    Aztec population growth have been found in recent and still unpublished
    regional surveys outside of the Valley of Mexico (e.g., Hare 2001).
7   Aztec foods and diet are discussed by S. D. Coe (1994) and Ortiz de Montellano
    (1990).
8   Sahagún 1950–82:bk.6:235. Modern peasant maize rituals with Aztec paral-
    lels are described by Lewis (1951), Sandstrom (1991), and Taggart (1983).
9   Díaz del Castillo 1963:233. Parsons (1996) discusses modern traditional
    methods of harvesting insects and algae; the nutritional value of the algae is

discussed in Furst (1978) and Ortiz de Montellano (1990:102–6).

10 Harner 1977. These arguments are countered by Price (1978) and Ortiz de Montellano (1990:85–94); see chapter 9.

11 Katz et al. 1974; Ortiz de Montellano 1990:98–102.

12 Cook and Borah (1979), Sanders et al. (1979), Whitmore and Williams (1998), and Williams (1989) all argue that the Aztec population exceeded their carrying capacity, whereas Blanton et al. (1993:155–6, 201–3) and Ortiz de Montellano (1990:72–97) take an opposing stance. I favor the former interpretation. The nutritional status of individuals as determined from osteological analyses of skeletal remains could help clarify the situation, but to date very few Aztec burials have been excavated.

13 Johnson and Earle 2000; Trigger 1993.

14 Sahagún 1950–82:bk.10:41–2.

15 Aztec terracing is described by Charlton (1970), Donkin (1979), Evans (1990), Sanders et al. (1979:242–51), and Smith and Price (1994).

16 Doolittle (1990) and Sanders et al. (1979:252–73) describe the technology and archaeological evidence for Aztec canal irrigation. Ethnohistorical accounts are discussed in Palerm (1972).

17 Aztec *chinampas* are discussed by Calnek (1972; 1976), Nichols and Frederick (1993), Sanders et al. (1979:273–81), and Wilken (1987).

18 Evans 1990.

19 Netting 1993; Wilken 1987.

20 Lees 1994; Wilkin 1987; Sanders et al. 1979:252–73.

21 M. E. Smith 1994b.

22 Parsons (1991) and Sanders et al. (1979:280) argue for centralized control of *chinampa* construction, although Wilken's (1987) research suggests that households could have built and maintained the system. The *chinampas* built around the edges of Tenochtitlan appear to have been small plots, each with a nearby house for the family of the farmers (Calnek 1972; 1974).

23 See discussion in M. E. Smith (1992a) and Smith and Price (1994). The continuous and dispersed nature of these settlement patterns calls into question the very concept of archaeological site as a discrete bounded unit of settlement.

24 This fieldwork is described in M. E. Smith (1992a; 1997b), Smith and Heath-Smith (1994), and Smith and Price (1994). The sites are difficult to reach today without a local guide.

25 Random sampling is a mathematical method for selecting items to study. It is designed to ensure that the items selected – the sample – are representative of the larger collection of items – the population. By using random sampling, we could generalize from our sample of excavated houses to the entire population of houses at these sites.

26 All houses at Capilco and most houses at Cuexcomate were simple structures corresponding to the residences of peasants or commoners, so we applied a household size figure of 5.5 persons (taken from Early Colonial census documents). Cuexcomate also had seven small elite residences, and we used a household size of 11 persons, also from the census documents. The census figures are discussed in P. Carrasco (1976) and S. L. Cline (1993); our meth-

ods of population estimate are described in M. E. Smith (1992a; 1994a).
27 These excavations were directed by T. Jeffrey Price, who conducted many of the technical analyses; see Smith and Price (1994). The example discussed in the text is unit 230.
28 Osvaldo Sterpone of the Instituto Nacional de Antropología e Historia made this discovery.

4   Artisans and their Wares

1 Brumfiel (1987) discusses patterns of craft production. See also Hodge (1998) and papers in Hodge and Smith (1994). The best ethnohistoric descriptions of artisans are in books 9 and 10 of Sahagún (1950–82). My use of the terms "utilitarian" and "luxury crafts" is imprecise; technically these terms refer to the consumption (uses) of goods, not to their production. But as Brumfiel (1987) points out, utilitarian and luxury goods had contrasting patterns of production, and these are handy labels to organize the diversity of Aztec crafts.
2 Important studies of craft production in early states include Costin and Wright (1998) and Wailes (1996).
3 Mesoamerican obsidian technology is discussed by Clark (1982; 1987), Pastrana (1998), and papers in Gaxiola and Clark (1989).
4 Other major Mesoamerican obsidian sources are located in the mountains east of the Basin of Mexico, in the Tarascan territory of Michoacan, and in the highlands of Guatemala (Charlton and Spence 1982; Cobean 1991).
5 Archaeologist Don Crabtree was the first to perfect a method for prismatic blade removal. He used a wooden "chest-punch" from a standing position, with the core between his feet. John Clark (1982) later worked out an alternative method, probably closer to the Aztec technique, in which the blade was produced from a sitting position, again with core between the artisan's feet.
6 Sahagún 1950–82:bk.10:83.
7 There is no comprehensive study of Aztec pottery. The best descriptions are provided by Séjourné (1970; 1983). Pottery production is discussed by Hodge et al. (1993) and Minc et al. (1994).
8 Anawalt (1981), Berdan (1987), and Hicks (1994) discuss the uses of cotton cloth. Techniques of cloth production are described by Fauman-Fichman (1999), McCafferty and McCafferty (2000), Smith and Hirth (1988), and Turok (1996).
9 The term "maguey" refers to several closely related species of the genus *Agave* that grow above 1,800 m elevation in central Mexico.
10 Hernández 1959:v.2:349 (translated by Parsons and Parsons 1990:276). Parsons and Parsons (1990) and Mendoza Cerón and Canger (1993) discuss the use of the maguey plant in both ancient and modern times.
11 On the *pulque* cult, see Anawalt (1993), Bruman (2000), and Nicholson (1991).
12 Dorothy Hosler (1994) is the best source for information on copper and

bronze metallurgy in Mesoamerica. My discussion is based upon that work plus conversations with Hosler, who has analyzed copper/bronze artifacts from my excavations in Morelos and from numerous other sites in Mesoamerica. Descriptions of copper objects for sale in the Tlatelolco market are found in Sahagún (1950–82:bk.8:67–9).

13   My interpretation of the economic context of part-time craft specialists differs from that of Brumfiel (1987; 1998b), who suggests that specialists decided to take up farming to ensure a secure source of food. Numerous historical and ethnographic studies from around the globe, however, reveal the opposite pattern – peasant farmers in times of economic hardship typically take up part-time crafts in order to supplement their income (e.g., Cook 1982; Thirsk 1961). This well-documented cross-cultural pattern seems to fit the available Aztec data: farming families added part-time craft production rather than crafting families adding part-time farming.

14   Sahagún 1950–82:bk.9:83–97. See also Berdan (1982:26–8, 154–5) and Pasztory (1983:278–80).

15   Codex Mendoza 1992:f.70r. See also Rojas (1986:116, 184) on the hereditary nature of Aztec crafts.

16   Aztec goldworking is described by Nicholson and Quiñones Keber (1983:152–61) and Saville (1920). Sahagún (1950–82:bk.9:73–8) describes the goldsmiths of Tenochtitlan. Mixtec gold from Oaxaca is described and illustrated in Caso (1969).

17   Sahagún 1950–82:bk.9:80.

18   Aztec mosaics are described by Nicholson and Quiñones Keber (1983:170–7) and Saville (1922). See ethnohistoric descriptions by Durán (1994:417) and Sahagún (1950–82:bk.8:80).

19   See Brumfiel (1980; 1987) and Hodge and Smith (1994).

20   My discussion of the Otumba project is based upon the following sources: Charlton et al. (1991; 2000), Neff et al. (2000), Nichols (1994), and Nichols et al. (2000). Conversations with Thomas Charlton, Deborah Nichols, Cynthia Otis Charlton, and Timothy Hare have contributed greatly to my knowledge of this project, and I thank Charlton and Otis Charlton for tours of the Otumba site and labs in 1989 and 1993.

21   The Otumba project archaeologists have identified a central core area of the site that was probably an elite residential zone, and a number of the workshops were located in or near this area. This may suggest elite control over at least some craft production.

5   The Commercial Economy

1   For descriptions of traditional peasant markets in modern Mesoamerica, see Carmack et al. (1996), Castillo Nechar (1995), or Cook and Diskin (1976).

2   The Inca of South America, contemporaries of the Aztecs, are an example of a civilization where trade and exchange were heavily controlled by the central imperial state. Both production and exchange were managed by state bureaucrats, and marketplaces only existed on the fringes of the Inca empire.

See D'Altroy (1992).

3   Cortés 1962:87–9. For other first-hand descriptions of the Tlatelolco market, see Díaz del Castillo (1963:232–4), Sahagún (1950–82:bk.8:67–9), and Torquemada (1975–83:v.4, 348–52).

4   Torquemada 1975–83:v.4, 345. Anderson et al. (1976:138–49) publish documents describing the Coyoacan market.

5   Durán 1971:278. Durán (1971:277–9) also describes the Cholula market. See Berdan (1985:346–9) for a discussion of specialized markets in general.

6   C. A. Smith 1974.

7   The friar Motolinía (1950:59) describes the specifics of the market schedules. Most ethnohistoric descriptions of markets pertain to the Valley of Mexico, but available evidence suggests that markets and market systems were similar throughout Aztec central Mexico. Areas outside the valley also had markets in most cities, towns, and villages; market hierarchies; and periodic schedules with merchants traveling among markets (M. E. Smith 1994a).

8   Durán 1971:274–5.

9   Sahagún 1950–82:bk.9:31.

10 Sahagún 1950–82:bk.9:17.

11 The reliance of Mesoamerican commerce on human carriers, made necessary by the lack of draft animals and wheeled transport, placed severe constraints on the nature of goods that could be traded over long distances. The human carriers could only carry limited loads over modest daily distances, and they had to be fed along the way. Although wealthy nobles could finance the transport of any type of good over any distance, merchants were limited to high-value, low-bulk goods if they were to profit from their ventures. See discussions of the economic and social conditions of Mesoamerican transport systems in Drennan (1984).

12 Durán 1971:138. Sahagún (1950–82:bk.9:1–19) lists the goods sold by the pochteca.

13 Olivier (1999) discusses the aspects of Aztec merchant gods.

14 Berdan 1988:645–6.

15 Aztec money in the forms of cacao beans and cotton textiles resembled modern currency in several respects. These items served to store value in that they could be saved for use at a later occasion, and they functioned as media of exchange in that they could be traded for a variety of other goods. Aztec money was not universally exchangeable like modern currency, however. One could use it to buy food, household items, or jewelry in the market, but land could not be purchased with cacao or textiles, and the use of money to pay for labor services was quite limited. Einzig (1966) discusses various types of nonwestern currency.

16 Coe and Coe (1996) is the best general treatment of cacao, including its cultivation, its use as currency, its use as a beverage, and its symbolism and significance in Aztec and Maya cultures. See also Bergmann (1969) and Rojas (1998).

17 Anderson et al. 1976:208–13. Rojas (1986:261; 1998) provides extensive information on prices and equivalents.

18 Molina 1972:f.37r (translated by Dibble 1988:72).

19   These more limited Postclassic currencies are discussed in the chapters of Smith and Berdan (2002). The T-shaped bronze "axe-monies" that were common in west Mexico are a fascinating form of currency. These were imitation bronze axes manufactured in standard shapes and sizes but so thin that they could not possibly have been used as axes. Groups of 20 or more were bundled together and tied with cord. See Hosler et al. (1990).

20   Most of the analytical techniques require expensive, specialized equipment, and the analyses can be quite costly. Only a few studies have been done to date on Aztec obsidian exchange. The success of chemical analyses of obsidian for other Mesoamerican cultures (e.g., Cobean et al. 1991) augurs well for the future application of these methods to Aztec sites and artifacts.

21   This discussion is based upon Hodge (1998), Hodge and Minc (1990), Hodge et al. (1993), and Minc et al. (1994).

22   Díaz del Castillo 1963:226. For discussion of Cholula Polychrome ceramics, see papers in Nicholson and Quiñones Keber (1994).

23   The Valley of Mexico salt industry is discussed by Sanders et al. (1979:171–5) and Parsons (1994).

24   Appadurai (1986) is a good introduction to commodities and luxury goods. Economic processes in Late Postclassic Mesoamerica are treated more fully in the chapters in Smith and Berdan (2002). Some archaeologists have turned to the distribution of broken pots and obsidian and other former commodities among houses of the elite and commoners as a way of inferring the existence of market systems in past societies (e.g., Hirth 1998).

25   Molina 1972:f.39v, 36v (translated by Dibble 1988:73, 71).

26   The distinction between a capitalist economy and a precapitalist commercialized economy – such as the Aztec, Roman, or ancient Assyrian economies – is not always recognized. The influential economic historian Karl Polanyi never fully grasped this distinction and devoted considerable effort to trying unsuccessfully to demonstrate the lack of commercial institutions in ancient societies (Polanyi et al. 1957); for critiques see Figueira (1984), Kuhrt (1998), Silver (1983), or Snell (1997). An article I published on the Aztec empire in the magazine *Scientific American* (M. E. Smith 1997b) was criticized by *The People* – newspaper of the Socialist Labor Party – for attributing capitalist institutions and behavior to ancient peoples. In fact, they compared my account of the Aztecs to the cartoon "The Flintstones"! In a reply to their article, I responded that the Aztec economy was *not* a capitalist economy and I emphasized the distinction between capitalism and ancient commercial economies.

6   Family and Social Class

1   By social class, I mean a category of people who stand in a similar relationship with respect to the basic resources of society. Among the Aztecs, nobles controlled most of the resources, particularly land and labor, and commoners had to work for nobles and pay them tribute. Some definitions of social class require the members to be conscious of their class membership and

allegiance to one another (e.g., Mann 1986); from such a perspective, Aztec nobles constituted a class, whereas commoners did not.

2   See the Codex Mendoza (1992). Modern discussion of the Aztec life cycle may be found in Berdan (1982:73–96), Clendinnen (1991a), and Soustelle (1961:163–202). Rosemary Joyce (2000a:144–65; 2000b) presents a particularly insightful analysis of the production of gender identity through specific rituals during childhood.

3   Codex Mendoza 1992:v.4:118.

4   Codex Mendoza 1992:v.4:120.

5   Codex Mendoza 1992:v.4:122.

6   These quotations are from the Codex Mendoza (1992:v.4:123, 122, and 124).

7   Information on these schools is found in the Codex Mendoza (1992:v.4:126–35; v.3:f.60v–65r), Durán (1971:289–95), and Sahagún (1950–82:bks.3, 8).

8   Durán 1971:293.

9   Weddings and their preparations are described in Sahagún (1950–82:bk.8:127–30). McCaa (1994; 1996) discusses the young age at which girls married.

10 Sahagún 1950–82:bk.8:130.

11 Codex Mendoza 1992:v.4:126.

12 Although some scholars have argued that women were dominated and severely exploited by men and by the state in Aztec society (e.g., Nash 1978), the predominant view today emphasizes the complementary nature of male and female roles in Aztec society. See Brumfiel (1991), Burkhart (1997), Clendinnen (1991a), Joyce (2000a), Kellogg (1995; 1997), Klein (1994), and McCafferty and McCafferty (1991).

13 For the role of women in Aztec domestic ritual see M. E. Smith (n.d.-b).

14 Useful disussions of Aztec social classes include Evans (2000), Hicks (1996), Lockhart (1992), and M. E. Smith (1986).

15 Preliminary data on these issues are assembled by Berdan (1987), Fauman-Fichman (1999), and Hicks (1994).

16 Lockhart (1992) is the best source on the *calpolli*; see also P. Carrasco (1976) and Hicks (1986). These and other recent studies present a very different view of the *calpolli* than that found in many older works. In place of an egalitarian body that owned land unconnected to nobles, the new view points out inequalities within the *calpolli* and the position of members under the control of a lord. I am using the term "ward" for the subdivision of a *calpolli* sometimes called *tlaxilacalli* or *chinamitl* in the sources.

17 Lockhart 1992:154.

18 Lockhart (1992) is also the best source on the *teccalli*, and differences in social organization between the eastern and western Nahua areas. Chance (2000) provides a new interpretation of the eastern Nahua *teccalli*.

19 This discussion is based upon our excavations at Cuexcomate and Capilco. We used written documents from other settlements in Morelos to interpret aspects of social organization at these sites; see M. E. Smith (1992a; 1994b) and Smith and Heath-Smith (1994). Other descriptions of Aztec village life may be found in Brumfiel (1991) and Evans (1993).

20 Aztec kinship and household organization are discussed by Kellogg (1986;

1995) and Lockhart (1992:59–93). The Aztec kinship system was of the bilateral type, meaning that individuals traced descent through both the maternal and paternal lines.

21   Sahagún 1950–82:bk.6:35–6. The Nahuatl term for potsherd, *tapalcatl*, is still used in central Mexico today, even among Spanish-speakers.

22   This argument is developed in Smith and Heath-Smith (1994). We used domestic artifact inventories to define quantitative measures of the standard of living at each excavated house (see also Olson 2001).

23   Fieldwork at Yautepec is described in greater detail in chapter 8; see Smith et al. (1994), Smith et al. (1999), and Olson (2001).

24   My view of the initial emergence of a new middle class parallels that of Sanders (1992). Like Sanders, I see the Aztecs as unique in ancient Mesoamerica in this respect; the Classic Maya and other Mesoamerican societies are best viewed as having two social classes. Hicks (1999) also argues for an Aztec middle class, but he bases his interpretation on the strange notion that all state-level societies must have three classes.

25   There is no comparative analysis of known Aztec palaces. Susan T. Evans has assembled information from ethnohistoric sources (Evans 2000; 2001) and described a small palace from Sihuatecpan (Evans 1988; 1991).

26   Excavation of this palace is described in M. E. Smith (1992a).

27   This census, which dates to the 1530s, is published in Nahuatl and German in Hinz et al. (1983); much of the pertinent information is summarized by P. Carrasco (1972; 1976). The census quoted at the start of this chapter is a related document from another town (see also S. L. Cline 1993; McCaa 1994; 1996).

28   Many works on the Aztecs state that nobles were exempt from tribute. This incorrect interpretation comes from an uncritical reading of early written sources. After the Spanish Conquest, the Aztec nobility managed to convince the Spaniards (including many of the chroniclers) that they had not paid tribute in ancient times and therefore should not have to pay tribute to the Spanish crown. This misrepresentation is exposed by Lockhart (1992:106), who notes that "lords and nobles paid tribute to the altepetl [city-state] as a matter of course."

29   Initial preservation efforts were coordinated by the Sociedad Cultural Yautepec; later a new organization was formed to continue this work, the Patronato Pro-Restauración de la Zona Arqueológica de Yautepec, Morelos. Reports on the excavations include de Vega Nova (1996) and de Vega Nova and Mayer (1991). García Payón (1936; 1979) excavated a large palace compound (ca. 3,500 sq m) at Calixtlahuaca. Although he called it a *calmecac*, it conforms to the standard layout of Aztec palaces; this may have been the royal palace of Calixtlahuaca (see chapter 8).

30   Alva Ixtlilxochitl 1975:v.2, 92–100. My description is based on this source; see also Hicks (1982; 1984).

31   Calnek 1976. Unlike Tenochtitlan, Texcoco did not have a shortage of land, so Nezahualcoyotl's palace may have been larger than Motecuhzoma's. The large size of Alva Ixtlilxochitl's estimate for the compound (84 ha) suggests that he may have been describing the entire downtown area of Texcoco,

including the palace area, central plaza, temples, and market, and not just the palace compound itself.

32   Townsend 1992:137–44. See also Evans (2000). Agricultural terraces at Texcotzinco are shown in figure 3.4.

33   The themes of Aztec political ideology that I list are taken from Hicks (1996), an excellent study of the subject. Other important studies of Aztec ideology include Brumfiel (1998a) and López Austin (1988).

34   Brumfiel (1987), P. Carrasco (1984), Pohl (1998), and M. E. Smith (1986) discuss the social connections within the nobility.

35   Durán 1994:331.

7   City-State and Empire

1   Aztec city-states are discussed by Hodge (1984; 1994; 1997), Lockhart (1992), and M. E. Smith (2000). Lockhart (1992) and Schroeder (1991) analyze the native Nahua concept of *altepetl*.

2   Sahagún 1950–82:bk.10:15. See Davies (1973) or Lockhart (1992) on the *tlatoani*.

3   Zorita 1963:126.

4   Examples include Berdan et al. (1996), Hicks (1992), and Hodge (1984; 1994).

5   Gibson (1964) first pointed out the interspersed subjects of Tepechpan and other city-states in the Teotihuacan Valley. The ruler-oriented nature of political organization is discussed by Grube (2000), Martin and Grube (2000), and M. E. Smith (2000). The *Relaciones Geográficas* are published in Acuña (1984–7).

6   Examples of political geography include P. Carrasco (1999), García Castro (1999), Gerhard (1993), and Smith and Berdan (1996). For Hodge's research, see Hodge (1984; 1994; 1997).

7   Comparative city-states are analyzed in Hansen (2000).

8   Durán 1994:406.

9   Hassig (1988) provides the most complete account of Aztec warfare; other sources include Davies (1987) and Isaac (1983a; 1983b). The ideology and iconography of Aztec warfare are discussed by D. Carrasco (1999) and Taube (2000a). Clendinnen (1991a) discusses the effects of warfare on Aztec society and culture.

10   Davies 1973:110; this view is echoed by Conrad and Demarest (1984:53) and other authors.

11   Variations in ancient empires are discussed by Mann (1986) and the chapters in Alcock et al. (2001). Hassig (1985) first applied the hegemonic empire model to the Aztecs, and Berdan et al. (1996) refined this approach. My discussion of the Aztec empire is based primarily upon Berdan et al. (1996) and M. E. Smith (2001).

12   Imperial control in the Valley of Mexico is discussed in Berdan et al. (1996), Hicks (1992), and Hodge (1994).

13   The expansion of the empire outside of the Valley of Mexico is covered by Berdan et al. (1996) and Davies (1987).

14   Other unconquered enemy states included Metztitlan to the north of the Valley of Mexico, the Yope state and Tututepec along the Pacific coast, and various Maya polities south of the empire. See Berdan et al. (1996:ch.6) and Davies (1968). The best source on the Tarascans is Pollard (1993).
15   Acuña 1984–7:v.6:328 (author's translation).
16   The Oztuma fortress is discussed by Armillas (1944) and Silverstein (2001). Other fortresses along the Tarascan frontier are discussed by Hernández Rivero (1994). These sites are isolated and difficult to reach without a local guide.
17   Silverstein (2001) has clarified some of the confusion in the native historical sources concerning the fortress and region of Oztuma. Sources from the Mexica tradition apparently confused the local Chontal fortress at Ixtepec with the new Aztec fortress at Oztuma. The Mexica sources state that the Chontal people were entirely wiped out in the battle, and this was the reason for sending immigrants to take their place. Local documents from the Oztuma area, however, make it clear that many Chontals survived, and the distinction between the local Chontal and the immigrant Mexica in this region remains important to their descendents even today.
18   The major excavations at Malinalco are described in García Payón (1947), who first proposed the Eagle-Warrior Temple interpretation of Structure 1. Townsend (1982) suggested the interpretation of the site stressing rulership and coronation. Hernández Rivero (1997) reviews these and all other published views of Structure 1; he favors García Payón's original interpretation. Malinalco is a popular tourist destination today; there is a new museum with many interesting objects from the site.
19   The excavations at Quauhtochco are described in Medellín Zeñil (1952). The role of the fortress is discussed in Berdan et al. (1996:142–6) and the implications of the Aztec ceramics at the site are discussed in M. E. Smith (1990). This site, known as Huatusco Viejo, can be visited today.
20   The major fieldwork at Zempoala is described in Brüggemann (1991) and García Payón (1949). Zempoala was the first major Mesoamerican city visited by the expedition of Cortés, and its armies joined the Spaniards in their expedition to Tlaxcala and Tenochtitlan (see chapter 12). The site is a major tourist attraction today.
21   Durán 1994:336. See M. E. Smith (1986) for further discussion of this passage and its implications.
22   Tapia 1971 (translated by Isaac 1983a:416).
23   Díaz del Castillo (1963:179) reports the Tlaxcallan viewpoint. The flowery war remains a controversial subject. In spite of its obviously propagandistic nature, many modern authors take the Mexica explanation at face value. See discussion in P. Carrasco (1999:404), Davies (1987), Isaac (1983a), and Plunket and Uruñuela (1994).

8   Cities and Urban Planning

1   Here I am following the functional approach to urbanism as outlined by Fox (1977) and Trigger (1972). Marcus (1983) applies this model to Mesoamerican

cities.

2 The city described in this fictionalized account is a composite picture of a typical city-state capital drawn from archaeological and ethnohistorical sources on various Aztec towns. Very little information survives on the city of Amecameca beyond its size (10,000 inhabitants in an area of 4 sq km) and political status (Hodge 1984; Parsons et al. 1982b; Schroeder 1991).

3 There is no single comprehensive study of ancient Mesoamerican urbanism and urban planning. Good introductions include Marcus (1983) and Sanders and Webster (1988). My discussion of Aztec urban planning is based upon my fieldwork at Cuexcomate (chapter 3) and Yautepec (see below), visits to other Aztec towns in the Valley of Mexico and Morelos, and scattered references in the documentary and archaeological literature.

4 The *pochteca*, for example, lived in their own *calpolli*, as did many of the luxury artisans described by Sahagún (see chapter 4). The localized distribution of craft workshops at Otumba (see figure 4.11) also suggests *calpolli* organization (Charlton et al. 1991; Nichols 1994). Not all cities fit this model; for example, Huexotla does not appear to have had many craft specialists nor distinguishable *calpolli* divisions (Brumfiel 1980; 1987).

5 Alva Ixtlilxochitl (1975) describes Texcoco; see Hicks (1982; 1984). Davies (1973:40–78) presents some of the scattered documentary information on Azcapotzalco, and Angulo Villaseñor (1976) describes archaeological work in Cuauhnahuac (modern Cuernavaca).

6 Fieldwork at Coatetelco is described by Arana Alvarez (1984). Ceramics from the site are discussed in M. E. Smith (2002). The site today is an official archaeological zone open to the public; there is a small museum with many of the excavated artifacts.

7 Fieldwork at Calixtlahuaca by García Payón was never properly published. Some information is provided in García Payón (1936; 1979); see also Marquina (1964) or Anonymous (1960). Ethnohistoric sources relating to the site are reviewed in García Castro (1999), Hernández Rodríguez (1988), and Quezada Ramírez (1972). The site is open to the public today. There is a small museum at the site, but most of the finds are at the Museo de Antropología in Toluca.

8 At the time of writing, our analyses of the Yautepec excavations are not complete. Preliminary descriptions of our fieldwork at Yautepec may be found in Hare and Smith (1996), Smith et al. (1994), and Smith et al. (1999). The palace excavations are described in de Vega Nova (1996) and de Vega Nova and Mayer (1991).

9 We had planned to concentrate our efforts in a large open area just west of the palace (probably an elite residential neighborhood), but between the first and second field seasons this area was the setting for a planned invasion by squatters. Local government officials were unable to evict the squatters, so we changed our tactics and found other places to dig around town. Instead of an intensive study of one part of Yautepec, we ended up with a larger number of smaller excavations distributed more widely throughout the site. I describe our experiences excavating in the midst of this political conflict in M. E. Smith (1997c).

10   An early colonial census permits the reconstruction of the population of Yautepec in 1519 at around 15,000 inhabitants (M. E. Smith 1994a). When this figure is divided by the areal extent of the city – 210 ha – the resulting population density of 71 persons per hectare is not too different from that of Cuexcomate (55 persons per hectare).

11   The reconstruction painting of Tenochtitlan (figure 8.7) gives a fairly accurate idea of the look of the city. At this scale, however, the city would have been about twice as large as depicted in the painting. See figure 8.8 for a more accurate scale.

12   My discussion of Tenochtitlan is based on Calnek (1972; 1976), Marquina (1960), and Rojas (1986). Archaeological excavations are described by Matos Moctezuma (1979; 1988; 1999) and Vega Sosa (1979). Although native historical sources state that Tenochtitlan was founded as a new settlement in the swamp, archaeological findings now suggest that there was a pre-Mexica settlement at that location (see chapter 2).

13   Umberger (1996) discusses these aspects of urban planning at Tenochtitlan. The role of the concept of Tollan as a model for Tenochtitlan is discussed by Boone (2000b). My model of the Mexica differentiating Tenochtitlan from other Aztec cities by drawing on their knowledge of ancient imperial capitals contrasts with previous discussions of Aztec urbanism, where smaller cities are considered to be copies of Tenochtitlan. Other aspects of urban planning at Tenochtitlan are discussed by Aveni (2001:235–44), Calnek (1976), D. Carrasco (1999), and M. E. Smith (1997a).

14   Excavations at Tlatelolco are described in González Rul (1996; 1998) and Guilliem Arroyo (1999). The skull rack is described in González Rul (1963) and Pijoan et al. (1989). The native historical record for Tlatelolco is based primarily on the document known as the *Anales de Tlatelolco* (Barlow 1989; Klaus 1999). The excavations at Tlatelolco are open to the public at the "Plaza of the Three Cultures" in Mexico City.

15   The conqueror Hernando Cortés said of the narrower southern causeway, "This causeway was as broad as two lances and very stoutly made such that eight horsemen could ride along it abreast" (Cortés 1962:68).

16   I discuss the sacred precinct and Templo Mayor at greater length in chapter 10.

9   Creation, Death and the Gods

1   Good discussions of Aztec religion include Burkhart (1989), D. Carrasco (1999), Clendinnen (1991a), Graulich (1997b; 1999), León-Portilla (1963; 1993), and Nicholson (1971). There is a vast amount of ethnohistorical information on Aztec religion, thanks to the efforts of priestly chroniclers like Sahagún and Durán. Most of this material comes from Tenochtitlan and, therefore, my discussion of religion pertains primarily to the Mexica people, unless noted otherwise.

2   The most complete treatment of Aztec myths is Graulich (1997b); see also León-Portilla (1963), Nicholson (1971), and Taube (1993). "The Fifth Sun"

is an excellent video by Patricia Amlin that portrays Aztec myths through the animation of images from the codices.

3 From the *Leyenda de los Soles*; quoted in León-Portilla (1963:107–8).

4 Bierhorst 1992:148.

5 Sahagún 1950–82:bk.3:2.

6 Sahagún 1950–82:bk.3:4.

7 In a classic study Soustelle (1961:115) attributed much of the complexity of Aztec religion to the incomplete synthesis of the diverse historical traditions; Graulich (1997b), on the other hand, stresses the incomplete attempts by the Mexica kings to transform the religion to a more imperial and centralized form. In an alternative view, León-Portilla (1963) finds more cohesiveness and integration in Aztec thought.

8 Several papers in Berlo (1992) discuss these deities; see also Taube (2000a).

9 Chimalpahin, quoted in León-Portilla (1963:161). Michel Graulich (1997) has done the most to distinguish late Mexica innovations from the older traditional central Mexican religion. He suggests, for example, that earlier Mesoamerican mythology describes four suns or creations, whereas the notion of a fifth sun was a Mexica innovation. Graulich's important study of Aztec rituals (Graulich 1999) has yet to appear in English translation, although parts of it have been published in English (Graulich 1992a).

10 See Nicholson (1971). It should be stressed that this scheme is a great simplification of a very complex situation. As Nicholson points out, the Aztecs themselves viewed the gods as more fluid and dynamic than this seemingly well-organized scheme might suggest.

11 For a detailed study of Tezcatlipoca, see Olivier (1997b). Taube (2000a) includes a discussion of Xiuhtecuhtli. León-Portilla (1963) discusses Ometeotl.

12 Durán 1971:99.

13 Sahagún 1950–82:bk.6:5.

14 Arnold (1999) and López Austin (1997) discuss Tlaloc. Nicholson (1991) analyzes the iconography of Ometochtli, and Vié-Wohrer (1999) that of Xipe Totec. The goddesses of the Teteoinnan complex are discussed by Klein (2000), Milbrath (2000), and Sullivan (1982).

15 Nicholson (1993) reviews the iconography of Tonatiuh in relation to the Aztec calendar stone (chapter 11). For Huitzilopochtli, see Boone (1989). Brotherston (1994) and Ragot (2000) discuss Mixcoatl.

16 There is an enormous literature on Quetzalcoatl, much of it attempting to separate the Aztec deity from the Quetzalcoatl of the Toltecs, a deity and/or ruler of Tollan (e.g., López Austin 1973; Nicholson 2001). Graulich (1992d) is a good introduction to Quetzalcoatl, and Guilliem Arroyo (1999) discusses circular temples dedicated to Ehecatl. On Yacatecuhtli, see Olivier (1997a).

17 The similarity of the Aztec motif (the skull and crossbones) to the Jolly Roger flag of the Caribbean pirates is fortuitous. The pirates most likely adopted this symbol in the eighteenth century from Christian iconography, probably from tombstone designs in the Kent/Sussex area of Britain (Dr. Richard Pennell, personal communication 2001). See Pennell (2001) and his website, "Death's Head and Pirates Flags": http://www.history.unimelb.edu.au/coursematerials/pirates/flags/pirate%20intro.htm.

18   The symbolism and iconography of death are discussed by Baquedano (1998), Brotherston (1994), and Ragot (2000). The ceramics from royal feasts are discussed by Smith et al. (n.d.). The platforms decorated with skulls and crossbones, found at several sites and depicted in the ritual codices, are often incorrectly identified as skull racks (*tzompantli*). Klein (2000) has shown that these were more likely platforms used for curing and fertility ceremonies, associated with the Tzitzimime deities.

19   Aztec concepts of the afterlife are discussed by Graulich (1997b:248–52), León-Portilla (1963:124–33), and Ragot (2000).

20   Durán 1971:122. For discussion of funeral practices and burials, see León-Portilla (1963: 124–133), Nagao (1985), and M. E. Smith (1992a).

21   An intriguing aspect of the burials at Cuexcomate and Capilco is the absence of adults. Burials in general are rare at Aztec sites, and some archaeologists think this is due to the prevalence of cremation. I disagree, because cremated remains were buried in ceramic jars or urns, and few such urn burials have been excavated outside of palaces and temples. Documentary sources such as the above quotation from Friar Durán mention the jars used to bury the charred bones from a cremation. Several of these urn burials, probably of Mexica kings or leaders, were recovered in the excavations at the Templo Mayor of Tenochtitlan (Matos Moctezuma 1988); they are quite rare at other sites, however. In my view most Aztec commoners were buried in cemeteries outside of settlements, but archaeologists have yet to find or excavate any of these.

22   The urn burials at the Templo Mayor may pertain to one of the Mexica kings. The Eagle-Warrior Hall burial is described by Román Berrelleza and López Luján (1999). The Calixtlahuaca burials are described in García Payón (1941).

23   Notched bones, often called "bone rattles," are discussed by Beyer (1934) and Seler (1990–98a). They were used as musical instruments in ceremonies.

10   Temples and Ceremonies

1   Priests are discussed by Alberti Manzanares (1994), Brundage (1985), and Nicholson (1971).

2   Sahagún 1950–82:bk.2:184–5.

3   Klein 1987:297.

4   The identification of Aztec deities with the devil, made by Sahagún and his assistants, is not a very accurate interpretation of their nature or role within Aztec religion.

5   Sahagún 1950–82:bk.2:184.

6   Durán 1971:81.

7   Aztec cannibalism in this respect was similar to other reported cases of cannibalism around the world. The eating of human flesh in most cases is a sacred act, done to close relatives in order to honor them and incorporate something of their essence into their living kin. This ethnographic reality contrasts sharply with the popular image of antagonistic cannibalism in which blood-

thirsty tribes capture their enemies (or perhaps missionaries and anthropologists) to cook for dinner in a big stewpot. The ritual use of the femurs of sacrifical victims is discussed by Broda (1970:231).

8   Sahagún 1950–82:bk.2:185.

9   I should note that it is very hard to determine the actual frequency of human sacrifice. The Spanish conquerors deliberately exaggerated the extent of human sacrifice to make the Aztecs appear more barbaric; this helped justify their conquest and domination. Although we cannot make a quantitative estimate, however, most scholars agree that sacrifice was widespread and frequent in Aztec central Mexico. In an interesting cross-cultural study, Winkelman (1998) reports that societies that practice human sacrifice tend to suffer from population pressure, they tend to engage in warfare to capture land and resources, and they tend to have non-hierarchical religions. The Aztecs fit the first two characteristics but not the third.

10 Much has been written on the symbolism and significance of human sacrifice in Aztec religion and society. The dominant scholarly interpretation for over a century has been that sacrifice was viewed as feeding the sun with blood and hearts to ensure the health and continuity of the sun and the gods (e.g., D. Carrasco 1999; León-Portilla 1993). Recently Michel Graulich (1997b; 2000) has suggested that an alternative view of sacrifice was more important to the Aztecs. He notes that sacrifice was initiated by the gods in mythical time as a means of atonement for their transgressions. It was carried out on earth by humans in the belief that sacrifice helps them atone for their own transgressions, enabling individuals to reach a more favorable afterlife.

11 See Harner (1977). Ortiz de Montellano (1978; 1990:85–94) published the strongest of several refutations of Harner's protein deficiency theory of cannibalism.

12 For the sacred precinct and Templo Mayor, see Boone (1987), Marquina (1960), Serrato-Combe (2001), and Vega Sosa (1979).

13 There are numerous publications on the Templo Mayor project. Some of the major works are Bonifaz Nuño and Robles (1981), González González and Olmedo Vera (1990), López Luján (1994; 1998), Matos Moctezuma (1979; 1982; 1988; 1999), and Olmos Frese (1999).

14 Matos Moctezuma (1988) and Graulich (1992b) propose alternative chronologies for the stages of construction of the Templo Mayor.

15 Excavations at the Eagle-Warrior Hall were done by López Luján (1998); a burial at this structure is reported by Román Berrelleza et al. (1999). The Cathedral excavations are described in Matos Moctezuma (1999).

16 The offerings are described and analyzed by López Luján (1994). Recent excavations in the sacred precinct continue to uncover offerings. Perhaps the most spectacular is Offering 102, which by chance had been sealed airtight, resulting in outstanding preservation of organic materials. In addition to the incense burners, sculptures, and other nonperishable objects found in most offerings, Offering 102 yielded a dyed cloth cape and numerous other pieces of textile and plant remains. The contents of this offering appear to represent the complete outfit and paraphernalia of an Aztec priest (Barrera Rivera et al. 2001). Artifacts and other objects excavated by the Templo Mayor project

are on display at the Templo Mayor Museum, a stunning museum recently built at the site. Many of the objects are illustrated in Bonifaz Nuño and Robles (1981), Carrasco and Matos (1992), and Matos Moctezuma (1989).

17   Umberger (1987; 1996) discusses the way Aztec artists drew upon earlier imperial styles. López Luján (1994) describes the Templo Mayor offerings; the burial at the Eagle-Warrior Hall is particularly noteworthy for containing heirloom ceramic vessels from both Teotihuacan and Tula (Román Berrelleza and López Luján 1999). See discussion in chapter 8.

18   Codex Telleriano-Remensis, f.8v (Quiñones Keber 1995:258)

19   Gussinyer (1969a; 1969b) discusses the Pino Suárez temple; Marquina (1964) describes the Calixtlahuaca example, which was excavated by García Payón (1979); and Guilliem Arroyo (1999) discusses the Tlatelolco temple and its offerings. Pollock (1936) describes circular temples throughout Mesoamerica, and their association with Ehecatl is discussed by Graulich (1992d).

20   Lagunas and Serrano (1972) describe the Teopanzolco skulls. In this and other cases we know that these were decapitated heads – rather than skulls removed from earlier graves and reburied – because they were accompanied by the top cervical vertebrae. This only occurs when the head is cut off at the time of death. Severed skulls like this have also been found at other Aztec sites. While we were excavating at Yautepec, for example, construction workers digging a trench for a water pipe near the excavations uncovered a large bowl containing a severed skull with cervical vertebrae. The Tlatelolco skull rack is described by Pijoan et al. (1989) and Pijoan and Mansilla (1997). A similar deposit of perforated skulls from a skull rack was excavated at the site of Zultepec in Tlaxcala (Martínez Vargas 1993).

21   M. E. Smith 1992a:327–33.

22   Durán 1971:412–70. Sahagún devoted an entire book of the *Florentine Codex* to the monthly ceremonies (1950–82:bk.2). The Toxcatl ceremonies are described in Durán (1971:426–9) and Sahagún (1950–82:bk.2:64–73); see also Heyden's (1991) analysis. Descriptions and analyses of selected monthly ceremonies may be found in Broda (1970) and Graulich (1992a).

23   The timing of the monthly ceremonies with respect to the agricultural cycle is the subject of some debate. While some of the ceremonies seem appropriate to their seasonal timing at the time of the Spanish Conquest, others seem out of step with the seasons (e.g., harvest rituals during the dry season). Graulich (1992a) is of the opinion that the failure of the Aztecs to add extra days for leap years led to a slippage in the timing of the monthly ceremonies to the point where they were many months out of tune with the seasons by 1519. Other scholars disagree with him (e.g., Hassig 2001), and this is still an open question that needs more research.

24   Sahagún 1950–82:bk.2:64.

25   Durán 1971:426.

26   Sahagún 1950–82:bk.7:27.

27   Elson and Smith (2001) describe these deposits and others excavated by George Vaillant at Chiconautla and Nonoalco in the Valley of Mexico.

28   For the Mesoamerican ballgame, see Scarborough and Wilcox (1991).

29   Durán 1971:318. People also gambled on the board game *patolli*, in which

beans were moved around a course in a manner similar to the game *pachisi*.
30   Durán 1971:463, 452.
31   Burkhart (1997) explores the reasons why the early Spanish priests were usually quite ignorant of what happened within the confines of the house and home. Archaeological evidence for domestic ritual is discussed by M. E. Smith (n.d.-b).
32   Seler (1990–98b) provides a brief introduction to magic and divination, and mentions modern survivals. Boone (2000a) and Anders et al. (1993) discuss calendrical divination. These are the primary themes of most of the ritual codices (see chapters 1 and 11). Of the chroniclers, Sahagún (1950–82) and Ruiz de Alarcón (1982) have the most information on magic and divination. There are some fascinating survivals of Aztec magic practices, in modified form, among some of the Nahua peoples of today (Knab 1997; Sandstrom 1991; 2001).
33   Ruiz de Alarcón 1982:213–14.

11   Science and Art

1   The Nahuatl term for the wild fig is *amatl*; the trees are *Ficus benjamina* or *Ficus involuta*. Aztec books and paper are discussed in von Hagen (1944) and Sandstrom and Sandstrom (1986).
2   Sandstrom and Sandstrom (1986) describe modern Otomi papermaking, and Stromberg (1976) describes the Guerrero tourist paper industry.
3   Important Aztec books mentioned in the text include the Codex Borbonicus (1974), the Codex Borgia (1976; see also Díaz and Rogers 1993), the Codex Telleriano-Remensis (Quiñones Keber 1995), the Codex Magliabechiano (1983), the Codex Mendoza (1992; Berdan and Anawalt 1997) the *Tira de la Peregrinación* (1944) and the *Tira de Tepechpan* (Noguez 1978). For general discussion of Aztec codices, see Berger (1998), Boone (2000c), Leibsohn (1994), and Robertson (1959).
4   Díaz del Castillo 1963:227–8.
5   Sahagún 1950–82:bk.10:28. See also Alva Ixtlilxochitl (1975–7:v.1:527).
6   Classic Maya writing is discussed by Kelley (1976) and Coe (1992). Justeson and Kaufman (1993) describe their decipherment of Epi-Olmec writing. Marcus (1992) covers Maya, Aztec, Mixtec, and Zapotec writing, with an emphasis on the Oaxaca scripts. Systems of signs at Teotihuacan and Xochicalco are discussed in the chapters in Diehl and Berlo (1989); Taube (2000b) is an important recent study.
7   For discussions of Aztec writing see Berdan (1992b), Marcus (1992), and Prem (1992). Berdan (1992a) is a catalog, description, and translation of all of the glyphs in the Codex Mendoza (1992), the single largest corpus of Aztec glyphs.
8   In English, rebus writing is often used in children's games. For example, the sentence "I saw Aunt Rose" can be written with four glyphs: an eye, a carpenter's saw, an ant, and a rose; similarly the word "belief" can be depicted by a bee and a leaf. Marcus (1992:20, 65) discusses the use of the rebus

principle in Mesoamerican writing systems.

9 Aztec calendars are discussed by Aveni (2001), Caso (1971), and Hassig (2001).

10 A common misunderstanding concerning the use of ancient calendars in Mesoamerica and in other civilizations is that peasant farmers were dependent upon priests or other leaders to interpret the calendar in order to guide their farming. Unless instructed by leaders, peasants would not know when to plant their fields, which must be done just before the rainy season starts. This secret knowledge is said to have been the basis for the power of priests over peasants. Anyone familiar with traditional farmers in Mesoamerica or other parts of the world, however, knows that they do not need to consult priests or formal calendars to know when to plant and cultivate their fields. Peasants are very aware of weather and the seasons. They make decisions about planting based upon their observations, experience, and the benefit of many generations of accumulated practical knowledge of the environment and technology. Leaders achieve and maintain domination over subjects through their control over more tangible factors such as land and labor, not calendars.

11 Torquemada 1975–83:v.1:260 (bk.2:ch.64) (translated by León-Portilla 1963:142).

12 Archaeoastronomy is the study of ancient astronomy. Aveni's research provides the best introduction to the astronomical accomplishments of the Aztecs and other Mesoamerican cultures; see Aveni (1992; 2001) and Aveni and Calnek (1999).

13 Motolinía 1971:24, ch.16 (translated by Aveni 1992:150).

14 Aztec conceptions of time and history are discussed by León-Portilla (1963) and Hassig (2001). Boone (2000c) has the most complete discussion of the various types of historical codices and their implications for conceptions of time and history.

15 Unfortunately there is no systematic work on the ancient technology of the Aztecs or the other peoples of Mesoamerica. The notes to chapters 3 and 4 contain references to the technology of Aztec agriculture and craft industries.

16 Gussinyer (1974) discusses lime plaster. Much of Roys' (1934) discussion of Maya construction methods applies equally to the Aztecs. The engineering of the Tenochtitlan aqueduct is described by Bribiesca Castrejón (1958).

17 For Aztec arithmetic and mathematics, see Closs (1997), Harvey and Williams (1980), and Payne and Closs (1986). Castillo F. (1972) discusses measurement systems.

18 Aztec medicine is discussed by Ortiz de Montellano (1990) and López Austin (1988). The Aztecs owed their good health in part to the lower levels of infectious disease in the ancient New World when compared with the premodern Old World. With the exception of the llama of Andean South America, the New World lacked the large domesticated animals that were often vectors of disease transmission and contributors to poor sanitation in the Old World. Also, in the New World urbanism developed later and was less widespread than in the Old World. Dense, urbanized populations are the prime breeding ground for infectious disease. The Aztecs and other native

peoples, however, paid a heavy price for the lack of these diseases when Old World epidemics swept the New World in the sixteenth and seventeenth centuries; see Crosby (1972) and McNeill (1976).

19 Sahagún 1905–7:v.3:f.119r (translated by León-Portilla 1963:26).
20 Sahagún 1950–82:bk.10:161–2.
21 Motolinía 1971:160 (translated by Ortiz de Montellano 1990:181).
22 Ruiz de Alarcón 1982:267–9.
23 Nicholson and Quiñones Keber 1994:vii. A number of authors have confused the Mixteca-Puebla style with the earlier coastal tradition, treating the two as manifestations of a single phenomenon. My wife and I have criticized this approach, however, because the coastal style occurred earlier in time and was not present in the Mixteca-Puebla area (Smith and Heath-Smith 1980). The chapters in Nicholson and Quiñones Keber (1994) provide numerous examples and analyses of the Mixteca-Puebla style proper.
24 Mixteca-Puebla style murals are discussed by Robertson (1970), Smith and Heath-Smith (1980), and the papers in Nicholson and Quiñones Keber (1994). Painted manuscripts from the outer imperial provinces are discussed in Berdan et al. (1996) and Boone (2000c). The Mesoamerican world system is discussed in chapter 12 below.
25 Aztec stone sculpture is discussed in Baquedano (1984), Nicholson and Quiñones Keber (1983), and Pasztory (1983). Monumental imperial sculptures and their religious and political significance are analyzed by Townsend (1979) and Umberger (1996).
26 There is a debate over the identity of this deity. The traditional view – that this god is Tonatiuh – was challenged by Townsend (1979) and Klein (1977), who argued that it was the earth lord Tlaltecuhtli. I follow the interpretations of Graulich (1992c) and Nicholson (1993), who favor a return to the traditional view.
27 The best introductions to Aztec literature and poetry are the books of León-Portilla (1963; 1969; 1992). See also *Cantares Mexicanos* (1985).
28 Sahagún 1905–7:v.6:f.122 (translated by León-Portilla 1969:27).
29 Aztec song (translated by León-Portilla 1969:68).
30 *Cantares Mexicanos* 1985:f.35v (translated by León-Portilla 1963:77).
31 *Cantares Mexicanos* 1985:f.16v (translated by León-Portilla 1963:78).
32 *Cantares Mexicanos* 1985:f.26r (translated by León-Portilla 1963:73).
33 Martí and Kurath (1964), although dated, is the most comprehensive introduction to Aztec music and dance. Musical instruments are discussed in Castañeda and Mendoza (1933) and Martí (1969).
34 Durán 1971:295.

12   Final Glory, Conquest, and Legacy

1 For Tzintzuntzan see Pollard (1977; 1993) or Marquina (1964).
2 Processes of long-distance communication in Late Postclassic Mesoamerica are discussed in the chapter in Smith and Berdan (2002); see also Blanton and Feinman (1984), M. E. Smith (2001), and Smith and Berdan (2000).

Important works on Late Postclassic Mesoamerica outside of the Aztec domain include Carmack (1981), Masson (2000), Pollard (1993), Spores (1984), and papers in Nicholson and Quiñones Keber (1994).

3   Fieldwork at Iximche' was conducted by Jorge Guillemín (1965; 1977), who died before publishing a full report on his research. An excellent discussion of the site, relating native historical records to the architecture, is found in Schele and Mathews (1998); see also Braswell (2001).

4   We are fortunate to have two views of the Spanish conquest of the Aztecs. The Spanish story was told by two of the participants, Hernando Cortés (1962), and Bernal Díaz del Castillo (1963), and summarized in the nineteenth-century account of Prescott (2000). The Aztec side of the story, contained in Sahagún (1950–82:bk.12), Durán (1994:483–563), and many scattered accounts, has been assembled by León-Portilla (1962) and Lockhart (1993). Many modern books summarize the events of the conquest and several recent works contain insightful analyses of the context and implications of the conquest (e.g., Clendinnen 1991b; Gillespie 1989:173–230; Graulich 1994; 1995; 1996; Hassig 1988:236–50; 1994; Thomas 1993). I base my discussion on these sources. See G. D. Jones (1999), Lovell (1985), and Warren (1985) on the Spanish conquest of other Mesoamerican peoples.

5   Sahagún 1950–82:bk.12:31.

6   Durán 1994:529.

7   Díaz del Castillo 1963:218, 219.

8   Sahagún 1905–7 (translated by León-Portilla 1962:92–3). See also Sahagún (1950–82:bk.12:81).

9   Translated from the Nahuatl by León-Portilla (1962:137–8).

10 Michel Graulich (1994; 1997a) puts less stress on Motecuhzoma's hesitation than many authors. He suggests that the massacre at Cholula was the response to an ambush deliberately promoted by Motecuhzoma. Its failure to stop the Spaniards may be due to the fact that Cholula was more often an enemy than a friend of Tenochtitlan.

11 Most modern authors apparently believe this story, which is repeated in numerous accounts of the Spanish Conquest. Gillespie (1989:173–201) provides a detailed historiographic analysis showing it to be a sixteenth-century fabrication, created in the attempt to make sense out of the cataclysm of the Spanish Conquest.

12 Hassig 1988:242–4 (the quotation is on p. 243). Graulich (1996) is highly critical of a later work of Hassig's (Hassig 1994) on the Spanish Conquest. Graulich's interpretations are found in Graulich (1994; 1996; 1997a).

13 Sixteenth-century epidemics are discussed by McCaa (1995), Prem (1991), Sanders (1970), and Whitmore (1992). In a fascinating book, McNeill (1976) analyzes the role of epidemics in world history, including the Aztec case.

14 Whitmore 1992. This initial epidemic reached Peru by 1526, where it killed the Inca emperor Huayna Capac long before any Europeans had arrived on the scene.

15 Sahagún 1950–82:bk.12:31.

16 Lockhart 1992:1. For general treatments of Nahua culture in the century after the Spanish Conquest, see Burkhart (1989), S. L. Cline (2000), Gibson

(1964; 1966), and Lockhart (1992). Gibson (1964) and Lockhart (1992) provide extensive overviews of the subject.

17 Early Mexican *encomienda*s are discussed by Gibson (1964; 1966). Gibson (1964:83) lists typical *encomienda* tribute goods.

18 Gerhard 1993; Gibson 1964; Lockhart 1992.

19 The role of the church is discussed by Gibson (1964; 1966). For the responses of the Nahuas to Christianity, see Burkhart (1989), Carmack et al. (1996:ch.5), and Lockhart (1992).

20 These early churches and monasteries, most of which still stand today, are fascinating structures. See Kubler (1948) and Perry (1992).

21 Carmack et al. 1996:165. See Burkhart (1989) for a detailed analysis of this situation.

22 Burkhart 1989; Ingham 1986.

23 Lockhart 1992; see also S. L. Cline (1993; 2000) and Kellogg (1995).

24 The archaeology of Early Colonial central Mexico is discussed by Charlton (1972), Charlton and Fournier (1993), Fernández Dávila and Gómez Serafín (1998), and Lister and Lister (1982).

25 Lockhart 1992:201–2. See also Gibson (1964), Haskett (1991), and Wood (1990).

26 A few of the many excellent anthropological descriptions of modern Nahua peoples today are Friedlander (1975), Ingham (1986), Lewis (1951), Sandstrom (1991), and Taggart (1983). See also Carmack et al. (1996).

27 Friedlander 1975:130, 71, 75.

28 Modern traditional houses are discussed by Moya Rubio (1982), Sandstrom (1991), and Smith et al. (1992). The house being built in figure 12.9, when completed, resembled that shown in figure 6.4.

29 See Lewis (1951) and Redfield (1929).

30 Foster (1960) discusses many examples of this phenomenon.

31 Friedlander 1975. For handspinning wool, the women of Hueyapan use large Aztec spindle whorls that they find in the fields. These whorls were originally used by the Aztecs to spin maguey fiber. Berdan and Barber (1988) also discuss modern Nahua textiles. Other modern Indian crafts and their historical development are discussed by Foster (1960), Friedlander (1975), Sandstrom and Sandstrom (1986), and Stromberg (1976). For modern use of the Nahuatl language, see Canger (1988) and Kaufman (1976).

32 The tortilla made of wheat flour is a northern Mexican food that originated well after the Spanish Conquest. Wheat flour tortillas are available in central Mexican grocery stores, but they are not nearly as prevalent in the diet as the maize tortilla.

33 Modern lessons from archaeological fieldwork on ancient states are discussed by Erickson and Candler (1989), Hudson and Levine (1999), Lentz (2000), Redman (1999), and Rice and Rice (1984).

34 Alvarado Tezozomoc 1975a:4–5 (translated by Marcus 1992:271–2).

Glossary of Nahuatl Terms

altepetl   City-state or kingdom consisting of a town and surrounding rural area ruled by a *tlatoani* (chapter 7).

calmecac   School for nobles or promising commoners (chapter 6).

calpolli   A group of families who lived near one another and were subject to a single lord. Most *calpolli* had between 100 and 200 families. In cities *calpolli* formed neighborhoods, whereas rural *calpolli* were either towns or collections of villages. The term *calpolli* is sometimes used in documents to designate a smaller residential unit, the ward (chapter 6).

Chichimec   Member of a hunter-gatherer band of northern Mexico. The ancestors of the Aztecs were Chichimecs who migrated south into central Mexico (chapter 2).

chinampa   Raised field bed; a form of intensive agriculture used to cultivate swampy areas (chapter 3).

ixiptla   God impersonator. Priests or planned sacrificial victims dressed in the regalia of a god and who were venerated as that god during key ceremonies (chapter 9).

macehualli (pl. *macehualtin*)   Commoner who was a member of a *calpolli* (chapter 6).

maguey   Plant of the genus *Agave* with many economic and medicinal uses (chapter 3).

maquahuitl   Sword made of a wood handle with two cutting edges of sharp obsidian blades (chapter 7).

metate   Stone slab used to grind maize to make tortillas and *tamales* (chapters 3 and 6).

patolli   Game of chance often played by gamblers (chapter 10).

pilli (pl. *pipiltin*)   Hereditary noble of a lower rank than a *tlatoani* or *tecuhtli* (chapter 6).

pochtecatl (pl. *pochteca*)   Professional merchant belonging to a specialized trading guild (chapter 5).

pulque   Fermented alchoholic beverage made from the sap of the maguey plant (chapter 3).

quachtli   Cotton cape or blanket of a standard size used as currency and for tribute payments (chapters 4 and 5).

quauhpilli   Special social category of nobles by achievement created by Motecuhzoma I to reward outstanding commoner accomplishments in war (chapters 2 and 7).

teccalli   Literally, "noble house," an institution in the eastern Nahua area consisting of a noble family, its land and other property, and the labor obligations of resident commoners (chapter 6).

tecpan   Palace; residence of a noble (chapter 6).

tecuhtli (pl. *tetecuhtin*)   High-ranking lord or noble who controlled a major estate and usually served in an important administrative or military position (chapter 6).

telpochcalli   School for commoner children (chapter 6).

teotl   Deity (chapter 9).

tequitl   Goods and labor service owed to lords by commoners (chapter 6).

tianquiz   Marketplace (chapter 5).

tlachtli   The Aztec ballgame, an event that combined ritual, sport, and entertainment (chapter 10).

tlacotli (pl. *tlacotin*)   Slave (chapter 6).

tlamama   Professional carriers or load-bearers, usually employed by merchants on trade expeditions (chapter 5).

tlatoani (pl. *tlatoque*)   King of a city-state. A *tlatoani*, literally "he who speaks," was always of the noble class (chapter 7).

tonalpohualli   260-day ritual calendar used for divination, astrology, and rituals (chapter 11).

tzompantli   Skull rack for public display of the skulls of sacrificial victims (chapter 10).

Note: The best modern Nahuatl-English dictionary is Karttunen (1983). The most complete sources on sixteenth-century Nahuatl are Friar Alonso de Molina's Nahuatl-Spanish and Spanish-Nahuatl dictionary from 1571 (Molina 1970) and Friar Sahagún's *Florentine Codex* (Sahagún 1950–82).

References

Acuña, René
  1984–7. *Relaciones geográficas del siglo XVI*. 9 vols. Universidad Nacional Autónoma de México, Mexico City.
Alberti Manzanares, Pilar
  1994. Mujeres sacerdotisas aztecas: las cihuatlamacazque mencionadas en los manuscritos inéditos. *Estudios de Cultura Náhuatl* 24:171–217.
Alcock, Susan E., Terence N. D'Altroy, Kathleen D. Morrison, and Carla M. Sinopoli (eds.)
  2001. *Empires: Perspectives from Archaeology and History*. Cambridge University Press, New York.
Alva Ixtlilxochitl, Fernando de
  1975–7. *Obras históricas*. Translated by Edmundo O'Gorman. 2 vols. Universidad Nacional Autónoma de México, Mexico City.
Alvarado Tezozomoc, Hernando de
  1975a. *Crónica mexicáyotl*. Translated by Adrián León. Universidad Nacional Autónoma de México, Mexico City.
  1975b. *Crónica Mexicana*. Edited by Manuel Orozco y Berra. Porrúa, Mexico City.
Anawalt, Patricia Rieff
  1981. *Indian Clothing Before Cortés: Mesoamerican Costumes from the Codices*. University of Oklahoma Press, Norman.
  1993. Rabbits, *Pulque*, and Drunkenness: A Study of Ambivalence in Aztec Society. In *Current Topics in Aztec Studies: Essays in Honor of H. B. Nicholson*, edited by Alana Cordy-Collins and Douglas Sharon, vol. 30, pp. 17–38. Papers. San Diego Museum, San Diego.
Anders, Ferdinand, Maarten E. R. G. N. Jansen, and Luis Reyes García
  1993. *Manual del adivino: libro explicativo del llamado Códice Vaticano B, Codex Vaticanus 3773, Biblioteca Apostólica Vaticana*. Códices mexicanos, vol. 4. Sociedad Estatal Quinto Centenario, Akademische Druck- u. Verlagsanstalt, Fondo de Cultura Económica, Madrid, Graz, Mexico City.
Anderson, Arthur J. O., Frances F. Berdan, and James Lockhart (eds.)
  1976. *Beyond the Codices: The Nahua View of Colonial Mexico*. University of California Press, Berkeley.

Angulo Villaseñor, Jorge
1976. Teopanzolco y Cuauhnahuac, Morelos. In *Los señoríos e estados militaristas*, edited by Román Piña Chán, pp. 183–208. Instituto Nacional de Antropología e Historia, Mexico City.

Anonymous
1935. *Tenayuca: estudio arqueológico de la pirámide de este lugar*. Departamento de Monumentos de la Secretaría de Educación Públic, Talleres Gráficos del Museo Nacional de Antropología, Historia y Etnografía, Mexico City.
1960. *Calixtlahuaca: Official Guide*. Instituto Nacional de Antropología e Historia, Mexico City.

Appadurai, Arjun
1986. Introduction: Commodities and the Politics of Value. In *The Social Life of Things: Commodities in Cultural Perspective*, edited by Arjun Appadurai, pp. 3–63. Cambridge University Press, New York.

Arana Alvarez, Raúl M.
1984. El juego de pelota en Coatetelco, Morelos. In *Investigaciones recientes en el área maya, XVII Mesa Redonda, Sociedad Mexicana de Antropología*, vol. 4, pp. 191–204. Sociedad Mexicana de Antropología, Mexico City.

Armillas, Pedro
1944. Oztuma, Guerrero: forteleza de los mexicanos en la frontera de Michoacán. *Revista Mexicana de Estudios Antropológicos* 6:157–65.
1969. The Arid Frontier of Mexican Civilization. *Transactions, New York Academy of Science* 31(6):697–704.

Arnold, Philip P.
1999. *Eating Landscape: Aztec and European Occupation of Tlalocan*. University Press of Colorado, Niwot.

Aveni, Anthony F.
1992. Moctezuma's Sky: Aztec Astronomy and Ritual. In *Moctezuma's Mexico: Visions of the Aztec World*, edited by Davíd Carrasco and Eduardo Matos Moctezuma, pp. 149–58. University Press of Colorado, Niwot.
2001. *Skywatchers*. 2nd edn. University of Texas Press, Austin.

Aveni, Anthony F., and Edward E. Calnek
1999. Astronomical Considerations in the Aztec Expression of History: Eclipse Data. *Ancient Mesoamerica* 10:87–98.

Baird, Ellen T.
1993. *The Drawings of Sahagún's Primeros Memoriales: Structure and Style*. University of Oklahoma Press, Norman.

Baquedano, Elizabeth
1984. *Aztec Sculpture*. British Museum, London.
1998. Aspects of Death Symbolism in Aztec Tlaltecuhtli. In *The Symbolism in the Plastic and Pictorial Representations of Ancient Mexico*, edited by Jacqueline de Durand-Forest and Marc Eisinger, vol. 21, pp. 157–80. Bonner Amerikanistische Studien, Bonn.

Barlow, Robert H.
1945. Some Remarks on the Term "Aztec Empire". *Americas* 1:345–9.
1989. *Tlatelolco: fuentes e historia*. Obras de Robert H. Barlow, vol. 2. Edited by Jesús Monjarás-Ruiz, Elena Limón, and María de la Cruz Paillés H. Instituto

Nacional de Antropología e Historia and Universidad de las Américas, Puebla, Mexico City and Puebla.

Barrera Rivera, José Alvaro, Maraí de Lourdes Gallardo Parrodi, and Aurora Montúfar López

2001. La ofrenda 102 del templo mayor. *Arqueología Mexicana* 8(48):70–7.

Berdan, Frances F.

1982. *The Aztecs of Central Mexico: An Imperial Society*. Holt, Rinehart, and Winston, New York.

1985. Markets in the Economy of Aztec Mexico. In *Markets and Marketing*, edited by Stuart Plattner, pp. 339–67. University Press of America, Lanham, MD.

1987. Cotton in Aztec Mexico: Production, Distribution, and Uses. *Mexican Studies / Estudios Mexicanos* 3:235–62.

1988. Principles of Regional and Long-Distance Trade in the Aztec Empire. In *Smoke and Mist: Mesoamerican Studies in Memory of Thelma D. Sullivan*, edited by J. Kathryn Josser and Karen Dakin, vol. 402, part 1, pp. 639–56. BAR International Series. British Archaeological Reports, Oxford.

1992a. Appendix E: The Place-Name, Personal Name, and Title Glyphs of the Codex Mendoza: Translations and Comments. In *The Codex Mendoza*, edited by Frances F. Berdan and Patricia Rieff Anawalt, vol. 1, pp. 163–239. University of California Press, Berkeley.

1992b. Glyphic Conventions of the Codex Mendoza. In *The Codex Mendoza*, edited by Frances F. Berdan and Patricia Rieff Anawalt, vol. 1, pp. 93–102. University of California Press, Berkeley.

Berdan, Frances F., and Patricia Rieff Anawalt

1997. *The Essential Codex Mendoza*. University of California Press, Berkeley.

Berdan, Frances F., and Russell J. Barber

1988. *Spanish Thread on Indian Looms: Mexican Folk Costume*. University Art Gallery, San Bernardino.

Berdan, Frances F., Richard E. Blanton, Elizabeth H. Boone, Mary G. Hodge, Michael E. Smith, and Emily Umberger

1996. *Aztec Imperial Strategies*. Dumbarton Oaks, Washington, DC.

Berger, Uta

1998. *Mexican Painted Manuscripts in the United Kingdom*. Occasional Paper, vol. 91. British Museum Press, London.

Bergmann, Richard F.

1969. The Distribution of Cacao Cultivation in Pre-Columbian America. *Annals of the Association of American Geographers* 59:85–96.

Berlo, Janet C. (ed.)

1992. *Art, Ideology, and the City of Teotihuacan*. Dumbarton Oaks, Washington, DC.

Berrin, Kathleen, and Esther Pasztory (eds.)

1994. *Teotihuacan: Art from the City of the Gods*. Thames and Hudson, New York.

Beyer, Hermann

1934. Mexican Bone Rattles. In *Studies in Middle America*, edited by Maurice Ries, vol. 5, pp. 321–49. Tulane University, Middle American Research Institute, New Orleans.

Bierhorst, John

1992. *History and Mythology of the Aztecs: The Codex Chimalpopoca*. University of Arizona Press, Tucson.

Blanton, Richard E., and Gary M. Feinman

1984. The Mesoamerican World System. *American Anthropologist* 86:673–82.

Blanton, Richard E., Stephen A. Kowalewski, Gary M. Feinman, and Laura M. Finsten

1993. *Ancient Mesoamerica: A Comparison of Change in Three Regions*. 2nd edn. Cambridge University Press, New York.

Bonifaz Nuño, Rubén, and Fernando Robles

1981. *El arte en el templo mayor: México-Tenochtitlan*. Instituto Nacional de Antropología e Historia, Mexico City.

Boone, Elizabeth H.

1983 (see *Codex Magliabechiano* 1983)

1987 (ed.). *The Aztec Templo Mayor*. Dumbarton Oaks, Washington, DC.

1989. *Incarnations of the Aztec Supernatural: The Image of Huitzilopochtli in Mexico and Europe*. Transactions, vol. 79 (2). American Philosophical Society, New York.

2000a. Guides for Living: The Divinatory Codices of Mexico. In *In Chalchihuitl in Quetzalli, Precious Greenstone Precious Quetzal Feather: Mesoamerican Studies in Honor of Doris Heyden*, edited by Eloise Quiñones Keber, pp. 69–82. Labyrinthos, Lancaster, CA.

2000b. Venerable Place of Beginnings: The Aztec Understanding of Teotihuacan. In *Mesoamerica's Classic Heritage: From Teotihuacan to the Aztecs*, edited by Davíd Carrasco, Lindsay Jones, and Scott Sessions, pp. 371–96. University Press of Colorado, Niwot.

2000c. *Stories in Red and Black: Pictorial Histories of the Aztecs and Mixtecs*. University of Texas Press, Austin.

Borah, Woodrow, and Sherburne F. Cook

1963. *The Aboriginal Population of Central Mexico on the Eve of the Spanish Conquest*. Ibero-Americana, vol. 45. University of California Press, Berkeley.

Braswell, Geoffrey E.

2001. Post-Classic Maya Courts of the Guatemala Highlands: Archaeological and Ethnohistorical Approaches. In *Royal Courts of the Ancient Maya*, vol. 2: *Data and Case Studies*, edited by Takeshi Inomata and Stephen D. Houston, pp. 308–34. Westview Press, Boulder, CO.

Bribiesca Castrejón, José Luis

1958. El agua potable en la república Mexicana: los abastecimientos en la época prehispánica. *Ingeniera Hidraúlica en México* 12(2):69–82.

Broda, Johanna

1970. Tlacaxipehualiztli: A Reconstruction of an Aztec Calendar Festival from 16th Century Sources. *Revista Española de Antropología Americana* 5:197–273.

Brotherston, Gordon

1994. Huesos de muerte, huesos de vida: la compleja figura de Mictlantecutli.

Cuicuilco 1 (n.s):85–98.

Brüggemann, Jürgen Kurt (ed.)
1991. *Zempoala: el estudio de una ciudad prehispánica.* Colección Científica, vol. 232. Instituto Nacional de Antropología e Historia, Mexico City.

Bruman, Henry J.
2000. *Alcohol in Ancient Mexico.* University of Utah Press, Salt Lake City.

Brumfiel, Elizabeth M.
1980. Specialization, Market Exchange, and the Aztec State: A View From Huexotla. *Current Anthropology* 21:459–78.
1983. Aztec State Making: Ecology, Structure, and the Origin of the State. *American Anthropologist* 85:261–84.
1986. The Division of Labor at Xico: The Chipped Stone Industry. In *Economic Aspects of Prehispanic Highland Mexico*, edited by Barry Isaac, vol. 2, pp. 245–79. Research in Economic Anthropology, Supplement. JAI Press, Greenwich, CT.
1987. Elite and Utilitarian Crafts in the Aztec State. In *Specialization, Exchange, and Complex Societies*, edited by Elizabeth M. Brumfiel and Timothy K. Earle, pp. 102–18. Cambridge University Press, New York.
1991. Weaving and Cooking: Women's Production in Aztec Mexico. In *Engendering Archaeology: Women and Prehistory*, edited by Joan M. Gero and Margaret W. Conkey, pp. 224–51. Blackwell, Oxford.
1992. *Postclassic Xaltocan: Archaeological Research in the Northern Valley of Mexico (1991 Annual Report).* Unpublished field report. Albion College, Albion, MI.
1998a. Huitzilopochtli's Conquest: Aztec Ideology in the Archaeological Record. *Cambridge Archaeological Journal* 8:3–14.
1998b. The Multiple Identities of Aztec Craft Specialists. In *Craft and Social Identity*, edited by Cathy Lynne Costin and Rita P. Wright, vol. 8, pp. 145–52. Archaeological Papers of the American Anthropological Association. American Anthropological Association, Washington, DC.

Brundage, Burr C.
1985. *The Jade Steps: A Ritual Life of the Aztecs.* University of Utah Press, Salt Lake City.

Burkhart, Louise M.
1989. *The Slippery Earth: Nahua–Christian Moral Dialogue in Sixteenth-Century Mexico.* University of Arizona Press, Tucson.
1997. Mexica Women on the Home Front: Housework and Religion in Aztec Mexico. In *Indian Women of Early Mexico*, edited by Susan Schroeder, Stephanie Wood and Robert Haskett, pp. 25–54. University of Oklahoma Press, Norman.

Caballero, Margarita, and Beatriz Ortega Guerrero
1998. Lake Levels Since about 40,000 Years Ago at Lake Chalco, Near Mexico City. *Quaternary Research* 50:69–79.

Calnek, Edward E.
1972. Settlement Pattern and Chinampa Agriculture at Tenochtitlan. *American Antiquity* 37:104–15.
1974. Conjunto urbana y modelo residencial en Tenochtitlan. In *Ensayos sobre*

el desarollo urbano de México, edited by Woodrow Borah, pp. 11–65. Secretaría de Educación Pública, Mexico City.

1976. The Internal Structure of Tenochtitlan. In *The Valley of Mexico: Studies of Pre-Hispanic Ecology and Society*, edited by Eric R. Wolf, pp. 287–302. University of New Mexico Press, Albuquerque.

1978. The City-State in the Basin of Mexico: Late Pre-Hispanic Period. In *Urbanization in the Americas from its Beginnings to the Present*, edited by R. P. Schaedel, J. E. Hardoy, and N. S. Kinzer, pp. 463–70. Mouton, The Hague.

1982. Patterns of Empire Formation in the Valley of Mexico. In *The Inca and Aztec States, 1400–1800: Anthropology and History*, edited by George A. Collier, Renato I. Rosaldo, and John D. Wirth, pp. 43–62. Academic Press, New York.

Canger, Una
1988. Nahuatl Dialectology: A Survey and Some Suggestions. *International Journal of American Linguistics* 54:28–72.

Cantares Mexicanos
1985. *Cantares Mexicanos: Songs of the Aztecs*. Translated by John Bierhorst. Stanford University Press, Stanford.

Carmack, Robert M.
1981. *The Quiché Mayas of Utatlan: The Evolution of a Highland Guatemala Kingdom*. University of Oklahoma Press, Norman.

Carmack, Robert M., Janine Gasco, and Gary H. Gossen (eds.)
1996. *The Legacy of Mesoamerica: History and Culture of a Native American Civilization*. Prentice-Hall, Englewood Cliffs, NJ.

Carrasco, Davíd
1999. *City of Sacrifice: The Aztec Empire and the Role of Violence in Civilization*. Beacon Press, Boston.

Carrasco, Davíd, Lindsay Jones, and Scott Sessions (eds.)
2000. *Mesoamerica's Classic Heritage: From Teotihuacan to the Aztecs*. University Press of Colorado, Niwot.

Carrasco, Davíd, and Eduardo Matos Moctezuma
1992. *Moctezuma's Mexico: Visions of the Aztec World*. University Press of Colorado, Niwot.

Carrasco, Pedro
1972. La casa y hacienda de un señor tlahuica. *Estudios de Cultura Náhuatl* 10:235–44.

1974. Introducción: la matrícula de Huexotzinco como fuente sociológica. In *Matrícula de Huexotzinco (Ms. mex. 387 del Bibliothèque Nationale Paris)*, edited by Hanns J. Prem, pp. 1–16. Akademische Druck- u. Verlagsanstalt, Graz.

1976. The Joint Family in Ancient Mexico: The Case of Molotla. In *Essays on Mexican Kinship*, edited by Hugo Nutini, Pedro Carrasco and James M. Taggert, pp. 45–64. University of Pittsburgh Press, Pittsburgh.

1984. Royal Marriages in Ancient Mexico. In *Explorations in Ethnohistory: Indians of Central Mexico in the Sixteenth Century*, edited by Herbert R. Harvey and Hanns J. Prem, pp. 41–81. University of New Mexico Press, Albuquerque.

1999. *The Tenochca Empire of Ancient Mexico: The Triple Alliance of*

Tenochtitlan, Tetzcoco, and Tlacopan. University of Oklahoma Press, Norman.

Casas, Bartolomé de las
1957–8. *Obras escogidas.* 5 vols. Atlas, Madrid.

Caso, Alfonso
1969. *El tesoro de Monte Albán.* Memorias, vol. 3. Instituto Nacional de Antropología e Historia, Mexico City.
1971. Calendrical Systems of Central Mexico. In *Archaeology of Northern Mesoamerica*, part 1, edited by Gordon F. Ekholm and Ignacio Bernal, vol. 10, pp. 333–48. Handbook of Middle American Indians. University of Texas Press, Austin.

Castañeda, Daniel, and Vicente T. Mendoza
1933. Los pequeños percutores en las civilizaciones precortesianos. *Anales del Museo Nacional de Arqueología e Historia, Epoca 4* 8(3):449–576.

Castillo F., Victor M.
1972. Unidades nahuas de medida. *Estudios de Cultura Náhuatl* 10:195–223.

Castillo Nechar, Marcelino
1995. *El tianguis de Toluca: una reminiscencia de los mercados prehispánicos.* Cuadernos de Cultura Universitaria, vol. 10. Universidad Autónoma del Estado de México, Toluca.

Castro, Casimiro
1855–7. *México y sus alrededores: colección de vistas, trajes y monumentos, por C. Castro, J. Campillo, L. Auda y G. Rodriguez.* Collection of lithographs. Decaen, Mexico City.

Chance, John K.
2000. The Noble House in Colonial Puebla, Mexico: Descent, Inheritance, and the Nahua Tradition. *American Anthropologist* 102:485–502.

Charlton, Thomas H.
1970. Contemporary Agriculture in the Teotihuacan Valley. In *The Natural Environment, Contemporary Occupation and 16th Century Population of the Valley*, by Anton Kovar, Thomas H. Charlton, Richard A. Diehl, and William T. Sanders. The Teotihuacan Valley Project Final Report, vol. 1, pp. 253–86. Occasional Papers in Anthropology, no. 3. Pennsylvania State University, Department of Anthropology, University Park.
1972. *Post-Conquest Developments in the Teotihuacan Valley, Mexico*, part 1: *Excavations.* Office of the State Archaeologist, Iowa City.

Charlton, Thomas H., and Patricia Fournier G.
1993. Urban and Rural Dimensions of the Contact Period, Central Mexico, 1521–1620. In *Ethnohistory and Archaeology: Approaches to Postcontact Change in the Americas*, edited by J. Daniel Rogers and Samuel M. Wilson, pp. 201–20. Plenum Press, New York.

Charlton, Thomas H., Deborah L. Nichols, and Cynthia Otis Charlton
1991. Aztec Craft Production and Specialization: Archaeological Evidence from the City-State of Otumba, Mexico. *World Archaeology* 23:98–114.
2000. Otumba and its Neighbors: Ex Oriente Lux. *Ancient Mesoamerica* 11:247–66.

Charlton, Thomas H., and Michael W. Spence

1982. Obsidian Exploitation and Civilization in the Basin of Mexico. In *Mining and Mining Techniques in Ancient Mesoamerica*, edited by Phil C. Weigand and Gretchen Gwynne, vol. 6, pp. 7–86. Anthropology, Stony Brook, NY.

Chimalpahin Cuauhtlehuanitzin, Domingo Francisco de San Antón Muñón
1965. *Relaciones originales de Chalco Amequemecan.* Translated by Silvia Rendón. Fondo de Cultura Económica, Mexico City.
1997. *Codex Chimalpahin: Society and Politics in Mexico Tenochtitlan, Tlatelolco, Texcoco, Culhuacan, and Other Nahua Altepetl in Central Mexico: The Nahuatl and Spanish Annals and Accounts Collected and Recorded by Don Domingo de San Antón Muñón Chimalpahin Quauhtlehuanitzin.* Edited by Arthur J. O. Anderson, Susan Schroeder, and Wayne Ruwet. 2 vols. University of Oklahoma Press, Norman.

Clark, John E.
1982. Manufacture of Mesoamerican Prismatic Blades: An Alternative Technique. *American Antiquity* 47:355–76.
1987. Politics, Prismatic Blades and Mesoamerican Civilization. In *The Organization of Core Technology*, edited by Jay K. Johnson and Carol A. Morrow, pp. 259–84. Westview Press, Boulder, CO.

Clark, John E., and Stephen D. Houston
1998. Craft Specialization, Gender, and Personhood among the Post-Conquest Maya of Yucatan, Mexico. *In Craft and Social Identity*, edited by Cathy Lynne Costin and Rita P. Wright, pp. 31–49. Archaeological Papers of the American Anthropological Assocation, vol. 8. American Anthropological Association, Washington, DC.

Clendinnen, Inga
1991a. *Aztecs: An Interpretation.* Cambridge University Press, New York.
1991b. "Fierceness and Unnatural Cruelty": Cortés and the Conquest of Mexico. *Representations* 33:65–100.

Cline, Howard F.
1972. The *Relaciones Geográficas* of the Spanish Indies, 1577–1648. In *Guide to Ethnohistorical Sources*, part 1, edited by Howard F. Cline, vol. 12, pp. 183–242. Handbook of Middle American Indians. University of Texas Press, Austin.

Cline, S. L.
1993. *The Book of Tributes: Early Sixteenth-Century Nahuatl Censuses from Morelos.* UCLA Latin American Center, Los Angeles.
2000. Native Peoples of Colonial Central Mexico. In *The Cambridge History of the Native Peoples of the Americas*, vol. 2: *Mesoamerica*, part 2, edited by Richard E. W. Adams and Murdo J. MacLeod, pp. 187–222. Cambridge University Press, New York.

Closs, Michael P.
1997. Mathematics of the Aztec People. In *Encyclopaedia of the History of Science, Technology, and Medicine in Non-Western Cultures*, edited by Helaine Selin, pp. 622–5. Kluwer Academic Publishers, Dordrecht.

Cobean, Robert H.
1990. *La cerámica de Tula, Hidalgo.* Instituto Nacional de Antropología e

Historia, Mexico City.

1991. Principales yacimientos de obsidiana en el altiplano central. *Arqueología* 5:9–31.

Cobean, Robert H., James R. Vogt, Michael D. Glascock, and Terrence L. Stocker

1991. High-Precision Trace Element Characterization of Major Mesoamerican Obsidian Sources and Further Analysis of Artifacts from San Lorenzo Tenochititlan, Mexico. *Latin American Antiquity* 2:69–91.

Codex Borbonicus

1974. *Codex Borbonicus. Bibliothéque de l'Assemblée Nationale, Paris (Y 120).* Edited by Karl Anton Nowotny and Jacqueline de Durand-Forest. Akademische Druck- u. Verlagsanstalt, Graz.

Codex Borgia

1976. *Codex Borgia (Cod. Gorg. Messicano 1).* Edited by Karl Anton Nowotny. Akademische Druck- u. Verlagsanstalt, Graz.

Codex Fejérváry-Mayer

1971. *Codex Fejérváry-Mayer: 12014 M. City of Liverpool Museums.* Edited by Cottie A. Burland. Codices selecti phototypice impressi, vol. 26. Akademische Druck- u. Verlagsanstalt, Graz.

Codex Magliabechiano

1983. *Codex Magliabechiano and the Lost Prototype of the Magliabechiano Group.* Edited by Elizabeth H. Boone. 2 vols. University of California Press, Berkeley.

Codex Mendoza

1992. *The Codex Mendoza.* Edited by Frances F. Berdan and Patricia R. Anawalt. 4 vols. University of California Press, Berkeley.

Códice Tudela

1980. *Códice Tudela: José Tudela de la Orden.* 2 vols. Ediciones Cultura Hispánica, Madrid.

Coe, Michael D.

1992. *Breaking the Maya Code.* Thames and Hudson, New York.

1994. *Mexico: From the Olmecs to the Aztecs.* 4th edn. Thames and Hudson, New York.

1999. *The Maya.* 6th edn. Thames and Hudson, New York.

Coe, Sophie D.

1994. *America's First Cuisines.* University of Texas Press, Austin.

Coe, Sophie D., and Michael D. Coe

1996. *The True History of Chocolate.* Thames and Hudson, New York.

Conrad, Geoffrey W., and Arthur A. Demarest

1984. *Religion and Empire: The Dynamics of Aztec and Inca Expansion.* Cambridge University Press, New York.

Cook, Scott

1982. *Zapotec Stoneworkers: The Dynamics of Rural Simple Commodity Production in Modern Mexican Capitalism.* University Press of America, Lanham, MD.

Cook, Scott, and Martin Diskin (eds.)

1976. *Markets in Oaxaca.* University of Texas Press, Austin.

Cook, Sherburne F., and Woodrow Borah

1979. Indian Food Production and Consumption in Central Mexico Before and After the Conquest (1500–1650). In *Essays in Population History: Mexico and California*, vol. 3, pp. 129–76. University of California Press, Berkeley.

Cortés, Hernando
1962. *Five Letters of Cortés to the Emperor*. Translated by J. Bayard Morris. Norton, New York.

Costin, Cathy Lynne, and Rita P. Wright (eds.)
1998. *Craft and Social Identity*. Archaeological Papers of the American Anthropological Assocation, vol. 8. American Anthropological Association, Washington, DC.

Cowgill, George L.
1997. State and Society at Teotihuacan, Mexico. *Annual Review of Anthropology* 26:129–61.
2000. The Central Mexican Highlands from the Rise of Teotihuacan to the Decline of Tula. In *Mesoamerica*, part 1, edited by Richard E. W. Adams and Murdo J. MacLeod, pp. 250–317. The Cambridge History of the Native Peoples of the Americas, vol. 2. Cambridge University Press, New York.

Crosby, Alfred W.
1972. *The Columbian Exchange: Biological and Cultural Consequences of 1492*. Greenwood Press, Westport, CT.

Cruz y Moya, Juan de la
1954–5. *Historia de la santa y apostólica provincia de Santiago de Predicadores de México en la Nueva España*. 2 vols. Manuel Porrúa, Mexico City.

D'Altroy, Terence N.
1992. *Provincial Power in the Inka Empire*. Smithsonian Institution Press, Washington, DC.

Davies, Nigel
1968. *Los señoríos independientes del imperio azteca*. Instituto Nacional de Antropología e Historia, Mexico City.
1973. *The Aztecs: A History*. University of Oklahoma Press, Norman.
1977. *The Toltecs Until the Fall of Tula*. University of Oklahoma Press, Norman.
1987. *The Aztec Empire: The Toltec Resurgence*. University of Oklahoma Press, Norman.

de Vega Nova, Hortensia
1996. Proyecto de investigación arqueológico en Yautepec, Morelos. In *Memoria, III Congreso Interno del Centro INAH Morelos, Acapantzingo, Cuernavaca, 1994*, pp. 149–68. Instituto Nacional de Antropología e Historia, Centro INAH Morelos, Cuernavaca, Morelos.

de Vega Nova, Hortensia, and Pablo Mayer Guala
1991. Proyecto Yautepec. *Boletín del Consejo de Arqueología* 1991:79–84.

Díaz del Castillo, Bernal
1963. *The Conquest of New Spain*. Translated by J. M. Cohen. Penguin, New York.

Díaz, Gisele, and Alan Rogers
1993. *The Codex Borgia: A Full-Color Restoration of the Ancient Mexican Manuscript*. Dover Publications, New York.

Dibble, Charles E.

1988. Molina and Sahagún. In *Smoke and Mist: Mesoamerican Studies in Memory of Thelma D. Sullivan*, edited by J. Kathryn Josserand and Karen Dakin, pp. 69–76. BAR International Series, vol. 402, part 1. British Archaeological Reports, Oxford.

Diehl, Richard A.

1983. *Tula: The Toltec Capital of Ancient Mexico*. Thames and Hudson, New York.

Diehl, Richard A., and Janet Berlo (eds.)

1989. *Mesoamerica After the Decline of Teotihuacan, AD 700–900*. Dumbarton Oaks, Washington, DC.

Donkin, R. A.

1979. *Agricultural Terracing in the Aboriginal New World*. Viking Fund Publications in Anthropology, vol. 56. University of Arizona Press, Tucson.

Doolittle, William E.

1990. *Canal Irrigation in Prehistoric Mexico: The Sequence of Technological Change*. University of Texas Press, Austin.

Drennan, Robert D.

1984. Long-Distance Transport Costs in Pre-Hispanic Mesoamerica. *American Anthropologist* 86:105–12.

Dupaix, Guillermo

1834. *Antiquités Mexicaines: relation des trois expeditions du Capitaine Dupaix, ordonnées en 1805, 1806, et 1807, pour la recherche les antiquités du pays, notamment celles de Mitla et de Palenque*. 2 vols. Jules Didot l'ainé, Paris.

Durán, Diego

1967. *Historia de las Indias de Nueva España*. Edited by Angel M. Garibay K. 2 vols. Porrúa, Mexico City.

1971. *Book of the Gods and Rites and the Ancient Calendar*. Translated by Fernando Horcasitas and Doris Heyden. University of Oklahoma Press, Norman.

1994. *The History of the Indies of New Spain*. Translated by Doris Heyden. University of Oklahoma Press, Norman.

Edmonson, Munro S. (ed.)

1974. *Sixteenth-Century Mexico: The World of Sahagún*. University of New Mexico Press, Albuquerque.

Einzig, Paul

1966. *Primitive Money*. Pergamon Press, New York.

Elson, Christina M., and Michael E. Smith

2001. Archaeological Deposits from the Aztec New Fire Ceremony. *Ancient Mesoamerica* 12:157–74.

Erickson, Clark L., and Kay L. Candler

1989. Raised Fields and Sustainable Agriculture in the Lake Titicaca Basin of Peru. In *Fragile Lands of Latin America: Strategies for Sustainable Development*, edited by John O. Browder, pp. 230–48. Westview Press, Boulder, CO.

Evans, Susan T.

1988. *Excavations at Cihuatecpan, an Aztec Village in the Teotihuacan Valley*. Vanderbilt University Publications in Anthropology, vol. 36. Department of

Anthropology, Vanderbilt University, Nashville.

1990. The Productivity of Maguey Terrace Agriculture in Central Mexico During the Aztec Period. *Latin American Antiquity* 1:117–32.

1991. Architecture and Authority in an Aztec Village: Form and Function of the Tecpan. In *Land and Politics in the Valley of Mexico: A Two Thousand Year Perspective*, edited by Herbert R. Harvey, pp. 63–92. University of New Mexico Press, Albuquerque.

1993. Aztec Household Organization and Village Administration. In *Prehispanic Domestic Units in Western Mesoamerica: Studies of the Household, Compound, and Residence*, edited by Robert S. Santley and Kenneth G. Hirth, pp. 173–89. CRC Press, Boca Raton.

2000. Aztec Royal Pleasure Parks: Conspicuous Consumption and Elite Status Rivalry. *Studies in the History of Gardens and Designed Landscapes* 20:206–28.

2001. Aztec Noble Courts: Men, Women, and Children of the Palace. In *Maya Royal Courts*, edited by Takeshi Inomata and Stephen Houston, vol. 1, pp. 237–73. Westview Press, Boulder, CO.

Evans, Susan T., and William T. Sanders (eds.)

2000. *The Teotihuacan Valley Project, Final Report*, vol. 5: *The Aztec Period Occupation of the Valley*, part 1: *Natural Environment, 20th Century Occupation, Survey Methodology, and Site Descriptions*. Occasional Papers in Anthropology, vol. 25. Department of Anthropology, Pennsylvania State University, University Park.

Fauman-Fichman, Ruth

1999. Postclassic Craft Production in Morelos, Mexico: The Cotton Thread Industry in the Provinces. PhD dissertation, Department of Anthropology, University of Pittsburgh.

Fernández Dávila, Enrique, and Susana Gómez Serafín (eds.)

1998. *Primer Congreso Nacional de Arqueología Histórica: memoria (Oaxaca, 1996)*. Consejo Nacional para la Cultura y las Artes, and Instituto Nacional de Antropología e Historia, Mexico City.

Figueira, Thomas J.

1984. Karl Polanyi and Ancient Greek Trade: The Port of Trade. *Ancient World* 10:15–30.

Flannery, Kent V. (ed.)

1976. *The Early Mesoamerican Village*. Academic Press, New York.

Florescano, Enrique

1993. The Creation of the Museo Nacional de Antropología of Mexico and its Scientific, Educational, and Political Purposes. In *Collecting the Pre-Columbian Past*, edited by Elizabeth H. Boone, pp. 81–103. Dumbarton Oaks, Washington, DC.

Foster, George M.

1960. *Culture and Conquest: America's Spanish Heritage*. Viking Fund Publications in Anthropology, vol. 27. Wenner-Gren Foundation for Anthropological Research, New York.

Fowler, William R., Jr.

1996. Special Section: Recent Chronological Research in Central Mexico. *An-*

cient Mesoamerica 7:215–331.

Fox, Richard G.
1977. *Urban Anthropology: Cities in their Cultural Settings*. Prentice-Hall, Englewood Cliffs.

Friedlander, Judith
1975. *Being Indian in Hueyapan: A Study of Forced Identity in Contemporary Mexico*. St. Martin's Press, New York.

Furst, Peter T.
1978. Spirulina. *Human Nature* 1:60–5.

García Castro, René
1999. *Indios, territorio y poder en la provincia matlatzinca: la negociación del espacio político de los pueblos otomianos, siglos XV-XII*. CIESAS, Instituto Nacional de Antropología e Historia, and El Colegio Mexiquense, Mexico City and Toluca.

García Payón, José
1936. *La zona arqueológica de Tecaxic-Calixtlahuaca y los matlatzincas: etnología y arqueología (primera parte)*. Talleres Gráficas de la Nación, Mexico City.
1941. Manera de disponer de los muertos entre los matlatzincas del Valle de Toluca. *Revista Mexicana de Estudios Antropológicos* 5:64–78.
1947. Los monumentos arqueológicos de Malinalco. *Revista Mexicana de Estudios Antropológicas* 8(1):5–63.
1949. Zempoala: compendio de su estudio arqueológico. *Uni-Ver (Universidad de Veracruz)* 1:449–76.
1979. *La zona arqueológica de Tecaxic-Calixtlahuaca y los matlatzincas: etnología y arqueología (textos de la segunda parte)*, edited by Wanda Tommasi de Magrelli and Leonardo Manrique Castañeda, vol. 30. Biblioteca Enciclopédica del Estado de México, Toluca.
1981. *La zona arqueológica de Tecaxic-Calixtlahuaca y los matlatzincas: etnología y arqueología (tablas, planos e ilustraciones de la segunda parte)*, edited by Wanda Tommasi de Magrelli and Leonardo Manrique Castañeda, vol. 31. Biblioteca Enciclopédica del Estado de México, Toluca.

Gaxiola G., Margarita, and John E. Clark (eds.)
1989. *La obsidiana en Mesoamérica*. Instituto Nacional de Antropología e Historia, Mexico City.

Gerhard, Peter
1993. *A Guide to the Historical Geography of New Spain*. revised edn. University of Oklahoma Press, Norman.

Gibson, Charles
1964. *The Aztecs Under Spanish Rule: A History of the Indians of the Valley of Mexico, 1519–1810*. Stanford University Press, Stanford.
1966. *Spain in America*. Harper and Row, New York.

Gillespie, Susan D.
1989. *The Aztec Kings: The Constitution of Rulership in Mexica History*. University of Arizona Press, Tucson.

González González, Carlos Javier, and Bertina Olmedo Vera
1990. *Esculturas mezcala en el templo mayor*. Instituto Nacional de Antropología

e Historia, Mexico City.

González Rul, Francisco

1963. Un tzompantli en Tlatelolco. *Boletín del INAH* 13:3–5.

1996. *Tlatelolco: lugar en el montículo de tierra*. Instituto Nacional de Antropología e Historia, Mexico City.

1998. *Urbanismo y arquitectura en Tlatelolco*. Serie Arqueología, Colección Científica, vol. 346. Instituto Nacional de Antropología e Historia, Mexico City.

Graulich, Michel

1992a. Aztec Festivals of the Rain Gods. *Indiana (Berlin)* 12:21–54.

1992b. Mexico City's "Templo Mayor" Revisited. In *Ancient America: Contributions to New World Archaeology*, edited by Nicholas J. Saunders, pp. 19–32. Oxbow Books, Oxford.

1992c. La piedra del sol. In *Azteca–Mexica*, edited by José Alcina Franch, Miguel León-Portilla and Eduardo Matos Moctezoma, pp. 291–5. Lunwerg, Madrid.

1992d. Quetzalcoatl-Ehecatl, the Bringer of Life. In *Ancient America: Contributions to New World Archaeology*, edited by Nicholas J. Saunders, pp. 33–8. Oxbow Books, Oxford.

1994. *Montezuma, ou l'apogée et la chute de l'empire aztèque*. Fayard, Paris.

1995. La conquête de Mexique: une nouvelle interprétacion. *Bulletin des Séances, Académie Royale des Sciences d'Outre-Mer* 40:365–74.

1996. Review of *Mexico and the Spanish Conquest* by Ross Hassig. *Nahua Newsletter* 22:19–23.

1997a. La matanza de Cholula. *Memorias de la Academia Mexicana de la Historia* 40:5–27.

1997b. *Myths of Ancient Mexico*. Translated by Bernard R. Ortiz de Montellano and Thelma Ortiz de Montellano. University of Oklahoma Press, Norman.

1999. *Fiestas de los pueblos indígenas: ritos aztecas, las fiestas de las veintanas*. Instituto Nacional Indígenista, Mexico City.

2000. Aztec Human Sacrifice as Expiation. *History of Religions* 39:352–71.

Grube, Nikolai

2000. The City-States of the Maya. In *A Comparative Study of Thirty City-State Cultures*, edited by Mogens Herman Hansen, pp. 547–66. The Royal Danish Academy of Sciences and Letters, Copenhagen.

Guillemín, Jorge F.

1965. *Iximché, capital del antiguo reino cakquiquel*. Instituto de Antropología e Historia, Guatemala City.

1977. Urbanism and Hierarchy at Iximché. In *Social Process in Maya Prehistory: Studies in Honour of Sir Eric Thompson*, edited by Norman Hammond, pp. 227–64. Academic Press, New York.

Guilliem Arroyo, Salvador

1999. *Ofrendas a Ehecatl-Quetzalcoatl en México-Tlatelolco: proyecto Tlatelolco, 1987–1996*. Colección Científica, vol. 400. Instituto Nacional de Antropología e Historia, Mexico City.

Gussinyer, Jordi

1969a. Hallazgos en el metro: conjunto de adoratorios superpuestos en Pino Suárez. *Boletín del INAH* 36:33–7.

1969b. Una escultura de Ehecatl-Ozomatli. *Boletín del INAH* 37:29–32.

1974. La cimentación de edificios prehispánicas en la Ciudad de México (algunas anotaciones). *Boletín del INAH, Epoca II* 8:31–40.

Hansen, Mogens Herman (ed.)

2000. *A Comparative Study of Thirty City-State Cultures.* The Royal Danish Academy of Sciences and Letters, Copenhagen.

Hare, Timothy S.

2001. Political Economy, Spatial Analysis, and Postclassic States in the Yautepec Valley, Mexico. PhD dissertation, Department of Anthropology, University at Albany, State University of New York.

Hare, Timothy S., and Michael E. Smith

1996. A New Postclassic Chronology for Yautepec, Morelos. *Ancient Mesoamerica* 7:281–97.

Harner, Michael

1977. The Ecological Basis for Aztec Sacrifice. *American Ethnologist* 4:117–35.

Harvey, Herbert R., and Barbara J. Williams

1980. Aztec Arithmetic: Positional Notation and Area Calculation. *Science* 210:499–505.

Haskett, Robert

1991. *Indigenous Rulers: An Ethnohistory of Town Government in Colonial Cuernavaca.* University of New Mexico Press, Albuquerque.

Hassig, Ross

1985. *Trade, Tribute, and Transportation: The Sixteenth Century Political Economy of the Valley of Mexico.* University of Oklahoma Press, Norman.

1988. *Aztec Warfare: Imperial Expansion and Political Control.* University of Oklahoma Press, Norman.

1994. *Mexico and the Spanish Conquest.* Longman, New York.

2001. *Time, History and Belief in Aztec and Colonial Mexico.* University of Texas Press, Austin.

Healan, Dan M.

1989. *Tula of the Toltecs: Excavations and Survey.* University of Iowa Press, Iowa City.

Henige, David P.

1998. *Numbers from Nowhere: The American Indian Contact Population Debate.* University of Oklahoma Press, Norman.

Hernández, Francisco

1959. *Historia natural de Nueva España.* 2 vols. Universidad Nacional Autónoma de México, Mexico City.

Hernández Rivero, José

1994. La arqueología de la frontera tarasco-mexica: arquitectura bélica. In *Contribuciones a la arqueología y etnohistoria del Occidente de México,* edited by Eduardo Williams, pp. 115–55. El Colegio de Michoacán, Zamora.

1997. *Ideología y práctica militar mexica: el cuauhcalli de Malinalco.* Private Publication, Mexico City.

Hernández Rodríguez, Rosaura

1988. *El Valle de Toluca: época prehispánica y siglo XVI.* Colegio Mexiquense,

Toluca.

Heyden, Doris

1991. Dryness Before the Rains: Toxcatl and Tezcatlipoca. In *To Change Place: Aztec Ceremonial Landscapes*, edited by Davíd Carrasco, pp. 188–202. University Press of Colorado, Niwot.

Hicks, Frederic

1982. Tetzcoco in the Early 16th Century: The State, the City and the Calpolli. *American Ethnologist* 9:230–49.

1984. Rotational Labor and Urban Development in Prehispanic Tetzcoco. In *Explorations in Ethnohistory: Indians of Central Mexico in the Sixteenth Century*, edited by Herbert R. Harvey and Hanns J. Prem, pp. 147–74. University of New Mexico Press, Albuquerque.

1986. Prehispanic Background of Colonial Political and Economic Organization in Central Mexico. In *Ethnohistory*, edited by Ronald Spores, vol. 4, pp. 35–54. Handbook of Middle American Indians, Supplement. University of Texas Press, Austin.

1992. Subject States and Tributary Provinces: The Aztec Empire in the Northern Valley of Mexico. *Ancient Mesoamerica* 3:1–10.

1994. Cloth in the Political Economy of the Aztec State. In *Economies and Polities in the Aztec Realm*, edited by Mary G. Hodge and Michael E. Smith, pp. 89–111. Institute for Mesoamerican Studies, Albany, NY.

1996. Class and State in Aztec Official Ideology. In *Ideology and the Formation of Early States*, edited by Henri J. M. Claessen and Jarich G. Oosten, pp. 256–77. E. J. Brill, Leiden.

1999. The Middle Class in Ancient Central Mexico. *Journal of Anthropological Research* 55:409–27.

Hinz, Eike, Claudine Hartau, and Marie Heimann-Koenen

1983. *Aztekischer Zensus: Zur Indianischen Wirtschaft und Gesellschaft im Marquesado um 1540*. Verlag für Ethnologie, Hanover.

Hirth, Kenneth G.

1998. The Distributional Approach: A New Way to Identify Marketplace Exchange in the Archaeological Record. *Current Anthropology* 39:451–76.

2000. *Archaeological Research at Xochicalco*, vol. 1: *Ancient Urbanism at Xochicalco: The Evolution and Organization of a Pre-Hispanic Society*; vol. 2: *The Xochicalco Mapping Project*. 2 vols. University of Utah Press, Salt Lake City.

Hodge, Mary G.

1984. *Aztec City-States*. Memoirs, vol. 18. Museum of Anthropology, University of Michigan, Ann Arbor.

1994. Polities Composing the Aztec Empire's Core. In *Economies and Polities in the Aztec Realm*, edited by Mary G. Hodge and Michael E. Smith, pp. 43–71. Institute for Mesoamerican Studies, Albany, NY.

1997. When Is a City-State? Archaeological Measures of Aztec City-States and Aztec City-State Systems. In *The Archaeology of City-States: Cross-Cultural Approaches*, edited by Deborah L. Nichols and Thomas H. Charlton, pp. 209–28. Smithsonian Institution Press, Washington, DC.

1998. Archaeological Views of Aztec Culture. *Journal of Archaeological Re-*

search 6:197–238.

Hodge, Mary G., and Leah D. Minc
1990. The Spatial Patterning of Aztec Ceramics: Implications for Prehispanic Exchange Systems in the Valley of Mexico. *Journal of Field Archaeology* 17:415–37.

Hodge, Mary G., Hector Neff, M. James Blackman, and Leah D. Minc
1993. Black-on-Orange Ceramic Production in the Aztec Empire's Heartland. *Latin American Antiquity* 4:130–57.

Hodge, Mary G., and Michael E. Smith (eds.)
1994. *Economies and Polities in the Aztec Realm*. Institute for Mesoamerican Studies, Albany, NY.

Hosler, Dorothy
1994. *The Sounds and Colors of Power: The Sacred Metallurgical Technology of Ancient West Mexico*. MIT Press, Cambridge.

Hosler, Dorothy, Heather Lechtman, and Olaf Holm
1990. *Axe-Monies and Their Relatives*. Dumbarton Oaks Studies in Pre-Columbian Art and Archaeology, vol. 30. Dumbarton Oaks, Washington, DC.

Hudson, Michael, and Baruch A. Levine (eds.)
1999. *Urbanization and Land Ownership in the Ancient Near East*. Peabody Museum Bulletin, vol. 7. Peabody Museum of Archaeology and Ethnology, Harvard University, Cambridge.

Ingham, John M.
1986. *Mary, Michael, and Lucifer: Folk Catholicism in Central Mexico*. University of Texas Press, Austin.

Isaac, Barry L.
1983a. The Aztec "Flowery War": A Geopolitical Explanation. *Journal of Anthropological Research* 39:415–32.
1983b. Aztec Warfare: Goals and Battlefield Comportment. *Ethnology* 22:121–31.

Johnson, Allen W., and Timothy K. Earle
2000. *The Evolution of Human Societies: From Foraging Group to Agrarian State*. 2nd edn. Stanford University Press, Stanford.

Jones, Grant D.
1999. *The Conquest of the Last Maya Kingdom*. Stanford University Press, Stanford.

Jones, Lindsay
1995. *Twin City Tales: A Hermeneutical Reassessment of Tula and Chichen Itza*. University Press of Colorado, Niwot.

Joyce, Rosemary A.
2000a. *Gender and Power in Prehispanic Mesoamerica*. University of Texas Press, Austin.
2000b. Girling the Girl and Boying the Boy: The Production of Adulthood in Ancient Mesoamerica. *World Archaeology* 31:473–83.

Justeson, John S., and Terrence Kaufman
1993. A Decipherment of Epi-Olmec Hieroglyphic Writing. *Science* 259:1703–11.

Karttunen, Frances

1983. *An Analytical Dictionary of Nahuatl.* University of Oklahoma Press, Norman.

Katz, Solomon H., M. L. Hediger, and Linda A. Valleroy
1974. Traditional Maize Processing Techniques in the New World. *Science* 184:765–73.

Kaufman, Terrence
1976. Mesoamerican Indian Languages. In *Encyclopedia Britannica, Macropedia*, vol. 11, pp. 956–63. Encyclopedia Britannica, New York.

Keen, Benjamin
1971. *The Aztec Image in Western Thought.* Rutgers University Press, New Brunswick.

Kelley, David H.
1976. *Deciphering the Maya Script.* University of Texas Press, Austin.

Kellogg, Susan
1986. Kinship and Social Organization in Early colonial Tenochtitlan. In *Ethnohistory*, edited by Ronald Spores, pp. 103–21. Handbook of Middle American Indians, Supplement, vol. 4. University of Texas Press, Austin.
1995. *Law and the Transformation of Aztec Culture, 1500–1700.* University of Oklahoma Press, Norman.
1997. From Parallel and Equivalent to Separate but Unequal: Tenochca Mexica Women, 1500–1700. In *Indian Women of Early Mexico*, edited by Susan Schroeder, Stephanie Wood, and Robert Haskett, pp. 123–44. University of Oklahoma Press, Norman.

Kirchhoff, Paul
1943. Mesoamérica: sus límites geográficas, composición étnica, y caracteres culturales. *Acta Americana* 1:92–107.

Klaus, Susanne
1999. *Anales de Tlatelolco: los manuscritos 22 y 22bis de la Bibliotèque de France.* Fuentes Mesoamericanas, vol. 2. Verlag Anton Saurwein, Markt Schwaben.

Klein, Cecelia F.
1977. The Identity of the Central Deity on the Aztec Calendar Stone. In *Pre-Columbian Art History: Selected Readings*, edited by Alana Cordy-Collins and Jean Stern, pp. 167–89. Peek Publications, Palo Alto.
1987. The Ideology of Autosacrifice at the Templo Mayor. In *The Aztec Tempo Mayor*, edited by Elizabeth H. Boone, pp. 293–370. Dumbarton Oaks, Washington, DC.
1994. Fighting with Femininity: Gender and War in Aztec Mexico. *Estudios de Cultura Náhuatl* 24:219–50.
2000. The Devil and the Skirt: An Iconographic Inquiry into the Pre-Hispanic Nature of the Tzitzimime. *Ancient Mesoamerica* 11:1–26.

Klor de Alva, Jorge, H. B. Nicholson, and Eloise Quiñones Keber (eds.)
1988. *The Work of Bernardino de Sahagún: Pioneer Ethnographer of Sixteenth-Century Aztec Mexico.* Institute for Mesoamerican Studies, Albany, NY.

Knab, Timothy J.
1997. *A War of Witches: A Journey into the Underworld of the Contemporary Aztecs.* Westview Press, Boulder, CO.

Konieczna Z., Bárbara
1992. *Coatetelco, Morelos: mini-guia*. Instituto Nacional de Antropología e Historia, Mexico City.

Kubler, George
1948. *Mexican Architecture of the Sixteenth Century*. 2 vols. Yale University Press, New Haven.

Kuhrt, Amalie
1998. The Old Assyrian Merchants. In *Trade, Traders and the Ancient City*, edited by Helen M. Parkins and Christopher Smith, pp. 16–30. Routledge, London.

Lagunas Rodríguez, Zaid, and Carlos Serrano Sánchez
1972. Decapitación y desmembramiento corporal en Teopanzolco, Morelos. In *Religión en Mesoamérica. XII Mesa Redonda*, edited by Jaime Litvak King and Noemí Castillo Tejero, pp. 429–34. Sociedad Mexicana de Antropología, Mexico City.

Lees, Susan H.
1994. Irrigation and Society. *Journal of Archaeological Research* 2:361–78.

Leibsohn, Dana
1994. Primers for Memory: Cartographic Histories and Nahua Identity. In *Writing Without Words: Alternative Literacies in Mesoamerica and the Andes*, edited by Elizabeth Hill Boone and Walter D. Mignolo, pp. 161–87. Duke University Press, Durham.

Lentz, David L. (ed.)
2000. *Imperfect Balance: Landscape Transformations in the Precolumbian Americas*. Columbia University Press, New York.

León-Portilla, Miguel
1962. *The Broken Spears: The Aztec Account of the Conquest of Mexico*. Beacon Press, Boston.
1963. *Aztec Thought and Culture: A Study of the Ancient Náhuatl Mind*. University of Oklahoma Press, Norman.
1969. *Pre-Columbian Literatures of Mexico*. University of Oklahoma Press, Norman.
1992. *Fifteen Poets of the Aztec World*. University of Oklahoma Press, Norman.
1993. Those Made Worthy by Divine Sacrifice: The Faith of Ancient Mexico. In *South and Meso-American Native Spirituality*, edited by Gary H. Gossen, pp. 41–64. Crossroad, New York.

Lewis, Oscar
1951. *Life in a Mexican Village: Tepoztlan Restudied*. University of Illinois Press, Urbana.

Limón Boyce, Morrison
1997. Tenayuca: primer sede de los chichimecas en la cuenca de México. *Expresión Antropológica (Instituto Mexiquense de Cultura)* 3:7–15.

Lister, Florence C., and Robert H. Lister
1982. *Sixteenth Century Majolica Pottery in the Valley of Mexico*. Anthropological Papers, vol. 39. Anthropological Papers of the University of Arizona, Tucson.

Lockhart, James
  1992. *The Nahuas After the Conquest: A Social and Cultural History of the Indians of Central Mexico, Sixteenth Through Eighteenth Centuries*. Stanford University Press, Stanford.
  1993. *We People Here: Nahuatl Accounts of the Conquest of Mexico*. University of California Press, Berkeley.
Lockhart, James, Frances F. Berdan, and Arthur J. O. Ancerson (eds.)
  1986. *The Tlaxcalan Actas: A Compendium of the Records of the Cabildo of Tlaxcala (1545–1627)*. University of Utah Press, Salt Lake City.
López Austin, Alfredo
  1973. *Hombre-díos: religión y política en el mundo náhuatl*. Instituto de Investigaciones Antropológicas, Universidad Nacional Autónoma de México, Mexico City.
  1988. *The Human Body and Ideology: Concepts of the Ancient Nahuas*. Translated by Bernard R. Ortiz de Montellano and Themla Ortiz de Montellano. 2 vols. University of Utah Press, Salt Lake City.
  1997. *Tamoanchan, Tlalocan: Places of Mist*. Translated by Bernard R. Ortiz de Montellano and Thelma Ortiz de Montellano. University Press of Colorado, Niwot.
  2001. Aztec. In *The Oxford Encyclopedia of Mesoamerican Cultures: The Civilizations of Mexico and Central America*, edited by Davíd Carrasco, vol. 1, pp. 68–72. Oxford University Press, New York.
López Luján, Leonardo
  1994. *The Offerings of the Templo Mayor of Tenochtitlan*. Translated by Bernard R. Ortiz de Montellano and Thelma Ortiz de Montellano. University Press of Colorado, Niwot.
  1998. Anthropologie religieuse du templo mayor, Mexico: la maison del aigles. 2 vols. PhD dissertation, Department of Archaeology, Université de Paris X-Nanterre.
López Luján, Leonardo, Hector Neff, and Saburo Sugiyama
  2000. The 9-Xi Vase: A Classic Thin Orange Vessel Found at Tenochtitlan. In *Mesoamerica's Classic Heritage: From Teotihuacan to the Aztecs*, edited by Davíd Carrasco, Lindsay Jones, and Scott Sessions, pp. 219–49. University Press of Colorado, Niwot.
Lovell, W. George
  1985. *Conquest and Survival in Colonial Guatemala: A Historical Geography of the Cuchumatán Highlands, 1500–1821*. McGill-Queen's University Press, Kingston and Montreal.
Mann, Michael
  1986. *The Sources of Social Power*, vol. 1: *A History of Power from the Beginning to A.D. 1760*. Cambridge University Press, New York.
Marcus, Joyce
  1983. On the Nature of the Mesoamerican City. In *Prehistoric Settlement Patterns: Essays in Honor of Gordon R. Willey*, edited by Evon Z. Vogt and Richard M. Leventhal, pp. 195–242. University of New Mexico Press, Albuquerque.
  1992. *Mesoamerican Writing Systems: Propaganda, Myth, and History in Four Ancient Civilizations*. Princeton University Press, Princeton.

Marcus, Joyce, and Kent V. Flannery
  1996. *Zapotec Civilization: How Urban Society Evolved in Mexico's Oaxaca Valley.* Thames and Hudson, New York.
Marquina, Ignacio
  1951. *Arquitectura prehispánica.* Instituto Nacional de Antropología e Historia, Mexico City.
  1960. *El templo mayor de México.* Instituto Nacional de Antropología e Historia, Mexico City.
  1964. *Arquitectura prehispánica.* 2nd edn. Instituto Nacional de Antropología e Historia, Mexico City.
Martí, Samuel
  1969. *Instrumentos musicales precortesianos.* Instituto Nacional de Antropología e Historia, Mexico City.
Martí, Samuel, and Gertrude Prokosch Kurath
  1964. *Dances of Anahuac: The Choreography and Music of Precortesian Dances.* Aldine, Chicago.
Martin, Simon, and Nikolai Grube
  2000. *Chronicle of the Maya Kings and Queens: Deciphering the Dynasties of the Ancient Maya.* Thames and Hudson, New York.
Martínez Vargas, Enrique
  1993. Trascendental hallazgo en Zultepec. *Arqueología Mexicana* 1(4):62–4.
Masson, Marilyn A.
  2000. *In the Realm of Nachan Kan: Postclassic Maya Archaeology at Laguna de On, Belize.* University Press of Colorado, Niwot.
Mastache, Alba Guadalupe, Robert H. Cobean and Dan M. Healan
  2002, *Ancien Tollan: Tula and the Toltec Heartland.* University Press of Colorado, Boulder.
Matos Moctezuma, Eduardo (ed.)
  1979. *Trabajos arqueológicos en el centro de la ciudad de México.* Instituto Nacional de Antropología e Historia, Mexico City.
  1982. *El templo mayor: excavaciones y estudios.* Instituto Nacional de Antropología e Historia, Mexico City.
  1988. *The Great Temple of the Aztecs.* Thames and Hudson, New York.
  1989. *The Aztecs.* Rizzoli, New York.
  1999. *Excavaciones en la catedral y el sagrario metropolitanos: programa de arqueología urbana.* Instituto Nacional de Antropología e Historia, Mexico City.
McCaa, Robert
  1994. Child Marriage and Complex Families Among the Nahuas of Ancient Mexico. *Latin American Population History Bulletin* 26:2–11.
  1995. Spanish and Nahuatl Views on Smallpox and Demographic Catastrophe in Mexico. *Journal of Interdisciplinary History* 25:397–431.
  1996. Matrimonia infantil, cemithualtin (familias complejas) y el antiguo pueblo nahua. *Historia Mexicana* 46:3–70.
McCafferty, Sharisse D., and Geoffrey G. McCafferty
  1991. Spinning and Weaving as Female Gender Identity in Post-Classic Central Mexico. In *Textile Traditions of Mesoamerica and the Andes: An Anthology,*

edited by M. Schevill, Janet C. Berlo, and E. Dwyer, pp. 19–46. Garland, New York.

2000. Textile Production in Postclassic Cholula, Mexico. *Ancient Mesoamerica* 11:39–54.

McClung de Tapia, Emily, and Evelyn C. Rattray (eds.)

1987. *Teotihuacán: nuevos datos, nuevas síntesis, nuevos problemas.* Instituto de Investigaciones Antropológicas, Universidad Nacional Autónoma de México, Mexico City.

McNeill, William H.

1976. *Plagues and Peoples.* Academic Press, New York.

McVicker, Donald

1989. Parallels and Rivalries: Encounters Between Boas and Starr. *Curator, Quarterly Publication of the American Museum of Natural History* 32:212–28.

Medillín Zeñil, Alfonso

1952. *Exploraciones de Quauhtochco.* Gobierno del Estado de Veracruz, Jalapa.

Mendoza Cerón, Isaías, and Una Canger

1993. *In Tequitl de Morrales: Working with Maguey.* Bianco Luno, Copenhagen.

Metcalfe, S. E., F. A. Street-Perrott, R. B. Brown, P. E. Hales, R. A. Perrott, and F. M. Steininger

1989. Late Holocene Human Impact on Lake Basins in Central Mexico. *Geoarchaeology* 4:119–41.

Milbrath, Susan

2000. Xochiquetzal and the Lunar Cult of Central Mexico. In *In Chalchihuitl in Quetzalli, Precious Greenstone Precious Quetzal Feather: Mesoamerican Studies in Honor of Doris Heyden*, edited by Eloise Quiñones Keber, pp. 31–54. Labyrinthos, Lancaster, CA.

Millon, René

1973. *Urbanization at Teotihuacan, Mexico*, vol. 1: *The Teotihuacan Map.* University of Texas Press, Austin.

Minc, Leah D., Mary G. Hodge, and M. James Blackman

1994. Stylistic and Spatial Variability in Early Aztec Ceramics: Insights into Pre-imperial Exchange Systems. In *Economies and Polities in the Aztec Realm*, edited by Mary G. Hodge and Michael E. Smith, pp. 133–73. Institute for Mesoamerican Studies, Albany, NY.

Molina, Alonso de

1970. *Vocabulario en lengua castellana y mexicana, y mexicana y castellana.* Porrúa, Mexico City.

1972. *Confesionario mayor en la lengua mexicana y castellana (1569).* Edited by Roberto Moreno. Instituto de Investigaciones Bibliográficas, Mexico City.

Morrison, Kathleen D.

1996. Typological Schemes and Agricultural Change: Beyond Boserup in Precolonial South India. *Current Anthropology* 37:583–608.

Motolinía, Toribio de Benavente

1950. *History of the Indians of New Spain.* Translated by Elizabeth A. Foster. The Cortes Society, Berkeley.

1971. *Memoriales, o libro de las cosas de la Nueva España y de los naturales de ella*. Edited by Edmundo O'Gorman. Universidad Nacional Autónoma de México, Mexico City.

Moya Rubio, Victor José

1982. *La vivienda indígena de México y del mundo*. Universidad Nacional Autónoma de México, Mexico City.

Nagao, Debra

1985. *Mexica Buried Offerings: A Historical and Contextural Analysis*. BAR, International Series, vol. 235. British Archaeological Reports, Oxford.

Nash, June

1978. The Aztecs and the Ideology of Male Dominance. *Signs* 4:349–62.

Neff, Hector, Michael D. Glascock, Thomas H. Charlton, Cynthia L. Otis Charlton, and Deborah L. Nichols

2000. Provenience Investigation of Ceramics and Obsidian from Otumba. *Ancient Mesoamerica* 11:307–22.

Netting, Robert McC.

1993. *Smallholders, Householders: Farm Families and the Ecology of Intensive, Sustainable Agriculture*. Stanford University Press, Stanford.

Nichols, Deborah L.

1994. The Organization of Provincial Craft Production and the Aztec City-State of Otumba. In *Economies and Polities in the Aztec Realm*, edited by Mary G. Hodge and Michael E. Smith, pp. 175–93. Institute for Mesoamerican Studies, Albany, NY.

1996. An Overview of Regional Settlement Pattern Survey in Mesoamerica: 1960–1995. In *Arqueología Mesoamericana: Homenaje a William T. Sanders*, edited by Alba Guadalupe Mastache, Jeffrey R. Parsons, Robert S. Santley, and Mari Carmen Serra Puche, vol. 1, pp. 59–95. Instituto Nacional de Antropología e Historia, Mexico City.

Nichols, Deborah L., and Charles D. Frederick

1993. Irrigation Canals and Chinampas: Recent Research in the Northern Basin of Mexico. In *Research in Economic Anthropology, supplement*, vol. 7, pp. 123–50. JAI Press, Greenwich, CT.

Nichols, Deborah L., Mary Jane McLaughlin, and Maura Benton

2000. Production Intensification and Regional Specialization: Maguey Fibers and Textiles in the Aztec City-State of Otumba. *Ancient Mesoamerica* 11:267–92.

Nicholson, H. B.

1971. Religion in Pre-Hispanic Central Mexico. In *Archaeology of Northern Mesoamerica*, part 1, edited by Gordon F. Ekholm and Ignacio Bernal, pp. 395–446. Handbook of Middle American Indians, vol. 10. University of Texas Press, Austin.

1991. The Octli Cult in Late Pre-Hispanic Central Mexico. In *To Change Place: Aztec Ceremonial Landscapes*, edited by David Carrasco, pp. 158–87. University Press of Colorado, Niwot.

1993. The Problem of the Identification of the Central Image of the "Aztec Calendar Stone". In *Current Topics in Aztec Studies: Essays in Honor of H. B. Nicholson*, edited by Alana Cordy-Collins and Douglas Sharon, vol. 30, pp. 3–

15. San Diego Museum, San Diego.

2001. *Topiltzin Quetzalcoatl*. University Press of Colorado, Boulder.

Nicholson, H. B., and Eloise Quiñones Keber

1983. *Art of Aztec Mexico: Treasures of Tenochtitlan*. National Gallery of Art, Washington, DC.

1994. *Mixteca-Puebla: Discoveries and Research in Mesoamerican Art and Archaeology*. Labyrinthos, Culver City, CA.

Noguez, Xavier (ed.)

1978. *Tira de Tepechpan: códice procedente del Valle de México*. Biblioteca Enciclopédica del Estado de México. 2 vols. Estado de México, Mexico City.

O'Hara, Sarah L., and Sarah E. Metcalfe

1997. The Climate of Mexico Since the Aztec Period. *Quaternary International* 43/44:25–31.

O'Hara, Sarah L., Sarah E. Metcalfe, and F. Alayne Street-Perrott

1994. On the Arid Margin: The Relationship Between Climate, Humans and the Environment: A Review of Evidence from the Highlands of Central Mexico. *Chemosphere* 29:965–81.

Olivier, Guilhem

1997a. Acercamiento al estudio de los dioses de los mercaderes en el atliplano central del México prehispánico. *Trace* 31:35–43.

1997b. *Moqueries et métamorphoses d'un dieu aztèque: Tezcatlipoca, le "seigneur au miroir fumant"*. Mémoires, vol. 33. Institut d'Ethnologie, Musée de l'Homme, Paris.

1999. Espace, guerre y prosperérité dans l'ancient Mexique central: les dieux des marchands à l'époque postclassique. *Journal de la Société des Américanistes* 85:67–91.

Olmos Frese, Laura del

1999. *Análisis de la ofrenda 98 del templo mayor de Tenochtitlan*. Colección Científica, vol. 384. Instituto Nacional de Antropología e Historia, Mexico City.

Olson, Jan Marie

2001. Unequal Consumption: A Study of Domestic Wealth Differentials in Three Late Postclassic Mexican Communities. PhD dissertation, Department of Anthropology, University at Albany, State University of New York.

Ortiz de Montellano, Bernard R.

1978. Aztec Cannibalism: An Ecological Necessity? *Science* 200:611–17.

1990. *Aztec Medicine, Health, and Nutrition*. Rutgers University Press, New Brunswick.

Palerm, Angel

1972. *Agricultura y socieded en Mesoamérica*. Secretaria de Educación Pública, Mexico City.

Parsons, Jeffrey R.

1991. Political Implications of Prehispanic Chinampa Agriculture in the Valley of Mexico. In *Land and Politics in the Valley of Mexico: A Two-Thousand-Year Perspective*, edited by Herbert R. Harvey, pp. 17–42. University of New Mexico Press, Albuquerque.

1994. Late Postclassic Salt Production and Consumption in the Valley of Mexico:

Some Insights from Nexquipayac. In *Economies and Polities in the Aztec Realm*, edited by Mary G. Hodge and Michael E. Smith, pp. 257–90. Institute for Mesoamerican Studies, Albany, NY.
1996. Tequesquite and Ahuauhtle: Rethinking the Prehispanic Productivity of Lake Texcoco-Xaltocan-Zumpango. In *Arqueología Mesoamericana: Homenaje a William T. Sanders*, edited by Alba Guadalupe Mastache, Jeffrey R. Parsons, Robert S. Santley, and Mari Carmen Serra Puche, vol. 1, pp. 439–59. Instituto Nacional de Antropología e Historia, Mexico City.
Parsons, Jeffrey R., Elizabeth M. Brumfiel, Mary H. Parsons, Virginia H. Popper, and Mary Taft
1982a. *Late Prehispanic Chinampa Agriculture on Lake Chalco-Xochimilco: Preliminary Report*. Report submitted to the Instituto Nacional de Antropolgía e Historia, Mexico City.
Parsons, Jeffrey R., Elizabeth M. Brumfiel, Mary H. Parsons, and David J. Wilson
1982b. *Prehispanic Settlement Patterns in the Southern Valley of Mexico: The Chalco-Xochimilco Region*. Memoirs, vol. 14. Museum of Anthropology, University of Michigan, Ann Arbor.
Parsons, Jeffrey R., and Mary H. Parsons
1990. *Maguey Utilization in Highland Central Mexico: An Archaeological Ethnography*. Anthropological Papers, vol. 82. Museum of Anthropology, University of Michigan, Ann Arbor.
Pastrana, Alejandro
1998. *La explotación azteca de la obsidiana en la Sierra de las Navajas*. Colección Científica, vol. 383. Instituto Nacional de Antropología e Historia, Mexico City.
Pasztory, Esther
1983. *Aztec Art*. Harry N. Abrams, New York.
1997. *Teotihuacan: An Experiment in Living*. University of Oklahoma Press, Norman.
Payne, Stanley, and Michael P. Closs
1986. A Survey of Aztec Numbers and their Uses. In *Native American Mathematics*, edited by Michael P. Closs, pp. 213–35. University of Texas Press, Austin.
Pennell, C. Richard (ed.)
2001. *Bandits at Sea: A Pirate Reader*. New York University Press, New York.
Perry, Richard
1992. *Mexico's Fortress Monasteries*. Espadaña Press, Santa Barbara.
Pijoan, Carmen María, and Josefina Mansilla Lory
1997. Evidence for Human Sacrifice, Bone Modification and Cannibalism in Ancient Mexico. In *Troubled Times: Violence and Warfare in the Past*, edited by Debra L. Martin and David W. Frayer, pp. 217–40. Gordon and Breach, Amsterdam.
Pijoan, Carmen María, Alejandro Pastrana, and Consuelo Maquivar
1989. El tzompantli de Tlatelolco: una evidencia de sacrificio humano. In *Estudios de antropología biológica*, edited by Carlos Serrano and M. Salas, pp. 561–83. Universidad Nacional Autónoma de México, Mexico City.
Plunket, Patricia, and Gabriela Uruñuela

1994. The Impact of the Xochiyayotl in Southwestern Puebla. In *Economies and Polities in the Aztec Realm*, edited by Mary G. Hodge and Michael E. Smith, pp. 434–46. Institute for Mesoamerican Studies, Albany, NY.

Pohl, John M. D.

1998. Themes of Drunkenness, Violence, and Factionalism in Tlaxcalan Altar Paintings. *Res: Anthropology and Aesthetics* 33:184–207.

Polanyi, Karl, Conrad M. Arensburg, and Harry W. Pearson (eds.)

1957. *Trade and Market in the Early Empires*. Henry Regnery, Chicago.

Pollard, Helen Perlstein

1977. An Analysis of Urban Zoning and Planning in Prehispanic Tzintzuntzan. *Proceedings of the American Philosophical Society* 121:46–69.

1993. *Tariacuri's Legacy: The Prehispanic Tarascan State*. University of Oklahoma Press, Norman.

Pollock, Harry E. D.

1936. *Round Structures of Aboriginal Middle America*. Publication, vol. 471. Carnegie Institution of Washington, Washington, DC.

Prem, Hanns J.

1991. Disease Outbreaks in Central Mexico During the Sixteenth Century. In *"Secret Judgments of God": Old World Disease in Colonial Spanish America*, edited by Noble David Cook and W. George Lovell, pp. 20–48. University of Oklahoma Press, Norman.

1992. Aztec Writing. In *Epigraphy*, edited by Victoria R. Bricker, pp. 53–69. Handbook of Middle American Indians, Supplement, vol. 5. University of Texas Press, Austin.

Prescott, William H.

2000. *History of the Conquest of Mexico and History of the Conquest of Peru*. Cooper Square Press, New York.

Price, Barbara J.

1978. Demystification, Enriddlement, and Aztec Cannibalism: A Materialist Rejoinder to Harner. *American Ethnologist* 5:98–115.

Quezada Ramírez, María Noemí

1972. *Las matlatzincas: epoca prehispánica y epoca colonial hasta 1650*. Serie Investigaciones, vol. 22. Instituto Nacional de Antropología e Historia, Mexico City.

Quiñones Keber, Eloise

1995. *Codex Telleriano-Remensis: Ritual, Divination, and History in a Pictorial Aztec Manuscript*. University of Texas Press, Austin.

1996. Humboldt and Aztec Art. *Colonial Latin American Review* 5:277–97.

Ragot, Nathalie

2000. *Les au-delàs aztèques*. Paris Monographs in American Archaeology, 7. BAR, International Series, vol. 881. Edited by Eric Taladoire. British Archaeological Reports, Oxford.

Redfield, Margaret Park

1929. Notes on the Cookery of Tepoztlan, Morelos. *Journal of American Folk-Lore* 42:167–96.

Redman, Charles L.

1999. *Human Impact on Ancient Environments*. University of Arizona Press,

Tucson.

Renfrew, Colin, and Paul Bahn

2000. *Archaeology: Theories, Methods and Practice*. 3rd edn. Thames and Hudson, New York.

Rice, Don S., and Prudence M. Rice

1984. Lessons from the Maya. *Latin American Research Review* 19(3):203–15.

Robertson, Donald

1959. *Mexican Manuscript Painting of the Early Colonial Period: The Metropolitan Schools*. Yale University Press, New Haven.

1970. The Tulum Murals: The International Style of the Late Post-Classic. In *Verhandlunger del XXXVIII Internationalen Amerikanisten-Kongres, Stuttgart-München, 1968*, vol. 2, pp. 77–88. Kommissionsverlag Klaus Renner.

Rojas, José Luis de

1986. *México Tenochtitlan: economía e sociedad en el siglo XVI*. Fondo de Cultura Económica, Mexico City.

1998. *La moneda indígena y sus usos en la Nueva España en el siglo XVI*. Centro de Investigaciones y Estudios Superiores en Antropología Social, Mexico City.

2001. El abastecimiento de Tenochtitlan: un modelo probablemente poco modélico. In *Reconstruyendo la ciudad maya: el urbanismo en las sociedades antiguas*, edited by Andrés Ciudad Ruiz, María Josefa Iglesias Ponce de León, and María del Carmen Martínez Martínez, pp. 491–502. Sociedad Española de Estudios Mayas, Madrid.

Román Berrelleza, Juan Alberto, and Leonardo López Luján

1999. El funeral de un dignatorio mexica. *Arqueología Mexicana* 7(40):36–9.

Roys, Lawrence

1934. The Engineering Knowledge of the Maya. In *Publication 436*, vol. 6, pp. 27–105. Carnegie Institution of Washington, Washington, DC.

Ruiz de Alarcón, Hernando

1982. *Aztec Sorcerers in Seventeenth Century Mexico: The Treatise on Superstitions by Hernando Ruiz de Alarcón*. Translated by Michael D. Coe and Gordon R. Whittaker. Institute for Mesoamerican Studies, Albany, NY.

Sahagún, Bernardino de

1905–7. *Historia de las cosas de la Nueva España, edición parcial en facsimile de los códices matritenses*. 4 vols. Hauser y Menet, Madrid.

1950–82. *Florentine Codex: General History of the Things of New Spain*. 12 books. Translated and edited by Arthur J. O. Anderson and Charles E. Dibble. School of American Research and the University of Utah Press, Santa Fe and Salt Lake City.

1993. *Primeros Memoriales*. (Facsimile edn.). Edited by Ferdinand Anders. University of Oklahoma Press, Norman.

1997. *Primeros Memoriales. Paleography of Nahuatl Text and English Translation*. Translated by Thelma D. Sullivan. University of Oklahoma Press, Norman.

Sanders, William T.

1956. The Central Mexican Symbiotic Region: A Study in Prehistoric Settlement Patterns. In *Prehistoric Settlement Patterns in the New World*, edited by

Gordon R. Willey, pp. 115–27. Viking Fund Publications in Anthropology, vol. 23. Wenner-Gren Foundation for Anthropological Research, New York.

1970. The Population of the Teotihuacan Valley, the Basin of Mexico, and the Central Mexican Symbiotic Region in the 16th Century. In *The Teotihuacan Valley Project, Final Report*, edited by William T. Sanders, Anton Kovar, Thomas H. Charlton, and Richard A. Diehl, pp. 385–452. Occasional Papers in Anthropology, vol. 3. Department of Anthropology, Pennsylvania State University, University Park.

1992. Ranking and Stratification in Prehispanic Mesoamerica. In *Mesoamerican Elites: An Archaeological Assessment*, edited by Diane A. Chase and Arlen F. Chase, pp. 278–91. University of Oklahoma Press, Norman.

1999. Three Valleys: Twenty-Five Years of Settlement Archaeology in Mesoamerica. In *Settlement Pattern Studies in the Americas: Fifty Years Since Virú*, edited by Brian R. Billman and Gary M. Feinman, pp. 12–21. Smithsonian Institution Press, Washington, DC.

Sanders, William T., Jeffrey R. Parsons, and Robert S. Santley
1979. *The Basin of Mexico: Ecological Processes in the Evolution of a Civilization*. Academic Press, New York.

Sanders, William T., and David Webster
1988. The Mesoamerican Urban Tradition. *American Anthropologist* 90:521–46.

Sandstrom, Alan R.
1991. *Corn is Our Blood: Culture and Ethnic Identity in a Contemporary Aztec Indian Village*. University of Oklahoma Press, Norman.

2001. Shamanism: Contemporary Cultures. In *The Oxford Encyclopedia of Mesoamerican Cultures: The Civilizations of Mexico and Central America*, edited by Davíd Carrasco, vol. 3, pp. 142–4. Oxford University Press, New York.

Sandstrom, Alan R., and Paula E. Sandstrom
1986. *Traditional Papermaking and Paper Cult Figures of Mexico*. University of Oklahoma Press, Norman.

Saville, Marshall H.
1920. *The Goldsmith's Art in Ancient Mexico*. Indian Notes and Monographs, vol. 7. Museum of the American Indian, Heye Foundation, New York.

1922. *Turquoise Mosaic Art in Ancient Mexico*. Indian Notes and Monographs, vol. 8. Museum of the American Indian, Heye Foundation, New York.

Scarborough, Vernon L., and David R. Wilcox (eds.)
1991. *The Mesoamerican Ballgame*. University of Arizona Press, Tucson.

Schele, Linda, and Peter Mathews
1998. *The Code of Kings: The Language of Seven Sacred Maya Temples and Tombs*. Simon and Schuster, New York.

Schroeder, Susan
1991. *Chimalpahin and the Kingdoms of Chalco*. University of Arizona Press, Tucson.

Séjourné, Laurette
1970. *Arqueología del Valle de México, I: Culhuacan*. Instituto Nacional de Antropología e Historia, Mexico City.

1983. *Arqueología e historia de Valle de México: de Xochmilco a Amecameca*.

Siglo Veintiumo, Mexico City.

Seler, Eduard

1963. *Comentarios al Códice Borgia*. 3 vols. Fondo de Cultura Económica, Mexico City.

1990–98a. Ancient Mexican Bone Rattles. In *Collected Works in Mesoamerican Linguistics and Archaeology*, vol. 3, pp. 62–73. Labyrinthos, Culver City.

1990–98b. Magic in Ancient Mexico. In *Collected Works in Mesoamerican Linguistics and Archaeology*, vol. 2, pp. 43–7. Labyrinthos, Culver City.

Serrato-Combe, Antonio

2001. *The Aztec Templo Mayor: A Visualization*. University of Utah Press, Salt Lake City.

Silver, Morris

1983. Karl Polanyi and Markets in the Ancient Near East: The Challenge of the Evidence. *Journal of Economic History* 43:795–829.

Silverstein, Jay

2001. Aztec Imperialism at Oztuma, Guerrero: Aztec–Chontal Relations During the Late Postclassic and Early Colonial Periods. *Ancient Mesoamerica* 12:1–30.

Smith, Carol A.

1974. Economics of Marketing Systems: Models from Economic Geography. *Annual Review of Anthropology* 3:167–201.

Smith, Michael E.

1984. The Aztlan Migrations of the Nahuatl Chronicles: Myth or History? *Ethnohistory* 31:153–86.

1986. The Role of Social Stratification in the Aztec Empire: A View From the Provinces. *American Anthropologist* 88:70–91.

1990. Long-Distance Trade Under the Aztec Empire: The Archaeological Evidence. *Ancient Mesoamerica* 1:153–69.

1992a. *Archaeological Research at Aztec-Period Rural Sites in Morelos, Mexico*, vol. 1: *Excavations and Architecture / Investigaciones Arqueológicas en Sitios Rurales de la Epoca Azteca en Morelos*, tomo 1: *Excavaciones y Arquitectura*. University of Pittsburgh Memoirs in Latin American Archaeology, vol. 4. University of Pittsburgh, Pittsburgh.

1992b. Rhythms of Change in Postclassic Central Mexico: Archaeology, Ethnohistory, and the Braudellian Model. In *Annales, Archaeology, and Ethnohistory*, edited by A. Bernard Knapp, pp. 51–74. Cambridge University Press, New York.

1993. Houses and the Settlement Hierarchy in Late Postclassic Morelos: A Comparison of Archaeology and Ethnohistory. In *Prehispanic Domestic Units in Western Mesoamerica: Studies of the Household, Compound, and Residence*, edited by Robert S. Santley and Kenneth G. Hirth, pp. 191–206. CRC Press, Boca Raton.

1994a. Economies and Polities in Aztec-period Morelos: Ethnohistoric Introduction. In *Economies and Polities in the Aztec Realm*, edited by Mary G. Hodge and Michael E. Smith, pp. 313–48. Institute for Mesoamerican Studies, Albany, NY.

1994b. Social Complexity in the Aztec Countryside. In *Archaeological Views from the Countryside: Village Communities in Early Complex Societies*, edited by Glenn Schwartz and Steven Falconer, pp. 143–59. Smithsonian Institution Press, Washington, DC.

1997a. City Planning: Aztec City Planning. In *Encyclopaedia of the History of Non-Western Science, Technology, and Medicine*, edited by Helaine Selin, pp. 200–2. Kluwer Academic Publishers, Dordrecht.

1997b. Life in the Provinces of the Aztec Empire. *Scientific American* 277(3):56–63.

1997c. Working Together: Archaeology in the Middle of Political Conflict in Yautepec, Mexico. *Society for American Archaeology Bulletin* 15(4):12–14.

2000. Aztec City-States. In *A Comparative Study of Thirty City-State Cultures*, edited by Mogens Herman Hansen, pp. 581–95. The Royal Danish Academy of Sciences and Letters, Copenhagen.

2001. The Aztec Empire and the Mesoamerican World System. In *Empires: Perspectives from Archaeology and History*, edited by Susan E. Alcock, Terence N. D'Altroy, Kathleen D. Morrison, and Carla M. Sinopoli, pp. 128–54. Cambridge University Press, New York.

2002. *Tlahuica Ceramics: The Aztec-Period Ceramics of Morelos, Mexico.* IMS Monographs, vol. 13. Institute for Mesoamerican Studies, Albany, NY.

n.d.-a. La cerámica postclásica de Morelos. In *La producción alfarera en el México antiguo*, edited by B. Leonor Merino Carrión and Angel García Cook. Colección Científica. Instituto Nacional de Antropoloía e Historia, Mexico City.

n.d.-b. Domestic Ritual at Aztec Provincial Sites in Morelos. In *Domestic Ritual in Ancient Mesoamerica*, edited by Patricia Plunket. UCLA Institute of Archaeology, Los Angeles.

Smith, Michael E., and Frances F. Berdan
1996. Appendix 4: Province Descriptions. In *Aztec Imperial Strategies*, Berdan et al., pp. 265–349. Dumbarton Oaks, Washington, DC.

2000. The Postclassic Mesoamerican World System. *Current Anthropology* 41:283–6.

2002. *The Postclassic Mesoamerican World.* University of Utah Press (in press), Salt Lake City.

Smith, Michael E., and John F. Doershuk
1991. Late Postclassic Chronology in Western Morelos, Mexico. *Latin American Antiquity* 2:291–310.

Smith, Michael E., and Cynthia Heath-Smith
1980. Waves of Influence in Postclassic Mesoamerica? A Critique of the Mixteca–Puebla Concept. *Anthropology* 4:15–50.

1994. Rural Economy in Late Postclassic Morelos: An Archaeological Study. In *Economies and Polities in the Aztec Realm*, edited by Mary G. Hodge and Michael E. Smith, pp. 349–76. Institute for Mesoamerican Studies, Albany, NY.

Smith, Michael E., Cynthia Heath-Smith, Ronald Kohler, Joan Odess, Sharon Spanogle, and Timothy Sullivan
1994. The Size of the Aztec City of Yautepec: Urban Survey in Central Mexico. *Ancient Mesoamerica* 5:1–11.

Smith, Michael E., Cynthia Heath-Smith, and Lisa Montiel

1999. Excavations of Aztec Urban Houses at Yautepec, Mexico. *Latin American Antiquity* 10:133–50.

Smith, Michael E., and Kenneth G. Hirth
1988. The Development of Prehispanic Cotton-Spinning Technology in Western Morelos, Mexico. *Journal of Field Archaeology* 15:349–58.

Smith, Michael E., and Marilyn A. Masson (eds.)
2000. *The Ancient Civilizations of Mesoamerica: A Reader.* Blackwell, Oxford.

Smith, Michael E., and Lisa Montiel
2001. The Archaeological Study of Empires and Imperialism in Prehispanic Central Mexico. *Journal of Anthropological Archaeology* 20:245–84.

Smith, Michael E., and T. Jeffrey Price
1994. Aztec-Period Agricultural Terraces in Morelos, Mexico: Evidence for Household-Level Agricultural Intensification. *Journal of Field Archaeology* 21:169–79.

Smith, Michael E., Osvaldo Sterpone, and Cynthia Heath-Smith
1992. Modern Adobe Houses in Tetlama, Morelos. In *Archaeological Research at Aztec-Period Rural Sites in Morelos, Mexico*, part 1: *Excavations and Architecture*, edited by Michael E. Smith, pp. 405–18. University of Pittsburgh Monographs in Latin American Archaeology, vol. 4. University of Pittsburgh, Pittsburgh.

Smith, Michael E., Jennifer Wharton, and Jan Marie Olson
n.d.. Aztec Feasts, Rituals, and Markets: Political Uses of Ceramic Vessels in a Commercial Economy. In *Pots as Political Tools: The Culinary Equipment of Early Imperial States in Comparative Perspective*, edited by Tamara Bray (book in preparation).

Snell, Daniel C.
1997. Appendix: Theories of Ancient Economies and Societies. In *Life in the Ancient Near East, 3100–332 BCE*, edited by Daniel C. Snell, pp. 145–58. Yale University Press, New Haven.

Soustelle, Jacques
1961. *Daily Life of the Aztecs on the Eve of the Spanish Conquest.* Stanford University Press, Stanford.

Spores, Ronald
1984. *The Mixtecs in Ancient and Colonial Times.* University of Oklahoma Press, Norman.

Stromberg, Gobi
1976. The Amate Bark-Paper Painting of Xalitla. In *Ethnic and Tourist Arts*, edited by Nelson H. H. Graeburn, pp. 149–64. University of California Press, Berkeley.

Suárez, Jorge A.
1983. *The Mesoamerican Indian Languages.* Cambridge University Press, New York.

Sullivan, Thelma D.
1982. Tlazolteotl-Ixcuina: The Great Spinner and Weaver. In *The Art and Iconography of Late Post-Classic Central Mexico*, edited by Elizabeth H. Boone, pp. 7–35. Dumbarton Oaks, Washington, DC.

Taggart, James M.

1983. *Nahuat Myth and Social Structure*. University of Texas Press, Austin.
Tapia, Andrés de
1971. Relación hecha por el Sr. Andrés de Tapia, sobre la conquista de México. In *Colección de documentos para la historia de México*, edited by Joaquín Icazbalceta, vol. 2, pp. 554–94. Porrúa, Mexico City.
Taube, Karl A.
1993. *Aztec and Maya Myths*. University of Texas Press, Austin.
2000a. The Turquoise Hearth: Fire, Self Sacrifice, and the Central Mexican Cult of War. In *Mesoamerica's Classic Heritage: From Teotihuacan to the Aztecs*, edited by Davíd Carrasco, Lindsay Jones, and Scott Sessions, pp. 269–340. University Press of Colorado, Niwot.
2000b. The Writing System of Ancient Teotihuacan. *Ancient America* 1:1–56.
Thirsk, Joan
1961. Industries in the Countryside. In *Essays in the Economic and Social History of Tudor and Stuart England, in Honor of R. H. Tawney*, edited by F. J. Fisher, pp. 70–88. Cambridge University Press, Cambridge.
Thomas, Hugh
1993. *Conquest: Montezuma, Cortés and the Fall of Old Mexico*. Hutchinson, London.
Tira de la Peregrinación
1944. *Tira de la peregrinación mexicana*. Libreria Anticuaria G. M. Echaniz, Mexico City.
Torquemada, Juan de
1975–83. *Monarquia indiana*. Edited by Miguel Leon-Portilla. 7 vols. Universidad Nacional Autónoma de México, Mexico City.
Townsend, Richard F.
1979. *State and Cosmos in the Art of Tenochtitlan*. Studies in Pre-Columbian Art and Archaeology, vol. 20. Dumbarton Oaks, Washington, DC.
1982. Malinalco and the Lords of Tenochtitlan. In *The Art and Iconography of Late Post-Classic Central Mexico*, edited by Elizabeth H. Boone, pp. 111–40. Dumbarton Oaks, Washington, DC.
2000. *The Aztecs*. rev. edn. Thames and Hudson, New York.
Trigger, Bruce G.
1972. Determinants of Urban Growth in Pre-Industrial Societies. In *Man, Settlement, and Urbanism*, edited by Peter J. Ucko, Ruth Trigham, and G. Dimbleby, pp. 579–99. Schenkman, Cambridge.
1993. *Early Civilizations: Ancient Egypt in Context*. The American University in Cairo Press, Cairo.
Turok, Marta
1996. Xiuhquilitl, nocheztil y tixinda: tintes del México antiguo. *Arqueología Mexicana* 3(17):26–33.
Umberger, Emily
1981. Aztec Sculptures, Hieroglyphs, and History. PhD dissertation, Department of Art History, Columbia University.
1987. Antiques, Revivals, and References to the Past in Aztec Art. *RES: Anthropology and Aesthetics* 13:62–105.
1996. Art and Imperial Strategy in Tenochtitlan. In *Aztec Imperial Strategies*,

Berdan et al., pp. 85–106. Dumbarton Oaks, Washington, DC.

Umberger, Emily, and Cecilia Klein

1993. Aztec Art and Imperial Expansion. In *Latin American Horizons*, edited by Don S. Rice, pp. 295–336. Dumbarton Oaks, Washington, DC.

van Zantwijk, Rudolf

1985. *The Aztec Arrangement: The Social History of Pre-Spanish Mexico*. University of Oklahoma Press, Norman.

Vega Sosa, Constanza (ed.)

1979. *El recinto sagrado de Mexico-Tenochtitlan: excavaciones 1968–69 y 1975–76*. Instituto Nacional de Antropología e Historia, Mexico City.

Vié-Wohrer, Anne-Marie

1999. *Xipe Totec, notre seigneur l'écorché: étude glyphique d'un dieu Aztèque*. 2 vols. Centre Français d'Études Mexicaines et Centraméricaines, Mexico City.

von Hagen, Victor W.

1944. *The Aztec and Maya Papermakers*. J. J. Augustin, New York.

Wailes, Bernard (ed.)

1996. *Craft Specialization and Social Evolution: In Memory of V. Gordon Childe*. University Museum Monograph, vol. 93. University Museum, Philadelphia.

Walsh, Jane MacLaren

1997. Crystal Skulls and Other Problems, Or, "Don't Look it in the Eye". In *Exhibiting Dilemmas: Issues of Representation at the Smithsonian*, edited by Amy Henderson and Adrienne L. Kaeppler, pp. 116–39. Smithsonian Institution Press, Washington, DC.

Warren, J. Benedict

1985. *The Conquest of Michoacan: The Spanish Domination of the Tarascan Kingdom in Western Mexico, 1521–1530*. University of Oklahoma Press, Norman.

Weaver, Muriel Porter

1993. *The Aztecs, Maya, and their Predecessors: Archaeology of Mesoamerica*. 3rd edn. Academic Press, San Diego.

West, Robert C., and John P. Augelli

1989. *Middle America: Its Lands and Peoples*. 3rd edn. Prentice-Hall, Englewood Cliffs.

Whitmore, Thomas

1992. *Disease and Death in Early Colonial Mexico: Simulating Amerindian Depopulation*. Westview Press, Boulder, CO.

Whitmore, Thomas M., and Barbara J. Williams

1998. Famine Vulnerability in the Contact-Era Basin of Mexico: A Simulation. *Ancient Mesoamerica* 9:83–98.

Wilk, Richard R., and Priscilla Stone

1998. Introduction to a Very Human Ecology: Celebrating the Work of Robert McC. Netting (introduction to theme issue). *Human Ecology* 26:175–88.

Wilken, Gene C.

1987. *Good Farmers: Traditional Agricultural Resource Management in Mexico and Central America*. University of California Press, Berkeley.

Williams, Barbara J.

1989. Contact Period Rural Overpopulation in the Basin of Mexico: Carrying-Capacity Models Tested with Documentary Data. *American Antiquity* 54:715–32.

Winkelman, Michael

1998. Aztec Human Sacrifice: Cross-Cultural Assessments of the Ecological Hypothesis. *Ethnology* 37:285–98.

Wood, Stephanie

1990. Adopted Saints: Christian Images in Nahua Testaments of Late Colonial Toluca. *Americas* 47:259–94.

Zorita, Alonso de

1963. *Life and Labor in Ancient Mexico: The Brief and Summary Relation of the Lords of New Spain*. Translated by Benjamin Keen. Rutgers University Press, New Brunswick.

Index